Truth in Motion

Truth in Motion

The Recursive Anthropology of
Cuban Divination

MARTIN HOLBRAAD

THE UNIVERSITY OF CHICAGO PRESS   CHICAGO AND LONDON

MARTIN HOLBRAAD teaches social anthropology at University College London. He is co-editor of *Thinking Through Things: Theorising Artefacts Ethnographically* and *Technologies of the Imagination*.

The University of Chicago Press, Chicago 60637
The University of Chicago Press, Ltd., London
© 2012 by The University of Chicago
All rights reserved. Published 2012.
Printed in the United States of America

21 20 19 18 17 16 15 14 13 12   1 2 3 4 5

ISBN-13: 978-0-226-34920-6 (cloth)
ISBN-13: 978-0-226-34921-3 (paper)
ISBN-10: 0-226-34920-9 (cloth)
ISBN-10: 0-226-34921-7 (paper)

Library of Congress Cataloging-in-Publication Data

Holbraad, Martin.
    Truth in motion : the recursive anthropology of Cuban divination / Martin Holbraad.
        p. cm.
    Includes bibliographical references and index.
    ISBN-13: 978-0-226-34920-6 (hardcover : alkaline paper)
    ISBN-13: 978-0-226-34921-3 (paperback : alkaline paper)
    ISBN-10: 0-226-34920-9 (hardcover : alkaline paper)
    ISBN-10: 0-226-34921-7 (paperback : alkaline paper)   1. Ifá (Religion)—Cuba.
2. Divination—Cuba. 3. Cuba—Religion.   I. Title.
    BL2532.I33H65 2012
    299.6'833302097291—dc23

                                                          2011037298

♾ This paper meets the requirements of ANSI/NISO z39.48–1992 (Permanence of Paper).

Contents

Acknowledgments

L ong in the making, this book is based on fieldwork that I conducted in Havana between 1998 and 2000 for my doctoral thesis, completed at the University of Cambridge in 2002, and a series of subsequent field trips to Cuba throughout the 2000s. I thank the Economic and Social Research Council, King's College, Cambridge, and the Department of Social Anthropology at Cambridge for financially supporting my doctoral studies. For funding on subsequent visits to Cuba, I thank the Arts and Humanities Research Council and the British Academy. Pembroke College, Cambridge, where I was a Research Fellow from 2002 until 2004, provided an optimal environment for sustained postdoctoral research. A magnificent place to do anthropology, the Department of Anthropology at University College London has since been my academic home. I am grateful to the department's administrative staff, and particularly to Helen Cooper, Diana Goforth, Chris Hagisavva, Alena Kocourek, and Martin O'Connor, for their part in making it a pleasure to work there.

Of the many friends and acquaintances who helped me in my research on Afro-Cuban religion in Havana, I would like to mention in particular Victor Bentancourt and his family and associates, Lázaro and Anaïris Panfét, Mira Petrunic, and Carlos and Mayra Torrens. Mette Berg and Lloyd Rundle made all the difference in the early stage of my doctoral fieldwork in Havana and Dimitris Kerkinos was a close companion throughout. For their love, friendship, and guidance for now well over a decade, I am profoundly grateful to Jacinto Herrera and Eloanél, Juana and her family, and especially Maritza Díaz and her family. Of the many academic and administrative staff at the Centro (now Instituto) de Antropología who helped me during my original fieldwork in Havana in 1998–2000, as well as in subsequent visits, I give special thanks to my two academic advisors, Juan

Alvarado Ramos and Rafael Robaina Jaramillo. Without their friendship, anthropological insight, and ethnographic guidance my research in Cuba would have been impossible.

Since our wedding in Havana in 2004, Zoraima Segón Valdés has been a constant support and source of inspiration, first as wife and now as life-long friend and confidante. Her family, and particularly Remédios (Tata), Euclides, Ernesto, Leonardo, and Dorka, have in recent years been my first port of call in Havana, and I am immensely grateful for their immutable affection. The same goes for my Havana soul-mate Javielito Alfonso, whose passion for music, books, Ifá, and friendship opened new horizons for me. As initiates of Ifá, Javielito and his father, Javier, provided the main anchor of my research. As can be seen in the pages of this book, most of what I know about Ifá life comes from the many hours I spent with them and their extended family and ritual associates in Havana, Matanzas, and Unión de Reyes. Javier himself became my Ifá godfather (*padrino de guerreros* and *mano de Orula*) in 1999 and, until his death in 2004, was as wise, perceptive, and tender a mentor as one could hope for, in life as in Ifá. This book is dedicated to his memory.

Of the many teachers and friends in Cambridge whose help I recorded in the acknowledgments of my doctoral thesis, here I would like to single out Caroline Humphrey, my PhD supervisor. Her unflagging support and intellectual stimulation during my studies, and in the years since, have been of immense value to me. I would also like to thank Stephen Hugh-Jones, my second PhD supervisor, as well as Marilyn Strathern and Maurice Bloch, my internal and external PhD examiners respectively. All three were of major inspiration as teachers, and the influence of their work is amply evident in the pages of this book. The same goes for Morten Pedersen who, as fellow student in Cambridge and anthropological soul-mate ever since, has been my closest intellectual companion throughout the writing of this book. While our friendship is in so many ways more encompassing than anthropology, our common sense of anthropological fun has perhaps been its most abiding feature.

I also owe thanks to Eduardo Viveiros de Castro, whom I first met in 1998 during his visiting professorship at Cambridge, and who has since become my most steadfast anthropological mentor and interlocutor. Having followed my research from its beginning, he has been my most engaged reader and critic throughout the writing of this book, acting also as reviewer of the manuscript for the publisher. His profound influence is amply evident in the final product. In fact, his inspiration, support, and guidance at all stages of the book's development have made me come to regard him as something of a godfather to the whole endeavor. I dedicate the book to him, as well as to my own godfather, in recognition of this and in gratitude for his friendship.

For mind-bending conversations, recommendations on literature, and all-round inspiration and moral support I would like to record my gratitude to Ben Alberti, Viorel Anastasoaie, Alex Argenti-Pillen, Alexandra Bakalaki, Alessandra Basso Ortíz, Barbara Bodenhorn, Casper Bruun Jensen, Victor Buchli, Phil Burnham, Matt Candea, David Cooper, Alberto Corsín Jiménez, Ludovic Coupaye, Magnus Course, Giovanni da Col, Philippe Descola, Piero di Giminiani, Sev Fowles, Luke Freeman, Alice Forbes, Sergio González Varela, Keith Hart, Lars Højer, Bruce Kapferer, Jose Kelly, Babis Kondarakis, Susanne Küchler, James Laidlaw, Murray Last, Jerome Lewis, Geoffrey Lloyd, Yvonne Marshall, Lucia Michelutti, Peter Morton-Williams, Andrew Moutu, Marjorie Murrey, Chloe Nahum-Claudel, Becky Nastou, Morten Nielsen, Chris Pinney, Ato Quayson, William Rea, Nanneke Reclift, Adam Reed, Rodney Reynolds, Balkis Rouached, Ami Salmond, Buck Schieffelin, Matan Shapiro, Barrie Sharpe, David Sneath, Tânia Stolze Lima, Alan Strathern, Tao Sule, Soumhya Venkatesan, Henrik Vigh, Sari Wastell, Graham Were, Jo Whiteley, Rane Willerselev, and Chris Witmore. For also reading and commenting on draft chapters I thank Patrick Curry, René Devisch, Terry Evens, Marcio Goldman, David Hillel-Ruben, Jamie Leach, the late Peter Lipton, Maria Livanou, John Peel, Lise Philipsen, and Michael Scott.

Much of the thinking presented in the book took shape in the anthropology department at UCL, particularly in conversation with participants in the research group on Cosmology, Religion, Ontology and Culture (CROC) and students on my course on Alterity and Experiment. Of friends and colleagues in the department, I would like to single out Allen Abramson, Alice Elliot, Rebecca Empson, Diana Espirito Santo, Danny Miller, David Napier, Sara Randall, Ellie Reynolds, Mike Rowlands, Julia Sauma, Dan Sherer, and Charles Stewart for their friendship and support, not least at the very final stages of writing. Jenny Adejayan, Nikos Giannakakis, Panos Giannakakis, Hera Karagianni, Giorgos Papagiannopoulos, Dimitris Psimaras, Joe Rodriguez, and Dimitris Vassos and his daughters Nefeli and Rallou have been there throughout.

As well as to Eduardo Viveiros de Castro, thanks are due to two anonymous reviewers for the University of Chicago Press for their invaluable comments, and to David Brent, the Press's editor, who brought the project to fruition. Piers Vitebsky helped to put me in contact with the Press, and I am supremely grateful for his advice, as well as for his inspiring influence as teacher. I am also grateful to Priya Nelson at University of Chicago Press for her assistance in the book's production, as well as to Therese Boyd for her thorough editorial work on the manuscript. In chapters 3, 5, and 8 I draw on two previously published papers of mine: "The Power of Powder: Multiplicity and Motion in the Divinatory Cosmology of Cuban Ifá (or *Mana* Again)," which appeared in *Thinking Through Things: Theorising Artefacts Ethnographically*, edited by A. Henare, M. Holbraad, and S. Wastell (London: Routledge, 2007), 189–225; and "Relationships in Motion: Oracular Recruitment and Ontological Definition in Cuban Ifá Cults," *Cahiers Systèmes de Pensée en Afrique Noire* 18 (2009): 219–64. I thank the publishers for permission to reprint parts of these texts.

Finally, I would like to make explicit my deep sense of gratitude to my family for their love and support during the years of the book's gestation. My sister Sonya and her joyful family—Matt, Anna, Samuel, Alexander, Mae!—have been my most solid emotional anchor in Britain during what has felt like a period of incessant shuttling between the UK, Cuba, Denmark, Greece, and elsewhere. My mother, Christina, and father, Carsten, also shuttlers by nature as well as necessity, have nevertheless always been there for me. Both of them intellectuals, they have each read multiple versions of the chapters that follow and have contributed immensely to their content as well as their form. Having dedicated my doctoral thesis to them, here I would like to record my unconditional gratitude for standing by me at every turn of this book's production. A big thing for me.

Preface

The Book's Agenda

This work addresses what I regard as the central question of anthropology as an intellectual project, namely, how to make sense of others. As shown in the following chapters, that question presents a profound *problem* for anthropology, with far-reaching implications for the way we imagine what it is we do as anthropologists, the turns of thinking in which we are most invested, and the particular challenges their whole operation poses.

The basic thought is this. In saying that anthropology's task is to make sense of others, we may well see an analogy with other disciplines that also seek to make sense of things, albeit in quite different fields of study. While biologists make sense of living organisms, economists of markets, and literary critics of books and poems, anthropologists make sense of others—particularly other peoples, societies, or cultures. Such an apparently unremarkable analogy, however, may easily be extended into a series of corollaries that, as I contend, are deeply problematic. For imagining anthropology by analogy to other disciplines all too naturally gives rise to the idea that its task of making sense of others is also analogous to that of making sense of organisms, markets, or novels. In particular, it gives rise to the notion that, as with such objects of inquiry, anthropology's attempt to make sense of other people must in some sense or other take the form of providing appropriate representations (descriptions, interpretations, explanations, and so on). Anthropology, in other words, must be in the business of what would ordinarily be called truth, understood (as broadly as one might wish, and in whatever sense one might prefer) as the attempt to provide representations that get their object right, as it actually is. Where biologists, say, seek to offer true representations of living organisms, we must be after true representations of other people's lives.

My thesis is that this way of thinking of anthropology, intuitive and perhaps even uncontroversial as it may seem, is basically wrong. My basic claim is that what makes other people "other" is precisely the fact that they cannot be represented. Alterity, if you like, is the challenge to which representation cannot rise: it is just when we are *unable* even to describe (let alone interpret, explain, translate, or analyze) aspects of people's lives that they become other to us. Things that are also people, people that are also gods, gods that are also wafers, twins that are also birds: these are the kinds of contradictory descriptions in which attempts to make sense of others by representing them may land us. The problem of alterity, then, is just the problem of nonsense: when even your best attempt to make sense of people's lives by representing them in terms you understand fails, you know you have hit upon it.

As discussed in the chapters that follow, this way of understanding anthropology's flagship problem is confluent with the work of a critical mass of scholars, notably including Terry Evens, Bruno Latour, Marilyn Strathern, Eduardo Viveiros de Castro, Roy Wagner, and their associates and students.[1] Arguably what brings these authors together is a desire to think (and do) anthropology beyond representation. Drawing and building on this body of work, my aim here is to further its agenda in a direction in which it has tended to be reluctant to move, namely toward the question of truth. This characteristic ambivalence toward truth is not difficult to understand. Insofar as the aspiration to truth (so emotive and grand!) has been bound up with the project of representation, such that the two are deemed to be each other's corollaries, attempts to move anthropology beyond representation can easily be thought ipso facto as attempts to move it beyond truth, too.

Still, the basic proposal of this book is that the question of truth in anthropology ought to be disentangled from that of representation. Indeed, the best way to defuse the grandiose conceits that the word *truth* often evokes is to disembed it from the assumptions about representation it so typically carries. For, as I suggest, the importance of truth as an aspiration for anthropology is not exhausted in the conceit of a discipline that imagines it can know everything and everyone. Thus, the abiding questions this book addresses are these: If the goal of representation is anthropologically problematic, or even untenable, where does this leave anthropologists' aspiration to truth? Can we have truth without representation? What might it look like? And how might it relate to the representationist assumptions about truth it seeks critically to bring into view?

Rudiments of Argument and Strategy

Since the question of truth, taken here in its peculiarly anthropological guise, is provoked by the challenge of ethnographic alterity, my attempt to address it in this book runs it up against just such an ethnographic exposure. Hence, the book's engagement with theoretical debates about truth and its status in anthropological inquiry takes the form of an ethnographic journey to the Afro-Cuban practice of Ifá divination in Havana, where I have conducted ethnographic research since 1998. The guiding idea is that assumptions about the nature, provenance, and value of truth that are deeply entrenched in anthropological debates on the subject, when set against the backdrop of a radically different set of concepts and practices associated with the pursuit of truth in Afro-Cuban divination, can be brought into view, examined critically, and then revised. The exploration of what Cuban religious practitioners take for granted when they use their oracles to "get to the truth of things," as they say, provides a repertoire of concepts with which to question and recast our own anthropological assumptions about truth.

In its form, such a strategy exemplifies a manner of reasoning that is perhaps quintessentially anthropological. Rendering "relative" familiar assumptions about truth by examining them from the unfamiliar vantage point of Cuban divination is analogous to what anthropologists have always been doing with all manner of concerns—looking at Maori gifts to think about modern markets, making Zande witchcraft speak to European ideas about causation, and so forth. But if the form of my analysis follows a well-trodden path, its substance leads elsewhere. Performing such an ethnographically driven operation on the notion of truth has consequences for the project of anthropology itself. Unlike gifts, witchcraft, and so on, the notion of truth pertains directly to the very nature of anthropological reasoning. When anthropologists address questions of truth, after all, they do so chiefly as a matter of methodology—positivism versus interpretivism, realism versus constructivism, and so on. So the move to render truth "relative" by setting it up as an ethnographic object is a fortiori a move to relativize anthropology itself.

It is this strategy that I call "recursive." Such a strategy lies at the heart of the antirepresentationist agenda of the authors I have mentioned: what Strathern, Viveiros de Castro, Wagner, and others who pursue this line of thinking share is an abiding interest in the impact that the content of ethnography may have on the form of its analysis—how ethnography may act to transform the very activity of anthropology. So my question is how the notion of truth might be revamped in the light of this agenda. In a nutshell, what notion of truth do we imply when we say that, rather than using analysis to represent ethnography, we use ethnography to transform analysis?

Exemplifying the very argument it seeks to articulate, my attempt to answer this question draws its impetus recursively, from the substance of my analysis of Cuban Ifá divination. My central claim in doing so is that familiar assumptions about truth as a property of representations that reflect reality are inadequate for understanding these practices' own claims to truth. Rather than producing representations, diviners' truth-claims induce something resembling a eureka moment, by bringing the rich mythical narratives on which Ifá divination is based to bear on the personal circumstances of the client. So, oracular truth does not depend on the possibility of comparing the oracle's pronouncements with the world as it is, as a representationist image of truth might have it. Rather than representing the world, the oracle transforms it by interfering with its very meaning—an ontological rather than an epistemic operation.

This broad idea, that what may seem to be epistemic representations are better analyzed as ontological transformations, surfaces in a variety of ways in the work of antirepresentationist scholars such as the aforementioned, and has ramifying roots in late twentieth-century poststructuralism. As already suggested, however, if my divination-led analysis adds something to this basic thought, it does so by casting it in relation to, and in favor of, a notion of truth. To the extent that Cuban diviners are, as it were, both anti-representation and pro-truth, they furnish a useful corrective to the tendency in the literature to throw the baby of truth out with the bathwater of representation. Indeed, cast in the mold of divination, truth acquires characteristics that are quite different to the ones antirepresentationist theorists prefer to disclaim. One of my aims is to show that keeping the notion of truth in the fray in this manner ultimately provides a way of *relating* matters of transformation to matters of representation in ways that are more complex than mere displacement, substitution, or repudiation.

Indeed, the particular ways in which the ethnography of Cuban divination slants the concept of truth also take the antirepresentationist argument in contingent and therefore potentially novel directions. For example, the idea of truth that my ethnography precipitates entails a particular reconceptualization of the role of meaning in the production of truth. The dynamic transformations of meaning that oracles bring about suggest a basic analytical reversal: rather than thinking of meaning in a state of rest, as we do also when we think of its role in reflecting the state of the world representationally, we see meaning in divinatory practice as the kind of thing that moves, quite literally, so as to be transformed—that is, what I call its inherent "motility." Again, this is an idea that resonates with much contemporary work in anthropology, and not least that of Roy Wagner. At the heart of my analysis, however, is a demonstration of how such a "motile logic" is supported by a nexus of concepts, objects, and practices that are associated with Ifá divination, which together provide the logical coordinates for the motility of meaning and truth in the workings of the oracle in particular ways. Such a motile nexus connects the notion of truth with a series of further analytical concerns that have to do with the conceptualization of, among other things, the relationship between transcendence and immanence in Ifá divination, the nature of the ontological transformations that divination effects, and how these entail forms of obligation that compel particular actions, not least in matters of initiation.

These ventures ultimately raise the question of how the reconceptualization of truth upon which they turn, and to which they also contribute, might exemplify *itself*. For if our anthropological attempt to make sense of Cuban divination issues in a series of reconceptualizations, then it too, like the diviners and their truths, must in some sense be in the business of transforming meaning. Hence the book's meta-anthropological dividend: how might the novel repertoire of concepts generated by the analysis of Ifá divination provide the ground for conceptualizing anthropological truth itself in motile terms—that is, conceptualizing anthropology as a generator of concepts? This, I take it, is to heed the call for "an anthropological concept of the concept," made by Viveiros de Castro nearly a decade ago (2003, 14; see also Corsín Jiménez and Willerslev 2007): how far and in what sense, is my question, can the notion of divinatory truth as reconceptualization yield a concept of anthropological truth as reconceptualization also? Since this kind of conceptual yield is just what is at stake in this manner of thinking of anthropological truth in the face of alterity, the truth of my argument, one might say, is in the eating of the pudding.

Recursive Structure

The task of manufacturing a concept of truth that is appropriate to a particular way of arguing (in this case, the tack of anthropological analysis I have branded as recursive) could be taken as essentially philosophical. It is philosophers, after all, who are most dedicated to the study of concepts— according to some, the very activity is defined by the love of making them (Deleuze and Guatarri 1996; cf. Bruun Jensen and Rödje 2009). Indeed: there can be little doubt that the concept of truth that this book sets out to articulate could be arrived at by a philosophical route, and that both the critique of representationism that it advances and the alternative conceptual framework that it proposes could be seen in light of philosophical treatments of these topics. Nevertheless, while the chapters that follow will make reference to such treatments where helpful (mainly by way of orientation), and thus sometimes take turns reminiscent of a philosophical style, the book is designed to make explicit the specifically anthropological tenor of its argument. The idea, in other words, is to demonstrate that anthropology is equipped to advance its own answers to its own questions in its own way, by showing, recursively, how this can be done.

The book's structure reflects this agenda. Having set out the overall argument of the book in this preface, in the introduction I proceed to relate it to the lively literature on Ifá divination, both in West Africa, where the practice originated, and in Cuba, where I studied it ethnographically. Providing the historical and ethnographic background for the main body of my argument on divination, such a review of the literature on Ifá also serves to articulate the basic tenet of the book's ethnographic strategy, namely that of focusing on Ifá divination in order to make the question of truth and its alterity ethnographically visible. Divination in general, and Ifá in particular, provides a privileged site for rendering truth an object of ethnographic inquiry. My discussion of existing approaches to the study of Ifá in West Africa and Cuba, as well as of the literature on Afro-American religion and culture more broadly, positions my orientation toward the question of truth in relation to some of the central debates in the West Africanist and Afro-Americanist literature, including questions of cultural continuity and change in the so-called Black Atlantic, and the political stakes with which such debates have been invested.

Chapter 1 continues the essentially preliminary task of motivating the overall argument of the book by placing it in the context of the long anthropological conversation about the role and status of truth in anthropological inquiry. The first part of the chapter offers what could be viewed as a microhistory of the discipline, presented from the point of view of anthropologists' shifting preoccupations with truth. The main claim here is that the question of truth in the discipline has always been bound up with the question of representation, which in turn has received a specifically anthropological treatment in terms of the distinction between nature and culture. The second part of the chapter turns the attention on attempts by scholars such as Wagner, Strathern, and Viveiros de Castro to recast the anthropological nature/culture dichotomy with reference, recursively, to ethnographic instances in which its purchase appears limited. Building on this body of work, and in view of its aforementioned ambivalence toward the idea of truth, my discussion ends with a plea to rethink the notion of truth in line with these full-hog overhauls of the discipline's infrastructure.

The main body of the book (chapters 2–8) takes up this task, showing how representationist assumptions about truth can be recast with reference to the ethnography of Ifá divination in Cuba—the kind of ethnographically driven analytical percolation I outlined earlier. Exemplifying the recursive relationship between truth as an analytical concept and truth as an ethnographic concern, the argument develops in three steps.

The first step, taken in chapter 2, is to characterize the assumptions about truth that underlie the longstanding anthropological debate about divination, and particularly about the analysis of so-called divinatory beliefs. Anthropologists who worry about the epistemic legitimacy of divination do so because they assume that its claim to truth is representational—an assumption that carries with it the corollary that diviners' claims to truth are inherently open to doubt. Pre-empting the ethnography presented in subsequent chapters, I then argue that this discounts the possibility that what might make divination so peculiar from the point of view of representationist expectations is not that people might "believe" its claims to truth, but rather that they might take them as the kind of statements that one *cannot but* believe. Such a prospect, I suggest, would have immediate (recursive) implications about how we think of the very idea of truth in this context. In order to be able to describe divination as issuing indubitable truths, the habitual notion of truth as a property of representations, which are inherently doubtful, would have to be fundamentally rethought.

Chapters 3–7 develop the second step of the overall recursive argument, in which the initial assumptions about divinatory truth outlined in chapter 2 are exposed ethnographically to the alterity of truth in Ifá divination. Chapter 3 sets the ethnographic coordinates of this procedure by providing an in-the-round account of the salience of the concern with truth in the life of *babalawos*, as the fully initiated diviners of Ifá are called. The account is anchored ethnographically in the lives of Javier Alfonso Isasi and his son Javielito, the two babalawos who provided me with my entry into the world of Ifá during my fieldwork, and with whom I worked most closely. With reference to their personal trajectories within the religion, as well as to their life at home as I witnessed it, the chapter charts the ways in which divination, and the concern with truth that lies at its heart, shapes key aspects of initiates' lives.

Chapters 4 and 5 chart the cosmological coordinates of Ifá, exploring the ways in which they inform the practice of divination. The key concern here is to articulate the way in which the distance between the worlds of gods and of humans is posited in Ifá cosmology, and how otherwise absent deities are elicited into presence in the ceremony of divination. Chapter 4 explores the contrasting roles of myth and ritual in this context, providing a detailed account of the divinatory ceremony itself. Drawing on this material, and framing it in relation to broader assumptions about the relationship between "transcendence" and "immanence," in chapter 5 I argue that making sense of the elicitation of deities in Ifá divination requires a basic analytical reversal: rather than thinking of deities as entities that may "travel" across worlds, we may think of them in what I call "motile" terms, as vectors of ontological transformation in their own right.

Chapters 6 and 7 extend and develop the implications of this motile logic with reference to an ethnography of the divinatory consultation itself. Framed with reference to anthropological discussions on the fluidity of "symbolic" meanings, and drawing on extracts from divinations conducted by Javier for his clients, chapter 6 is devoted to showing the importance to the process of consultation of what babalawos call "interpretation." Crucially, this turns on the babalawo's ability to bring the mythical narratives on which Ifá divination is based to bear on the personal circumstances of his client. I then go on, in chapter 7, to formulate a motile account of the process of divinatory interpretation, as well as of the truths that emerge from it. Meaning, on this account, is conceived as a motile trajectory that is defined by its capacity to metamorphose, to use a word Javier once used to explain how divination "works." On such a premise, truth too needs to be conceptualized in motile terms, as an event of collision—a meeting—between previously unrelated strands of meaning.

Chapter 8, finally, draws on the ethnographic and analytical discussions of the preceding chapters in order to bring the recursive transformation of the concept of truth in divination into fruition—the third step of the overall argument's recursive strategy. Addressing the question of indubitability that motivated the argument from the outset, the discussion focuses on a series of ethnographic indications of the significance babalawos accord to the indubitable quality of their oracles. Taking up the analytical challenges that this ethnography presents, I venture a reconceptualization of truth drawing on the motile analytic advanced in the previous chapters. The key claim here is that, in order to make sense of the constitutive indubitability of truth in Ifá, divinatory truths must be conceived as acts of definition (rather than representation) that effectively transform the world upon which they purport to comment. To underline the analytical departure, I use the neologism "infinition" to brand this motile conceptualization of truth.

The conclusion is devoted to exploring the metatheoretical dividends of the analysis of divination offered in the main body of the book. It does so by placing the concept of truth as infinition, yielded by the recursive analysis of Ifá, side by side with the claims to truth that this analysis itself has made. Suggesting that anthropology too, like divination, is in the business of infinition, I develop a model of anthropological analysis that I call "ontographic," thus connecting the ontological force of infinition with the epistemic concern with charting things. The chapter ends by exploring some of the breakdowns in the analogy between anthropology and divination, not least in relation to what I consider to be the characteristic humility of anthropological endeavor—something of which babalawos, as we shall see, could hardly be accused. This notion of humility as a constitutive principle of anthropological analysis is taken up in a brief epilogue, drawing out some of its implications for broader questions about the role of ethnographic contingency in anthropology, and the fundamentally tentative character of the motile truths to which it gives rise.

The Question of Truth in the Historiography and Ethnography of Ifá Divination

Truth as an Ethnographic Object

As an object of ethnographic inquiry truth is elusive. Certainly, unlike gifts or witchcraft, truth has not made it onto the canon of ethnographic concerns, so the idea of doing "an ethnography of truth" is hardly self-explanatory. Perhaps part of the difficulty is that if one decides to see truth as an ethnographer, one sees it everywhere. What aspect of people's lives is not impinged upon by concerns about truth? Locating truth in the ethnographer's world, one has to reckon not only with the apparent truism that all claims are truth-claims (to say "roses are red," some philosophers suggest, is to claim that it is true that roses are red), but also with the substantive matter that truth, as an object of concern for people, is never far from the surface of life. From the broadest ambits of political rhetoric ("our society is multicultural") to the confessional moments of a personal relationship ("I love you!"), questions of truth are always at stake. In this sense truth is a little like an ethnographic tautology.

Such a tautology tends to inhibit the study of truth in a properly ethnographic way (cf. Steiner 1954). For if the claim is that concerns for truth are latent everywhere by implication, one may well wonder whether their detection, if you like, in a variety of social settings is owing more to the ethnographer's own analytical preconceptions than to the ethnographic data themselves. Sure, questions of truth may be *assumed* to be relevant both to political slogans and to declarations of love, but only in the sense that whatever the ethnographer has already decided is truth can be read into them. Like with ghosts, it would seem that to see truth you have first to believe in it.

The tautology of detecting truth everywhere, using its a priori relevance to bring disparate phenomena under a single heading, has certainly made truth an attractive concern for anthropologists interested in abstracting general principles for the analysis of social interaction. For example, this is the meeting point of classical anthropological debates about the so-called rationality of indigenous beliefs with concerted attempts by ethnomethodologists and, more recently, cognitive and semantic anthropologists to investigate the principles that underlie people's inferences in particular social settings (e.g., Garfinkel 1967; Hallpike 1979; Hutchins 1980; Sperber 1985, 1996; Boyer 1990; Rappaport 1999). The power of the analytical vocabulary of rationality, belief, inference, knowledge, and so on depends on the stipulation that, whatever they say or do, people ipso facto make claims to what the analyst recognizes as truth. I shall return to this point in the next chapter, when I come to discuss some of these anthropological preoccupations.

Still, in direct contrast to such analytical stipulations about truth (or, if you like, meta-ethnographic ones), my interest here is in examining truth as a squarely ethnographic concern.[1] As has been explained in the preface, the overall aim of this book is precisely to render anthropological assumptions about truth vulnerable, by exposing them ethnographically to an altogether different way of engaging with truth. An ethnography of divination, I now want to show, is ideal for this task. Unlike politics, love, or what-have-you, divinatory practices provide a firm ethnographic handle onto truth since in them truth, and people's concern for it, features not as an implicit corollary but as an explicit and overriding objective. As David Zeitlyn puts it, based on his long-term study of varied forms of divination in Cameroon, "Divination must be recognised as being a means of obtaining true answers. Only if it is held to be a truth-telling exercise is it worth performing" (1995, 189). One might say, then, that divination provides an opening for an ethnography of truth because in it truth is recognized first by the diviner and his clients, and only afterwards, if at all, by the anthropologist and his or her readers. Crucially, as with gifts, witchcraft, and other topics of the ethnographic canon, this raises the possibility that what diviners recognize as truth might be very different from what we take truth to be when we think anthropologically—a possibility explored throughout this book. To set us on this path, we may now turn to the history and ethnography of Ifá divination, beginning with the literature on its practice in West Africa, where Cuban Ifá originates.

Ifá in West Africa and the Prestige of Truth

With reference to E. E Evans-Pritchard's famous observation that different divinatory methods vary in prestige depending on how reliable they are perceived to be,[2] Ifá can be placed squarely at the pinnacle of the many divinatory forms that have for centuries been practiced in West Africa (practitioners of Ifá in Cuba, too, we shall see later, make much of this traditional esteem). As can be gleaned from historical accounts of religious practice in the region that nineteenth-century colonial administrators called "Yorubaland" (today a part of the state of Nigeria), the majestic sophistication of this form of divination, which probably developed on the basis of geomantic practices originating in the Near East (Brenner 2000, 54–56), has always been deemed an index of its prestige among practitioners (Abimbola 1997a; Bascom 1991).

The rich literature on the religious life of the polities whose political and military rivalry dominates the history of the region roughly from the tenth until the late nineteenth century, reveals a patchwork of more or less localized cults focused on the worship of particular deities, called *orisa* (e.g., Peel 2000, 107–16; Barber 1981; Apter 1995).[3] The distribution and relative prestige of distinct orisa cults in different areas was intimately bound up with the political and military fortunes of regional polities, since the prominence of cults in local life was contingent partly on the patronage of royals and other local rulers, for whom, in turn, such ritual associations were a key source of political authority (Matory 2005, 4–22; Barnes and Ben-Amos 1997).

While many orisa cults were centered primarily on the practice of spirit possession, initiates were also able to perform divinations using a variety of methods (e.g., see Bascom 1991, 7–11). Indeed they often became professional diviners, typically by mastering the *owo merindinlogun* oracle, which is based on the casting of sixteen cowry shells and is often seen by practitioners as a simplified version of Ifá (Bascom 1980; Akinnaso 1992, 84–88).[4] Such divinatory practices were distributed unevenly, however, and their prestige varied according to local ritual and political allegiances. By contrast, the appeal of the oracle of Ifá might best be described as "ecumenical" (Peel 1990, 344). Maintaining its ritual and spiritual epicenter at

Ile-Ife, a town that was revered as holy even by competing polities, the cult of Ifá spread across the groups that later came to be known collectively as Yoruba, and became popular also with some of their neighbors, such as the kingdom of Dahomey (see Maupoil 1943). The babalawo, the full initiates of the cult, resided in all major towns in the region and were well-nigh universally regarded as the ultimate authorities in matters of divination.[5] Their divinatory authority was considered superior not only by lay people, who paid the babalawo to divine for them on all manner of personal matters, but also by initiates of other orisa cults, in whose rituals babalawo were often called upon to participate, as well as by political rulers for whom they divined on matters of state, including on questions of royal and chiefly succession (Horton 1979, 121–28; Bascom 1991, 91–102).

A number of excellent studies show that what John Peel calls the "hegemonic" role of Ifá (1990, 342) was owing to a combination of mutually constitutive political and cosmological factors (see particularly Horton 1979; Peel 1990; Apter 1992). Such analyses focus primarily on the historical and cosmological association of the cult of Ifá with the town of Ile-Ife (also referred to as Ife), the cradle of humanity according to some origin myths (Willet 1967, 121–24; Law 1973; Apter 1987, 1992, 15). Ife was historically the first major kingdom in the region, reigning supreme from roughly the tenth century to the fifteenth, when its dominance was eroded by the rise of the Edo kingdom of Benin in the east as well as that of Oyo in the north (Horton 1979). While versions of these myths differ widely, Ife-centric cosmogonies detail how Olodumare, the supreme god of the heavens (*orun*), dispatched his son Oduduwa to create the world with the help of a rooster and a calabash filled with sand. Descending from the sky on a chain, Oduduwa encountered a vast primordial sea on which he emptied out the contents of his calabash, placing the rooster on top of the sand. As the rooster began to scratch the surface of the sand, tracts of land began to emerge. Oduduwa went on to found a kingdom at Ife, close to the site of his original descent from heaven, and the sons he fathered (sixteen of them according some accounts) are said to have founded other kingdoms further afield (cf. Apter 1992, 16–23).

Despite the demise of its political dominion from the fifteenth century onward, Ife retained its cosmogonic status as what scholars have called a "Yoruba spiritual capital" (following Johnson 1921; cf. Horton 1979, 79). Indeed, it has been argued that the prestige of Ifá divination was intimately bound up with babalawo's role in sustaining Ife's status as a "father state" whose cosmogonic authority radiated out to otherwise more powerful polities (e.g., Horton 1979; cf. Apter 1992, 31–34).[6] However, it is important for the present argument to note that the babalawo's capacity to play such a ritual-*cum*-political role was itself premised on underlying assumptions about the relationship between authority and truth, and particularly about babalawo's authority as brokers of truth par excellence. In other words, while the status of Ife acted as a historical condition for babalawo's prestige, it is as well to bear in mind that the babalawo's authority as arch-diviners was itself constitutive of their ritual-*cum*-political power and, by extension, of the sacred status of Ife: it was by virtue of their privileged access to truth that babalawo were socially powerful rather than the other way round.

Like the stories of the foundation of Ife, myths regarding the origin of Ifá vary a great deal. On many accounts Ifá, personified as Orunmila, the wise deity of Ifá divination who is the principal focus of worship for babalawo, was himself one of the deities sent by Olodumare to Ife to establish order in the world. In other myths Ifá (or Orunmila) is presented as having been born in Ife as a mortal, later to become a diviner-king of another town (e.g., see Abimbola 1997a, 4–8; 1973, 41–44) or, according to other versions, of Ife itself (Dennett, as quoted in Apter 1992, 26). Interestingly, as Andrew Apter remarks, examples of myths that justify the ritual structure of the cult with reference to the kingship of Ife "invert rather neatly the myths of princely dispersion which describe the origins of Yoruba kingdoms. Whereas Oduduwa sent out sixteen sons (according to Ife traditions) to found the first kingdoms, Ifá selected sixteen apprentices, one from each of the kingdoms, to come to Ife for training and to return with the powers of Ifá divination" (1992, 26).

The theme of babalawo's original apprenticeship with Ifá/Orunmila is a key component of their claim to divinatory supremacy. Wande Abimbola, who as a foremost scholar of Ifá and a senior babalawo himself, acts as a figurehead of contemporary Yoruba religion (cf. Peel 1992, 341), provides the following account of the mythical foundations of Ifá divination:

According to the myths, there were occasions when, there being no physical barrier between heaven and earth at that time, Ifá was summoned by Olodumare (God Almighty) to heaven to use his great wisdom to solve problems for Him. Ifá finally returned to heaven in annoyance due to an insult given to him by one of his children. Shortly after this, the earth was thrown into great confusion. Famine and pestilence raged throughout the earth. . . . After some time, the people of the earth decided to seek remedy for the hardship by sending the eight children of Orunmila [viz. Ifá] to heaven to go and beg their father to return to earth. The children went accordingly. When they reached heaven, they found Ifá "at the foot of the much-climbed palm-tree which branched this way and that until it had sixteen hut-like branches." They begged Ifá to come back to the earth but he refused. Ifá, however, gave each of his eight children sixteen palm-nuts. . . . When the children of Ifá returned to earth, they started to use the sixteen palm-nuts for divination. . . . The absence of Ifá from earth no longer mattered, since his children and disciples could communicate with him through [the sixteen palm-nuts] and the other instruments of divination. (Abimbola 1997a, 6–7)

The instruments of Ifá divination and how they facilitate babalawo's communication with the divinities will be explored in detail in subsequent chapters. However, Abimbola's mythical narrative serves to establish the central point I wish to make here, namely that by attributing the divinatory powers of babalawo to their privileged access to the divinatory authority of Orunmila himself, such cosmological accounts relate the prestige of Ifá divination directly to its supremacy as a source of truth. Indeed, as we shall see, in Ifá myths that are current in Cuba, Orunmila's trademark claim to wisdom is typically depicted in terms of his position beyond the contrasting and sometimes conflicting claims of other orisa. In such accounts, Orunmila's ability to dispel "confusion" and thus to "solve problems" for divinities and mortals alike turns on his role as an impartial arbitrator, specifying the partial claims of other orisa or other divine entities in particular circumstances, and prescribing appropriate ways to satisfy them, typically by means of offerings or sacrifices. So, insofar as babalawo's divinatory expertise draws its authority from Orunmila's mythical role as impartial arbitrator, their position vis-à-vis the cults of other orisa is similarly encompassing.

One might say, then, that what distinguishes babalawo's appeals to the mythical precedents of cosmogony is a peculiar coincidence of form and content. In form the babalawo's cosmological argument matches analogous claims by the devotees of other deities. Just as babalawo source their prestige as diviners back to the impartial wisdom of Orunmila—"witness to the creation of all things," as they say—devotees of Sango may claim ritual authority (e.g., for their cowry-oracle) by appeal to the power of the orisa himself as virile god of thunder, or a royal pretender may affirm his political clout by tracing his lineage back to the founder-god Oduduwa. From the point of view of their form, such cosmologically motivated arguments, enacted in ritual, exemplify what Apter has called a "Yoruba hermeneutics of power," in which appeals to cosmology serve to sustain contrasting claims to authority "within deeper and necessary visions of the truth" (1992, 7; cf. Apter 1991). In such a context, however, babalawo's claims to divinatory supremacy become ecumenical precisely because their content pertains, as it were, to their form. Unlike that of Sango or Oduduwa, Orunmila's divine power is that of revealing just those visions of truth that Yoruba cosmology provides, including those that relate to all the other divinities. The truth to which babalawo lay claim is that of laying claim to truth. Hence their authority as divinely sanctioned truth-brokers becomes all-encompassing, making Ifá "the point of articulation of the cults of the other *orisa*" (Peel 1990, 342).

As Apter shows, truth itself is a marked concept in Yoruba cosmology: "Deep truths (*imojinle*), secret mysteries (*awo*), even history (*itan*) and tradition (*asa*) gloss the sacred foundations of Yoruba social life into divisions of an archive of knowledge" (Apter 1992, 7). Ifá diviners' authority rested on the fact that as "fathers of secrets," which is what the term *babalawo* means literally, they were deemed to have privileged access to this "archive of knowledge." As we shall see in detail with reference to its practice in Cuba, Ifá divination turns on the babalawo's intimate knowledge of a vast body of myths—what Abimbola famously called the "Ifá literary corpus" (1997a, 32; cf. Abimbola 1973). Called *ese Ifá*, these myths took the form of verses and were regarded as secret. Neophyte babalawo were required to memorize and learn to interpret them in arduous apprenticeships that lasted fifteen years or more and involved a series of initiatic steps—a form of schooling, as Akinnaso has argued (1992; see also Abimbola 1973, 1997a, 18–25). It was precisely by virtue of the "truths" that the ese contained that the babalawo were deemed able to dispel "confusion" in divination. As Peel explains, "Ifá narratives [viz. the ese] are reckoned as *itan* ("history"), true stories which yield historical precedents for current situations. Ifá presumes and promotes the view that all significant events are the replication of archetypes" (Peel 1990, 341). Babalawo's divinatory supremacy—their unequaled ability to account for events by relating them to the truths of myth—was founded in the all-encompassing character of the ese, which addressed all aspects of cosmology, including each of the other orisa and a host of other divine entities. Karin Barber emphasizes this point in her classic study of the social dynamics that underlie the competition between different orisa cults:

[T]he Yoruba have a great variety of spiritual forces to deal with. The pantheon as a whole and the relationships between all these forces are mainly the concern of the *babalawo*, the highly-trained specialist Ifá priests, who master a great corpus of divination verses dealing with every aspect of the cosmology. Ordinary individuals, though they consult Ifá constantly, have a more partial view of the cosmology determined by the particular powers and cults they are involved with. These are drawn principally from among the *egungun* [ancestor spirits] and the *orisa*. (Barber 1981, 729; accents omitted)

While, as David Brown has argued, this account downplays to a certain extent the variations that the ese may have displayed in different localities (Brown 2003, 144; see also Bascom 1991, 43; Abimbola 2000), Barber's image captures one of the chief premises of babalawo's own claim to superiority, expressed in pan-Yoruba terms as the ability to act as a "mouthpiece of Yoruba traditional religion taken as a whole" (Abimbola 1965, 4). As babalawos in Cuba today also say, "everything is in Ifá."

As I have already indicated, the core argument of this book is concerned with elucidating the understanding of truth that this magisterial form of divination implies, and comparing it with notions of truth in anthropology. And as we shall see in following chapters, such a comparative project must take what I am calling a "recursive" form: to compare the notion of truth in Ifá and in anthropology is necessarily an exercise in self-comparison, since, by making a claim to anthropological truth, the comparison itself is an example of one of its own two legs. In this connection, it is worth drawing attention to a theme that often surfaces in the historiography of Ifá, namely the analogy between babalawo and "intellectuals." Early European accounts of what came to be known as "Yoruba traditional religion" are replete with depictions of the babalawo as local sages, whose education in the mythical knowledge of the ese lent them an aura of learnedness that commanded scholarly respect—albeit one that was usually mixed with a good deal of condescension toward its "heathen" and "superstitious" character (e.g., Johnson 1921). Indeed, recent studies that explore the emergence of the idea of a "Yoruba nation"[7] in the late nineteenth century have emphasized the role of babalawo as part of a literate intelligentsia who actively promoted it, affirming the totalizing cosmological horizon of Ifá as an abiding source of a pan-Yoruba identity (Peel 1990, 2000; Matory 1999, 2001; Cohen 2002). In fact, the metaphor of babalawo as intellectuals has long since been literalized, with prestigious babalawo such as Wande Abimbola working also as international academics and promoting the image of a modern-day "Yoruba diaspora" with roots that can be traced back to the ancient polities of West Africa—a kind of second-order rendition of Ife-centric origin myths, fitting for the contemporary era of identity politics (e.g., see Abimbola 1997b; cf. Matory 2005, 127–28).

The suggestion that babalawo's learnedness makes them equivalent to intellectuals raises questions that go to the heart of the agenda of this book. Given that babalawo's investment in truth is nevertheless very different from that of intellectuals (the gulf between the two does seems like a version of the fabled contrast between *mythos* and *logos*), how are we to think of the relationship between Ifá's claims to truth vis-à-vis that of the intellectuals who study them academically? In fact, would the presence of apparently differing truth-stakes on either side not imply a sort of confrontation? Whose truth, as it were, should trump whose? As will be argued more closely later, addressing the notion of truth upon which Ifá practice turns involves reckoning fully with these questions. Here, however, we may note that such concerns with the conceptualization of truth in Ifá divination place the present book's agenda at right angles to much of the recent literature on Yoruba religion and its "diaspora" in what has come to be known as the Black Atlantic (Thompson 1983; Gilroy 1993; Matory 2005; Nicolau Parés and Sansi Roca 2011). To see this, we may briefly discuss this body of work as it has developed over the past century or so.

Afro-American Religion and the Politics of Its Representation

While the trajectory of the literature on Afro-American culture and religion is too complex to review fully here, its broad arc can be plotted as a gradual shift from classical anthropological concerns with describing and comparing sociocultural structures and traits, toward an increasing emphasis on locating historiographically the processes through which they emerge.[8] The political and epistemic rationale of this shift in twentieth-century anthropology is well known, and well reflected in the West Africa–based research so far discussed. Early studies that presented "Yoruba traditional religion" as a local system of beliefs and practices (e.g., Frobenius 1913; Morton-Williams 1964, 1966; Parrinder 1970; Bascom 1991), largely abstracted from their broader historical and, particularly, colonial context, began in the era of postcolonial critique to be viewed as unduly "essentialist." Among the many complaints that rode on this charge was the suggestion that by presenting their ethnographic subjects as little more than carriers of palpably exotic beliefs, rituals, social arrangements, and so on, anthropologists reinforced racist prejudices about the irrationality, backwardness, and general inferiority of Africans, obfuscating the historical setting of their colonial domination, and denying them an active role (or "agency") in forging the conditions of their existence. Following the classical period's zenith in intense debates about the peculiar "logics" of African "modes of thought" in the 1960s and 1970s (e.g., Fortes and Dieterlen 1965; Horton and Finnegan 1973), studies of Yoruba religion took a sharp critical/historiographic turn, emphasizing the dynamic and creative character of Yoruba religious practices (e.g., Barber 1981; Drewal 1992), as well as their tractable historical contingency as we have seen earlier (e.g., Apter 1992; Peel 2000).

The recent deconstruction of the very idea of a "Yoruba traditional religion" is perhaps the clearest expression of the historiographic impulse that has been engendered by this line of research—a tendency to account for the kinds of data earlier generations of scholars would call beliefs, cultural traits, indigenous logics, and so on as deliberate and historically situated responses to social, political, and economic conditions. Lorand Matory's sophisticated account of how Yoruba traditional religion as well as the putatively Yoruba-based Afro-Brazilian religious practice of Candomblé emerged in the cross-Atlantic traffic of slaves and freed returnees from the nineteenth century onwards is perhaps the most influential example in the current literature (Matory 1999, 2005). Presented as a corrective to the "outmoded supposition that internal integration and isomorphism of cultures with local populations are the normal conditions of social life," Matory's account seeks to "understand supposedly local and primordial 'folk' cultures and 'primitive' religions not primarily in terms of their roots in a pristine past but in the context of the dynamic politics, economics, and long-distance communication that are the lived realities of the 'folk.'" Such a story, notes Matory, serves to "restore the . . . subject, or agent, to the narrative" (2005, 1, 2, 7).

What Matory also notes is that the shift to a translocal perspective will appear more radical to scholars of West African religion that to those working from within the tradition of Afro-American studies (2005, 12–16). Attempts to trace the "African roots" of Afro-American cultures in the "New World"—a project that was put on the anthropological agenda in the early twentieth century by, among others, Raimundo Nina Rodrigues in Brazil (1988), Fernando Ortíz in Cuba (1906), and Melville Herskovits in the United States (1958)—had an obviously translocal slant from the start. Nevertheless, a shift from sociocultural primordialism toward detailed historiography, analogous to the one we saw in the West Africanist literature, is also characteristic here. Recent writings on Afro-American religions have been centrally concerned with repudiating the idea that the religious (and other cultural) practices that emerged in different parts of the Americas following the trans-Atlantic slave trade and its aftermath can be understood in terms of their continuities and discontinuities with putatively original African traditions, as earlier generations of scholars had assumed they could. As Stephan Palmié writes, such attributions "provide a poor substitute for a historiography of Atlantic cultural transmission, let alone New World ways of demarcating and socially organising cultural difference" (Palmié 2002, 161).

Before explaining the sense in which this tendency is orthogonal to the concerns of this book, and in view of the book's Cuban remit, we may pause here briefly to consider how the tendency has played out in the lively literature on Afro-Cuban religion. As with the broader trends of research already mentioned, the large body of scholarship on Afro-Cuban religion has from the start centered on questions of continuity and change. Focusing on phenomena of acculturation, Creolization, syncretism, hybridization and so on, the central concern in this literature has been with apportioning the relative weight of African origins and American innovations in the wide variety of religious practices that have developed on the island since the massive importation of slaves associated with the sugar boom of the eighteenth and nineteenth centuries.

As reviews of these debates show (e.g., Brown 2003, 3–14), scholarly arguments about the relative contribution of the African-origin part of the population to Cuban society and culture have from the start been deeply embedded in the politics of racial relations, as they unfolded on the island since the abolition of slavery in 1880 and formal independence in 1902. Taking a politically complex stance toward "black culture," derogatory and emancipatory in turns, founders of Afro-Cuban studies such as Fernando Ortíz and his students sought to chart the different formations of Afro-Cuban "folklore" in relation to its origins in different parts of West and Central Africa. This produced a wealth of literature published primarily within Cuba in the first half of the twentieth century, and further expanded by research in folklore under the auspices of Fidel Castro's cultural policy since the Revolution in 1959 (see Ayorinde 2004). What

emerged from this research was a patchwork of distinct, though intertwin-
ing, traditions, understood in religious-*cum*-ethnic terms with reference
to the *naciones*, as they were called, into which slaves were organized in
colonial times. Ifá and Santería, linked to each other cosmologically and
ritually in the complex of Regla de Ocha, were designated as "Lucumí,"
which was the ethnonym given to slaves deemed to be descendants of West
African Yoruba speakers; the complex of Palo Monte, or Regla de Congo,
was associated with Bantu speakers of the "Congo" *nación* (see Ochoa
2010); the secret male fraternities of *Abakuá* were traced to the "Carablí"
nación (see Miller 2009), which was meant to comprise primarily people
from the Cross-River Delta; and finally there were the religious practices
of the nación of "Arará," in which people from the Dahomey area were
included (see Andreu Alonso 1995; cf. Basso Ortíz 2005). In addition,
there was research on *vodú* practices brought to Cuba from Haiti, as well
as interest in putative survivals of Amerindian rituals, such as the practice
of Espiritismo de Cordon in the eastern part of the island, which drew on
Kardecian Spiritism, popular in various forms throughout Cuba since the
nineteenth century (see also Espirito Santo 2009, 2010).

   A major task in this literature has been to chart the distinctive cosmology and ritual, as well as the material and linguistic features of each of
these traditions, exploring both the relationships between them and their
so-called syncretic links to popular Catholicism. On the back of these empirical concerns (putatively so, inasmuch as they reified "traditions" as dis-
cernable objects of study), questions of continuity and change have been
the central theoretical agenda in this literature. Much as with the classical
phase of the West Africanist scholarship, these questions were broached
for most of the twentieth century in terms of an economy of cultural traits
and dispositions, whose varying formations and transformations in Cuba
were to be explained mainly with reference to the changing fortunes of the
African descendants who carried them. Much debate centered on the role
of colonial institutions in providing the social conditions for reconstituting
African religious practices, and not least the so-called *cabildos de nación*,
modeled on Spanish religious fraternities (*cofradias*), in which the different naciones were permitted a degree of autonomy.

   For example, the apparently pre-eminent position of Ifá and Santería,
compared to other Afro-Cuban religious practices throughout the twentieth century, is often explained with reference to the prominence of the
Lucumí nación. In the first half of the nineteenth century, slaves designated as Lucumí, who comprised Yoruba speakers as well as people from

neighboring West African areas, swelled in numbers owing to the influx of slaves that followed the disintegration of the Oyo empire in West Africa (Brandon 1993, 55–59; cf. Thornton 1992; Palmié 2002, 312–13). Lucumí cabildos in Havana and other western towns became particularly prominent. Many studies have sought to show how these organizations provided conditions for Lucumí religious practices to be preserved, reorganized, and transmitted to subsequent generations (e.g., Ortíz 1921; Montejo 1968; Guanche 1983; Dianteill 2002). For example, the structure of Ifá and Santería which, as we shall see, has developed since the nineteenth century in the form of ramifying ritual lineages of initiates, is shown to have resulted from the admixture of different social and cultural elements within the cabildos. West African principles of initiation are inflected by the royal imagery and hierarchy that were integral to the internal administration of the cabildos as encouraged by the colonial authorities, and combined with the Iberian principle of *compadrazgo* (co-parenthood) to generate the distinct lineage "branches" (*ramas*) that have reproduced themselves through the generations, as they still do today, on the basis of hierarchical godparent-to-godchild relationships (cf. Brandon 1993, 75–76; Dianteill 2000).

While such arguments remain influential, much recent scholarship in the field has been motivated by dissatisfaction with the passive model of transmission that they presuppose. Palmié puts the point fairly:

> Such interpretations are by no means invalid, particularly when phrased as testable hypotheses about the relation between cultural forms and the history of their social enactment. Much too often, however, have they taken the form of presuppositions about the formal determination of contemporary African American religious practice by forces of "tradition" or similar empirically elusive dei ex machina. (Palmié 2002, 160)

Combining the strengths of long-term ethnographic fieldwork with detailed historical research and historiography, recent studies have presented more sophisticated accounts. In line with the shift away from more or less speculative models of cultural transmission and social reproduction in the broader Black Atlantic literature, these studies present fine-grained images of the historical events and forces through which these practices have been and continue to be formed, emphasizing practitioners' role as agents, rather than mere carriers, of cultural, social, and historical transformation. Questions of memory (Brandon 1993), ritual performance

(Hagedorn 2001; Mason 2002), identity politics (Ayorinde 2004), structures of power and community (Wirtz 2007; Hearn 2008), and historical
agency and imagination (Palmié 2002; Routon 2008) have been central in
such accounts. Equally, we now have detailed historical reconstructions of
the role of prominent individuals in the institution and transformation of
Afro-Cuban religious forms—a story of ramifying relationships of power,
prestige, and influence, as well as persecution and dislocation, emerging
out of a complex transnational web of people, practices, and objects, linking Cuba, West Africa, and, increasingly, the United States, where Afro-
Cuban religions have been gaining ground in recent decades as the result
of the activities of Cuban émigrés in Miami, New York, and elsewhere
(e.g., Palmié 1995 and, on Ifá in particular, Brown 2003). Ethnographically
perspicacious, this body of work conveys a nuanced image of the historical
fortunes and contemporary position of Afro-Cuban religion. The current
vibrancy of these practices is explored in relation to a past forged in the
face of official persecution, marginalization, and folkloric "sanitization"
in different periods of the postcolonial and Revolutionary era. The relative renaissance of Afro-Cuban religion on the island in recent decades
is accounted for with reference, not only to changes in the revolutionary
government's social and cultural policy in post-Soviet times, but also to
the role of transnational developments such as tourism, immigration, and
the emergence of "diasporic" discourses, not least on the Internet (e.g.,
Capone 1999; Hagedorn 2001; Holbraad 2004a; Argyriadis, de la Torre,
Gutiérrez Zúniga, and Aguilar Ros 2008; Hearn 2008).

I shall be drawing on much of this body of research in my ethnography
of various aspects of the religious life of babalawos in Havana. On the
other hand, by focusing on the conceptual universe that is constituted in
Ifá worship, and particularly on the concept of truth around which it re-
volves, I sidestep the dominance of this research agenda. Indeed, if in this
book I say so much about such traditional-looking topics as cosmology, ritual, and myth, ignoring for the large part their many sociological, political,
and historical instantiations, that is because I assume (and want to demonstrate in the context of the anthropology of Afro-American religion) that
such concerns can do more than merely bolster outdated anthropological
assumptions about the role of cultural tradition. In other words, one may
well agree with Matory when he argues that anthropologists' old concerns
with "cultural logics," "systems of belief," and the like provide—at least
on their own—a flimsy basis for understanding how African American

religions came to be as they are (Matory 2005, 17), and still maintain that, suitably recast, such a focus holds interest for other reasons.

This may sound complacent. As already noted, a chief motivation for the historiographically oriented shift away from "essentializing" (and thereby also "exoticizing") approaches has been political—a restitution of African Americans as agents in world history, modernity, and so on (processes in which they have for too long been given the role of opposite pole—what Michel-Rolph Trouillot called the "savage slot" [2002]). So, from the viewpoint of political rectitude, my move away from this agenda may appear more backward than sideways. Yet it is not self-evident that the most politically responsive way to think about those whom colonial (imperial, Western, rationalist) imaginaries have denigrated as savage is to accord them their rightful share of agency in world history. At the very least, one can point out that the image of the world's peoples tussling for position in a global political economy is itself historically contingent, as is the notion that "agency" is necessarily everyone's idea of political dignity (e.g., see Strathern 1988; Mahmood 2004; Kirsch 2006; and Kelly 2011 for alternatives). True: conferring agency to erstwhile "savages" in our scholarly narratives of what matters is politically desirable in our own terms. But how far it is in theirs, and if so in what ways, are open ethnographic questions.

Obviously it would be absurd to suggest that the history and politics of slavery, colonialism, and social injustice do not matter to practitioners of Afro-Cuban religion. Apart from everything else, studies such as the aforementioned show the many and complex ways in which this is so (from images of slavery in ritual symbolism, to active political participation in each of the momentous phases of Cuban revolutionary struggle—see also Fernández Robaina 1990). What I am suggesting is that the study of Afro-Cuban religion is not exhausted by these concerns, and that exploring their remainder may be as politically responsive an analytical agenda as focusing upon them. The point can be put with reference to my earlier suggestion that the study of Ifá divination presents an image of confrontation between different ideas of truth—a confrontation, that is, borne of conceptual alterity. The impulse to rehabilitate the position of African American subjects as historical agents in our academic narratives turns on our concern, as anthropologists, for our own idea of truth—in particular, our concern with how best to "represent" the people we study. My question is what happens when the people we study have their own concerns

with truth, and, to boot, these concerns do not coincide with ours because
they turn on a different concept of truth altogether—one that that relates
to phenomena that have for so long been represented by anthropologists
as irrational, albeit understandable once other constituents of "their culture" and "their society" are brought to light. To assume that raising this
question is a return to an outmoded essentialism of cultural logics and the
like is to ignore this possibility, substituting our own concerns for those of
the people in whose name we perpetuate them.

So I suggest that attending to the substance of the conceptual economy
of Afro-Cuban religion, rather than, if you like, to the political economy
of its translations across the Atlantic, is itself a political act. As I shall be
showing throughout this book, it is through this kind of attention—taking
the alterity of the conceptual universe of Ifá seriously—that outmoded
ideas about culture, belief, cognition, and so on, all of which have indeed
bolstered forms of political oppression, can be combated. To invoke Eduardo Viveiros de Castro's manifesto for the kind of agenda I wish to pursue, concerns for the political self-determination of the people we study
cannot be furthered without also taking into account questions about their
"conceptual self-determination" (2003). At issue, as he says elsewhere, is
the "permanent decolonization of thought" (2011, 128; see also 2010).

It will be noted that such an agenda brings the book's approach into the
vicinity of lively and politically loaded debates about what has been called
"African philosophy" (e.g., Hountondji 1983; Mudimbe 1988; Hallen and
Sodipo 1997; Hallen 2000). As reviews of this literature show (e.g., Appiah
1992; Masolo 1994; Karp and Masolo 2000), discussions among professional philosophers and cultural critics about the philosophical content
of African thought are intimately bound up with wider debates about the
position of African peoples in what Achille Mbembe calls the postcolony
(2001). Investigations into the ontological, epistemological, ethical, and
aesthetic tenets of African discourse in a variety of fields (from cosmology and mythology to oral poetry, literature, and everyday discussion),
and debates about how and how far these forms of expression should be
considered philosophical, have been framed by the concern to combat
the longstanding derogation of African forms of thought as irrational, superstitious, and so on. Clearly, then, an anthropological agenda oriented
toward conceptual self-determination is sympathetic to many of the premises and goals of this literature.

Nevertheless, the distinctively anthropological tack I wish to take here
is also rather different. The point can be put by analogy to my commen-

tary on the political imaginary underlying the Afro-Americanist concern with according agency to African American subjects. If the image that drives that intellectual agenda is of peoples striving for political recognition on the stage of world history, the concern for intellectual emancipation that drives much of the literature on African philosophy conjures a picture of people striving for a place in the canon of human intellectual achievement. So, inspirational as they are, attempts to mine African culture and discourse for philosophical insight share in the same impulse to "recognize" in it ideas and values that derive at the first instance from our own standards of what is worthy and significant.[9]

What, then, of my stated aim to take seriously the analogy between babalawos and intellectuals? As an anthropological endeavor this does not turn on a worry about philosophical credentials. I take it that babalawos' activities as diviners are what they are, and that the degree to which philosophical insights may be found in what they do and say (explicitly in their "wisdom" or implicitly in their manner of thinking, talking, and acting) is an ethnographic matter. Most relevantly, I see no reason to suppose that babalawos' abiding concern with truth (the major ethnographic premise of this book) should be construed as philosophical. Its nature is divinatory, and much of this book is about explaining what this entails. My concern with conceptual self-determination turns on *our* credentials, as analysts, in describing how and what truth matters to babalawos. This, as we shall see, involves a concerted attempt to rid the analysis of Ifá divination of a series of presuppositions that have their roots in Western philosophical traditions. In this sense, matters pertaining to philosophy may indeed be relevant, but only to our own anthropological preoccupations with the ethnography of Ifá. To ascribe such preoccupations onto Ifá itself is, I would contend, an ethnographic distortion. In order to show the distinctively anthropological character of the problems this book seeks to address, the next chapter examines the role and character of the notion of truth in anthropological research.

CHAPTER ONE

Truth in Anthropology: From Nature and Culture to Recursive Analysis

In contrast to babalawos' characteristic confidence about their ability to pronounce truth, anthropologists in recent years have tended to view such questions with a mixture of anxiety and boredom. The story of how we got to this point of truth-weariness in anthropology is often told and sometimes lamented (e.g., Gellner 1985; Spiro 1987; Wilson 2004; cf. Myhre 2006b). My purpose in retelling it here is not so much to comment on the rights and wrongs of current attitudes to truth, but rather to articulate the concept of truth that they presuppose. My central claim in this respect is that while in the relatively short history of the discipline attitudes to truth have shifted dramatically, the notion of truth with which they have been concerned has remained the same, namely the familiar idea that truth is a matter of representing the world as it actually is. Pivotal to longstanding debates about anthropology's status as a social science, this commonsense understanding of truth has been cast within the discipline in terms of the distinction between society and culture on the one hand and nature on the other. Since, from an anthropological point of view, people's representations pertain to culture and society, while the world as it actually is pertains to nature, truth is a function of this foundational anthropological distinction.

The changing attitudes toward truth in anthropology—from confidence through skepticism to apathy—can be understood with reference to shifting conceptions of the relationship between culture/society and nature, including the notion of "human nature," which, along with "culture" and "society," has played such an important role in attempts to demarcate the intellectual remit of the discipline. This, however, raises the question of what happens to the concept of truth when the distinction between culture/society and nature is rescinded altogether, as it has been in recent strands of anthropological thinking. Can the concept of truth withstand such a negation of its major premise or does it fall with it? This question poses a major challenge to the discipline of anthropology at its current juncture—the challenge that lies at the heart of this book's agenda. In particular, I shall show that while the move away from taking the culture/society versus nature distinction as the analytical starting point is anthropologically imperative, its implications for the role of truth in anthropological reasoning remain unexplored.

I begin by examining three broad stages in the conceptualization of the relationship between culture/society and nature. Borrowing from Maurice Bloch's idiosyncratic periodization in a recent overview of the discipline's history (2005), I use the terms *evolutionism* and *diffusionism* to label the first two stages, and add *constructivism* to label the third one.[1] Of course much has been written about the tenets of each of these currents and about the specific manner in which each defined the anthropological project. My review of this familiar ground is not intended to clarify my own theoretical position but to show what each of these theoretical positions entails for the conceptualization of truth in anthropology. Thus, I present the story of truth in anthropology in three installments, each corresponding to a particular period in the history of the discipline. This three-stage trajectory can be seen as a progressive weakening of the link between the concepts of culture and society and that of nature, particularly human nature. While evolutionist anthropology posited a substantive relationship between sociocultural phenomena and human nature, diffusionist approaches turned this relationship into a purely formal one, and thus opened the way for the constructivist turn, which severed the relationship altogether. Inasmuch as truth in anthropology has been deemed to depend on just this relationship, the stock of truth has fallen as the relationship has weakened.

Evolutionism, "Diffusionism," Constructivism: The Fall of Truth

At its inception as a professional discipline in the nineteenth century, anthropology was supremely confident about its ability to make truth-claims about human beings. Working within the parameters of the broader field of natural history that was so invigorated by Darwin's theory of evolution, anthropologists embarked on elucidating the basic features of human nature by comparing its manifestations in different parts of the world. Alongside the study of human beings' physical and ecological features, research on their varied social and cultural characteristics was considered a major part of this enterprise. That sociocultural variation could be taken as an index of an underlying human nature was guaranteed by the evolutionist premise that deemed that different forms of social organization and cultural expression were natural inasmuch as they corresponded to different stages in human beings' development as a species. Indeed, establishing an isomorphic relationship between stages of natural evolution and sociocultural "advancement" was a central concern, involving, for example, attempts to correlate differences in biometric measurements with distinct social or cultural characteristics.

This naturalism enabled nineteenth-century evolutionary anthropology to think of itself as a scientific enterprise capable of delivering truths about human phenomena: its methods and procedures (the use of empirical evidence, experimental methods, explicit rules of inference, and so on) placed it on par with other sciences that had been established as professional academic fields since the Enlightenment. Like them anthropology could represent the natural world correctly, as it is, which was to say that anthropology could arrive at the truth.

In order to understand the particular character of evolutionary anthropology's claim to truth, however, it is important to note its peculiarly "reflexive" quality. The term *reflexivity* here should not be confused with *reflexivism*, which we associate with much more recent developments in the discipline (although, as we shall see, the two are indeed connected). Rather, evolutionary anthropology was reflexive in that, unlike other natural sciences, its own activities themselves had to be understood, in a broad and basic sense, as forming part of the field of phenomena it set out to investigate. Anthropology, after all, was a human phenomenon in its own right: it was an example of a highly distinctive sociocultural manifestation that was characteristic of the "advanced" societies in which anthropologists lived and worked. So if anthropology was the study of human phenomena in general, not least the study of sociocultural variation, then it would, in some sense, have to include itself in its own remit of study.

As we shall see, this irreducibly self-referential quality of anthropology had far-reaching consequences for the development of the discipline, ultimately feeding into the kind of postpositivist skepticism about truth that has become so familiar in recent decades. But here we may note that, without necessarily undermining them, the requirement of reflexivity at minimum placed an added constraint on anthropologists' claims to truth. Like other scientists, anthropologists could claim truth for their propositions (e.g., hypotheses, theories, refutations) only if they represented the facts of nature, and particularly the facts of human nature, as they are. But unlike other natural scientists, anthropologists had also to be sure that whatever claims they made about (human) nature were coherent with the one fact of which they had to be certain, namely the human ability to represent nature as it is—in other words, the human capacity for truth which they themselves, and modern science in general, exemplified. Anthropological accounts of human nature that failed to account for their own possibility, in this sense, were at least incomplete and at worst self-contradictory. Hence, the justification of anthropological truth-claims could not only be a matter of methodological procedure. It also had to be one of substantive anthropological argument. For truth to be the form of anthropological inquiry, if you like, it had also to be part of its content. This meant that the conceptual machinery of truth—the very distinction between the natural world and human beings' representations of it, notions of evidence, of reason, and so on—doubled up on itself reflexively, becoming as much an object of anthropological scrutiny as it was a matter of methodological deliberation.

Evolutionary anthropology amply met the requirements of reflexive justification. It did this by putting questions of truth and falsehood, and particularly different peoples' propensity toward them, at the heart of the story it told about human beings' natural evolution through different stages of sociocultural development. According to this story, all human beings, from the most primitive to the most advanced, had the capacity to represent the world around them as it is, that is, they all had the capacity for truth.[2] However, alongside other obvious markers (such as degrees of technological sophistication, social complexity, and moral refinement), one of the things that made human beings naturally different from each other was that they had developed this capacity to different degrees. At the earliest stages of evolution humans were hostage to intellectual confusions of various kinds. Manifest in such pervasive "superstitions" as animism and magic, these confusions included a difficulty with abstract thought and a tendency to misattribute causation (e.g., ascribing agency to natural forces), as well as a proclivity toward category mistakes of various sorts (e.g., treating things as people or confusing signs with their referents). As humans moved to more advanced stages of evolution these confusions were lifted step by step. So, the more advanced a society was, the more it was able to represent the world transparently, as it actually is. The apogee of this evolutionary trajectory from false superstition toward reasoned truth was modern-day science, understood as the systematic attempt by humans to offer true accounts of the world around them. Hence the reflexive justification: anthropologists could tell the truth about human nature because they themselves exemplified a stage of human evolution that was characterized, precisely, by the ability to tell the truth. Human beings, in other words, could tell the story of their own evolution by virtue of it, so anthropological truth-claims were, if you like, self-justified.

Except that this version of anthropological reflexivity was tautological. The idea that truth comes naturally to anthropologists by virtue of their advanced state of evolution as civilized humans was circular, since the difference between civilization and the evolutionary stages that were supposed to lead up to it was already defined in terms of, among other factors, the propensity to truth. To be primitive *was* (partly) to be prone to error, and to be civilized *was* (partly) to be inclined to truth. So attempts to periodize social and cultural differences into evolutionary stages served not to reveal the underlying natural differences that cause them, but rather to "naturalize," as we would say today, social and cultural differences that anthropologists, for social and cultural reasons of their own, deemed significant. The natural superiority of modern civilization, by virtue of which evolutionary anthropologists could lay claim to it reflexively, was, to recall Bronislaw Malinowski's famous criticism, a "conjecture" that said lots about the Victorian anthropologists who made it and little about the facts of human nature (1926, 132).

The failure of evolutionary anthropologists to clinch their argument about natural stages of sociocultural evolution by empirical means left the way open to alternative ways of accounting for the variety of people's social and cultural arrangements, which professional anthropology was now beginning to record with the help of increasingly systematic methods. Evolutionists' main critics in the nineteenth century, the so-called diffusionists, argued that, rather than being mapped on to a putative natural sequence of evolution, social and cultural variation should be seen as the result of patterns of diffusion, in which particular social and cultural traits travelled differentially across the world depending on contingent circumstances (demographic flows, ecological and adaptive factors, particular historical circumstances, and so forth). Here I follow Bloch (2005, 6–7) in using the term *diffusionism* in a broader sense, to refer to the key idea that underlay the nineteenth-century arguments about global patterns of diffusion, namely that the varied ways in which people live in different parts of the world are the result, not of natural necessity, but of historically contingent processes of sociocultural transmission. Taking this as a core premise, the forefathers of social and cultural anthropology as we know it today—emblematically Boas in America, Malinowski and Radcliffe-Brown in Britain, and Durkheim, Mauss, and their circle in France—effectively shifted the intellectual object of anthropology. By decoupling sociocultural phenomena from any correlation with natural evolutionary stages, they instituted society and culture as sui generis fields to be understood in terms of their own.

From the point of view of anthropological truth and its justification, this may seem like a major shift, since it appears to compromise the naturalist premise upon which the confidence of anthropology as a science of human nature rested. If the social and cultural variation in which anthropologists were so interested could not be explained as an expression of human beings' underlying nature, then in what sense could its study even be scientific? At the very least, understanding such phenomena in their own terms would imply anthropological methods whose ability to deliver truth would rest on more than the naturalist claim to be providing accurate representations of human nature. Furthermore, such a move away from naturalism also undermined the evolutionists' reflexive justification for anthropological truth-claims, ruling out of court any notion that anthropologists' privileged access to truth was natural: seen as itself an example of sociocultural variation, the propensity to truth or error became a matter of social and cultural contingency rather than natural necessity. It followed that, as far as this propensity was concerned, anthropologists and their "natives" were on the same boat, in principle capable of truth or error in equal measure.

From today's standpoint, it may seem as though this flattening move, which appears to obliterate the distance between anthropologist and native at the level of first principle, would open the floodgates for the kind of relativism we now associate with social constructivism and postmodern self-doubt. And certainly, in its twentieth-century versions, diffusionism involved foundational debates about anthropology's scientific credentials, with some arguing that the distinctively human subject-matter of the discipline (which entailed accounting for human values, subjective feelings, opinions, and so on) gave anthropological claims to truth a character that was vastly different from those of the natural sciences (e.g., Geertz 1973b).[3]

None of this, however, led to the kind of self-doubt that "science war-riors" of more recent years have come to associate with sociocultural contingency. Crucially, these methodological debates about scientific cre-dentials were not about *whether* sociocultural anthropology could con-tinue to be deemed a science, but about *how*. The diffusionist move did not shake anthropologists' confidence in their ability to offer true repre-sentations of the world, nor did it dent their assumption that in this respect they were better than the people they studied. Taking their claim to truth as given, what was at issue methodologically for anthropologists as they moved into the twentieth century was how best to articulate the particu-lar character of truth-claims about sociocultural phenomena and how to provide epistemological justifications for them that would be as robust as those of natural science. Even American cultural anthropologists, with all their insistence on "cultural relativism," saw no reason to give up the idea that the study of human culture was a scientific enterprise through and through (e.g., Boas 1940; Kroeber 1952). Understood as the idea that since particular cultural formations have to be interpreted in their own terms they do not lend themselves to universal generalizations, cultural relativism was proposed by Boas and his students as a point of scientific methodology—a proposal about the principles that would have to inform a properly exact study of human cultures.

Key to understanding why the move from evolutionism to diffusionism did not inhibit anthropologists' confidence as scientists is the role that the notion of human nature continued to play in their reasoning, albeit in a sparser guise. For while diffusionism hollowed out the concept of human nature from its explanatory power when it came to accounting for the diversity of human phenomena, it did not deprive the concept from its key heuristic role, namely that of singling out human phenomena as a distinct field of study. In a sense it strengthened it. Social and cultural diversity was no longer to be mapped on to an underlying axis of natural diversity that rendered differences between people analogous to differences between species. Rather, it was now taken as the index of our underlying unity as a species, which qualitatively marks us off from the rest of nature. What we all share by nature is the capacity to be socially and culturally different from each other—our unique nature, so to speak, is to be cultural.

Retaining naturalism in this purely formal sense, and enfolding within it the substantive concern with sociocultural diversity as a sui generis phe-nomenon, kept in place the analogy between anthropology and the natu-ral scientific approaches from which it was otherwise distinguished. Both the object of anthropology and its methods of study differentiated it from other sciences. Nevertheless, treating social and cultural orders as a part of nature meant that they could still be studied in the same sense, if not necessarily in the same way, as other natural phenomena. They could be described, as any other aspect of the world could, and analyzed, so as to form the basis for propositions that were as robust as those of the other sciences, subject as they were to similar standards of evaluation. In this way the notion of human nature continued to act as the ultimate guarantor for anthropological aspirations to truth.

This formal naturalism also allowed diffusionism to meet the requirement for a reflexive justification of anthropological truth (the idea that whatever claims anthropologists might make about their own ability to arrive at the truth should be compatible with the stories they tell about others'). Again, it did so by retaining the foil of the evolutionists' argument while discarding its substance. To be sure, the idea that people's propensity to truth or error is socially and culturally contingent nullified any notion that anthropologists' claim to truth is naturally superior. However, it left intact the basic premise that motivated the evolutionists' tautologies about natural superiority, namely the seemingly self-evident fact that, *qua* scientific, anthropologists' claims to truth were indeed superior to those of the people they studied. That this should still seem self-evident was a direct corollary of the role that naturalism continued to play in the definition of anthropology as a science. According to this image, people of all societies make sense of the natural world around them, including themselves as a part of that world, by means of their own cultural repertoires and according to their own social arrangements. However, only some societies have devoted themselves to developing systematic methods and techniques that may ensure that their representations of the world are actually correct. Science in modern Western societies is exactly that: a sophisticated sociocultural attempt to represent nature (or, in the case of anthropology, society and culture as a part of nature) as it actually is—that is, truly. Thus the very terms in which anthropological claims to truth were defined, namely as the ability to represent (human) nature as it is, pertained directly (and reflexively) to the substance of the diffusionist argument about the uniformity of human nature and the diversity of societies and cultures

In this way the propensity to truth or error continued reflexively to mark out the difference between anthropologists and natives respectively. What had changed was that the evolutionist tautology of postulating these propensities as natural was now replaced by the more tractably empirical task of explaining them with reference to social and cultural factors. While this task hardly exhausted anthropologists' preoccupations during this period, it was at the core of their endeavors throughout the discipline's "short twentieth century"—its golden age as a confident producer of knowledge about the social and cultural world, which lasted roughly until the 1970s. In fact, from the point of view of the requirement for reflexive justification, the story of the discipline during this period can be told as a series of competing attempts to account for the (always self-evident) fact that the people anthropologists studied should so often and in such varied ways get the world around them wrong (myths, rituals, magic, and all the other odd "beliefs" that went with them). Were these erroneous beliefs and practices perhaps useful to them in some way (functionalism)? Did they somehow help preserve the social structure of the group (structural-functionalism)? Did they express core values of its culture (cultural interpretivism)—its *gestalt* personality perhaps (culture and personality school)? Were they metaphors for basic social concerns (symbolism) or examples of people's false consciousness of them (Marxism)? Or were they in some deep sense expressions of how the human mind works in general (structuralism)?

For a long time, the self-evidence of their claims to truth as scientists prevented anthropologists from turning such questions onto themselves. Thus anthropologists failed to treat their own ostensive ability to represent the world truly as a phenomenon requiring explanation with reference to the particular features of modern Western society and culture. Nevertheless, the reflexive bent of anthropologists' abiding concern with explaining native errors was always present by implication, invariably framed in terms of a series of "master" contrasts and narratives that mapped directly onto the reflexive distinction between native error and anthropological truth: myth versus history, ritual versus technology, magic and religion versus science, or, the most encompassing, tradition versus modernity.

Staple to all forms of anthropological argumentation, these kinds of questions and distinctions received their most explicitly "reflexive" treatment in the so-called rationality debate that raged among anthropologists in the 1960s and 1970s, with some philosophers weighing in as well (e.g., Horton 1967; Wilson 1974; Hollis and Lukes 1982; cf. Lukes 2000). At issue in this debate was not only why "indigenous people" (as they were now often called) might get things wrong in the way that they do, but also how these errors, and the "modes of thought" that sustain them (Horton and Finnegan 1973), could be compared to the standards of reason and truth to which anthropologists themselves, as scientists, subscribed. Were indigenous peoples' "apparently irrational beliefs," as they were branded (e.g., Sperber 1985), simply the result of a misapplication of the universal standards of reason that science exemplifies or did they display a logic of their own?[4] If they did have their own logic, then how did this compare to the logic that informs scientific reason? And, crucially in terms of the reflexive justification of anthropology as a science, how might the latter be used to account for the former, thereby proving its superior claim to truth in the pudding?

Still, by the time these systematic comparisons between the inner workings of "indigenous" and "Western" (scientific) forms of reasoning were being debated, the confident assumption that the latter were superior to the former no longer went free of challenge. Within the rationality debate itself, some argued that if indigenous beliefs instantiate a logic that is coherent unto itself, with principles of reasoning that were different to those of Western science, then to judge those beliefs by the standards of Western science was inappropriate (e.g., Lévi-Strauss 1966; Winch 1967). For if anthropological analysis of indigenous systems of belief effectively reveals that there was not just one standard of reason but many (many "rationalities"), then to continue to uphold one of them as the standard for evaluating the rest is contradictory. Anthropology should give up the hubris of seeking to uphold the superiority of scientific claims to truth by showing how they could account for others' errors, and rather recognize that if others' beliefs appear erroneous to us that is because they are being held up against standards of truth that are alien (and therefore inappropriate) to them. Instead of being a cross-cultural Rottweiler for science, then, anthropology should adopt the standpoint of the people it studies in order to *counter* science's claims to universal validity, by showing that multiple and mutually incommensurate claims to truth are possible.

The ascendancy of such arguments for epistemological relativism, which began to be made across the board in anthropology roughly from the late 1960s onwards, mark the period I call "social constructivist" ("cultural constructivist" would also do). Under an assortment of influences, including phenomenology, hermeneutics and Weberian sociology, structuralism, poststructuralism and semiotics, Wittgenstein's philosophy of language, as well as critiques of natural scientific method itself (e.g., Kuhn 1962; Feyerabend 1975; Rorty 1979), the very idea of scientific truth began to be considered either naive or dogmatic. Specifically anthropological variants of such arguments gained pre-eminence within the discipline partly for contingent reasons that had to do particularly with the end of colonialism. Self-conscious about the role of anthropological knowledge in colonial projects, and working in an atmosphere of antiauthoritarian radicalism in intellectual circles (civil rights, student activism, opposition to cold warfare and so on), anthropologists on both sides of the Atlantic began to see political emancipation in the idea that Western scientific enterprises such as their own had no privileged claim to the authority of truth. Where previous generations had balked at treating anthropology on a par with the sociocultural phenomena it had purported to study scientifically (other than in the purely formal sense implied by diffusionism), in the postcolonial era anthropologists saw this as a move toward the kind of cross-cultural egalitarianism that could be embraced. To view anthropologists' claims to authoritative truth as social constructions was to place them on par with indigenous truth claims. If no truth is any less socially constructed than any other, then all societies' claims to truth are, at least in principle, equally valid.

However, for purposes of the present argument, it is important to emphasize that the conditions for such skepticism were already present in the diffusionist idea that what human beings have in common by nature is the capacity to be socioculturally different from one another. To be sure, this suggestion improved on the evolutionist tautology—that of first defining sociocultural differences as natural ones and then explaining them as such. Still, the suggestion is itself a paradox. Much like familiar anxiety-inducing paradoxes such as Socrates' knowing that he knows nothing, the "culture is natural" credo of diffusionism entails its own negation. Consider, after all, the twofold implication diffusionists drew from it: on the one hand all claims to truth are socially and culturally contingent and, on the other, some of them are better than others because they reflect nature as it actually is. While validly drawn, the two implications are mutually inconsistent—the bread-and-butter epistemological conundrum. If evaluating truth-claims involves testing them against nature, then there must after all be *some* truth-claims that are not socioculturally contingent, namely a set of statements that show how nature *really* is. Without such a set of statements, how could we ever decide which truth-claims actually get nature right? Conversely, holding on to the idea that *all* truth-claims are socioculturally contingent implies giving up the notion that they can nevertheless be evaluated with reference to nature as an objective benchmark. If all truth-claims are socioculturally contingent, then any statement about what nature is like (objectively, really, actually) must also be so, and therefore must itself require further evaluation, and so on to infinity, without ever getting to the putative rock-bottom benchmark of nature as it is. Hence the paradox: when either of the two entailments of diffusionism is true, the other one is false.

The move from diffusionism to social constructivism, then, can be understood with reference to this paradoxical dilemma. Diffusionist anthropology had chosen to uphold its claim to scientific truth by holding dogmatically onto the idea of a nature that stands outside the realms of society and culture. Social constructivists took the alternative option. Taking the diffusionist credo to its ultimate conclusion (if culture is natural, so to speak, then nature is cultural), they subjected nature under the realms of society and culture and thus relinquished anthropology's claim to scientific truths that could only be guaranteed by nature's objective reality. This, of course, obliterated any attempt at "reflexive" justification: the idea that each claim to truth is in its own way partial (in both senses of the word) went hand in hand with reducing to the absurd the notion of nature as a neutral benchmark for truth, and regarding all claims to truth as socially and culturally "situated."

In fact, one of the most significant effects of social constructivists' break with naturalism was to turn the requirement for reflexive justification squarely on its head. For evolutionists and diffusionists alike the point of whatever reflexive story they told about anthropology's claims to truth could only be to bear out their obvious superiority. With this superiority now denied in principle, the role of reflexive argument became the opposite, namely to place anthropologists and the people they studied on an equal footing by showing how their truth-claims were equally situated and partial. At the level of substantive ethnographic inquiry, this opened the floodgates for the study of all aspects of so-called Western societies, including that of science itself. To this day, however, this anthropological "symmetry," as Bruno Latour calls it (1993), has not been extended to proper ethnographic studies of anthropologists themselves—their daily life as professional academics, their conduct during fieldwork, its correlation to their claims to expertise, and so on.[5] Rather, much as with evolutionism and diffusionism, social constructivists' reflexive attention to their own practices as anthropologists has been limited to the level of epistemological and methodological discussion.

In particular, it has taken the form of an injunction to "reflexivism." I use the ending "-ism" here to highlight the ideological tenor of this rendition of anthropological reflexivity. A form of epistemological double vision, reflexivism seeks to incorporate into anthropological practice the idea that, as social constructions, the truth-claims anthropologists make about the societies they study are necessarily also a function of their own claim to authority as anthropologists. Hence, rather than taking (or offering) those truth-claims at face value, which would be to collude with the structures of authority that underpin them, anthropologists must make sure to situate such claims with reference to the conditions of their production—the power differentials of "West" versus "rest," issues of class, race, gender, and so on, and even, at the psychoanalytic level, the personal propensities of the researcher him- or herself. While binding anthropologists to what the philosopher of science Isabelle Stengers calls the stance of "irony" (2000), this effort to "deconstruct" anthropological knowledge brought with it a flurry of creative experimentation with the form of anthropological writing, as anthropologists strove to find ways to subvert their own authority so as to shift power to the people about whom they wrote ("giving voice," "speaking truth to power," and so on).

By the time I came of age in anthropology, at the turn of the twenty-first century in Britain, it had become fashionable to dismiss some of the grosser excesses of social constructivism—the potentially debilitating infinite regress of always having to deconstruct any attempt at positive knowledge; the danger of nihilism that lurked in giving up the level-headed intuition that some things are just truer than others, pure and simple; the sheer self-indulgence of making it a methodological imperative to talk about oneself before talking about others ("enough about you, now can we talk about me?" said the native to the reflexive anthropologist). All too often, it was felt, the reflexivist recipe for double vision (one eye outward, the other inward) produced a blur, in which sight of the original remit of anthropology—the exciting prospect of making sense of sociocultural phenomena the world over—was lost.

Perhaps unfair in its refusal to acknowledge the more anthropologically productive effects of bringing the self in to the fray of research in this way (e.g., Rosaldo 1989; Wikan 1990), the dissatisfaction with constructivist anxieties about truth led in some quarters to a call to arms in defense of science and "common sense." Indeed, if the most public controversies within the discipline in the 1980s and 1990s are anything to go by, the most prevalent rejoinder to social constructivism has been to insist on the time-honored idea that anthropology can aspire to scientific truth for as long as it holds fast to the basic facts of "human nature," which, as it is often asserted, must obviously act as a constraint upon the sociocultural variability that so dazzles the constructivists (e.g., Freeman 1983 *contra* Mead 1961; Obeyesekere 1992 *contra* Sahlins 1985).

This kind of level-headedness has in recent years become particularly prevalent in the field of cognitive anthropology, whose proponents are now probably the most vociferous critics of social constructivism (e.g., Sperber 1985, 1996; D'Andrade 1995; Bloch 2005). Effectively mirroring the constructivist aversion to the idea of human nature, cognitive anthropologists argue that the real chimera is culture, at least insofar as it is taken as a domain of phenomena that is somehow separate from or beyond nature. Yes, human beings have a peculiarly sophisticated capacity to represent the world around them, including the capacity to represent other representations (and in fact other species do have analogous, albeit in important respects more rudimentary, capacities). But this capacity is itself natural, not just in the formal sense admitted by earlier generations of anthropologists as we have seen, but rather in a fully substantive and scientifically tractable way: cultural representations are a function of human mental capacities, and these, as rapid advances in cognitive science now purport to show, are just the result of natural processes (neuronal and so on) that take place in the human brain. So to treat cultural representations as a domain unto itself and then worry whether or not nature as it is in *it*self can be accessed through them is unduly to mystify matters, since cultural representations are themselves as natural as trees. On a naturalist premise, truth pertains not to an ontological mismatch between culture and nature, but rather to scientifically tractable epistemic matches between some parts of nature (brain-instantiated representations) and others (the world, the people in it, their brain-instantiated representations). Not only can anthropology aspire to arrive at such truths in its own representations of sociocultural phenomena, but it can also set up questions regarding human beings' capacity for truth in this sense as a prime object of anthropological investigation (e.g., Boyer 1990).

Nevertheless, such returns to naturalistic defenses of scientific truth in anthropology have been a minority pursuit. Indeed, if truth was something of a battle-cry in the more polarized public controversies that culminated in the so-called science wars of the 1990s (see Herrnstein Smith 2005)—at that time, either you believed in truth or you didn't—the present attitude to such questions within the discipline seems to be weariness. This has partly to do with the fact that, as far as mainstream, bread-and-butter anthropological research is concerned, over the past couple of decades the skeptical message of constructivism has been largely absorbed. While by no means all anthropologists these days would pledge explicit allegiance to constructivism as a coherent theoretical doctrine, and many profess their awareness of its pitfalls, its basic tenets of relativism and reflexivism have arguably become professional reflexes within the discipline. In that sense, barring the cognitivists, we are all working constructivists.

Hence, for example, the strong tendency in recent years to refrain from comparative theoretical generalizations and to favor instead accounts of particular ethnographic instances for their own sake—"assemblages of anecdotes about this and that," as Bloch laments with a degree of hyperbole (2005, 9). Hence also the now-dominant idea that if theory is to be sought anywhere, that should be not at the level of supracultural propositions conceived in the analyst's unavoidably essentialist imagination, but rather at the level of concrete and historically contingent infracultural diffusions—the writ-large relativity of the globalized political economy of modernity, transnationalism, empire, and so on—of which the literature on Afro-American religion is, as we saw, one expression. And hence, finally, the marked tendency in recent years to supplant questions regarding the truth-value of particular anthropological arguments with concerns about their ethical credentials and political consequences—the move from objective models to moral ones, as Roy D'Andrade has put it (1995).

If the tendency to take constructivist tenets for granted in recent years has often been more a matter of basic instinct than of explicit argumentation, this is also because the familiar arguments from first principles in which the science and culture wars of the 1980s and 1990s so often exhausted themselves were seen to lead to sterile position-taking. No amount of constructivist irony could ever persuade a naturalist (or, more broadly, a "realist") to give up on his point-blank-obvious intuition that there's a world out there that both constrains and acts as a benchmark for the truth-claims we may make about it. And no amount of realist level-headedness could ever persuade a constructivist to give up her always-cleverer insight that since the world is given to us only in the ways we represent it, it cannot be conceived independently of the truth-claims we make about it. To the extent that anthropology's disciplinary niche as an explorer of social and cultural variety involves an inclination toward the latter position, anthropologists' broad tendency at present is to practice constructivism without, as it were, preaching it too much—or not, at least, if this involves engaging in, by now, apparently futile clashes at the level of first principles (Culture is natural! No, nature is cultural!).

Dissatisfaction with these ostrich tactics—the more-or-less conscious choice to ignore a debate that remains unresolved within the discipline—is one of the motivations for this book. Its aim, however, is decidedly not to resume the debate in the terms in which it has so far been conducted and, as it now seems, exhausted. On the contrary, the book adopts as a starting point that putting the question of truth back on the anthropological agenda requires a basic shift of the terms in which we discuss it. In particular, we need to depart from the central assumption that has remained constant throughout the trajectory of anthropologists' debates about truth, namely that the notion of truth itself is to be understood, broadly, in terms of the relationship between representations and the world they represent, or, in the more specifically anthropological terms set forth above, the relationship between culture and nature. Put in a nutshell, the story I have told about anthropologists' changing attitudes to truth over the past century and a half is about the gradual exhaustion of the epistemological implications of just this assumption—starting from anthropologists' initial confidence that the truth of their cultural representations of human nature was guaranteed by nature itself, and moving step by step to the ironic realization that nature cannot provide such guarantees since it must itself be a cultural construct. So the collective yawn with which the question of truth now tends to be greeted in anthropology will be fully justified for as long as the concept of truth is left suspended between the poles of nature and culture and the antinomous attractions that they exert.

Of course neither the injunction to break with so-called representationist assumptions about what truth is, nor the proscription of the so-called binary opposition of nature versus culture, will sound particularly original in the present intellectual climate.[6] On the former count, it should be remembered that a whole swathe of twentieth-century philosophy has been about presenting alternatives to representationist accounts of truth; American pragmatism, late Wittgenstein, and just about all of what Anglo-Saxons call "Continental" philosophy may serve as examples. Indeed, one response to the epistemological impasses of anthropology in recent decades has been to turn to such philosophies for inspiration, sometimes mining them (though rarely explicitly) for alternative visions of anthropological truth (e.g., Jackson 1989; Moore 2005; Myhre 2006b; Pina-Cabral 2009; cf. Morris 1997). Similarly, denying the universal validity of the distinction between nature and culture, and lumping it contemptuously together with a whole canon of offending "binaries" (mind/body,

West/rest, male/female, and so on), has been de rigueur in much anthropological teaching and writing for twenty years or more.

Nevertheless, I suggest that run alongside each other these two platitudes add up to something interesting. In particular, pursuing the anthropological platitude about the cultural variability of distinctions between nature and culture to its ultimate consequences, as has been done in recent writings that are anything but platitudinous, raises the prospect of formulating alternatives to the representationist account of truth in a manner that is *distinctly anthropological.* So, having framed the question of truth in terms of the quintessentially anthropological distinction between nature and culture, my strategy now is to pursue an "internal" anthropological critique of that distinction in order to reframe the question of truth without deferring to received (and of course only in that sense platitudinous) philosophical wisdoms—a point on which I shall comment further in due course.

Toward a Recursive Analysis of Truth

The nigh-on catholic renouncement of the distinction between nature and culture in contemporary anthropology as an odious binary indicates the sheer weight of influences that have made this attitude plausible. It is almost as though all major theoretical developments in late twentieth-century social theory—from phenomenology, semiotics and systems theory to poststructuralism, practice theory, actor network theory, and even some variants of cognitive theory[7]—had conspired to converge on a single point: Descartes was wrong, if not evil, and all vestiges of his, and any, dualism must be purged. As with all vilification, however, the problem is that the en masse adoption of this message has all too often been at the expense of its content—gaudily cutting down "Cartesianisms" like weeds while leaving their roots untouched in the soil. Perhaps the most blatant sign of this in anthropology is that the repudiation of the distinction between nature and culture is typically done in the name of cultural relativism. According to this view, the very concepts of nature and culture are themselves cultural constructions—a mark of our Cartesian mindset—and therefore should not be projected ethnocentrically onto others who may not classify the world in these particular terms. Once stated like this, the oddity of this position, which verges on self-contradiction, becomes obvious. It is only by relying on the distinction between nature and culture—precisely the form of "classifying the world" we are supposed not to project onto others—that we are able (indeed bound) to repudiate the "ethnocentrism" of the distinction itself. We should not universalize the distinction between nature and culture, we say, because other cultures do not make it, and thus we reinscribe its universality in the very act of denying it.

The strand of nature/culture debate I want to pursue here can be characterized as a concerted attempt to overcome this lazy paradox. The stakes in this line of anthropological thinking should not be underestimated. Insofar as the relativizing move of rendering the distinction between nature and culture culturally contingent is a special case of the kind of constructivism that lies at the heart of the current apathy toward questions of truth, resolving the paradoxes inherent in this move allows us a way to think ourselves out of the *impasses* of constructivism itself. At stake, then, is a position that goes beyond constructivism, not by striking a balance between it and the naturalist/realist intuitions it has sought to tutor, but rather by radicalizing it to such an extent as to come out, as it were, on its other side. The question is this: How might the "nonuniversality" of the distinction between nature and culture be conceptualized *without* recourse to that very distinction? And, following on from that, what might the implications of such a way of thinking be for the question of truth in anthropology, which has so far been wedded to this distinction?

Although charting the varied sources of debate that have led up to this type of question is too large a task to undertake here, it is worth noting that the critique of the anthropological matrix of nature versus culture has arisen within the discipline as an extension of anthropologists' longstanding investment in what has come to be known as "cultural critique"—a mode of anthropological argument that stems from the inclination to "relativize" things by using ethnography to show how they could be conceived differently. In an incisive discussion, Keith Hart shows that the task of relativizing assumptions, which other disciplines as well as the wider public may take for granted, has been a major part of anthropologists' intellectual mission from the early years of the discipline. Cultural critique in this inclusive sense has cut across the discipline's otherwise determining theoretical divides and national traditions (Hart 2001).[8] Nevertheless, with its abiding concern with cultural relativity, American cultural anthropology has arguably provided the most fertile ground for the cultivation of this kind of stance, as shown, for example, by the recordbreaking sales of such books as Ruth Benedict's *Patterns of Culture* (1934).

The rise of reflexivism in the 1980s in the United States, promoting a

"repatriation" of anthropology in which not only sundry aspects of modern Euro-American culture but also, crucially, anthropology itself become
the object of anthropological reflection, can be seen as the ultimate logical consequence of a cultural critique that is played out from within the
coordinates of cultural relativism (e.g., Marcus and Fischer 1986). Anthropology itself, including its *ur*-binary of nature versus culture, is thus relativized as one among myriad cultural constructs. Remarkably, however,
what often goes unmentioned when the story of late twentieth-century
cultural anthropology gets told (e.g., Kuper 2000) is that the same tradition of cultural critique that bore us reflexivism in the 1980s also delivered
a turn of thinking that was both less inward-looking and more radical in
its critical implications: instead of relativizing anthropology as a cultural
construct, this tack of research effectively relativized culture (and its opposition to nature) as an anthropological one.

The turning point arguably was David Schneider's *tout court* attempt to
debunk the anthropological concept of kinship. To be sure, Schneider's argument could be viewed as a straightforward example of relativist cultural
critique US-style, which is how Schneider himself presented it. Following
his original research in Micronesia on Yap kinship categories, Schneider
"repatriates" his project by examining the cultural construction of kinship
among middle-class residents of Chicago (1968). There he finds that the
"core symbols" of American kinship, as he called it, are organized around
a culturally elaborated distinction between what are deemed to be "facts
of nature" (particularly sexual intercourse and the blood-ties to progeny
it is supposed to engender) and the cultural conventions that are deemed
to bring them under control (particularly the codes of conduct that are
enshrined in marital law, and the kin-relationships to which they give rise).
To the extent that this distinction also informs the cross-cultural study
of kinship by anthropologists (from Lewis Henry Morgan's distinction
between descriptive and classificatory kin terms to Claude Lévi-Strauss's
contention that kinship systems offer varying solutions to the universal
problem of humans' passage from nature to culture), the very concept
of kinship is an ethnocentric projection of a Western cultural model (see
Schneider 1984; cf. Leach 2003, 21–32).

What brings Schneider's critique to the brink of something more than
just an argument from cultural relativism, however, is his willingness to
adumbrate the implications of the cultural contingency of the nature/
culture distinction for the infrastructure of anthropological analysis itself,
thus prefiguring the kinds of recursive arguments that came later, and for

which he arguably opened the way. While his critique was a pioneering example of an anthropological strategy that has since become very familiar, namely that of weighing up the ethnocentric baggage of all manner of categories that had previously been taken for granted as supracultural analytical tools ("religion," "ritual," "politics," "labor," "property" and so on), Schneider's critique amounted to more than that by virtue of the fact that its target was a category as foundational to the discipline as kinship. As borne out by his own subsequent reflections on the matter (1995), Schneider was well aware that to undermine the natural basis for the study of kinship was to undermine willy-nilly the most basic premise of the anthropological project of cross-cultural comparison itself. What made kinship different from religion, ritual, politics, and so on, giving it its privileged position as the bedrock for cross-cultural comparisons, was that it was assumed to be the most basic point of contact between the universal facts of human nature and their variable cultural elaborations by different social groups. For Schneider, to explode the study of kinship was to deal a blow on the foundational matrix through which anthropologists conceptualized similarity and difference itself. Of course, as Adam Kuper remarks in an acerbic review of Schneider's contribution to American cultural anthropology, it is unsurprising that Schneider did not take his maverick move the whole way so as to undermine the anthropological notion of culture alongside that of nature (Kuper 2000, 122–58). To do so would have nullified the premise of his critique, namely that kinship, and the distinction between nature and culture upon which it is based, is an American cultural construct. It would radicalize his relativism to such an extent that it would end up undoing itself.

This is exactly what Roy Wagner did in *The Invention of Culture*—a book dedicated to Schneider with an acknowledgment of the "germinal" character of its debt to him (Wagner 1981, ix). Like Schneider, Wagner is concerned with the work that the distinction between culture and nature does for anthropology and, again like Schneider, he contrasts this distinction to ways of thinking and acting elsewhere so as to show that it exemplifies distinctively Euro-American presuppositions. But what allows Wagner to escape the paradox of charting such contrasts in terms of cultural difference is that, unlike Schneider, he made the concept of culture itself the target of his critique. Here I shall dwell on the rudiments of his argument at some length, drawing not only on *The Invention of Culture* but also on its ethnographic prequel, *Habu: The Innovation of Meaning in Daribi Religion* (1972), where Wagner developed the core elements of his model with reference to his ethnography of ritual and cosmology among the Daribi people of the Highlands of Papua New Guinea.

In line with the discussion of the previous section—and in resonance with the word's etymological root in the Latin *colere*, "to cultivate" (Wagner 1981, 21)—anthropologists imagine "culture," in its broadest sense, as a set of conventions by which people order and make sense of themselves and the world around them (again, in the broadest sense, nature). Since conventions established at different times and places by different groups of people vary, and the very idea of a convention implies a particular social setting in which it is abided, we speak of "cultures" in the plural. The languages people speak, their social arrangements and political institutions, their means of subsistence, technological wherewithal, economic activities, ritual practices and religious beliefs, ways of seeing the world, perhaps even their ways of feeling in it—all these, we consider, are conventions that people establish and live by. So the job of the anthropologist is to describe the conventions of the people he studies, having learned something of their inner workings as he himself has lived by them during fieldwork. And since these conventions are ultimately "artificial" (49), in the sense that they are established in order to organize and make sense of a world that is prior to human action and is by this token "given" or "innate" (ibid), anthropologists are also charged with accounting for the conventions they describe. They may interpret how and why the conventions in question make sense to the people who live by them, explain how and why they emerged as they did, and even draw conclusions about humanity in more general terns—in short, they may engage in the project of anthropological analysis and theorization in its varied and competing guises.

Much as with Schneider on kinship, Wagner's critical move is to relativize this set of assumptions by showing their peculiarly Euro-American character and using ethnography from elsewhere to explore alternatives. On the former count, he observes that the assumption that human activity is directed toward gaining a handle on the vagaries of an otherwise disorderly and unpredictable world, or "nature," by establishing shared cultural conventions lies at the heart of the way we think of sundry aspects of life in Western societies. Schneider's own depiction of the regulation of natural urges by the moral and legal sanction of marriage in American kinship is one example, but Wagner's all-embracing account ranges over a vast cultural terrain, from ideas about artistic refinement and scientific classification to the artifices of advertising and the cultivation of personality.

To the extent that such varied domains of our culture (as we think of them, again, conventionally) are deemed to be different ways of rendering the world meaningful, they are also all underpinned by a particular way of thinking about meaning itself. Typified by the distinction between symbols and the things for which they stand, this "semiotic," as Wagner calls it, is a corollary of the opposition between culture and nature. Meaning, according to this view, arises from human beings' ability to represent the world by bringing to bear upon it sets of arbitrarily defined (and hence conventional) symbols. Thus cultural conventions order the world by deploying symbolic structures that organize it into distinct categories by means of their otherwise arbitrary relationships to "signs"—a take on meaning that is familiar to anthropologists from structuralist theory, and which endures in different ways, for example, in the otherwise divergent constructivist and cognitive approaches of contemporary anthropology (see also Holbraad 2007, 196). Indeed, it is just this view of meaning that is expressed in the basic idea that the job of the anthropologist must be to represent the culture he studies. Social structures, systems of exchange, modes of production, collective representations, indigenous beliefs, cultural logics, core symbols, local knowledge, cognitive schemata, logics of practice, world systems, transnational flows, political economies, multiple modernities, invented traditions—all are ways of expressing the results of anthropologists' efforts to depict and understand the conventions of the people they study by deploying and elaborating upon their own.

So this is the first sense in which culture is an "invention," as the title of Wagner's book would have it: supposing that the only way for people to have culture is to order the world by means of conventions, the anthropologist transfigures his experience of other people's lives by using his own conventions to enunciate a set for them, too.[9] But of course what the anthropologist finds when living with the people he studies are not structures, beliefs, symbols and so on, but just people living their lives and, when he is lucky, talking to him about them. And one possibility that emerges when one attends to how people actually live is that their activities might not, after all, be directed toward establishing, abiding by, or elaborating conventions. Accordingly, the counterpart to Wagner's argument about the sway that the notion of culture as convention holds in the West involves using his ethnography of the Daribi in Melanesia to show how culture could be conceived differently.

In *Habu*, named after a key Daribi curing ritual in which men impersonate ghosts, Wagner argues that the aspects of life the Daribi consider most salient (ritual, myth, exchange, magic, naming, and more) are directed not toward controlling the world by subjecting it to collective conventions, but rather toward the opposite, namely using conventions as a base-line from which to engage in acts that are meant to transform them by way of improvisation into something novel and unique. So, from the Daribi point of view, all the things that the anthropologist imagines as "culture"—"grammar, kin relationships, social order, norms, rules, etc." (1981, 87)—are not conventions for which people are responsible, but rather the taken-for-granted constituents of the universe that form the backdrop of human activity. They are "innate," in Wagner's terms, inasmuch as they belong to the order of what just is rather than that of what humans have to do. Conversely, the things that the anthropologist imagines as "nature," including not only the unpredictable facts and forces of the world around us but also our own incidental uniqueness as individual persons, for the Daribi constitute the legitimate sphere of human artifice (see also Strathern 1980). Human beings, according to this image, do not stand apart from the world, bringing it under control with their conventions, but rather partake in the world's inherent capacity to transform itself by transgressing the conventional categories that the Daribi take for granted.

So, for example, when in the habu ritual Daribi men impersonate ghosts that are held responsible for certain illnesses, they are not acting out a cultural convention—conforming to a cultural script, underpinned by indigenous categories ("ghost"), beliefs ("illnesses are caused by ghosts") and so on. Rather, like a jazz musician may "bend" a conventional scale to improvise a solo that sounds alive and unique, they subvert "innate" distinctions, and in this case particularly the distinction between living humans and dead ghosts, to bring about an effect that is powerful precisely because it *recasts* or, in Wagner's term, "differentiates" the categories they take for granted (Wagner 1981, 81; 1972, 130–43). Taking as the granted state of the world that dead ghosts are dead ghosts and living people are living people (the "collectivizing" categories of convention), in the habu men *take on* the characteristics of ghosts, temporarily enacting the startling possibility that dead ghosts can indeed come to life and interact with humans. In doing so, they artificially bring about a novel effect, namely ghosts that are also men, by temporarily transgressing ordinary distinctions between life and death, men and spirits, and so on.[10] So, much as with jazz or "true" acting in David Mamet's sense (1997), the success of the habu relates to people's capacity to render the predictable unpredictable, rather than the other way round (see also Holbraad 2010a). However many times the habu may have been done in the past, its power depends on the degree to which the participants can make it a fresh subversion of convention. In this sense—and contrary to anthropological arguments about ritual as a transfiguration of "structure," "culture," or "ideology" (e.g., Geertz 1973a; Sahlins 1985; Bloch 1992; Rappaport 1999)—the habu is an anticonvention par excellence, or, in Wagner's word, an *invention* (see also Wagner 1984; Strathern 1990).

So, for Wagner, the second sense in which culture is invented presents itself in direct contrast to the first. Anthropologists invent a culture for the people they study in assuming that what makes them different (viz. an example of "cultural variation") must be the particular way in which they organize their lives conventionally. By contrast, the Daribi are different in that their energies are focused on "differentiating" their conventions so as to bring about singular moments of invention. Hence if our slot for "culture" is the slot of what people "do," and our slot for "nature" is for that to which they do it, then in the case of the Daribi the slot for "culture" is taken by the activity of invention and that of "nature" is taken by "innate" conventions. In that sense Daribi culture *is* invention.

The question then arises: if what counts as culture in the case of the Daribi is in this way opposed to what counts as culture in anthropology, then what could an anthropological account of the Daribi look like? In other words, if what makes the Daribi "different" is their orientation toward invention, then how can an anthropology that brands all differences as divergences of conventions ("cultural variation") make sense of Daribi life without inventing for it a "culture" that distorts it? This goes to the crux of our original question: how can (in this case) the Daribi's radical divergence from our distinction between nature and culture be articulated without falling into the Schneiderian trap of thinking of it as "cultural"?

Wagner's solution to the conundrum relates to the third and final sense in which culture can be conceived as an invention for him. This is, effectively, an exhortation to move from the first sense in which culture has always been an invention for anthropologists (the idea that making sense of other people's lives must come down to formulating—and in that sense inventing—the conventions by which they live) to the second one (the Daribi-derived idea that human activities may be oriented toward subverting conventions in order to precipitate singularly novel effects). If the assumption that people like the Daribi must have a culture that consists of conventions gets in the way of making sense of the fact that culture in their case consists of processes of invention, then the onus is on the anthropologist to move away from his initial assumptions and conceive of new ones. Hence the ethnography of Daribi "invention" must precipitate a process of invention *on the part of the anthropologist.* Departing from the conventional anthropological notion of culture as convention, the anthropologist is called upon to transform the notion in a way that incorporates the possibility of invention as described for the Daribi—in other words, to invent the notion of "culture" as invention.

For purposes of my broader argument about the relationship between Wagner's discussion of invention and my own concern with truth, it is important to pause here to address a possible sticking-point regarding Wagner's strategy. If the critical suggestion is that to make anthropological sense of Daribi invention one has to recast the very act of making sense anthropologically as an act of invention, too, then one may wonder about this rather miraculous-looking coincidence. What is the significance, for Wagner's argument, of the convergence between the content of what seems basically a parochial ethnographic argument (the inventions involved in the Daribi's habu ceremonies) and the presumably broader form of its anthropological analysis (the invention of culture as invention)? If the idea is that anthropological assumptions are to be revised in light of the ethnography that stumps them, then are we to conclude from this convergence of content and form that for Wagner this revision is to be understood as a form of *derivation?* And would this imply that, had the Daribi diverged from anthropological assumptions about culture as convention in some different way (i.e. if what had stumped our assumptions was not their orientation toward invention but rather something else), we would then need (*somehow*) to think of the task of anthropological analysis along those lines, whatever *they* might be?

Wagner is not very clear on this point, and the pleasure he takes, as we shall see in a moment, in playing with the analogy between what people in Melanesia do and what anthropologists who study them could do probably contributes to the ambiguity. Nevertheless, I would suggest that at stake in his argument is *not* a straight "derivation" of anthropological form from ethnographic content. What necessitates the move of inventing anthropological analysis as an act of invention is not the content of Daribi ethnography as such, but rather its alterity—that is, the fact that its content (whatever this may be) contradicts the assumptions that anthropologists who treat culture as convention bring to it. After all, while Wagner's

Daribi ethnography is sufficient to precipitate the argument for anthropology as invention, it is demonstrably not necessary. Any ethnography that contradicts the initial assumption that culture is a matter of convention, that instantiates the challenge of "alterity" in this sense, would place the onus of invention on the analyst. This is borne out by the fact that a variety of anthropologists have advanced analyses that are as inventive as Wagner's, without necessarily dealing with ethnographic depictions of the processes of invention as such (among others, Marilyn Strathern's invention of "dividual" persons precipitated by the ethnography of Melanesian exchange [1988, 1992] and Eduardo Viveiros de Castro's invention or "multinaturalist" ontologies precipitated by Amerindian cosmology [1998a, 1998b]).

Neither necessary nor miraculous, the convergence between ethnographic content and analytical form in Wagner's argument is a matter of strategy. By using the Daribi's concern with invention as an *example* of the kind of analytical challenge presented by *all* ethnographic alterity as such, Wagner effectively redoubles the resources from which to draw in order to characterize that very challenge—which is to say, to invent it as the challenge of analytical invention. This, I would suggest, makes for the distinctively anthropological tenor of his invention—an important point to which I shall return later. Wagner could, after all, take the requirement for anthropological invention in the face of alterity as a purely methodological question, to be discussed, as is often the case with these things, in abstract quasi-philosophical terms. What he does instead is cast this discussion in the form of an *anthropological comparison:* the analogy between the Daribi's concern with invention and the anthropologist's need to adopt something analogous as an analytical tack allows Wagner to place the two alongside each other.

Set forth as the "epistemology" of the ethnographic argument presented in *Habu* (Wagner 1981, xv), *The Invention of Culture* does just that. Putting in place the conditions of possibility for invention on the part of the anthropologist, much of the argument of the book is devoted to showing that such processes of invention are as present in modern Western life as they are in Melanesia. The difference for Wagner is that whereas Melanesians take responsibility for their acts of invention while taking conventions for granted, for Westerners it is the other way round. Jazz and acting, which I have mentioned, are only particularly "marked" examples of this—displaying not only the presence of invention in our lives, but also its relegation to an irreducibly ineffable realm that lies beyond human control (we speak, significantly, of "natural talent," "inspiration," or even "genius," by which we mean "something . . . je ne sais quoi"). In fact, argues Wagner, the possibility of invention is implicated in everything we do and say. Even the simplest declarative sentence, insofar as it is not just a trivial statement of what we already know conventionally (e.g., literal statements about our accepted categories, such as "men are mortal," or definitions such as "bachelors are unmarried men"), involves an element of invention. For example, when I say that invention is part and parcel of all nontrivial communication, or if I suggest that Wagner is a genius, what I say is only interesting—it "says something"—insofar as it presents a *subversion* of what is already conventionally accepted. I am in effect asking you to conceive of communication and of Wagner differently from what (I assume) you already do. In this sense I am putting forth an invention in a way that is analogous to what Daribi men do when they impersonate ghosts (and compare this with such exemplarily boring claims as "communication involves mutual understanding" or "Mozart was a genius"—boring, precisely, because they say nothing "new": they merely state conventions that are already established and accepted). The same, argues Wagner, holds for all meaningful action that is not merely trivial.

Just as with conventional accounts of rituals such as the habu, the problem, Wagner suggests, is that the irreducibly inventive dimension of meaning remains opaque as long as it is viewed through the prism of convention. To equate the meaningful with the inventive is itself an example of invention insofar as the assumption "against" which this point gains its originality is that meaning pertains to convention—the "semiotic" of symbols that stand for things in the world that Wagner identifies, as we saw, as the key corollary of Euro-American distinctions between culture and nature. So if it is to be understood as more than such an act of trivial classification, the notion of invention requires an alternative account of meaning. Such an account lies at the heart of Wagner's own invention of the notion of invention and takes the form of a dialectical contrast with the semiotic of convention—a "figure/ground reversal," as he often puts it (e.g., Wagner 1987).

Convention relies on the assumption that the realm of symbols and the realm of the things for which they stand are opposed—culture to nature, representation to world. Conventions arbitrarily "fix" the meaning of symbols that can then be used to express things by being "applied" to the world. For example, I assume we know what "genius" means and who "Wagner" is, so when I say "Wagner is a genius" I apply the former to the latter—an operation that is formally indistinguishable from my doing the same for Mozart. Hence, in the semiotics of convention, the fixing of meaning and its application to the world to express something "about it" are logically separate, the former being the precondition for the latter. Invention, Wagner argues, turns this image inside out. When the Daribi impersonate ghosts, Benny Goodman goes off on a solo on his clarinet, and Wagner invents the semiotics of invention (and I call *him* a genius for it), meaning is not a precondition for expression but rather an *outcome of it.* According to this view, every act that the semiotic of convention would brand as an "application" of symbolic meaning to the world is in fact an *extension of meaning.* So, to stick to the discomfiting example, to say "Wagner is a genius" does not "apply" the notion of genius to the person we call Roy Wagner but rather extends what we mean by both: Wagner's particular form of brilliance putatively extends the notion of genius in a novel way and, equally, the notion of genius extends the conception of the kind of person (or anthropologist) we may think Wagner is. Instead of a "gap" of mutual independence between symbol and thing, representation and world, we have a relation of mutual dependence, whereby meanings modify each other in the act of being brought together. Just as with the habu, then, the semiotic of invention implies that everything ("representations" and "world" alike) is meaningful, and the task of expression is to mediate the relationships between meanings so as to engender novel ones—not to "convey" meanings representationally, but to *create* them by transforming the ones that are already given.[11]

We may conclude, then, that if making sense of the Daribi's divergence from our assumptions about nature and culture precipitates an act of invention on the part of the anthropologist, it must also precipitate *a departure from just those assumptions.* The anthropologist's task of making sense of people that are "different" can no longer be a matter of "representing" the differences in question—to do so, as we have seen, is effectively to obliterate them. Rather like the habu, the anthropologist's task on this view is to transform the categories he takes for granted in the very act of bringing them to bear on the differences of which he seeks to make sense. Making sense, in other words, must involve the semiotics of invention.

This way of thinking of the task of anthropology "solves" the Schneiderian paradox. Instead of trumping ethnographic alternatives to the distinction between nature and culture by branding them as cultural, Wagner's position allows them to trump that distinction itself by transforming it into an altogether different way of thinking about difference. Indeed, to

think about difference, on this view, *is to think differently:* to transform
one's most basic assumptions in light of the differences that trump them.
Adapting a term from Marilyn Strathern, whose own seminal critique of
anthropological assumptions about nature and culture was developed in
mutual influence with Wagner, I call this task of ethnographically driven
anthropological self-trumping, "recursive analysis" (Strathern 1980; cf.
Strathern 1988, 320).[12]

Bringing into focus the reciprocal relationship between anthropological analysis and ethnographic description (the form and the content of anthropological work, so to speak), the notion of recursivity is also meant to
signal this approach's basic departure from the dilemma between naturalism and constructivism. As we saw in the discussion of the "reflexivity" of
anthropological truth-claims, the move from naturalism to constructivism
in anthropology left intact the basic assumption that both anthropologists
and the people they study are in the business of representation: people in
different societies represent the world in different ways and the anthropologist's job is to represent (describe, interpret, explain, and so on) these
representations, which he calls "cultures" (construed, in Wagner's terms,
as sets of conventions). As we also saw, however, the turn to constructivism
shifted the balance between these two orders of representation. Where
naturalism had assumed that anthropological representations are superior
to indigenous ones since they are systematically geared toward reflecting the world as it actually is, constructivism countered that "the world
as it actually is" is necessarily also a cultural representation (a "cultural
construct"), so anthropological and indigenous representations are in this
respect no less or more valid than each other. The move to recursivity,
then, can be seen as the next step: an attempt to tip the balance in favor of
the "indigenous" yet further—so much so that it is made a vantage point
from which the very assumptions on which the dispute between naturalism and constructivism relies can be called into question and refigured or,
in Wagner's terms, "invented."

This book's concern with truth emerges directly out of this way of thinking about recursivity. Where, one wants to ask, does the move to recursive
analysis leave the notion of truth in anthropology? For it would seem that
such a move raises a major dilemma. On the one hand, seeing recursivity
as a further step on the trajectory from naturalism to constructivism would
appear to imply seeing it also as a further move away from the notion
of anthropological truth. In fact, thus construed, the move to recursivity
seems to amount to nothing less than an annihilation of the very idea of

truth as anthropologists have conceived it. Anthropological debates have relied on a concept of truth that is wedded to the distinction between nature and culture, as well as to the notion of representation, and these are precisely the assumptions that recursive analysis puts into question. How could one possibly hold on to the notion of truth while discarding the whole conceptual infrastructure in which it is embedded?

On the other hand, it would also seem that, more or less implicitly, recursive analysis does want to uphold at least some sort of appeal to truth. After all, what makes recursive analysis so different from constructivism is that, while the latter seeks to abstain from the kind of truth-judgments that characterize naturalism, the former proposes assertively to *invert* them. Where naturalist approaches privilege the "scientific" truth-claims of the anthropologist at the expense of the people he studies, recursive ones affirm the indigenous perspective as against that of the anthropologist (see also Argyrou 2002). To take the (recursive!) example, when Wagner uses his account of the habu as an ethnographic pivot with which to recast the anthropological concept of culture, is he not in some pertinent sense giving the "truth" to the Daribi? Furthermore, if this affirmation of Daribi ethnography is supposed to serve as an allocentric vantage point from which not only to criticize, but also to reinvent anthropological assumptions, does this not also imply an appeal to some sort of truth on the part of the anthropologist after all—on the part, say in this instance, of Wagner as both critic and innovator? The ethnographically led suggestion that the notion of culture as convention be replaced with a notion of culture as invention does, in fact, sound a lot like a claim to truth; it seems, for instance, to censure one view and propose another much like any ordinary, "representational" truth-claim would. But if part of the recursive effect of these very claims is to obliterate the notion of truth altogether, then what kind of claim is being made here and how could it even be articulated as such?

So, what concept of truth might a recursive anthropology entail? How might such a concept operate in the transformed (or better *transformational*) conceptual landscapes that recursive analyses are meant to engender? How, indeed, might it help to sustain such transformations— including, among other things, the transformation of anthropology itself, as a recursive tack would demand? And how open might such a concept be to being recursively transformed itself? In seeking to answer these questions I hope to complete the image of recursive analysis as it emerges not only in Wagner's own argument on invention, but also in a growing body of work that has developed in confluence with it in the past thirty years or so—be that through direct and mutual influence (e.g., Strathern 1988), or more indirectly (e.g., Viveiros de Castro 1998a, 1998b, 2010), or by a different route altogether (e.g., Latour 1993). While a review of this literature is beyond my present remit, it is worth noting that authors who, like Wagner, have used ethnography recursively to transform the infrastructure of anthropological analysis have not only had little to say about truth but have often done their best to distance themselves from it. It is remarkable, for example, that Wagner should call the conceptual apparatus presented in *The Invention of Culture* an "epistemology" and yet fail to incorporate in it an explicit discussion of the notion of truth—an abiding epistemological concern if ever there was one, not least for anthropologists. Seen in light of this silence, one may surmise that Wagner's emphasis on the notion of "invention" (viewed here as an antonym of truth as well as of convention) is meant to connote a move away from concerns with truth altogether.

Such a tendency is characteristic of the broader literature that can be said to develop, in one way or other, a recursive approach. This is illustrated in the work of the three aforementioned authors, Marilyn Strathern, Eduardo Viveiros de Castro and Bruno Latour, who, along with Wagner, have probably been the most influential in this field. In *The Gender of the Gift* (1988), for example, Strathern describes her attempt to use Melanesian ethnography recursively to refigure basic anthropological assumptions about society and the individual, as well as basic feminist assumptions about gender and power, as an exercise in analytical "fiction": "If my aims are the synthetic aims of an adequate description [of Melanesian ethnography], my analysis must deploy deliberate fictions to that end. . . . The question is how to displace [our metaphors] most effectively" (1988, 10, 12). Elsewhere she calls this activity "an exercise in cultural imagination" (1992a, xvii).

More explicitly, Latour's sustained attempt to use ethnographic and historiographic accounts of scientific practice "in action" to transform the epistemological framework that is assumed to inform it (e.g., 1987, 1988) results in a shift away from the vocabulary of truth, toward an analytical language that reflects the irreducibly "fabricated" character of scientific truth-claims: from fact to "factish" (1999, 266–92, 2010), from matters of fact to "matters of concern" (2004), and, most explicitly, from truth to "circulating reference" (1999, 69–74). So, for Latour, looking past what he famously calls a "modern constitution" bent on "purifying" nature from culture (1993) involves revealing scientists' truth-claims as fragile projects

of "construction," which are to be understood not as cultural constructions of nature but rather as hybrid and contingently negotiated amalga-
mations of elements from both—"naturecultures" (Haraway 2007).

My own account of anthropological truth, precipitated by an attempt
to account for the truth of Cuban divination, will bear substantial resemblances to Latour's concerted revamps of the truth-stakes in Western science more generally (as well as some differences, as we shall see in due
course). Still, from the point of view of overall strategy, what I seek to add
to this debate is a specific consideration of the truth-stakes in anthropologists' characteristic—in fact quite peculiar—reckonings with problems
of alterity. Seen in this light, the affinities between Latour's accounts of
science in general and my own analysis of anthropology in particular also
present a problem. Latour's ethnographic refutations of commonplace
assumptions about the representational character of scientists' activities
seeks explicitly to *efface* the difference between "modern" science and the
kinds of "non-modern" practices anthropologists have typically studied.
"We have never been modern," Latour says iconoclastically, and affirms
the continuity that this statement implies by eschewing the metaphysically
and politically loaded vocabulary of truth, and melding it with its putative
non-modern opposites. The characteristically "modern" choice between
fact and fetish, for example, gets translated into the decidedly hybrid neologism "factish" (1993; 2010, 21–22).

By contrast, my focus is on anthropology's constitutive investment in
tarrying analytically with precisely that divide Latour seeks symmetrically
to overcome (see also Holbraad 2004b). So while, in line with Latour, my
aim is hardly to *preserve* the putative asymmetry between anthropologists'
truth-claims and those of the people they study (such as the diviners I
worked with in Cuba), my task in nevertheless to examine it systematically in order to reveal its peculiar conceptual complexities, as well as the
precise contours of its limitations in relation to the analytical challenges
of alterity. Given the constitutive part it plays in the very set up of that
challenge, to give up on the notion of truth—let alone the word—by antirepresentationist credo, Latourian or other, would effectively foreclose
the analysis I wish to advance.

The significance of this strategic departure can be articulated most
clearly in relation to the work of Viveiros de Castro, in which the premises
and goals of the kind of anthropology I have been calling recursive have
arguably received their most explicit treatment. In a series of publications
over the past fifteen years or so, Viveiros de Castro has been charting

concertedly the "metatheoretical premises" of his analyses of Amerindian animism, exploring the particular demands that ethnographic alterity places upon anthropological analysis (2002, 113; cf. 1992, 1998a, 1998b, 2003, 2010, 2010).[13] My treatment of alterity as the major premise of anthropological analysis, as well as many of the conclusions I draw from this regarding the role of conceptualization and its ontological effects in anthropological thinking, draw heavily on this body of work. At the same time, my desire to put the question of truth at the center of such recursive endeavors is intended partly as a response to Viveiros de Castro's explicit refusal to do so. To articulate this divergence, it is worth examining Viveiros de Castro's argument against anthropological preoccupations with truth in some detail.

In "The Relative Native" (2002), a landmark in the development of Viveiros de Castro's metatheoretical perspective, the author presents the concern with truth as a key point of *contrast* between anthropologists' traditional project of interpreting and/or explaining indigenous "beliefs," and an anthropology that takes indigenous thinking seriously enough to "use it, draw out its consequences, and explore the effects it may have on our own" (2002, 113,129).[14] With reference to his research on Amerindian animism, he writes:

> Would taking the Amerindians seriously mean "believing" in what they say, taking their thought as an expression of certain truths about the world? Absolutely not; here is yet another of those questions that are famously "badly put." Believing or not believing in [indigenous] thought implies first imagining it as a system of beliefs. But problems that are properly anthropological should never be put either in the psychologistic terms of belief, or in the logicist terms of truth-value. . . . We know the mess anthropology made when it decided to define natives' relationship to their own discourse in terms of belief: culture instantly becomes a kind of dogmatic theology. And it is just as bad to shift from "propositional attitudes" to their objects, treating native discourse as a repository of opinions or a set of propositions: culture turns into an epistemic teratology—error, illusion, madness, ideology. (Viveiros de Castro 2002, 130)

Getting anthropology out of its mess must, for Viveiros de Castro, involve moving away from questions of truth altogether. Later on in the essay he develops the point with reference to the notion, typical of Amerindian animism, that peccaries might be human:

I am an anthropologist, not a swinologist. Peccaries . . . are of no special interest to me, humans are. But peccaries are of enormous interest to those humans
who say that the peccaries are human. . . . The native's belief or the anthropologist's disbelief has nothing to do with this. To ask (oneself) whether the
anthropologist ought to believe the native is a category mistake equivalent to
wondering whether the number two is tall or green. . . . When an anthropologist
hears from his indigenous interlocutor (or reads in a colleague's ethnography)
such things as "peccaries are human," the affirmation interests him, no doubt,
because he "knows" that peccaries are not human. But this knowledge (which
is essentially arbitrary, not to say smugly tautological) ought to stop there: it is
only interesting in having awoken the interest of the anthropologist. No more
should be asked of it. Above all, it should not be incorporated implicitly in the
economy of anthropological commentary, as if it were necessary (or essential)
to explain why the Indians *believe* that peccaries are human whereas *in fact* they
are not. What is the point of asking oneself whether the Indians are right in this
respect—do we not already "know" this? What is indeed worth knowing is that
to which we *do not* know the answer, namely what the Indians are saying when
they say that peccaries are human. . . . Hence, when told by her/his indigenous
interlocutors . . . that peccaries are human, the anthropologist should ask her
or himself, not whether or not "s/he believes" that they are, but rather what
such an idea could show her/him about indigenous notions of humanity and
"peccarity." (134–36)

This constitutes a trenchant analysis of the first horn of the truth-dilemma
I set out earlier: understood as a property of beliefs about the world, truth
is indeed incompatible with a turn to recursivity for precisely the reasons
Viveiros de Castro articulates (see also 2002, 116). True as it may be,
however (and note the incongruous locution), this still leaves open the
questions raised by the second horn of the dilemma: is it really possible
to advance recursive arguments without recourse to some (other, altered,
suitably recast) concept of truth? Replacing the tainted truth-vocabulary
of representationism with that of "invention," "fiction," "imagination,"
"factish," and so on is no help. What are the truth-stakes in such analytical activities, one wants to ask, and how do they relate to more traditional
ways of imagining the role of truth in anthropology? At any rate, it would
seem odd for proponents of the recursive approach, after having put the
reinvention of the distinction between nature and culture at the very center of their endeavor, to then stop short of also reinventing truth—a prime

corollary of that distinction, as we have seen. If a recursive approach allows anthropologists to go beyond merely criticizing prevailing concepts of nature and culture, by transforming them—positively—into something new, then why not try the same for truth?

While my central aim of the book is to demonstrate that such a venture holds interest in its own right, my motivation in doing so is also strategic. Showing that recursive analysis has a stake in truth (showing, that is, *what* truth it has a stake in) is important in order to articulate its potential contribution to anthropological thinking at the present juncture. As seen in the previous section, the question of truth has been at the heart of the most foundational theoretical debates in anthropology since its inception, and has oriented basic divergences of opinion regarding the discipline's role in the broader intellectual landscape (e.g., Are we supposed to participate in the project of science or stand outside it? Should we revel in human diversity for its critical potential or subsume it under the sign of the universal?). It is hard to see how the distinctive character and contribution of a recursive approach could be gauged properly without explicitly connecting it back to those debates about truth—that is, other than by sheer rejection.

More particularly, raising the question of truth afresh helps to combat the persistent tendency to mistake recursive analysis for a kind of extreme (or at least extremely self-referential) version of constructivism. Treating the recursive critique of nature/culture distinctions as a form of cultural relativism is only one example. At the risk of glossing over the diverse criticisms that the body of literature I have called recursive has attracted, it is worth noting that charges one associates with attacks on constructivism, relativism, and their theoretical cognates are a prominent feature of this critical repertoire. Suspicions of exoticism, for example, are typical (e.g., Carrier 1992). At their most extreme—usually in seminars and lectures—the rebukes go something like this: Surely Amazonians can tell a peccary from a human when they hunt! And don't Melanesian people, composed "dividually" of their relations to others according to Strathern, nevertheless go "ouch!" *in*dividually when pinched? And so on, in come-off-it *touché.*

Recalling Viveiros de Castro's analysis, it is clear that such "smugly tautological" appeals to common sense are misplaced. The accusation of preposterousness sticks only if you take notions of peccaries that are human, humans that are dividual, and so on, as representations (be they descriptive or analytical) of indigenous "beliefs," "propositions," "opinions," or indeed "constructions." However, the tendency to distance recursive arguments from considerations of truth is arguably a prime source of this misunderstanding. After all, when cast in purely negative terms (implicitly or explicitly), aversion to the concept of truth makes recursive arguments seem rather too similar to relativist/constructivist ones—such an aversion being as characteristic of the latter, though, as we have seen, in a different sense and for different reasons. Hence, from the point of view of critics invested in "common sense" and the facts of the world, the difference between recursivity and constructivism can easily appear slight: both seem to boil down to the lowly common denominator of denying that anthropology is in the business of ascertaining truth. To the contrary: I contend that what makes recursivity most different from constructivism is precisely the fact that it is able positively to uphold a claim to truth—one that is as rigorous and exact as any claim to truth ever was. And it can do so, not despite itself, but by its own virtue: by recursively transgressing representationist assumptions so as to arrive at a different concept of truth altogether. It is to this task that I turn in the next chapter, in which I characterize the assumptions about truth that are embedded in the anthropological literature on divination and specify the ethnographic conditions for their recursive revision.

CHAPTER TWO

Truth Beyond Doubt:
The Alterity of Divination

G etting an ethnographic handle on the question of truth—a question
that is so easily assumed to be essentially philosophical—is no easy
matter. If the baby in this case is the phenomenon of divination, inasmuch
as it demarcates an ethnographic arena where truth is at issue, the murky
bathwater is made of anthropologists' attempts to explain it. As we saw, it
is precisely the fact that anthropological explanations incorporate prejudicial assumptions as to what *counts* as truth that motivates us to look at divination afresh, as a strategy for bringing murky assumptions into view. So
this must be the first task: to create analytical elbow space for a new way
of looking at divination. In particular, what is required is a way of looking
at divination that reveals the peculiar character that truth acquires in this
context. So rather than commencing my attempt to convey the alterity of
divinatory truth with an evocative ethnographic image, as has become de
rigueur in contemporary anthropological writing ("hit the reader in the
gut!"), this chapter is deliberately concerned with "theory." If, as we shall
see, alterity is a function of the divergence between ethnographic materials and the initial assumptions the analyst brings to them, then the role of
this chapter is precisely to elucidate the assumptions anthropologists have
habitually brought to the study of divination, with a view to identifying
their points of conflict with the ethnography of Ifá in later chapters.

In fact, I argue, the fundamental alterity of divinatory truth has been
pretty much ignored by anthropologists who have sought to account for
the phenomenon of divination. In a nutshell the problem is this. Even the
most sophisticated anthropological accounts of divination—such as those
provided by Evans-Pritchard and Pascal Boyer, as we shall see—are un-

able to reflect a crucial fact, namely that practitioners of divination do not just take the verdicts that oracles deliver to be true, but rather take them to be the kinds of things that could not but be true. Diviners' claim, in other words, is not just to truth, but rather to a kind of truth that has also been something of a holy grail in the Western tradition of reasoning, namely *indubitable* truth. Having missed this distinction, anthropologists have effectively assumed that divinatory verdicts could only issue truths that are inherently open to doubt. This misinterprets the ethnography of divination and thereby also prejudices its analysis. A recurring theme in my discussion is that the discrepancy between divinatory practice and existing analytical presuppositions is a function of a broader incongruity between the practitioners' perspective—according to which verdicts are indubitable—and what I call the "skeptical" perspective, which *can only* recognize practitioners' truth-claims as doubtful at most (and in fact, as a rule, "actually" false). In this sense, existing anthropological analyses of divination err on the side of skepticism and thus tend to be locked in a smarter-than-thou stance vis-à-vis divinatory practice. It follows that if one's task is to analyze divination in its own terms, the analytical presuppositions that underlie the skeptical perspective—and which lead to the assumption that the truths of divination could only be seen as doubtful—need to be identified in order to be discarded. The ultimate aim of this chapter, then, is not only to offer a critique of the skeptical perspective, but also to turn the negative points made against its favor into positive desiderata for a more adequate analysis of divinatory truth, thus laying the groundwork for elaborating a new analytical perspective with regard to the ethnography of Ifá in Cuba.

Divination in Anthropology

Anthropological writings on divination tend to recapitulate the discipline's longstanding concern with alterity, discussed in the previous chapter under the heading of "cultural difference." In particular, they recapitulate the discipline's fascination with the exotic, as old as James Frazer's *Golden Bough*. By exotic, here, we may understand a peculiarly territorialized notion, according to which alterity resides in the cleavage between assumptions that may be taken as typical of "Western" forms of thinking (or "Western common sense," as we may brand it) and the assumptions that practices that are deemed to be alien to it, such as divination (or magic, or female circumcision, or divine kingship, and so on), appear to exemplify. Within this genre, writings on divination also recapitulate the strategies that anthropologists have traditionally adopted in the face of the analytical challenge that alterity poses, and particularly the broad tendency to predicate their own mystification by divination onto the practices themselves—projecting them, in one sense or other, as strange "beliefs" (what Viveiros de Castro called "epistemic teratology") that demand an explanation.

This is most clearly the case when it comes to three classical anthropological approaches to divination, which correspond respectively to debates about social function, symbolic expression, and epistemic credentials. With regard to the first, we may note Mary Douglas's comment that, largely as an effect of Evans-Pritchard's classic ethnography of oracles and their role in Zande social life, which we shall be discussing at length presently, there now exists a long line of studies that focus on the sociological and political role of divinatory practices (Douglas 1970, xvi; influential examples include Mitchell 1956, Moore 1957, Park 1963, Mendonsa 1982, and Shaw 1985). With regard to symbolist analyses, an analogous influence has been exerted by Victor Turner's groundbreaking interpretations of the symbolic language of Ndembu divination (Turner 1967, 1975). Often in conjunction with functionalist arguments, a number of scholars since Turner have sought to elucidate the often immensely rich symbolic content of divinatory practice, showing how it can be seen as a form of "rhetorical art" (Burke, cited in West 2007) that has particular characteristics that set it apart from other forms of expression (e.g., see Werbner 1973, Parkin 1991, and Abbink 1993; see de Boeck and Devisch 1994 for a critique).

There can be no doubt that a sound understanding of the social implications of divination, as well as a proper grasp of the universe of meanings upon which it may draw, are indispensable to the study of divination. Indeed, we shall have plenty of occasions to explore each of these dimensions in relation to Ifá in subsequent chapters. However, the argument of this book proceeds from the premise that neither of these approaches provides a satisfactory response to the analytical challenges that divinatory practices pose. While I do not propose to enter here into the broader, and by now somewhat hackneyed, methodological debates that have surrounded each of them, a deal-breaking shortcoming from the point of view of the present argument is common to them both. Whether one chooses to account for divination in terms of its social effects (functionalism) or to treat it as a symbolic expression (symbolism), one effectively fails to engage with what, at least in some cases, practitioners themselves consider to be so important about it. In particular, such approaches fail to provide insight into the central idea that has made divination appear most exotic to anthropologists in the first place, namely that it is, to recall Zeitlyn's phrase, "a truth-telling exercise" (1995, 189). While divination may very well have both social and symbolic effects, it is obvious that people who engage in these practices do not do so out of a desire to produce such effects. To convey the point too crudely perhaps, they do not see themselves as social engineers or as rhetoricians—or, if they do, they do so only by virtue of their truth-telling capacities. So classical functionalist and symbolist approaches to explaining divinatory beliefs, so called, at most succeed in explaining them away—displacing, as it were, the question of their truth.

Before addressing the third classical approach to divination, which takes on the question of truth directly, we may note that much recent writing on divination has tended to make a virtue of this kind of displacement for its own sake. Mirroring the broader methodological aversion to questions of truth in anthropology since the 1970s, and impatient with the ways in which divination had become embroiled in the "rationality" debate in particular (i.e., the third approach, addressed below), many anthropologists in recent decades have been reluctant to view divination as a matter of belief at all. Without necessarily denying that truth, in some sense, is at stake in these practices, such scholars have effectively opened up for investigation a whole range of further topics, exploring, as René Devisch calls them in a programmatic paper, the internal, semiotic, semantic, and praxeological dimensions of the divinatory process (1985, 68–78). With Devisch himself, as well as Michael Jackson (1978), Richard Werbner (1989), and Philip Peek (1991) setting much of this agenda, we now have a wealth of studies delving deep into the phenomenology of divinatory experiences (e.g., Jackson 1989), the intersubjective constitution of divinatory meaning (e.g., Graw 2009), its capacity for world-making (Devisch 1991; de Boeck and Devisch 1994), moral power (Stroeken 2010), psychoanalytic dimensions (Devisch forthcoming), role in healing (Winkelman and Peek 2004) and as shelter from social and personal uncertainty (Whyte 1997; Silva 2011), and plenty more.[1]

My own study of Cuban Ifá in the following chapters will broach a number of such topics, drawing inspiration from this growing body of work. Thus questions about the constitution of meaning during the divinatory consultation, the normative force of divinatory verdicts in regulating matters of worship, and the ontological—"world-making," if you like—effects which they precipitate, will feature prominently in the chapters that follow. Rather than treating these as concerns that go beyond the traditional anthropological debate about diviners' claims to truth, however, my aim is deliberately to *relate* them to it (see also Myhre 2006a). My tack, in other words, is to show that the concern with truth in divination is systematically bound up with such questions, such that addressing them becomes part of taking the debate about truth forward.

In this connection, it is worth remarking on the relationship between my concern with divinatory truth and broader arguments regarding the role of so-called performativity in ritual contexts. I am thinking here of influential proposals advanced by Maurice Bloch (1974) and Stanley Tambiah (1985) to the effect that, broadly put, ritual practices are characterized by uses of language that are aimed not at communicating things about the world, but rather at acting upon it. Drawing on philosophical theories about the power of "speech-acts" (particularly Austin 1962 and Searle 1969), these authors have argued that when, say, an elder chants during an initiation ceremony, or when a witch casts a spell, they are effectively bringing an initiation or a spell about, much like I can make a promise by saying "I promise that . . ." So according to this view, and using the terminology of speech-act theory, the role of ritual language is essentially "performative" rather than "assertive."

As we shall see in due course, my own argument regarding the alterity of truth in divination bears significant resemblances to this kind of approach. In my own way, I too shall be arguing that diviners' verdicts are forms of speech-act that precipitate transformations of a certain kind. The difference, however, is worth noting. Bloch and Tambiah's turn to performativity is proposed explicitly as a turn *away* from questions about the truth-value of ritual utterances, inasmuch as they adopt the philosophical assumption that truth must be, to recall Austin's famous distinction, a matter of words' capacity to say things rather than do them (a matter of "propositional" rather than "illocutionary" force). By contrast, my interest is in developing an analysis of divinatory speech-acts that places their claim to truth at the core of their performative character. Cutting against the Austinian axiom of saying versus doing, my question is about how divinatory utterances are able to *do truth*, and, following on from that, how a truth that is "done" in this way might be conceptualized.

This brings us to the third classical approach to divination, which addresses divinatory claims to truth directly—particularly, as it is sometimes said, as an "epistemological" question (e.g., Shaw 1991)—and thus comes closest to the concerns of this book. At least since Cicero's classic dialogue on the pros and cons of divination, *De Divinatione* (1997), scholars from a number of disciplines have sought to dissect diviners' abiding claims to truth. Examples here would include Karl Jung's analyses of "synchronicity" in Chinese I Ching divination (1989) and Marcel Detienne's marvelous account of the "enigmas" of divination in ancient Greece (1996; see also Vernant 1974). Within anthropology, this topic was long debated under the rather infelicitous heading of "rationality"—the idea being that, since to straight-thinking social scientists and philosophers people's "belief" in divination "appears irrational," as the catchy gloss on the issue has it,[2] the attempt to make sense of divination must turn on its rationality credentials (Sperber 1985; see also Horton and Finnegan 1973; Wilson 1974; Hollis and Lukes 1982). I do not propose to go into the ins and outs of the rationality debate as a whole here. As Tambiah outlined in his Morgan Lectures on the topic (1990), the debate can be seen in terms that are broad enough to include most major figures in European anthropology at least. In any case, as was also noted in the previous chapter, rationality-talk has waned within the discipline in recent years, having perhaps exhausted itself under the weight of divisive controversies in the 1980s and 1990s, such as the one about the rationality of Hawaiians' reaction to Captain Cook (Obeyesekere 1992; Sahlins 1995).

My interest here is only in identifying what is arguably the key failing of attempts to account for divinatory truth that have been associated with these debates, namely their constitutive blindness to the question of indubitability. To this end, the discussion that follows is anchored in the work of E. E. Evans-Pritchard and Pascal Boyer, and this for different reasons in each case. Of those "big name" anthropologists who have set the terms of the rationality debate, Evans-Pritchard is the only one to have focused specifically and at length on divination. Indeed, his analysis—so lightly scripted into his *Witchcraft, Oracles, and Magic Among the Azande* (1976)—is of such caliber that it allows for a sustained review of the most central issues regarding divinatory phenomena. Boyer, on the other hand, may not have set the terms of the rationality debate, not least because he is so critical of it. But his analysis, also conducted with detailed reference to divination, is Evans-Pritchard's match as far as scope and rigor are concerned, and touches upon some of the central concerns that motivate my own approach. Let us begin, then, by returning to Evans-Pritchard's classic.

Evans-Pritchard on Oracles

As Tambiah has shown, Evans-Pritchard's monumental ethnographic
study of the Azande's "mystical notions" (1976, 229) can be read fruitfully
as a response to the early work of the French philosopher and ethnologist Lucien Lévy-Bruhl on "primitive mentalities" (Tambiah 1990, 42–64,
84–93; cf. Lévy-Bruhl 1926). Lévy-Bruhl's argument was itself a reaction
to comparisons in Victorian anthropology between so-called primitive
magic and modern science, which placed magic at the earliest end of an
evolutionary progress toward rational explanation of natural phenomena,
and thus relegated magic to the position of the "bastard sister" of science
(e.g., Frazer 1911). Lévy-Bruhl's proposal was that rather than viewing
magic as a set of erroneous suppositions about the workings of nature, one
could interpret it as evidence that "primitives" collectively represent the
world in a manner that is qualitatively distinct from our own, because it is
founded on different principles. Whereas "civilized" rationality is geared
toward determining the causal connections between logically distinct aspects of reality, primitives view nature from within a "mystical mentality"
that fuses the world into an embracing unity, with reference to a logic
of "participation." It is in light of this logic, which sees continuity where
we posit distinction, so that "objects, beings, phenomena can be . . . both
themselves and something other than themselves," that magical beliefs
can be seen to make sense. We may find this incomprehensible because
the law of contradiction governs our logic. Primitive mentality is "indiffer-
ent" to such constraints (Lévy-Bruhl 1926, 76, 78).

    Evans-Pritchard's landmark discussion of Zande divination in *Witch-
craft, Oracles, and Magic* relies on a similar distinction between fundamentally different ways of thinking. The difference is that on Evans-Pritchard's
analysis—and this was his famous critique of Lévy-Bruhl—"mystical"
thought exists alongside "commonsense" causal thinking, in a complementary fashion. Much of the book is devoted to describing how divinatory
practices and the "beliefs" with which they are associated (in witchcraft,
sorcery, and so on) are pervasive in Zande daily life. All occasions that are
regarded as socially or personally significant are preceded by consultation
of an oracle, not least in order to find out whether the pernicious influence of witchcraft may be involved (Evans-Pritchard 1976, 121–22). But,
although Evans-Pritchard is emphatic about the fact that beliefs in witchcraft and the efficacy of oracles at detecting it are fallacious—"witches, as

the Azande conceive them, clearly cannot exist" (1976, 18)—he shows how
such beliefs can be held in conjunction with other explanatory strategies
that a Western audience would readily assent to. He writes: "In speaking
to the Azande about witchcraft and in observing their reactions to situations of misfortune it was obvious that they did not attempt to account for
the existence of phenomena, or even the action of phenomena, by mystical
causation alone" (21).

Hence, his famous example: A Zande man who happened to set fire
to his beer hut is well aware that the fire was caused by his torch. Yet, at
the same time, he may be equally convinced that the incident was brought
about by witchcraft. As soon as he can afford to do so, he will take a couple
of fowls to a diviner who, by the method of administering a special poison called *benge* to the birds and observing its effects on them, will be
able to refute or corroborate the suspicion, depending on whether the
poisoned birds survive or die in the process. The Zande man's reasoning,
explains Evans-Pritchard, runs something like this: "Every year hundreds
of Azande go and inspect their beer by night and they always take with
them a handful of straw to illuminate the hut. . . . Why then should [I] on
this single occasion have ignited the thatch of [my] hut?" (1976, 21–22).

Evans-Pritchard argues that what the Azande explained by appeal to
the oracle are not the causal conditions that led to the fire—these they can
identify as easily as anyone could, merely by using their common sense
(about the effects of flames on straw huts and so on). What the oracle accounted for "were the particular conditions in a chain of causation which
related an individual to natural happenings in such a way that he sustained
injury" (1976, 21). So, goes the famous argument, divinatory and commonsense explanations can be entertained side by side because they answer
fundamentally different kinds of questions. Whereas the latter account
for "how" events occur, the former explain "why" these events happen as
they do at a particular place and time and to a particular person. While
commonsense explanations and predictions tell causal stories, divinatory
verdicts relate events to personal histories. One may say, then, that for
Evans-Pritchard divination picks up where common sense leaves off. After all is said and done, the fire in the beer hut having been accounted for
even in the most exhaustive and hard-nosed manner possible, the owner
is still left with the questions: "Why *me*? Why *now*?" The only commonsense answer to such questions is a nonanswer: "coincidence" (23).

In later chapters I shall be developing an analysis of Ifá divination that
takes off from this rather profound distinction between "how" and "why"

questions. But just as one may be enthusiastic about Evans-Pritchard's insight on this point, one may lament the fact that its influence over subsequent debate has been outdone by an altogether separate analytic strategy in his work, which can be shown to be less enlightening. I have in mind here Evans-Pritchard's other famous argument, namely that witchcraft, oracles, and magic form a web of mutually supporting propositions and practices that sustains the Azande's mystical beliefs by virtue (or vice) of its circular character. No sooner, it seems, has Evans-Pritchard opened up the logical space for articulating the peculiar characteristics that set divination apart from commonsense causal reasoning, than he goes on squarely to capitulate to a much more conventional line of inquiry, which is premised on a logical homology between the two. So, despite having distanced divination from common sense by distinguishing their respective explanatory domains (why as opposed to how), Evans-Pritchard proceeds to extend criteria of truth and error that are applicable to commonsense accounts, to arbitrate (negatively) upon "mystical" accounts as well. The question, then, becomes the familiar one: how is it that practitioners of divination fail to see the error of their ways? And so, the answer: "Mystical notions are eminently coherent, being interrelated by a network of logical ties, and are so ordered that they never too crudely contradict sensory experience but, instead, experience seems to justify them" (1976, 150).

The key claim here is that the (closed) coherent order of "mystical notions" is sustained through circularity.[3] The belief that oracles work is supposed to furnish a prime example. In fact, at this juncture Evans-Pritchard makes two claims that sound rather similar, though they ought to be distinguished. First, he explains that the notion that oracles can be relied upon to identify the causes of personal misfortune is (mutually) reinforced by the Azande's beliefs in witchcraft, magic, and witch-doctorhood. "In this web of belief," he writes, "every strand depends upon every other strand" (109). Later on in the book, however, he goes on to add a more meticulous account of how Azande manage to sustain their belief that their oracles work in the face of varied contradictory data, as happens, for example, when the oracle fails to provide a definitive answer to a question. Paradoxically, he explains, these types of "errors" serve to *confirm*, for the Azande, the infallibility of the oracle, since they themselves are explained in terms of further mystical notions. Such "secondary elaborations of belief," as Evans-Pritchard calls them, include accounts of oracular errors in terms of breaches of taboos, the anger of ghosts and forest-deities, sorcery, or, indeed, malpractice on the part of diviners. Thus, he writes, "the contradiction between experience and one mystical notion is explained by reference to other mystical notions" (160).

Now, with reference to Viveiros de Castro's comments on the "smug tautologies" of anthropologists' belief-talk, we have already gauged the analytical slurs of this way of treating indigenous conceptions, and these are issues to which I shall return. In passing, we may also note that such ascriptions of the notion of belief to sundry natives have been questioned also on ethnographic grounds, with critics pointing out that they may have more to do with the Judeo-Christian provenance of the terminology than with indigenous ways of reckoning (e.g., Needham 1972 and South-wold 1979; see also Favret-Saada 1980, Latour 2005, and Stroeken 2008). However, for present purposes we need only focus on the fact that Evans-Pritchard's argument from circularity fails even on its own terms.

The difficulty comes down to a basic contradiction in Evans-Pritchard's approach. On the one hand he is keen to emphasize, contra Lévy-Bruhl, that mystical notions are held alongside commonsense ones. Yet at the same time he claims that the circular structure of the mystical edifice is sustained for lack of an alternative: "[The Azande's] blindness is not due to stupidity: they reason excellently in the idiom of their beliefs, but they cannot reason outside, or against, their beliefs because they have no other idiom in which to express their thoughts" (1976, 159).

This contradiction could perhaps be resolved with reference to the distinction between the how questions of common sense and the why questions of divination that we have already discussed. What one would then need to do is show that the two domains of interrogation are somehow insulated from each other, so that each domain corresponds to a distinct frame of belief (commonsense and mystical respectively) in such a way that the twain might never meet. Indeed, in a way, this is just the kind of argument I shall be developing in later chapters, though minus the notion of belief, which is fundamentally incompatible with Evans-Pritchard's characterization of why questions. Still, Evans-Pritchard himself develops no such argument, choosing rather to make the weaker point that mystical notions do not compete with common sense. In the absence of an argument, however, there is no reason to assume that the "how" logic of common sense could not mitigate the coherence of mystical notions. What is it, we may wonder, that renders commonsense accounts inappropriate when it comes to dealing with the kinds of questions that the oracles answer?

What is important to stress here is that this difficulty is a function of the role given to circularity in Evans-Pritchard's analysis. If beliefs in divination can only be made to appear reasonable in light of *other* suitably compatible beliefs, then it is hardly surprising that the presence of further *in*compatible beliefs (viz. those of common sense) should jeopardize the argument. In the absence of a way of keeping those non-truth-giving beliefs at abeyance, what we are faced with is an inconsistent triad.

Much of the rest of this book is geared toward avoiding this threat by accounting for divination without recourse to other "beliefs"—viewing divination, in other words, as a sui generis source of truth, to be understood in terms of its own. In preparation for this task, it pays to examine also a more recent analysis of divination, presented by Pascal Boyer (1994). This is not least because, with its sophisticated analytical framework, Boyer's argument serves well to pinpoint more precisely some of the key premises that also underlie Evans-Pritchard's account, particularly regarding the notion of truth as a property of so-called representations.

Boyer on Divination, Causal Indices, and Truth

Like his widely cited arguments on religious phenomena more generally (Boyer 1990, 1994, 2000), Boyer's argument on divination turns on what he calls a "cognitive" premise. This specifies that explaining why people think what they do—for example, why they might think that oracles give them the truth—must ultimately be a matter of showing how their minds are able and likely to entertain the notions in question. This, for him, is because the ideas that anthropologists usually summarily describe as "culture," such as ideas about divination, in fact boil down to highly complex aggregates of mental representations. These are distributed across human populations in accordance with constraints imposed by individual human brains—the instruments for mental representation par excellence (cf. Sperber 1996). Hence Boyer eschews the general (or, as he calls it, "epistemic") question of why people believe in divination (the kind of question that exercised Evans-Pritchard as well as subsequent contributors to the rationality debate), and sets out to analyze the cognitive processes involved when a given individual represents an oracular pronouncement as being true (Boyer 1994, 49–52). These processes, he argues, can be seen as a particular variant of the cognitive processes involved in ascribing truth to any ordinary representation, so the analysis of divination must begin from an understanding of human representational capacities in general.

The first point to note about the cognitive structure of truth ascription, argues Boyer, is that it is "meta-representational," that is, it turns on the mind/brain's ability to represent representations (1994, 243–45). Take the representations that are involved in an ordinary conversation. Representing such utterances as true involves spontaneously representing what cognitive psychologists call an "evidential account." This specifies two things. First, it specifies that the representation that the speaker is expressing was *caused* by the events or states of affairs that his utterance describes; or, in other words, that his mental representation emanates from the way things really are. Second, it specifies that the utterance in question is expressing *that representation*, and not some other. So if, for example, someone said to me, "The sky is cloudy," my default presumption that what that person said is true would be built on the spontaneous assumption that (1) his mental representation THE SKY IS CLOUDY was, somehow, caused by the sky actually being cloudy, and (2) that his utterance actually conveyed the mental representation that was thus caused, rather than some other representation that he might construct (e.g., a deceitful one that was, a fortiori, not caused by the way the sky actually is). In other words, I believe what he says because I believe that he knows what he is talking about, and that he is not lying about what he knows. The evidential sequence, then, takes the following form:

[fact] causes [MENTAL REPRESENTATION] expressed by [utterance]

So much for everyday communication. What is interesting about divinatory proceedings, argues Boyer, is that they explicitly preclude the possibility of constructing the second stage of the above sequence. What is so important about trance, "randomizing" techniques that diviners so often employ (such as cowries or cracked scapulae), references to supernatural agencies and so on is that they are all means through which the diviner is himself effectively divested of responsibility for the verdict (Boyer 1994, 246; see also Zempleni 1995 and Graw 2009). Hence, to take the Azande benge oracle as the example, when a man consults an oracle it is clear to him that it is the poison that is fed to the fowls that determines the verdict, not the oracle operator (Evans-Pritchard 1976, 146–49). It follows that the truth of the verdict cannot be evaluated with reference to a correspondence between the verdict uttered and the mental representation of the diviner. The diviner cannot lie because, properly speaking, *he* does not speak at all. If suspicion does arise that the diviner's mental representations are in fact deflecting the causal series that leads up to a given verdict, then the action simply does not count as a genuine divination (cf. Boyer 1994, 207). Bypassing mental representations, then, evidential accounts for divinatory verdicts correspond to immediate causal sequences:

[fact] causes [verdict]

Boyer develops this point with reference to the semiotic framework elaborated by the philosopher Charles Peirce. Genuine divination, he argues, is assumed by practitioners to deal in "indexical" utterances—utterances assumed to be caused directly by the states of affairs they express, like a smile is assumed to express goodwill because it is caused by it (Boyer 1990, 72–75; cf. Rappaport 1979). This point is of central importance to Boyer since for him the indexical character of divinatory verdicts lies at the heart of the answer as to why practitioners tend to deem such verdicts to be true. The causal nature of the connection between indices and the facts they describe, he argues, increases the probability that practitioners will suppose that the verdict is true. This is because from a very early stage of human cognitive development causal relationships are represented as stable connections (a point made famously also by David Hume [2000], minus the cognitive jargon), so that a given effect tends spontaneously to be conjoined in the mind/brain of the observer with its supposed cause. Consequently, to the extent that divinatory technologies coerce practitioners into assuming that their outcomes are indexical, they also tend to force the assumption that they are true. Boyer's logic on this last point is pivotal to his argument, so it is worth quoting his own words:

> If a causal connection is assumed between two events or states c and e, a subsequent occurrence of e will lead the subject to assume that c . . . Representing a connection as causal leads to conjecture that it may correspond to a stable pattern. . . . In metaphorical terms, the utterances [e.g., divinatory verdicts] are supposed to be true because they are construed as the stable symptoms or indices of the situations they describe. (1994, 251)

But the point hardly follows. All that anti-representational divinatory techniques can do is force upon practitioners the assumption that *were* the verdict to be true, it would be so because it was caused immediately by the facts that it describes, that is, it would be their index. Boyer's appeal to the stability of causation is in this sense question-begging. Spelling out

the correspondence between indices and stable causal connections motivates not the proposition that divinatory verdicts need to be taken as
indices, but only the tautology that were the verdicts to be so taken they
would be assumed to be true. So, to return to the Azande, the fact that
when verdicts are taken as true they are assumed to be caused by, let us
suppose, witchcraft, in no way explains why verdicts are taken as true in
the first place. Indeed, in light of Evans-Pritchard's aforementioned point
about the coexistence of divinatory and commonsense explanations, the
question remains: why do Azande presume that the poison kills fowls because of witchcraft rather than because of, say, its toxicity?

In more general terms one may say that this non sequitur itself indexes
a basic flaw in Boyer's cognitivist approach to the question of truth. To
see this, we may note first that one of Boyer's motives for adopting such a
strategy is his impatience with the old rationality debate. Arguing against
Southwold (1979) and Sperber (1985), Boyer identifies the idea that "in
order to explain why people hold some proposition true, it is enough to
show how its refutation is blocked" as a central assumption underlying rationalist attempts to account for the occurrence of religious beliefs (Boyer
1990, 55). This assumption is unjustified, he points out, since only a limited
subset of unrefuted or irrefutable ideas is actually entertained by religious
practitioners. Neutralizing the "apparent irrationality" of such beliefs,
in other words, may perhaps be necessary but is surely not sufficient for
explaining their occurrence. However, a similar argument can be made
against Boyer's own alternative. Outlining, as he does, the cognitive mechanisms that allow for representing religious ideas as true is insufficient for
showing why these ideas are actually held as true. By their very openness,
cognitive constraints may set the parameters for the occurrence of religious ideas as hypothetical assumptions, but, conceptually speaking, they
underdetermine practitioners' inclination to take those ideas to be true.

Divination and Indubitability

It is interesting at this point to note that this criticism of Boyer's argument
turns on the same premise as our earlier account of the shortcomings of
Evans-Pritchard's analysis. As we saw, the weakness of Evans-Pritchard's
account ultimately came down to the fact that the truth of Zande oracular
verdicts was seen as being derived in a circular fashion from other logically compatible cultural beliefs. The problem with this strategy is that,

by rendering the truth of certain beliefs dependent on that of others, one creates sufficient logical space for nontruth-giving beliefs, such as those of a putative common sense, to present themselves as alternatives. Note the formal similarity to the weakness of Boyer's cognitively minded argument. Practitioners' evidential accounts allow for divinatory verdicts to be represented as true because they posit a direct causal link back to the states of affairs that they describe. Here too divinatory truth is taken to be derived from something else (in this case the representation of a causal connection). And here too the posited connection between divination and that other thing that lends it its truth can be broken. There is nothing to stop practitioners from positing an alternative causal account that would connect the verdict, not to the state of affairs it describes, but to a more mundane cause like the toxicity of poison, or whatever. Hence, one might say, in both Evans-Pritchard's and Boyer's analyses of divination, divinatory verdicts are inherently open to doubt, where doubt can be understood, in this context, as a form of interference of common sense with the epistemic/cognitive sequencing of divinatory reasoning.

It may be objected that rather than a weakness, the window of doubt afforded by rendering the truth of verdicts "derivative" in such ways is more of a virtue, since these analyses manage to accommodate the fact that verdicts are indeed often doubted, not only by exceptious analysts, but also by skeptical practitioners. Certainly in Cuba (and perhaps in many other places too) there are plenty of people who do not "believe" in the oracles at all. Ideological Communists and converted Christians are most vehement in this respect in Cuba. Moreover, as we shall have occasion to see in more detail later, a significant proportion of Cuban practitioners attend diviners' consultations in what may best be described as an agnostic or half-hearted spirit, explaining, for instance, that, although they are interested in what the diviners have to say, they are not "really" sure whether to believe them (cf. Bascom 1941). In light of these possible attitudes, would go the objection, the aim of analysis cannot be to render beliefs in verdicts entirely foolproof, because, as skeptics know, they are not.

This is a point well worth taking, I would argue, but only for its irony, since it takes us to the heart of what is so wrong with Evans-Pritchard and Boyer's common "derivativist" strategy, if one may call it that. Taking a leaf out of the skeptic's book, one may admit straight out that divinatory verdicts are open to doubt—indeed anthropologists' own skeptically slanted theories, based as they are on the idea that divinatory beliefs are likely to be false and therefore require anthropological explanation, just prove this obvious point. Crucially, however, I want to argue that this is not how divinatory verdicts present themselves to practitioners. Insofar as practitioners do believe the verdicts, they take them as not only true but also *indubitably* so. Much of the rest of this book is directed toward showing that this is so, and *how* this is so, in the case of Ifá divination. First, however, it is necessary to explain what I mean by indubitability in this context, and to indicate the nature of the analytical challenges entailed and the way they may be addressed.

Consider the following hypothetical scenario. Say one of Evans-Pritchard's Azande told a friend of his that he—the friend—was being bewitched. In line with the considerations discussed already, the Zande man was making a doubtful statement. Indeed, his friend might well later report: "My friend told me that I am being bewitched, but I'm not so sure." This would be a perfectly straightforward and intelligible judgment to make—be it true or false as a matter of fact. Now think of a situation in which the same statement was delivered to the man as a verdict of the benge oracle. Imagine also that the man was a skeptic when it came to oracles. He would be inclined to make the same judgment: "The oracle told me that I am being bewitched, but I am not sure." Clearly, as a skeptic, the man would be perfectly within his logical rights, as it were, to cast doubt on the oracle's verdict in this way. However, as Evans-Pritchard illustrates so clearly in his discussion of "secondary elaborations," the committed practitioner of divination would have a bone to pick with him on this point. Imagine the reaction:

> When I told you yesterday that you are being bewitched you doubted me. Fair enough, I could have been wrong. But today you say you doubt the oracle. Others might accuse you of disrespect, I don't know, but I just think your thinking is confused. You may doubt that you're being bewitched like you did yesterday, or you may doubt whether that thing that gave this as a verdict (the thing I took to be an oracle) really is an oracle, or you may even doubt whether the things that we in Zandeland call oracles exist. But you cannot doubt that the *oracle* gave a true verdict. That is just a misnomer: the whole point about the oracle—the reason why I used it to confirm my suspicion that someone is bewitching you—is that, insofar as it is a genuine oracle at all, it *must* give true verdicts.

To doubt oracular truth is to doubt whether it is oracular.

Lest this way of presenting the argument appears too farfetched, the point can also be made with reference to a particularly popular argument in the anthropological literature on divination. A lot of anthropological attention has been focused on a characteristic typical of divinatory proceedings in many parts of the world (though by no means universally), namely that divinatory verdicts often resist clear-cut interpretation. The Pythic oracle of ancient Delphi with its masterfully paradoxical deliveries is something of an *ur*-example, but the ethnographic record is replete with comparable cases (Wood 2005, 29; Werbner 1973; Bascom 1991, 68–75; Abbink 1993). Some analysts have tended to suggest that the ascription of truth to divinatory verdicts actually turns on this characteristic—call it "interpretative openness" (e.g., Bascom 1941; Bohannan 1975; Parkin 1991; Zeitlyn 1990, 1995). According to such analyses, diviners' verdicts act as blank slates upon which practitioners are able to draw interpretations that they can reasonably represent as being true. Hence, it is suggested, divinatory truth can be accounted for in terms of intersubjective "negotiations" of meaning among communities of practitioners, whereby the truth of a particular divination is in one way or other "constructed" out of the rich semiotic materials that the process of divination furnishes (symbols, narratives, dialogues and so on).

Now, it will be clear that such approaches are premised on the idea that divinatory truth must be a function of the meaning that diviners and their clients ascribe to their oracles' pronouncements—an assumption that may appear reasonable on the more general premise that in order to decide whether something is true or false one should at least first understand it. However, divination turns on the denial of just such an assumption. Indeed, one of my central claims about the alterity of divinatory truth is that what makes divination so special is the fact that practitioners seem to be putting the cart before the horse in just this respect. The logic of divination, I claim, turns on the idea that what makes divinatory verdicts worth interpreting in the first place is the fact that they *must* be true. Rather than by negotiation, disbelief—though I argue that this is the wrong term—is suspended in principle.

So the claim I set out to substantiate in later chapters is that in contrast to ordinary statements that are in principle open to doubt, divinatory statements are true indubitably, since oracles (and other divinatory means) are taken to be things that can only give true answers. It follows that the skeptical assertion that verdicts could be false—whether as a matter of principle or as a matter of fact—just amounts to a denial that the verdicts in question are verdicts at all. Hence the old worry about the apparent irrationality of divination—why might practitioners believe that what their oracles tell them is true?—is off the mark. To set the problem up in terms of practitioners' beliefs is just to capitulate to the skeptical position, contradicting the putative indubitability of divination by raising the prospect that practitioners might not believe in it. There is certainly a sense in which practitioners can perfectly well "not believe" in any given divination, or indeed in divination in general. However, as my imaginary Zande dialogue is meant to demonstrate, the object of disbelief in such cases is not the truth of divination (or of any particular divination) but rather its divinatory character.

So, far from a worry about apparent irrationality, the real problem divinatory phenomena pose could be branded as an *apparently dogmatic stipulation.* Note the issue: Diviners and their clients may be free to stipulate as they please the kind of truth divination gives, defining it by fiat as indubitable. Such a putative premise for divination would have the status of what philosophers call an "analytic" statement, that is, equivalent to statements such as "bachelors are unmarried men," to use the standard example, which are true by virtue of their meaning alone. So, if you know what divination is, you know that its truths are indubitable, just as if you know what a bachelor is, you know he is an unmarried man. The problem is that such a definition of divinatory truth appears altogether perverse or, as I shall call it, dogmatic. For the verdicts diviners deliver seem to have none of the characteristics that would allow one to define them as indubitable. It is as if, having defined bachelors as unmarried men, one insisted on using the term to refer to boys, women, or even happily married men.

Consider the types of truth-claims to which philosophers have been inclined to accord the status of indubitability. Analytic statements, as we just saw, are one such type. Following the landmark argument by the philosopher Saul Kripke about "*a posteriori* necessity" (1980), another might include empirical statements such as "water is H_2O." According to Kripke, such statements fix the reference of terms by "rigidly designating" their "essential" properties, without which things would not be what they are. For example, once water has been found to be H_2O, fixing its essential molecular structure a posteriori (as opposed, for instance, to the a priori definition of bachelors as unmarried men), to wonder whether water is indeed H_2O is just to wonder whether water is water. Furthermore, depending on how far one would want to enter the exegetical debates about the validity of Descartes' famous cogito argument, one might extend indubitability to include statements like "I think, therefore I am," the truth of which may be supposed to be entailed by their very utterance. Or, finally, one could also mine indubitability in theological arguments for the existence of God (e.g., Plantinga 1964).

It is unnecessary, however, to discuss these matters at any length here since it is easy to see that divinatory truths cannot be construed as being indubitable in any of these familiar senses. Take our earlier example, the divinatory statement "you are bewitched." This hardly looks like an analytical statement, since there appears to be nothing in the definition of "you" (whether taken as a pronoun of indeterminate reference or as a designator of a particular person) that would entail witchcraft. Apart from anything else, if the presence of witchcraft could *per impossible* be ascertained merely by virtue of the meaning of terms, by analogy to "bachelors are unmarried men," then going to diviners to find such matters out would be quite redundant.[4] Nor does "you are bewitched" look anything like a Kripkean designation of essential properties. Unlike water and its molecular formula H_2O, presumably the person in question would still be himself even if he was not bewitched. And as for the Cartesian cogito and theological concerns with the nature God, it is hard to see their relevance in this context at all. Whatever it might be, a statement such as "you are bewitched" is not an example of the cogito argument, much less a statement about the perfection of God and so on.

Indeed, if it is feasible to bypass philosophically minded deliberations of this kind, it is because it seems obvious that divinatory statements are of a very familiar type, namely statements of fact—as "a posteriori," "synthetic," and "contingent" as any ordinary statement, such as "you are tired" or "the sun is shining." Certainly in terms of its form, a claim like "you are bewitched" is indistinguishable from a statement of fact. Just as with such ordinary statements, it would appear that the truth of the claim would depend on the facts of the matter. In other words, it would depend on whether the person in question was indeed bewitched. The problem, however, is that such matters are inherently doubtful. To render the divinatory verdict "you are bewitched" dependent on whether the person in question is indeed bewitched is just to render its truth doubtful, since there is always the possibility (a strong one, some would no doubt want to add) that the person might not be bewitched. Treating such verdicts as statements of fact, then, takes us straight back to the skeptical position.

So we are landed in a contradiction. Divinatory verdicts cannot both be indubitable (as I claim they are defined to be) and statements of fact (as they appear to be). Since one of the main ethnographic tasks of this book is to demonstrate that divination does indeed issue indubitable truths, it follows that, despite appearances to the contrary, divinatory truths cannot be statements of fact—unless one is prepared to charge practitioners of divination with a form of absurd dogmatism. The analytical task, therefore, must be to determine what kind of truths these are—a task or conceptualization that will be taken up with reference to the ethnography of Ifá in later chapters. To prepare for this task, however, it is worth dwelling just a little further on the problem of indubitability. In particular, it is worth setting out in more precise terms what it is about statements of fact that makes them inherently open to doubt. By doing so, one puts oneself in a position to see what a better take on divinatory truth might look like.

Desiderata for an Analysis of Divinatory Truth

We may keep this unavoidable excursion into traditionally philosophical stomping grounds tolerably simple and short by being clear on what it is we are looking for. We have just identified the notion of doubt as the prime sticking point when it comes to appreciating the difference between divinatory notions of truth and ordinary ones. Indeed, a narrow focus on the concept of doubt leads us directly to a distinction that lies at the heart of very familiar assumptions about truth, which arguably inform the way divinatory truth-claims have been compared to ordinary statements of fact in anthropology, namely the distinction between representations and facts.[5] The notion of doubt arises precisely in terms of this commonplace distinction.

One way to express difference between representations and facts is to point at a contrast philosophers would call modal, that is, a contrast pertaining to such concepts as possibility, necessity, and actuality. Facts, we may note, are just actual: they are what they are. Representations, by contrast, can equally well be about things that are not as they can be about things that are. Because of this difference it is natural to assume that representations rather than facts are the proper bearers of truth and falsehood. But if notions of truth and falsehood presuppose representations as bearers, then so does the very concept of doubt, since it in turn stands or falls by the distinction between truth and falsehood. The possibility that something may be false (upon which the notion of doubt depends) can only arise representationally: there are no false facts. So without a concept of representation we cannot have a concept of doubt.

Indeed, the entailment here is mutual: just as doubt implies representation, so representation implies doubt.[6] For as long as truth is conceived as a relationship between a representation and a fact, there is always the possibility that this relationship might be one of mismatch. It is always possible that the representation's truth-conditions, as philosophers say, are not satisfied by any fact. Indeed it is for this reason that an analysis that takes divinatory verdicts to be representations of facts must necessarily render their putative indubitability an absurd dogma. The practitioner of divination may insist, blue in the face, that doubtful verdicts are not verdicts. But if verdicts are taken to be representations they must be doubtful, so the practitioner's insistence makes no sense. It follows, then, that the central desideratum for a theory of divinatory truth must be to do away with the notion of representation.

The counterintuitive character of such a project is expressed by the seeming oxymoron "nonrepresentational truth." Indeed, look at its corollaries. If we want to keep the notion of truth and discard the notion of representations, truth must be defined as something other than a property of representations. But what could that be? Facts perhaps? But how can truth be predicated on a fact? Surely facts are just what they are, and to say that they are true is itself a truism. And the strangeness continues. For even if truth can somehow be redefined without recourse to representations, its opposite, falsehood, must be discarded. As with doubt, falsehood is a function of representation (there are definitely no false facts). But what is truth without its opposite, other than an empty concept? Surely the reason why one would even bother to redefine truth without representations would be that it is useful for distinguishing whatever it is that it predicates from corresponding falsehoods.

So the task that divination seems to force upon us is that of articulating an altogether counterintuitive conceptual repertoire for truth. This, of course, is not altogether surprising. As the literature on divination shows, our intuitions on these matters are inclined toward skepticism by default. After all, they are quite untutored in things divinatory. So the best place to begin to look for a conceptual repertoire that is adequate to divinatory phenomena must be among practitioners of divination. This will be my task for the next six chapters, where I explore ethnographically one of the most complex divinatory traditions in the world as I encountered it in my fieldwork in Havana, namely the practice of Ifá.

CHAPTER THREE

Living Ifá: The Matter of Truth

True Encounters

It is said that in personal relationships people tell you all you need to know about them within the first few minutes of acquaintance (the problem being that you find that out much later). Almost a decade and a half after my first visit to Cuba in 1998, I am wondering whether the same could be true of ethnography. What is certain is that when I sat for the first time with Javier Alfonso Isasi, the elderly man who during the following months would become my main interlocutor in my research on the role of divination in Afro-Cuban religion, I was quite unaware of the significance that afternoon's conversation would come to acquire for me, much later.

Although I had never actually met Javier before, I had arrived at his home in the inner city Havana *barrio* of Belén with a head full of plans. Two months into my doctoral fieldwork, I was still in search of what I imagined as a viable circle of "informants"—a family perhaps, or a ritual grouping of some sort, who would be involved in divination and willing to let me into their lives. Not that I had found it difficult up to that point to meet people who fulfilled both of those requirements. Afro-Cuban religion was enjoying an effervescent resurgence in the more open cultural climate of post-Soviet Cuba, and it seemed that almost every person I met was either themselves a diviner or could take me to meet somebody who was. Indeed, in the harsh economic climate of this "Special Period"—as Fidel Castro had euphemistically called Cuba's solitary socialist path following the end of the Soviet era—people were only too keen to bring a dollar-wielding foreigner into their lives. But I had felt hustled in these encounters. In the symmetry of our respective agendas of extraction—my search for ethnographic material, their struggle for dollars—I saw only tension. I held on to an image of informants who might be happy to share themselves with me, or at least to give me what I was after, out of sheer generosity of spirit—"the goodness of their heart." Then, I told myself, I too could be generous.

Javier was just that kind of person. Everyone who knew him—acquaintances of mine to whom Javier "attended" in religious matters, as diviners say—spoke of "the old man" with a tenderness of almost filial intensity. They spoke of his great expertise as a babalawo, a priest of Ifá, the prestigious male diviner-cult I had come to Cuba to study. Both his advanced age and the religious prestige of his ancestral family in Matanzas, a provincial town renowned as a stronghold of Afro-Cuban religion, were mentioned as reasons for his firm sense of integrity. The "humility" of his situation, as a widower sharing frugal living quarters with his adult son in a tenement flat (*solar*), was held up not only as an anachronism, at a time when babalawos in particular were perceived to be capitalizing on the regal prestige of their sacred office in the struggle for dollars (see Holbraad 2004a), but also as a mark of his personal virtue. "The old man is not up to anything" (*no está en nada*), one of his devoted clients had told me, "still attending to the same people as before [i.e., before the crisis of the Special Period], charging the same prices, working Ifá in the old style." If this was a stereotype, it fully coincided with my own idealized images (though, actually, it was true).

So when Javier's son, Javielito, suggested at the party where we first met that he could take me to meet his father "to talk Ifá," commenting offhand that this might just be something his father would enjoy doing, I felt on the verge of a breakthrough. Javielito was himself a babalawo of a number of years, though he made his living mainly as a professional bass player, and we had hit it off instantly talking about music as well as the religion. As I made my way to their solar the following day, a fifteen-minute walk from my own air-conditioned apartment, I was determined to make this relationship the key to my research. Almost upon my arrival, after having been invited to sit at the end of the old man's bed in which he spent most of his time since the onset of Parkinson's disease, I set on the path of carefully chosen words. I talked to Javier about my background, my anthropological interest in Afro-Cuban divination, and my hope that he might help me in my studies by allowing me to spend time with him. Would he be my informant, I was asking, as appealingly as I could.

His response was not what I had expected. Here, paraphrased from notes I took later, is what Javier said:

How would you know who's telling you the truth? A lot of people say they know these things and then they tell lies. You may come to me and I can tell you three things, and then you go to someone else and he tells you ten. Remember that this religion came from the Africans and they were not like what you see today. They were secretive and wouldn't let go of their knowledge—[laughing] they were real pieces of work! They were illiterate and from mouth to mouth things got distorted. In those times Ifá didn't have papers like it does today. Now people write books and they're full of lies. Look at what Lydia Cabrera did [referring to the renowned Cuban ethnologist who, as a woman, had caused some controversy among initiates by publishing data they considered secret]. Her book made people angry. When I was young people used to talk about what they had to do to extract things [*sacar les cosas*] from the babalawos, make them food, get them drunk, clean their house, or even build them one. But the old-timers weren't stupid either, so many of the things that are done today are badly done because people don't know what's true. You have to be careful what people tell you.

Had Javier not spoken in an entirely kindly tone, I would have been certain as I sat gazing into his face that this was all intended as a polite refusal of my proposition. Prepped in the hustling dynamics of earlier encounters, what I heard in Javier's words was an out-loud narration of my private ethnographic paranoia—albeit one substantiated with a certain historical depth. Was he not confirming what I had already experienced? You can't find what you're looking for because everyone is out to deceive you. Indeed, his disparaging comments about Cabrera's alleged ethnographic indiscretions seemed to me a fairly direct way of saying that he, at any rate, would be unwilling to cooperate in my project of ethnographic extraction.

Yet even at the time this interpretation seemed inadequate. For a start, his reaction appeared to involve a number of puzzling conflations. His worry about the truth-value of my research seemed first to run together the possibility of error with that of active deception. For example, his comment about the inevitable distortions of an oral tradition appears to be intended as an example of babalawos' propensity to tell lies, or at least to withhold truths. But then he was also implying that deception and error alike are a matter of indiscretion—the *excess* of truth. Lydia Cabrera's supposed publication of cult secrets constitutes, ipso facto, a straight case of "lies," while babalawos' own scheming extractions from furtive elders have made for a situation in which Ifá is done badly because "people don't

know what's true." In any case, it was unclear to me with whose capacity
for deception (or error, or indiscretion) Javier was primarily concerned—
that of the ethnographer, or that of the babalawo? My uncertainty on this
score was only increased by the fact that most of his reply to me seemed to
be directed at Javielito, a babalawo. "You should be careful what people
tell you." Was this intended for me, as friendly advice for my future research in this apparent ethnographic minefield, or was it meant for internal consumption—a comment between babalawos about the perils of
the economy of knowledge in Ifá, or even a subtle paternal warning to
Javielito about his relationship to prying outsiders?

I have little doubt, in retrospect, that with his elisions Javier was indeed expressing a certain amount of ambivalence toward my proposal.
One could also speculate whether some of the apparent jumbles in the
syntax of his thoughts were signs of an aging mind (in subsequent inter-
views Javier was open about the fact that our conversations sometimes
made him tired). Nevertheless, more than ten years later, and with Javier
having since died, I am convinced that his comments that afternoon, as
a first stake on our encounter, were significant in ways I could not have
deciphered at the time. The fact that the afternoon turned out, mysteri-
ously to me, a success, confirmed my sense even then that his words went
beyond my immediate pragmatic concerns (viz. the ethnographer's "will
he or won't he"). Even as I began to fumble a justification of my project
in response to his remarks, Javier was already inviting me to return in
coming days to discuss the history of his family in Matanzas—a suggestion I had made as part of my earlier pitch. Somehow, it seemed to me, his
perception of lying and truth in Ifá and in anthropology did not perturb
his inclination to be kind to strangers—the goodness of his heart. I was
privileged to enjoy this kindness for the rest of my year in Havana and on
every subsequent visit until Javier's death in 2004.

I begin with the story of my first encounter with Javier partly because in an
important sense it instantiates the overall strategy of this book. It will become apparent that behind the seeming symmetry between our respective
concerns with truth—my outsider's (anthropological) concern with secur-
ing "informants," his insider's (native) concern that I might be duped—
lies a deep (ontological) divergence between our respective *conceptions*
of truth itself, which would account for the puzzlement Javier's comments
caused me at the time. In order to prepare for the analysis of this conceptual divergence, however, this chapter dwells first on the surface of Javier's

comments. For, as it became clear to me the more time I spent in Javier's home, the concerns he expressed to me so vividly in our first encounter, involving notions of "truth," "error" and "deception," "transmission" and "distortion," "knowledge" and its "extraction," and so on, were entirely pervasive in his everyday life as a babalawo. As I hope to show with reference to my ethnography of life in Javier's home, questions of truth lie at the heart of babalawos' interactions with each other and with the world around them, providing both the form and the content of their social lives. In this sense, the fact that Javier should have prefaced our relationship by raising such concerns was just an indication of how much they mattered to him anyway.

This chapter, therefore, serves two purposes at once. It develops ethnographically the central premise of this study, which is that babalawos' abiding concern with truth plays a constitutive role in the practice of Ifá. In this sense the chapter can be seen as the ethnographic complement of my historically driven presentation of Ifá in the introduction, in which I argued that notions of truth, and of babalawos' privileged access to it, provide the cosmological underpinnings of the development of Ifá practice in West Africa and Cuba. At the same time, this chapter also serves to present the ethnographic setting of the study by introducing the reader to Javier and his son Javielito, whose daily lives as practicing babalawos provide the ethnographic anchor of my discussion of key facets of Ifá practice in Havana.

In line with my more concerted discussion of anthropological reasoning in later chapters, however, I should make clear here that this ethnographic acquaintance with Javier's home life should not be taken as an exercise in ethnographic "evocation." To the extent that the present ethnographic engagement is aimed at identifying the *alterity* of truth in Ifá, the idea that it should also serve as an evocation of life as a babalawo, bringing the reader closer to the "experience" of Ifá practice and so forth, is incongruous. If the notions of truth that I seek to identify are both abiding in Ifá practice (as shown in this chapter) and deeply divergent from those the reader can fairly be expected to take for granted (as shown later), then the idea that Ifá life could be evoked in an introductory way, before embarking on an analysis of the alterity of its conceptual underpinnings, has to be misguided. If anything, the role of ethnographic description under such conditions must be to render for the reader a sense of distance rather than familiarity—in a deliberate version of so-called exoticism, if you like. So the descriptive task of this chapter is to show how concerns with truth feature in the everyday life of babalawos like Javier, while preserving for the reader the sense in which these concerns seem puzzling, as a first step toward tackling the puzzle analytically in subsequent chapters.

Divinatory Regulation: Javier's Initiatory Career

In line with the supreme prestige of Ifá as a system of divination, practitioners of Afro-Cuban religions associate babalawos mainly with their office as professional diviners. Indeed, this public image dominates the exegetical and academic literature on the topic. As is overwhelmingly the case with the anthropological and historical literature on divination more generally, writings on Ifá divination tend to focus on what one might call the "consultative" role of the oracle, which allows babalawos to use Ifá to divine for uninitiated clients on all manner of personal matters in exchange for a fee. Having read much of this literature in preparation of my fieldwork, it was primarily the image of diviners' consultations for clients that I had in mind when I went in search for babalawos to work with in Havana.

Life in Javier's home certainly confirmed the image to an extent. During my research I soon discovered that a proportion of the visitors the two men received on a daily basis were paying clients who came to Javier for purposes of divinatory consultation. Javier himself would frequently emphasize the point. Unlike other babalawos, who dedicated themselves primarily to the varied ritual functions associated with the more esoteric aspects of Ifá practice, these days, as he would say, he was a *babalawo de consulta*, dedicated mainly to conducting divinatory consultations in the service of clients. In his time, he would explain, he had played a more active role in the internal affairs of "la religión," as he called it. Most important, he had sponsored the full initiation of a good number of younger babalawos (twelve to be precise), as well as officiating in initiations of a lower grade for tens more. While many of these "godchildren" (*ahijados*) still remained in regular contact with him, and the babalawos among them often invited him to participate in ceremonies that they conducted—the collective rituals that babalawos generically call *plantes*—in later years his health prevented him from leaving his home much. So he remained content to offer ordinary divinatory consultations to the daily traffic of clients, godchildren, and other friends and relatives who visited him, often at his bedside.

FIGURE 3.1. Javier drinking coffee in his home, Havana, 1999

These kinds of consultations were a central feature of Javier's everyday life, and understanding how divinatory truth is brokered in such sessions was a major aspect of my research. However, what I soon realized interacting with Javier, Javielito, and the many other babalawos that I met through them, is that the role of divination in Ifá goes well beyond the consultation of clients. Listening to babalawos talk, one comes to appreciate that behind the public image of professional consultation lies a much more pervasive concern with divination that has to do with its role in regulating the internal workings of the religion itself. To babalawos, far more absorbing than the incidental pronouncements the oracle makes for the benefit of clients is what the oracle says to *them*, effectively directing their own role in the affairs of worship and their personal comportment as babalawos. To give a first sense of the "divinatory regulation" of Ifá life, as we may call it, and to show how concerns with truth lie at its heart, I relay the story of Javier's initiation as a babalawo.

Javier was born in 1921 in Matanzas, into a poor family of dockworkers with a rich tradition in Afro-Cuban religious practices. His maternal grandfather, Mateo Isasi, was an influential initiate of Santería (*santero*) who had been brought up by the famous African-born babalawo Ño Blas Cardenas (see also Brown 2003, 76, 321). Javier's mother was initiated into Santería, as were a number of his uncles and aunts. His father's main allegiance, however, was with Uriabón Efí, a powerful lodge of Abakuá, a secret male fraternity (see Miller 2009). Javier himself was inducted as a member of Efí Dondá, another powerful Abakuá lodge in Matanzas, when he was still in his late teens, and later went on to form the subsidiary lodge Efí Ñumané in which he officiated at a high rank (namely as *ekueñón*). Much of his youth, as he would reminisce, was spent enjoying the rich social life that these male fraternities provided. For a young man about town, as he explained, the activities of Abakuá were more attractive than the life of Santería, which was viewed by Abakuá initiates as a mainly feminine affair, dominated by women and "effeminate men," as he put it, "full of gossip and women's stuff." Ifá, on the other hand, was practiced little in Matanzas at that time. The few babalawos who lived there when he was young tended to keep themselves to themselves.

Nevertheless, Javier knew from an early age that at some point he would become a babalawo. This, he explained, had been ordained by Orula himself, the patron oricha of divination, who is said to speak through the oracle of Ifá. After the death of Ño Blas, the famous Havana babalawo Asunción Villalonga, who was also born in Africa and had been a close friend and ritual associate of Ño Blas, began to visit Matanzas every year on November 25, in honor of Ño Blas's anniversary of initiation—his "birthday of Ifá" (*cumpleaños de Ifá*). The purpose of these visits was to attend ritually to Ño Blas's "fundaments" (*fundamentos*), the consecrated items associated with Ifá initiation. This had been ordained in a divination that had been conducted as part of Ño Blas's funerary rites (*ituto*). That Asunción, rather than Javier's grandfather Mateo himself, should be the one to attend to Ño Blas's fundamentos of Ifá was because only babalawos are sanctioned to perform such rituals. Although Ño Blas had trained his adopted son Mateo to become a babalawo, Orula had barred Mateo from Ifá initiation in a divination that Ño Blas had carried out on the matter. So when Asunción approached the end of his life, he asked Orula to determine who, if anyone, should take charge of Ño Blas's fundamentos after his own death. According to the divination this would have to be young Javier. That Orula should ordain so was no surprise, Javier explained, since, among his eight other siblings (four of them male), he had been Grandfather Mateo's favorite, and since the old man had been barred from inheriting Ño Blas's legacy, it stood to reason that Javier should do so in his place.

As is the case today, becoming a babalawo was hardly an easy matter at that time. Ifá initiation, as babalawos like to say, is the birth of a king—

an expensive seven-day ceremony of regal opulence, involving generous sacrifices and sumptuous feasts (Holbraad 2004a, 2005). In view of the scarcity of means in the family, Mateo later conducted a divination with his own cowry shells (*los caracoles*), as santeros do, and found out that Javier's guardian oricha (*angel de la guarda*) was Changó, the virile deity of thunder, and that Changó would help him secure the means to undergo initiation into Ifá. In line with the ritual requirement that Santería initiation should precede initiation into Ifá, this meant that Javier would have to be initiated into Santería before going on to become a babalawo.

However, unlike other santeros, who were loath to accept the authority of Ifá in matters of Santería initiation, Mateo had been taught by Ño Blas that decisions regarding the crucial matter of one's guardian oricha had to be ratified by the oracle of Ifá. So he promised to take Javier to Havana to consult Ifá with Asunción, Ño Blas' old friend. "This surprised me," Javier said as he recounted the story to me, "since it was quite normal then for santeros to use their shells for these things—it still is in Matanzas" (cf. Brown 2003, 76). At any event, the trip to Asunción never took place, partly because, growing up, Javier himself was more absorbed with the activities of Abakuá and was happy to delay the ceremonies of Santería and Ifá, which he could in any case ill afford.

Having migrated from Matanzas to Havana in search of work in 1939, Javier was in his forties and married to Javielito's mother before he began to take concrete steps toward Ifá initiation. Working in a factory and as a parking attendant among other jobs, he had become close to Isaias Mejias, stepfather of one of his brothers-in-law, who was a babalawo of some repute. "The sixties were a fun time in Havana," Javier recounted, "and my brother-in-law and I had formed a little group with a number of other babalawos." The group, he explained, included such figures as Mario Mendosa (Otuaché), Babél (Eyiobbe), Paulino from Matanzas (Osá Bara), and Marquetti (Okanawete). "We used to meet every Thursday at a bar on the corner of Jervasio and Reina [a central location in the inner city neighborhood of Centro Habana], opposite the Church of the Santisimo, to drink beer and talk Ifá. I enjoyed this a lot, listening to the babalawos talk, all the stories and so on, so I decided to enter the religion, as Orula had said."

So it was that in 1958 Javier underwent the first major step toward Ifá initiation, the ceremony of *awofaka*, with Mejias as godfather (*padrino*). Like all initiatory rites, this three-day ceremony involves an *itá*, which is a lengthy divinatory ceremony where neophytes are given key edicts relating to their life as initiates. Crucially, babalawos consider this itá ceremony as the only authoritative forum for ascertaining a neophyte's guardian oricha. Accordingly, and in line with Mateo's intentions, in Javier's itá Orula was asked to ratify Mateo's original cowry divination. To no one's surprise, given the memory of Mateo's standing, the oracle confirmed that Javier's tutelary oricha was indeed Changó, and that he would have to be initiated into Santería as Changó's "son" before going on to Ifá.

However, this second divinatory confirmation of Javier's "path" (*camino*), as babalawos and santeros call neophytes' trajectories in life, was not the end of the story. In view of his family's strong tradition in Santería in Matanzas, Javier chose as godmother (*madrina*) for his initiation into Santería a good friend of his grandfather Mateo known as La China, after her mother, "China Ecó," who had been a famous *santera* in Matanzas at the turn of the twentieth century. Notwithstanding her respect for Mateo, La China was unhappy with the prospect of presiding over Javier's initiation without confirming Changó's guardianship herself, using her own cowry oracle. As Javier commented to me, it was only Mejias's sense of honor and respect for the elderly santera that prevented him from obstructing such an unnecessary verification of Orula's divinatory edict. In any event, La China's divination duly corroborated what Ifá had already pronounced, and in 1963 Javier proceeded with Santería initiation. With Changó's help, as he liked to say when telling the story, and with Mejias as godfather, in 1967 he "made himself Ifá," as initiation as a babalawo is usually referred to (*hacerse Ifá*).

Divination and the Path of Initiation

Javier's story can, of course, be read in a number of ways—it presents the kind of ethnographic superabundance that could form the basis of what Clifford Geertz called "thick description" (1973). For example, one could take it as an old man's tale—an account of "Ifá old style" (*Ifá al antiguo*), as babalawos say. Certainly nostalgia for the times before the massive expansion of the religion from the 1980s onwards, times when being a babalawo was still something of which to be truly proud, was at the heart of Javier's narrations. For example, the emphasis he places on the protracted character of his initiatory journey can be understood partly by contrast to the speed with which Ifá has grown in recent decades. Javier's piecemeal movement from one initiatory step to the next, subject to multiple divinatory strictures and other ritual subtleties, as well as the abiding constraints of poverty, for him evokes an era quite different from the present one. These days, he and other elderly babalawos like to say, "Ifá is sooner sold than made" (*Ifá lo mismo se vende que se hace*). According to this view, increasingly unscrupulous babalawos now cut corners with ritual propriety when opportunities to gain dollar-wielding godchildren, including tourists and other foreign visitors, present themselves (see Hagedorn 2001; Palmié 2002, 260–89; Holbraad 2004a; Argyriadis 2005). Equally, Javier's narrative could be read as a commentary on the perennial tussle for ritual authority between babalawos and santeros that has been so central to the constitution of Ifá and Santería as parallel religious forms in Cuba. In particular, Javier's contrast between Mateo's "surprising" acceptance of babalawos' ultimate authority to ascertain a neophyte's guardian oricha, and La China's more typical resistance in the matter, exemplifies what is arguably the central point of contention that divides babalawos and santeros (see also Brown 2003, 153–55; Wirtz 2006, 186–94).

My interest here, however, is more in "thinning out" Javier's narrative than in thickening it interpretatively. Arguably, the string of events that Javier recounts, as well as the further interpretive resonances that I have just outlined, can be understood with reference to a single major premise, namely the role of divination in organizing the affairs of worship. The matter of initiation, on which Javier's narrative focuses, is particularly significant in this respect since it pertains to the very constitution of the social arrangements of worship. Effectively, Javier's story presents an image of a life of worship that is directed at each of its most crucial junctures by the edicts of divination. According to this image, it not so much people who make divination as divination that makes people. As the trajectory of Ño Blas's legacy of Ifá illustrates, bypassing Mateo despite his adopted father's own wishes and ending up with Javier's initiation via Asunción's and Mejias's divinations, it is the oracle of Ifá itself that decides who gets to "make himself Ifá." Indeed, the fundamental character of this principle of divinatory regulation is arguably basic both to Javier's nostalgic worries about the laxity of babalawos' initiations in recent years, and his somewhat macho dismissal of santeros' claims to authority in such matters. The notion that Orula's oracular edicts about a neophyte's initiation might be trumped by a babalawo's wish to earn dollars or a santera's assertion of her own divinatory authority is to him fundamentally improper.

The reliability of oracles as authoritative sources of truth is at the heart of this system of divinatory regulation, as shown by the story of Javier's triple divinatory confirmation as a son of Changó. Notwithstanding his prestige as a leading santero, Mateo accepts that his own cowry divination is not sufficient to establish Changó's guardianship of his grandson beyond doubt, and therefore cedes authority to the babalawos. Contrastingly, Javier's santera godmother denies the finality of the babalawo's verdict and insists on corroborating it with her own divination. While such conflicting claims to authority obviously have many dimensions (concerns with prestige, power, money, personal honor, and so on are all part of the fray), the common premise upon which they turn is that authority in matters of initiation depends on the credibility of the oracle used for the task. That this crucial question is conceived explicitly in terms of standards of truth is vividly illustrated by the myth babalawos commonly use to justify their exclusive prerogative to determine neophytes' guardian oricha—a claim that effectively expands the regulative remit of Ifá to include a key aspect of initiation into Santería. As far as babalawos are concerned, the divinatory supremacy of Ifá is a function of the superior transparency and impartiality of the truths Orula bestows on them in divination:

> It used to be the case that the *santos* [as the orichas are also referred to in Cuba] used their own cowries to determine whether a person was to be under their guardianship. But Obatalá [a major oricha], who was the governor at the time, accumulated many more godchildren than the rest of the santos. Taking Ochún and Ogún with him for support, Changó went to Obatalá's house to complain. As they arrived Obatalá heard them coming and came out of his palace to meet them. Changó stepped forward and told him, "Look, *baba* [father], we are here because we want to know why when you register *aleyos* [i.e., the uninitiated] to determine their guardian angel none of us ever emerge as the owners of his head." Obatalá responded, "That is how I do things." So Changó told him, "*Baba*, this is not legal, why don't we go to the house of Orula and he will tell us how to resolve the issue." Obatalá said, "So be it, you are right since Orunmila doesn't make santo, and you don't trust me but I too don't trust you either, for as long as this world exists let Orunmila be the one to determine the guardian angel of each person, since he is impartial." (from the divinatory "sign" Osa Roso)

Still, to present the regulatory power of Ifá divination as just a question of the impartiality of Orula's verdicts is to miss a crucial aspect of its authority for practitioners. Indeed, in line with the overwhelming tendency in the anthropological literature to focus on the "consultative" aspect of divination, one could imagine the oracle's role in directing the "paths" of neophytes as just a matter of identifying the "correct" initiatory course among the available options. This is not, however, how practitioners think about the matter. As they make clear, oracular pronouncements are as much edicts as they are verdicts, in the sense that the initiatory path that Orula marks for neophytes in divination is one that they are *required* to take. Divinatory regulation presents initiatory paths not as options but as obligations: paths have to be followed. In particular, having one's path marked by the oracle as being one of Ifá is conceived as an explicit "call" to initiation by Orula (*la llamada de Orula*). To illustrate what is at stake for practitioners in this connection, and also by way of introduction to the other half of the father-and-son Ifá partnership of Javier and Javielito, I present Javielito's own account of his path to Ifá, as he wrote it for me at my request:

In relation to my steps of initiation, I can tell you that at a very early age I received the Warrior deities (see below) from the hands of Isaias Mejias, my father's godfather. I suppose I must have been three or four years old, I do not remember the moment. At ten years of age in 1969 I received *mano de Ifá*, also without being aware of its significance. Only from that moment onwards did I begin to have notions of Ifá, though still in a rather indirect manner. I say this because Ifá was not my interest as such since at that time what really interested me were music groups of rock, pop, and soul of the '60s, and furthermore I was aware of the negative attitudes regarding the religions at the time. In my mano de Ifá it was determined that my guardian angel is Ogún. To the question whether I ought to "seat" the santo [viz. undergo the full initiation to Santería], Orunmila said no, so it was determined that I should wash[1] Ogún and make myself Ifá. My disinterest continued until finally I decided to make myself Ifá, influenced by the fascination of the stories [viz. the myths], listening to the babalawos speak, and seeing that many people with less background or none at all were beginning to enter the religion. Also, a principal aspect of the signo [i.e., one of the 256 divinatory configurations on which the divinatory practice of Ifá is based—see below] that I had drawn in my mano de Ifá is difficulty at advancing in life, or bringing one's aspirations to fruition. This signo speaks of the crab of whom there is the proverb that says that he walks backwards and has no head, so the babalawos tell you that you need to make yourself Ifá in order

FIGURE 3.2. Javier and his son Javielito in their home together with the author, Havana, 1999

to change and to be able to prosper in life, etc. Thus in 1988 I washed Ogún and on August of that year I made myself Ifá.

It is significant here that Javielito juxtaposes his initial "disinterest" with the normative vocabulary of the oracle ("it was determined that I should . . ."), implying that had he not been initiated he would have faced difficulties in his life. Such notions of obligation are key to understanding the regulative role of the oracle, not only in matters of initiation but, more generally, in all important aspects of worship (sacrifices, prohibitions, and so on). To disregard oracular imperatives—or, as practitioners say, to "fall into disobedience" (*caer en la desobedencia*)—is considered an affront to Orula himself. And, as the myths of Ifá continually reiterate, the deities' wrath can be awesome in such cases.

Initiation is particularly problematic in this context. With prices ranging from $1,000 to more than $5,000 during my fieldwork, Ifá is one of the most expensive of what is in any case an inordinately pricey set of ceremonies, so many practitioners have mixed feelings about the prospect of having the oracle mark them a path of Ifá. Notwithstanding its great prestige, only a small proportion of potential neophytes can actually afford to go through with the ceremony. For most, having a path of Ifá implies a long and frustrating period of waiting for a financial opportunity to come along, and this is by no means an easy matter given the economic situation in Cuba, particularly during the post-Soviet period. Indeed, frustration in this context is compounded by an element of fear. For it is understood that a pending initiation can anger the deities concerned, particularly if the chosen neophyte seems to be ignoring the oracle's call by procrastinating over his initiation, failing to save up, or to take advantage of the right circumstances when they come his way. In such cases all sorts of incidental misfortunes that might afflict the potential neophyte may be explained in terms of his failure to heed Orula's call, and this provides babalawos with a certain amount of emotional leverage when it comes to impressing the urgency of initiation upon potential godchildren.

It may also be noted that such notions of obligation make divination a prime instrument for the initial recruitment of neophytes. Neither Javier nor his son provides a particularly good example of this since, as Javier put it, both of them were "born into the religion," given the family history. However, the link that the idea of obligation establishes between divination and initiation means that well nigh any man who consults the oracle of Ifá as a client can find himself propelled into the orbit of initiation. To take a most typical scenario, an ordinary uninitiated client who consults a babalawo in relation to a health problem, an imminent court case, or some other urgent matter of this kind may have no thoughts of initiation until the oracle tells him that in order to overcome his difficulties he will have to make himself santo. Quickly he gets the money together to undergo the mano de Orula ceremony to determine which oricha will be his guardian. In the ensuing itá the oracle tells him his guardian oricha but also "calls" him to Ifá.

The pressure of obligation that the oracles exert in this way extends well beyond the matter of initiation to include pretty much all aspects of babalawos' lives, as we shall see. Moreover, I shall argue that this abiding normative power of Ifá divination is a function of the deeper ontological constitution of divinatory truth. The fusion of what one might want to call "epistemic" transparency with "normative" authority is one of the key ways in which divination subverts ordinary analytical assumptions about what counts as truth. To prepare for this, we may first chart out some of the consequences that the regulative role of divination has for the social organization of Ifá worship.

The Matrix of Initiation and the Propulsion of Paths

For reasons of clarity, my rendition of Javier's trajectory of initiation includes only his references to the more major ceremonies—particularly
the ceremony of mano de Orula in which an itá is held to determine the
neophyte's guardian oricha, the ceremony of full initiation into Santería
as a son (or daughter) of that oricha, and the ceremony of initiation as a
babalawo reserved only for those for whom Orula has "marked" (*marcar*)
a path of Ifá. However, these ceremonies are part of a more complex matrix of initiatory possibilities (see table 3.1).The table depicts initiation
as a gradual process that unfolds as a series of ceremonies over time—a
tota simul view of the space in which the piecemeal ascent in the initiatory
hierarchy Javier's story exemplifies takes place.

Not all the ceremonies listed, however, are properly considered as initiations. "Initiation" (*iniciación*), a term used by practitioners themselves,
refers to the more ceremonious rites—such as the three that frame my
presentation of Javier's narrative—which involve lengthy divinations that
regulate various aspects of the neophyte's further progress within the cult,
as we shall see.[2] Other ceremonies are best described as consecration rites,
whereby the neophyte "receives" various consecrated paraphernalia for
his or her personal protection (e.g., receipt of the so-called *guerreros*—the
popular "warrior" deities).[3] Indeed, while each step of initiation or consecration opens up for practitioners a correspondingly wider range of ritual
activities, the crucial leap from just being able to participate in rituals to
gaining the right to dispense them oneself is only achieved by those practitioners who "make themselves Ifá" by undergoing the weeklong initiation
ceremony. Only babalawos are entitled to dispense Ifá rituals, be they of
divination, magic, or consecration. From then on, additional consecration
ceremonies are referred to as "powers," which the babalawo "receives"
from more senior initiates who "have" them, allowing babalawos to perform additional ritual functions.

So the vertical axis of table 3.1 marks a hierarchical order, with Ifá initiation standing at the higher end of a plethora of possible initiatory paths.
The role of divination as an indispensable navigational instrument within
this matrix of possibilities, propelling neophytes in particular directions as
a matter of obligation, is constitutive of this hierarchy, since each step neophytes take on the path of initiation depends on divinatory selection. Indeed, as the notion of Orula's "call" to Ifá indicates, becoming a babalawo

TABLE 3.1 **The initiatory matrix of Ifá**

	CEREMONIES DISPENSED WITHIN IFÁ CULT (i.e., by babalawos)		CEREMONIES DISPENSED OUTSIDE IFÁ CULT (i.e., by initiates of other cults, Catholic priest)	
	Additional ceremonies (as prescribed by oracle)	Necessary stages for full initiation to Ifá (ordinary liturgical requirements, subject to oracular confirmation)	Necessary stages for full initiation to Ifá (ordinary liturgical requirements, subject to oracular confirmation)	Additional ceremonies (as prescribed by oracle)
PRE-INITIATION	*recibir Olokun* (Deity of deep seas) *recibir Oddúa* (Powerful creator deity)	*recibir guerreros* (Warrior deities): Elegguá, Ogún, Ochosi, with Osun *recibir mano de Orula* (*fa ka*) / *ko fa* For men/women respectively (idol-deity Orula received in "incomplete" form)	Catholic baptism *ka ri ocha* (*hacerse santo*) Full Santería initiation as devotee of particular *oricha*. Or alternatively, *lavar santo* ("washing" the *oricha* – simpler form of Santería initiation, as a stepping-stone to Ifá initiation)	*rayamiento* (Initiation to one of Palo Monte cults) *jurarse en Abakuá* (Initiation to one of secret male societies) *lavar/recibir collares* ("Wash/receive the necklaces," i.e., consecration of *oricha* paraphernalia by *santero*)

TABLE 3.1 **The initiatory matrix of Ifá** (*continued*)

	CEREMONIES DISPENSED WITHIN IFÁ CULT (i.e., by *babalawos*)		CEREMONIES DISPENSED OUTSIDE IFÁ CULT (i.e., by initiates of other cults, Catholic priest)	
	Additional ceremonies (as prescribed by oracle)	Necessary stages for full initiation to Ifá (ordinary liturgical requirements, subject to oracular confirmation)		Additional ceremonies (as prescribed by oracle)
INITIATION		*HACERSE IFÁ* FULL IFÁ INITIATION only for men (deity Orula received in "complete" form)		
POST-INITIATION	*Recibir guanaldo* ("The knife") and/or *poderes* (Extra "powerful" deities, including Osain, Oddúa, Olofin, etc.)		After full initiation, the *babalawo* is prohibited from undertaking further steps of consecration outside Ifá cult.	
DEATH RITES	*Honras* (Extra funerary rite undertaken by god-children of deceased)	*ituto* (Funerary rite for deceased *babalawo*)		

Note: Ceremonies that are considered absolute prerequisites for Ifá initiation appear in the central two columns of the table. Other ceremonies, which may emerge in any individual case as additional prerequisites if the oracle so ordains, are listed in the far left and far right columns.

is a prestigious achievement precisely because divinatory selection is an inherently exclusive process—as Javier's grandfather Mateo, for example, knew all too well. Apart from the generic rule that only heterosexual men can make Ifá (see also below), aspiring babalawos have to pass a whole series of divinatory hurdles, the most important of which is the itá divination of the mano de Orula ceremony, as we have seen. Whether the neophyte has the path of Ifá depends on which of the 256 possible divinatory configurations (*signos*) is drawn in this itá. While the details of this process are guarded as secret by babalawos, it is interesting to note that some babalawos spoke to me about the relevant criteria in terms of the gender associations of different categories of signos. "Masculine" signos mark a path of Ifá for the neophyte, while "feminine" ones bar him from it.

Be that as it may, the crucial corollaries of neophytes' hierarchical ascent along this initiatory order are the equally hierarchical *social* relationships that each stage of initiation articulates. From the first step of consecration practitioners are incorporated in networks of religious kinship, referred to as "families" (*familia de Ifá*), which from then on provide a primary context for worship. As we have seen with reference to Javier, at the heart of Ifá kinship lies the relationship between a padrino (godfather) and his ahijado/a (godson/daughter) (see fig. 3.3). This relationship arises because consecration always involves "receiving" (*recibir*) the crucial consecrated items from an initiator who "has" (*tener*) them and is able to act as godfather by "giving" (*dar*) them, usually in return for money. In the case of full initiation, the crucial item the neophyte babalawo receives from his padrino is Orula himself, in the form of a pot containing consecrated items including the paraphernalia of divination, which will be discussed in detail in the next chapter. For purposes of exposition, I shall refer to this consecrated deity/object as "the Orula/s," "his Orula," "an Orula" and so on. In reference to the cosmological role of Orula, conceived as an oricha who resides in the sky, in the mythical past of cosmogony, and so on, I shall speak simply of "Orula." As we shall see, the distinction is both subtle and crucial.

Once completed, the ritual transaction of "receiving" consecrated items engenders a lasting relationship that is cultivated in hierarchical terms: the godchild owes his or her padrino respect and is expected to visit him regularly, bringing gifts when possible. The padrino, in turn, is obliged to help and advise his godchildren on matters religious, both by coaching them through mythical knowledge and ritual practice, and by making his ritual services available to them according to their circumstances.

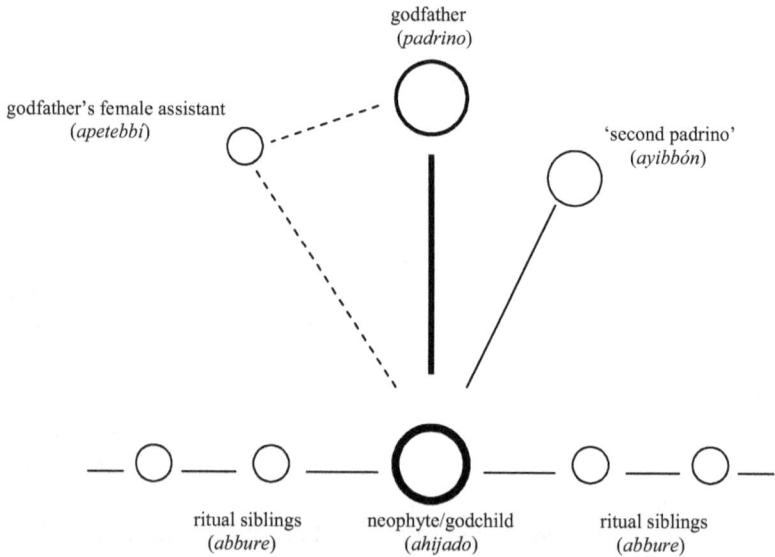

FIGURE 3.3. Ritual kinship relations in the religious family

While this vertical kinship relation (godfather to godchild) is as simple as it is fundamental, it can engender a large degree of complexity due to the fact that godfathers can have many godchildren and vice-versa. Babalawos have a free hand at attracting godchildren at quantity, and indeed tend to welcome as many as possible, since this is felt to enhance their personal prestige among practitioners, including considerable material accrual (money, gifts, and so on; see Holbraad 2005). Conversely, a single practitioner may have different godfathers corresponding to separate ceremonies. Furthermore, the ceremony of full Ifá initiation requires the ritual assistance of a "second padrino" (usually referred to as *ayibbón*) who subsequently may take a primary role if the godfather-godchild relationship is disrupted for some reason (e.g., the godfather's death or immigration, personal conflict). Finally, complexity accrues also on the horizontal dimension, since godchildren who share a godfather are viewed as siblings, and refer to each other as *abbure*, or, in Spanish, as "brothers/sisters in the religion" (*hermanos en la religión*).

Still, of all ego's ritual kin-relations by far the most important is with the godfather, not only because of its substantive ritual significance, but also because of its structural implications. Unlike other relations within

(*babalawos*)   (Orulas)

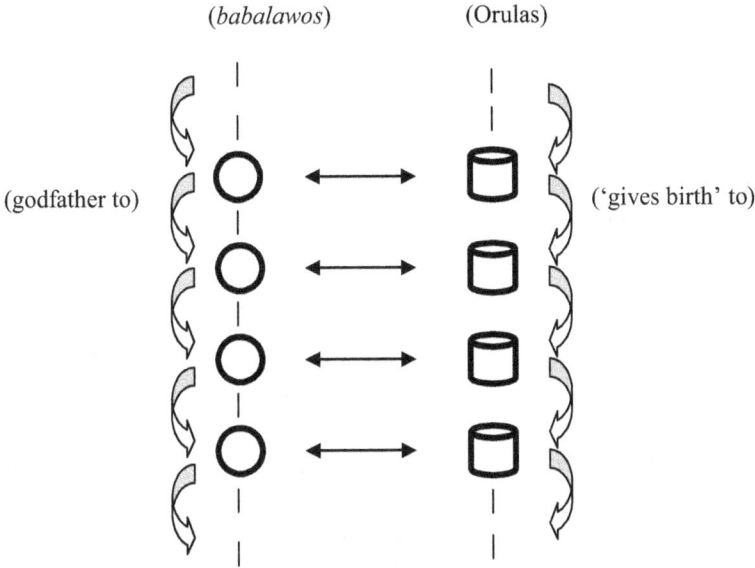

FIGURE 3.4. Ritual lineages and the births of consecrated Orulas

the ritual family, godfather-godchild relations can be iterated indefinitely through the generations, as godchildren who become fully initiated babalawos gain the right to acquire godchildren of their own, and so on. Referred to as *ramas* (branches), lineages of babalawos may in principle extend indefinitely into the past, although, given the relatively short history of Ifá in Cuba, babalawos will typically trace their genealogical line from three to maybe five or six generations back, often to an "African" of the nineteenth century (see Brown 2003, 76).

The genealogical reckoning involved in lineage affiliations is important to babalawos both ritually and politically. Ritually speaking, the lineage is considered sacred in its own right, and its efficacy is invoked at the outset of all rites by means of a ceremonious incantation of ancestors' names— the so-called *moyubba* (Menéndez Vásquez 1995), discussed in the next chapter. Babalawos explain this sacred quality of lineages in terms of the ritual of initiation itself: the Orulas that godfathers "give" during initiation are said to be "born" (*nacen*) out of their own Orula. Moreover, the consecration of the neophytes themselves as babalawos is also spoken of as a birth, and specifically as "the birth of a king," as we have seen. Lineages of babalawos, then, are coupled with isomorphic lineages of Orulas (see fig. 3.4).

The vocabulary of filiation here is significant, partly because it sheds some light on the traditional ban on women and homosexual men being initiated as diviners of Ifá. I say "traditional" because this topic has been provoking heated (and on occasion violent) conflicts in the ranks of babalawos in recent years, following the decision in the mid-2000s by the prominent babalawo Victor Betancourt to break with this stricture by conducting an initiation ceremony for women, called *iyanifá*, which he claims is "authentically African," and allows female initiates to progress beyond the *kofá* ceremony (traditionally the upper limit of Ifá initiation for women, as indicated in table 3.1) to become diviners of Ifá alongside male babalawos. While it is beyond the remit of my argument to describe this debate, we may note that the fierce resistance Victor has encountered from the majority of babalawos in Cuba speaks partly to the deep cosmological significance of gender in Ifá. Indeed, while babalawos guard the details of this matter with great care, it is significant to them that a key part of Ifá initiation is the bestowal upon the male neophyte of "the secret of *odu*," described to me by one babalawo as the "female principle of Ifá" and by another as "Orula's wife." As babalawos explain, it is by virtue of their affinity to odu that they are able to preside over the birth of Orulas during initiations. One may surmise that, cosmologically speaking, women and homosexual men are barred from Ifá initiation because, by definition, they cannot take odu as a wife. Indeed such an interpretation would accord with the fact that, as Victor often reiterates in defense of his innovation, the iyanifá ceremony only enables women to act as diviners and does not entitle them to preside over the "birth" of Orulas as, *per impossible*, "godmothers."

Be that as it may, we may note here that women nevertheless do play a prominent role in the ritual life even of babalawos who reject iyanifá (as I am sure Javier would have, had he lived to witness it), and this in two principal ways. Within the context of dispensing the more elaborate rituals, senior babalawos officiate with the help of a female assistant, referred to as *apetebbí*, who will often be a relative of the babalawo (such as wife, mother, sister). This is connected to the domestic character of the apetebbí's responsibilities. While apetebbí do participate in the liturgy of certain Ifá ceremonies, their main role during rituals is to attend to the babalawos, which mainly involves cooking, cleaning, and the like. Beyond the confines of the larger ceremonies, however, women are chiefly significant to babalawos as clients for divinatory consultation (my own data from recording clients' visits at Javier's house over a period of four months suggests a female/male ratio of about 7 to 3).

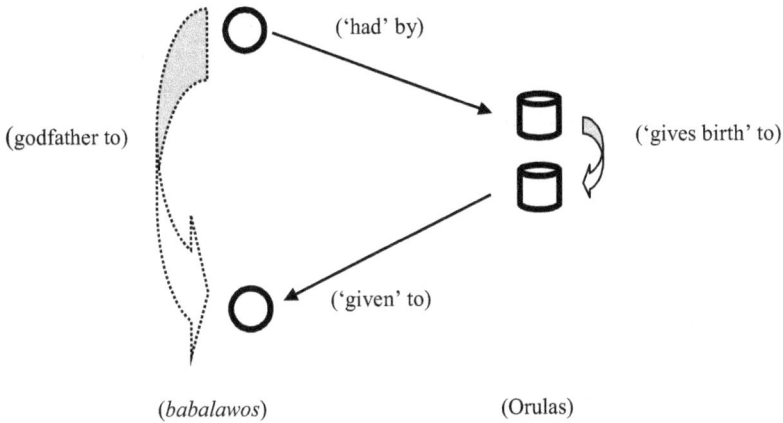

FIGURE 3.5. The logical priority of initiate : deity relationships over initiate : initiate relationships

So, in summary, Ifá initiation is articulated as a gradual transformation of relationships on two planes. On the one hand neophytes enter increasingly wide circles of divine influence by receiving various kinds of consecrated items, including the consecrated Orulas. In fact, what distinguishes the initiated from the uninitiated in this context is precisely the fact that while both groups are in principle subject to divine influence, the former are better equipped to enter into reciprocal relationships with the deities, by virtue of the care and attention they bestow on the consecrated items they receive during initiation. Each deity has likes and dislikes in terms of the position he or she should occupy in the initiate's home, offerings he or she should be given and, above all, the animals' blood with which he or she ought to be fed. Over and above the regular care that they owe their deities, initiates may also appeal to them on specific matters by making occasional requests. These are accompanied by appropriate offerings, which may be decided through divination.

As we saw, however, such human-deity relationships are connected to a second plane of relationships, namely ritual kin-ties between humans—be they immediate, in the family, or mediated along the lineage. Significantly, such human-human relations are a logical consequence of human deity relations. For example, in the constitution of lineages outlined above (in fig. 3.4), it is by virtue of having their own Orula that godfathers are able to preside over the birth of a new Orula, which subsequently the neophyte receives as a prerequisite for his own birth as a babalawo (see fig. 3.5).

The same priority holds for ritual "family" ties (as opposed to lineages). For example, you might be my sibling (*abbure*) because we both received our warrior deities, say, from the same babalawo, who in turn was only in position to give the warriors to us because he had his own. And note that the logical implication here is not mutual. With respect to this (and each) ceremony, the babalawo does not give us the deities by virtue of being our godfather, but rather becomes our godfather by virtue of giving us the deities. Recalling Van Gennep's famous thesis (1960) about the sacred character of social transitions in rites of passage, we may say that in Ifá relationships between people are both mediated and engendered by relationships with deities. This fundamental logical priority effectively recapitulates the logic of divinatory regulation, according to which the relationships that neophytes establish with deities during initiation are themselves dictated to them by Orula by means of the oracle.

Living Ifá

So far we have seen how the regulative role of divination gives form to the lives of initiates by organizing the relationships to deities and people that initiation involves. However, for babalawos the influence of the truths Orula reveals in divination extends much further than that, coloring all aspects of their everyday lives. At the most generic level, this just follows from the more general notion that all human experiences are in one way or the other under the sway of the orichas—an idea that is so fundamental to the divinatory logic of Ifá worship that one could call it the "divinatory principle" par excellence. Indeed it is on the basis of this general principle that Ifá practitioners, initiated and uninitiated alike, seek the advice of oracles so frequently, as a way of gauging the orichas' influence over the details of their lives.

In this connection we may note that while individual clients typically consult babalawos on personal matters, such as love affairs and other personal relationships, professional prospects, questions of health, and so on, the divinatory remit of babalawos also extends to global concerns. In line with their historical role as royal counsels in Ife, Oyo, and other West African polities, babalawos have on and off since the 1930s come together once a year to perform collectively a divination for the coming year—the so-called *letra del año* ceremony, which includes divinatory edicts that concern the fortunes of the Cuban nation as a whole, and often touches on even broader issues relating to international politics, technological innovations, climactic events, and so on. While in recent years there have been controversies between competing annual assemblies, which I shall not go into here, it is relevant to note that babalawos typically relay the results of the letra del año to their godchildren and clients in the beginning of each year, and often refer to it during their consultations.

In a sense one could say that becoming a babalawo involves an intensified commitment to the "divinatory principle." For example, I once asked a *babalawo* to explain what initiates mean when they say that "Ifá gives you protection." After first emphasizing the idea, which one often hears from babalawos, that Ifá initiation is inherently beneficial since it prolongs one's life (by sixteen years, as some babalawos specify) and ensures Orula's favor in all matters, he went on to explain that becoming a babalawo gives one the privilege to consult Orula directly on whatever issue one wishes, and thus to overcome life's difficulties (*superar a los problemas*). In this vein, babalawos are supposed to perform personal divinations every morning "to open the day" (*abrir el dia*), as they say. To illustrate the very quotidian effects of these auroral consultations, I recall one occasion in which Javielito and I were left waiting at an appointment we had with a babalawo friend of his. Some days later Javielito told me that his friend had later apologized to him for standing us up, explaining that Orula had ordained in that morning's consultation that he should not leave his home under any pretext—a perfectly reasonable excuse among fellow initiates.

However, the influence of divination over babalawos' lives also works at a deeper, more encompassing level. I refer here to the lasting effects of the itá, the long and to babalawos most significant divinatory consultations that are held for neophytes in all major initiation ceremonies, including the ceremony of "making oneself Ifá." As we have already seen with reference to Javier's story of initiation, the itá of the mano de Orula ceremony has a lasting influence since, depending on which one of the 256 signos is drawn for the neophyte, it may prescribe further steps of initiation that may be taken years later. But beyond matters of initiation, during the consultation of itá the babalawos also coach the neophyte in all manner of issues associated with his signo, providing a global characterization of his or her personality, prospects in life, particular issues of which to be aware, and so forth. Effectively, one's "sign of itá" (*signo de itá*) designates one's entire identity as a person. Indeed, when it comes to the itá of full Ifá initiation, this identification is enshrined in the fact that the name of one's signo is adopted informally as a personal name for the neophyte—Marquetti "Okanawete," Fran "Obbeché," and so on.

One might say, then, that one's signo de itá plays a role that is analogous to a horoscope in Western astrology. The difference, however, is that beyond merely describing one's life prospects and giving advice on how to act in light of them, for babalawos the itá also has a deeply prescriptive quality. In fact, the compulsory manner in which itá ceremonies direct neophytes' initiatory paths is just an instance of the basic idea that the truths that itá reveals about the neophyte also place obligations upon him. In the case of ceremonies anterior to Ifá initiation, such as mano de Orula, these prescriptions are typically spelled out by the babalawos for the benefit of the neophyte as a list of rules for living: for example, "you may not eat beans," "avoid loitering on street-corners," "attend to the spirit of your dead grandmother." When it comes to babalawos' own initiation, however, the normative force of the signo takes a more encompassing role. As discussed in more detail below, becoming a babalawo involves a long learning process in which babalawos verse themselves in the vast body of myths that are associated with each signo, which constitute the basis of divinatory interpretation, and are the source the more epigrammatic rules that are given to neophytes at lower levels of initiation. Given the personal significance of their own signo de itá, babalawos are expected to pay particular attention to the characteristics of that signo, amassing as much of the mythical knowledge associated with it as they can. The normative character of this process of self-discovery, which may unfold itself throughout a babalawo's life, is captured by the idea that one ought to "live" one's signo (*vivir el signo*). In an extreme version of what Marshall Sahlins calls "mythopraxis" (Sahlins 1985), babalawos are expected not only to learn the myths of their own signo, but also interpretatively to *emulate* them in their daily lives.

Javier's life as a babalawo provides a moving illustration. As he often used to explain, his *signo de Ifá*, Ogunda Tetura, is a "good" sign which speaks of great longevity. It is also, however, "a poor man's sign" (*signo de pobre*), which speaks of the importance of conforming oneself with the little one has in life. This, for him, had deep implications for his own comportment as a babalawo. In relation to longevity, Javier would sometimes point out that one of the stories of his signo described life as a hollow tree: "the tree lasts for years, even though it has less and less inside." While this for him was a good metaphor of his current circumstances, already

advanced in age and with his failing health, it was also how he would justify his reluctance to participate in ceremonies and other tiring activities.
"*Plantes* [viz. ceremonies] draw life from you, and due to my signo (*por
mi signo*) I need to preserve the little life I have left," Javier would say.
Indeed, it was with reference to this aspect of his signo that, during the
course of the itá of one of his godchildren some years earlier, babalawos
had determined that Javier should not preside over any further initiations
in his lifetime. Most strikingly, perhaps, from that time onward Javier con-
signed himself to living surrounded by half a dozen or so pigeons, which
would perch freely all over the deteriorating furniture in his home. "He
has those because of his signo," Javielito explained. "They bring peace
and stillness."

The emphasis on poverty in Ogunda Tetura was also normative for Javier. While the fact that he had always been poor was for him self-evidently
a reflection of his signo, it was also in a certain sense a source of content-
ment for him. Living an entirely frugal existence together with Javielito
in their single-room apartment, the only objects Javier owned, other than
the strictly utilitarian and a set of beautiful chinaware that had belonged
to Javielito's deceased mother, were books and the implements of his religion. On a number of occasions he contrasted his own circumstances
with babalawos' increasing reputation for showing off their regal prestige
with dollar purchases (cars and motorbikes, big stereos, trendy clothes,
and extravagant nights out). While that might be quite proper for them,
he reflected, his signo of Ogunda Tetura meant that he would always have
to stay poor. On these grounds he had long since contracted out of the
various competitive strategies babalawos adopt in order to attract wealthy
godchildren, and had refused to follow the successive price-hikes for clients' consultations, keeping his at the "pre-dollar" level of 3.15 Cuban
pesos. In line with the characteristics of his signo, his reputation among
clients as well as fellow babalawos was built on modesty.

It should be noted, however, that the perhaps rather Christian-sounding
ethical undertones of Javier's comportment are not in themselves a characteristic of the normative injunctions of the signos of Ifá. Just as Javier
tended to live out an ascetic and kindly ethos with reference to his interpretation of Ogunda Tetura, other babalawos justify quite different
behaviors that, as he said, "may be proper to them" owing to their own
signo. To take an infamous example, one of the most prominent babalawos working in Havana during my fieldwork had a reputation for having
amassed an exorbitant amount of godchildren, many of them dollar-paying

foreigners, occasionally performing initiations that were judged by other babalawos as variously inappropriate. Having heard many critical commentaries on the matter, I had assumed that this was an example of the kind of unscrupulous behavior Javier so often criticized—"selling" rather than "making" Ifá. When I raised the matter with him and Javielito, however, their circumspect response was rather more respectful than I had anticipated. A senior babalawo from a prestigious lineage, they explained, this was no mercenary youngster. Rather, his behavior aptly reflected his signo, which was that of a "bandit," and included a myth akin to the tale of Ali Baba and the forty thieves. So, all in all, for him it was proper to behave improperly.

Speaking Ifá and the Economy of Learning

One could summarize the foregoing discussion by saying that the abiding role of divination in the lives of babalawos makes for a peculiar form of wisdom, if one may speak in these terms. Premised on a divinatory principle, this wisdom resides in babalawos' ability to relate "the imponderabilia of everyday life," to coin the anthropological phrase, with the mythical realm of the signos of Ifá. To the extent that this activity, as we have seen, melds a concern for truth with a sense of obligation, babalawos' wisdom is measured partly by the extent to which their own actions can be seen to express the divine edicts of their signo. To "live" one's signo is a prime mark of one's prestige. Effectively, one might say, the mythopractical character of babalawos' actions is one in which life is raised to the power of myth.

One of the most fascinating aspects of doing fieldwork among babalawos is listening to them speak about the mythopractical universe into which their signos propel them. I have in mind here babalawos' expression "speaking Ifá" (*hablar Ifá*), by which they refer to the more-or-less informal manners of conversation that typically take place when babalawos meet socially, whether this be in an everyday context, such as a house-visit or a friendly meeting at a bar, or at the fringes of a collective ceremony, such as a *plante* of initiation. Magisterial forms of what one might want to call gossip, what makes these conversations so intriguing is how participants strive, often competitively, to bring their command of the mythical knowledge of Ifá signos to bear on the topic of discussion, however mundane, rather like intellectuals might discuss current affairs in terms of their

readings of their favorite philosophers, or like psychoanalysts might talk
about their personal relationships by appeal to Freud or Lacan. To give a
sense of how such conversations unfold, I adduce an extract from one that
I recorder at Javier's house, involving Javier, Javielito, and one of Javier's
more senior babalawo godchildren who was visiting at the time (I shall call
him Rogelio). Over a quick cup of coffee, as Javier liked it (others would
have preferred rum), the three men were discussing the recent disappear-
ance of one of Rogelio's own godchildren. As Javielito later explained to
me, the man was most likely hiding from Rogelio due to a severe ritual
infringement. It is customary, Javielito explained, that when a babalawo
performs the initiation of his first godchild he should invite his own godfather to participate in the ceremony, and particularly to manage the money
that is involved. It would appear, however, that Rogelio's miscreant godchild deliberately hid from his godfather the fact that he was performing
an initiation, effectively "breaking the relationship off," as Javielito put
it. Having heard rumors that his godchild had actually died, Rogelio had
come to discuss the matter with Javier, his own godfather, and to find out
what he and Javielito had heard about the case:

JAVIELITO: Well, our friend Alexis, you may know him, a young white guy, told me,
    "Listen, I saw that guy just yesterday, he greeted me" [laughing].
ROGELIO: So really he is the living dead! Seems the guy is on the run.
JAVIELITO: Yes, otherwise you'd have to pay for the cost of the funeral! [laughing].
    Alexis said, "That's the guy who got Obbesá in Ifá and in the [ceremony of
    the] knife as well" [referring to the man's initiatory signo in both ceremonies.
    Obbesá is considered a particularly "difficult" signo, associated with death, be-
    trayal, and the creation of enemies].
ROGELIO: It's true, though, that Orula make no mistakes (*Orula no se equivoca*).
JAVIER: No, boy, it's true that Orula makes no mistakes. We are the mistaken ones
    (*los equivocados somos nosotros*). If it isn't today it will be tomorrow . . .
ROGELIO: Obbesá says to you in the Ifá [in the initiation ceremony], do the knife
    ceremony to get rid of this signo [referring to the fact that in the itá of the knife
    ceremony the neophyte receives a further signo in addition to that of his origi-
    nal initiation]. So when he gets Obbesá all over again in the itá of the knife that
    means that he is being punished by Orula himself.
JAVIER: Yes, by the hand of Orula.
ROGELIO: It's Orula punishing him, not us.
JAVIER: And what's funny is that all Obbesás [babalawos of that signo] will tell you,
    "everyone betrays me, I have no friends."

ROGELIO: Well, he [referring again to his godchild-on-the-run] has no friends because he is friend to nobody.

JAVIELITO [in jest]: He probably wanted to do what Lion did in his funeral.

JAVIER [laughing as he tries to remember]: Ah, that story, hey, I don't think I remember this path (*camino*), do you know it?

ROGELIO: This sounds like it is in Irete File [another divinatory signo of Ifá], no?

JAVIELITO AND JAVIER TOGETHER: No, in Obbesá!

JAVIELITO: That was when the lion pretended he was dead to . . .

JAVIER: . . . to see who his enemies were.

JAVIELITO: So the animals all went to the wake and the lion was like this [imitating
an uncomfortable pose, playing dead], holding the position for a while . . .

JAVIER: And one of the animals goes, "He moved! Damn, he's alive!' . . . because the
lion was really bad and everyone was so afraid of him, so when the beast dies they
hold the wake not to feel the pain of his death, but to make sure he's dead!

ROGELIO: To confirm that he was dead! [laughing]

JAVIER: Listen to this! But it seems he moved, so the tiger goes, "Get out of here!,"
and the lion goes, "You get out, damn it!" [laughter subsides]. Listen, Obbesá
is betrayal. If the *osobbo* (bad fortune) gets you, you're in trouble. So, okay, he
[Rogelio's godchild] is applying this because he knows that there are a lot of
people who want him dead. So when these people hear it they go "the beast is
dead, there's no problem anymore" and he just disappears.

One could hardly wish for a more vivid display of the divinatory principle
in action—life understood in the light of myth. However, as the competitive dimension of such conversations shows (always subtle, never absent),
for babalawos "talking Ifá" is always also a personal display, and particularly a display of what they call *conocimiento*, a concept I propose to
translate as "learning" (it could also be translated as "knowledge," but
for analytical reasons that will emerge later I wish to avoid the philosophical baggage of that term). For babalawos, one's ability to operate in the
mythopractical universe of Ifá is a direct function of one's command of the
vast corpus of esoteric material that is associated with the 256 signos. It is
to this esoteric corpus, after all, that initiation gives them access, and their
standing as "fathers of secrets" depends on their ability to utilize it.

The life of a babalawo, then, is "a lifetime of study," as it is often said.
Unlike their Yoruba counterparts, however, Cuban babalawos do not
enjoy the benefit of formal training (cf. Bascom 1991, 84–90; Akinnaso
1992). Certainly neophytes can expect to learn much of what they need to
know directly from their elders, and particularly from their godfather. The

initiation ceremony itself involves teaching the neophyte crucial "secrets" (*secretos*), such as the mechanism of the oracle. But initiates generally seek to develop the overall competence required to practice Ifá by also visiting ceremonies conducted outside the context of the immediate ritual family. For recently initiated babalawos (*awó keké*), these occasions do not only provide an opportunity to learn ritual procedure through practice and observation, but also allow them to make themselves known in religious circles. Friendships and alliances formed during this period of apprenticeship may later flourish into collaborative relationships, and invitations to officiate in rituals in exchange for payment may well ensue.

Alongside oral interaction, which was the main mode of transmission of mythical and ritual knowledge from African slaves to their Creole progeny during the nineteenth century, written documents have become increasingly important for the training of babalawos. Cuban libraries as well as individual scholars have archives of "notebooks" (*libretas*) written by initiates of both Santería and Ifá, which go back at least to the turn of the previous century. Such records are still kept privately by individual initiates, both as an aide-mémoire for diverse information (e.g., myths, prayers, recipes, translations of Lucumí terms) and for registering personal data, such as divinatory verdicts associated with one's initiation, ritual prohibitions, and so on (Guanche 1983, 360–62; Menéndez Vásquez 1998, 3:3–15). In addition, babalawos also exchange documents with each other for the purpose of study (though, as we shall see below, babalawos can be rather guarded in these matters). These include "papers of Ifá" (*papeles de Ifá*), "Ifá say's" ("*dice Ifá*"), and "Treatments of Oddu" (*Tratados de Oddu*). The two latter types generally refer to manuals compiled by dedicated babalawos, and are often passed down the generations of Ifá lineages, or may be copied and sold commercially. "Papers of Ifá" usually consist of one or two sheets of information on a particular oddu, and are exchanged between babalawos informally (for an example, see appendix B). These days much of this material is stored on computer and exchanged electronically.

Babalawos emphasize the importance of Ifá documents with reference to a proverb associated with the divinatory signo Odilobbe: "write things down for memory cannot be trusted." During consultation, however, reading from papers is generally considered a faux pas, so an exceptionally good memory is nevertheless cited by babalawos as a prerequisite for success. This, for example, is how one babalawo illustrated to me the extraordinary abilities of Miguel Febles (Odí Ká), one of the most notorious babalawos of past generations (see Brown 2003, 88–92): "Miguelito didn't give papers out easily, but when he did, he'd give them complete, with their *ebbó* [secret recipes for offerings and sacrifices] and everything. . . . Then he'd start telling stories one after the other, and if you looked them up [in the papers] they'd be just like he told them. He was born for this."

At the same time, babalawos are keen to emphasize that learning is an open-ended project and that a good memory alone does not make a good diviner. Babalawos explain that however much one studies, one must also rely on Orula's help when it comes to recalling one's learning appropriately knowledge. Particularly during a formal divination such as an itá, it is understood that Orula often directly assists babalawos (and particularly the more inexperienced ones) by illuminating them while they speak. This process of illumination, referred to as *iporiawó*, does not, however, amount to a form of spirit possession. It is rather explained as an enhancement of the diviner's intuition, though its effects can be quite startling to babalawos. Javier told me the story that before he had even been initiated, he was talking over a drink with Mario Mendosa, a well-established babalawo at that time. During the conversation, Javier found himself speaking about Otuaché, Mendosa's own initiatory signo, claiming that it includes a story that speaks of an individual that kept magical powders (*acheses*) under his fingernails. "I wasn't even conscious of what I was saying,' Javier recalled. Having never come across such a story, Mendosa dismissed the suggestion. Years later, after Javier's own initiation, Mendosa admitted that he had recently found a "paper" of Otuaché that included the story of the powdered fingernails. A premature case of iporiawó, Javier explained.

Secrets

In the introduction, following a point made by Peel, I argued that babalawos' investment in the idea of truth makes them analogous to intellectuals. And as we have seen in the course of this chapter, a number of the ways in which truth features in babalawos' daily lives could be said to add dimensions to such an analogy—the commitment to lifelong study, the pleasure taken in competitive displays of learning, and so on. A crucial breakdown of the analogy, however, concerns the matter of secrecy. By contrast to intellectuals, for whom "publication" is so important, much of babalawos' energy is directed to making sure that the secrets to which they become privy are kept within the community of initiates—although it should be noted that, with the advent of the Internet and the growth of

Ifá-related websites based in the United States and elsewhere, this has become increasingly difficult to achieve.

A story that circulated among babalawos in Havana during my first stint of fieldwork in 1998 illustrates their preoccupation on this issue. Apparently an otherwise unremarkable babalawo had recently decided to eschew Ifá and proceeded to publish a pamphlet describing in detail a number of Ifá ceremonies, including that of full initiation, and "other secrets." Though invariably indignant about the episode, babalawos offered me different explanations of his motives. Some thought he had simply "lost it," others suggested that disowning religion may have ingratiated him with the state authorities, and many more assumed that this was a shameless attempt to make money by selling the secrets off. Be that as it may, the story had a revealing ending. When I visited Havana a couple of years later I asked Javielito for news on the matter and was told that the offending babalawo had recently been seen in Ifá ceremonies shamefacedly sweeping the floor in self-inflicted penitence. As Javielito explained, it was assumed by babalawos to whom he had spoken that, in the meantime, Orula must have punished him severely for his "disrespect" (*falta de respeto*).

A second sense in which babalawos are secretive has to do not with their relationship to noninitiates but rather with their relationships to each other. As we saw in relation to the notorious Miguel Febles, babalawos can be very reluctant to share what they learn with fellow initiates, and the relatively free exchange of Ifá documents has only recently become more common. Older initiates remember times when "it was hard work" to get a babalawo even to show his papers, let alone exchange them. We may recall that this was also how, in our first meeting, Javier framed his warning to me that in Ifá "you should be careful what people tell you." In the old days, as he said, to get babalawos to tell their secrets "you had to make them food, get them drunk, clean their house, or even build them one." Indeed, while more recently the exchange of papers has become freer than it was in those times, much of the old ethos of secrecy remains. For example, it is indicative that, like most babalawos, Javier and Javielito kept their own formidable collection of papers tucked away and out of sight—in their case in a wardrobe in the makeshift wooden loft (*barbacoa*) that served as Javielito's bedroom, which is the most private part of the apartment. Only rarely were these materials shown to visiting babalawos (or anthropologists), and when they were this was a sure sign of trust.

For babalawos there is a very pragmatic reason for being guarded with each other in this way, and that has to do particularly with sorcery—an activity to which practitioners generically refer as *brujería* (see also Lach-atañere 1961, contra Ortíz 1906). Indeed, it may be fair to say that while, as we have discussed, babalawos' public standing in the wider community of religious practitioners is associated primarily with their supreme abilities in divination, sorcery is the chief measure of the respect (premised, of course, on fear) that babalawos accord to each other. As has been mentioned already, the information associated with each signo extends beyond the myths that babalawos might recount in a public contexts such as divination. In particular, each signo includes esoteric instructions for achieving specific ends, which range from the remedial (e.g., a cure for a particular ailment) to the aggressive (how to inflict a particular ailment on an enemy). In this very literal sense, the more a babalawo learns, the more powerful (indeed dangerous) he becomes, and it is understood that babalawos may use this power against each other when a conflict arises. In fact, as my (invariably elliptical) conversations with babalawos on such matters made clear to me, the threat of sorcery is the hidden "underneath" (*sensu* Ferme 2001) of babalawos' accounts of their competitive relationships with each other. Joking to me about the diminutive physique of a particularly infamous babalawo of Miguel Febles's lineage, Javielito once remarked: "Still, this is an individual with whom you do not mess!" The competitive machismo of babalawos has, if you will, an irreducibly metaphysical dimension to it.

While the analysis of sorcery is beyond the immediate scope of this book's argument, babalawos' more general furtive attitude both to one another and to outsiders arguably speaks directly to our central concern with the nature of truth in Ifá. Indeed, I would argue that if babalawos' investment in secrecy is for them a matter of such pragmatic importance, that is just because the truths that are thus guarded—the "secrets" that babalawos "father"—are themselves of an essentially pragmatic nature. Fusing the mixed connotations of the word in its original Greek sense— fact, object, and deed all at once—the truths with which babalawos are so concerned are arguably very different in nature from what one might ordinarily assume truth to be. In order to begin to see this, we may now turn to the chief arena in which truth is brokered in Ifá, namely the ritual of divination and the cosmology in which it is embedded.

Mythical Transcendence and Ritual Elicitation: The Cosmo-Praxis of Ifá Divination

In the previous chapter we saw how babalawos' abiding concern with truth, which surfaces in so many ways in the everyday life of Ifá, is underpinned by what I called a divinatory principle. Potentially, every aspect of life is under the sway of the orichas in one way or other. With the help of Orula's counsel, babalawos are able to gauge this influence, not only by performing divinatory ceremonies, but also by mastering the deeper relationship, on which divination is based, between the mythical archetypes of the oddu and the everyday events that they illuminate. In this chapter, my task is to elucidate the cosmological coordinates that frame the divinatory principle, and to show how the ceremony of divination itself, which exemplifies this principle at the very heart of Ifá worship, is played out within them. In particular, I provide an account of the central cosmological "problem" upon which the divinatory principle turns, and which the ritual of divination is able to solve. For purposes that are, as we shall see, only heuristic, I call this "the problem of transcendence." Let me begin by explaining this choice.

The Problem with the Problem of Transcendence

As something of a snake oil in philosophical as well as theological deliberation, the distinction between transcendence and immanence and its many corollaries is pervasive in the anthropology of religion. Ever since

Emile Durkheim defined the field in terms of the difference between the sacred and the profane, distinctions that posit an ontological gap between a world "beyond," in which divinities dwell, and a world of "here and now," in which we humans do, have been used in various ways to describe the phenomena that have been treated under the banner of "religion." When and how such distinctions relate to philosophical and theological discussions of transcendence and immanence is a question about which it is difficult to be precise, since these concepts are themselves notoriously slippery, as the many and rarefied theological debates about them in the history of Christianity, for example, would indicate—angels dancing on the heads of pins. Whether explicitly or implicitly, however, their many resonances are felt across the anthropological literature, and not least in ethnographic descriptions of cosmologies and practices that are in many ways very different from the intellectual and theological tradition from which concerns with transcendence and immanence spring, namely, and broadly, the Judeo-Christian one.

West African religious forms, including the Yoruba, have often received such treatment, most militantly by Christian scholars interested in showing the continuities between "traditional" and Christian theological principles (e.g., Idowu 1962; Awolalu 1979; cf. Horton 1971). But less partial accounts also display some of the characteristics of this way of thinking. Consider for example Wyatt MacGaffey's commentary, provided as part of a synthesis of the cultural traditions of the forest regions of West and Central Africa, which includes Yoruba-speaking areas. Summing up the chief characteristics that are shared by cosmologies in this region, he writes of an abiding distinction between two worlds, the "visible" and the "invisible":

> [T]he other world is unseen cause, as opposed to visible effect; the past, as op-
> posed to the present; it is powerful and the source of power; it is an authori-
> tative model, opposed to the obscure and ambiguous sensual world; and it is
> the hidden interior and origin of things and people. Knowledge of it imposes
> moral and aesthetic order upon the medley of experience in the visible world,
> which masks the invisible world that both animates and explains it. (MacGaffey
> 2000, 18)

MacGaffey notes that similar cosmological coordinates are central to Ifá divination, and presently we shall see many ways in which he is right. Notable by its absence, however, is an attempt to disambiguate his account from its many resonances with Western theological and philosophical debates about similar cosmological and ontological bifurcations. Taken out of context, the quotation could rather comfortably be mistaken for an account of, say, Platonic philosophy or Christianity or some other so-called world religion—try substituting "Form" or "God" for "other world" to see how easily this can be mapped onto familiar transcendence/immanence distinctions.

In fact, such continuities have often been invoked by scholars who have sought to explain the contingent historical links between West African religion and Christianity (and Islam) in particular, especially in the context of conversion in Africa (e.g., Peel 1990) and, most relevantly, the Americas (see Brown 2003, 118–24, for a critical review). John Thornton's influential account of the corresponding roles of what he calls "revelation" in Christianity and West and Central African religions is a good instance of this (Thornton 1992, 236–62). Eschewing the idea that the conversion of Africans and their descendants to forms of Christianity in the Americas (as well as in Africa itself) was a matter of substituting one cosmology for another, Thornton emphasizes the compatibilities afforded by revelation in both forms of religious experience. If the truths of Christian doctrine are given through the divine revelations that are transmitted through prophets, apostles and their scriptures, the authoritative truths of West African religion are made manifest through the revelations of divination, spirit possession, omens, and the like. The difference between the two is only one of degree: while revelations in Christianity are rare and cherished events, in West Africa they are "continuous" (Thornton 1992, 256, cf. Eliade 1991). On the strength of this analogy, Thornton elaborates a sophisticated argument showing how revelation facilitated the complex dynamic of Africans' conversion and its recognition by missionaries and colonials. In a nutshell:

> Africans became Christians not because the priests or the converts sought to match or replace their cosmologies. Instead, they converted because they received "co-revelations," that is, revelations in the African tradition that dovetailed with the Christian tradition. The conversion was accepted because Christians also accepted this particular set of revelations as valid. (Thornton 1992, 255)

Such arguments are elegant and persuasive partly by virtue of the bridges they build between the ethnography of colonized peoples and the longstanding concerns that inform the intellectual traditions of their erstwhile colonizers. Note, for example, the implications of treating the revelations of divination by analogy to Christian theophany for our interest in the notion of truth. Matthew Engelke's discussion of Zimbabwean Friday Apostolics' concerns with what he calls the "problem of presence"—"the paradox of God's simultaneous absence and presence" (Engelke 2007, 12)—could furnish a bridge (see also Keane 2007, 59–82 and *passim*). For, as Engelke argues, the problem turns partly on questions of truth. Notwithstanding the much-fought-over differences between them, Christian traditions and denominations share an abiding concern with the transcendence of God, and this "problem" is also one of truth. Citing Paul Ricoeur's hermeneutically minded reading of Genesis (1998), Engelke frames the issue in terms of the separation between God and his human creations in the story of the Fall. If Adam and Eve in the Garden of Eden were separated from God as Created to Creator, the Fall introduces "suspicion" as a second order of transcendence. Distance from God is rendered as an opacity of communication, such that "a fault line is introduced into the most fundamental condition of language, namely, the relation of trust" (Ricoeur, cited in Engelke 2007, 13). Conversely, communion with God (or "immanence") is also communion with and in truth. So if divination can be conceived by analogy to the revelations that effect such communion in Christianity, the question of its truth would pan out as a variant of an age-old Christian concern with Original Sin.

Pre-empting the argument I shall be making in the next chapter, however, we may sound a note of caution here. There is no doubt that analogies between Christian and non-Christian religious forms are relevant to understanding historical situations of contact, syncretism, conversion, and so on.[1] Still, as a number of scholars working in these fields have pointed out, such comparisons confront an abiding analytical pitfall, namely that the conceptual vocabulary in which they are couched is often itself derived from Christian (or, more broadly, Judeo-Christian) theological preoccupations—a predicament that Fenella Cannell, writing of the anthropology of Christianity in particular, has called "the Christianity of anthropology" (2006; see also Asad 1993; Sahlins 1996). Part of the difficulty, as already noted, is that such notions as revelation, transcendence, and immanence or, indeed, truth carry such a heavy freight of Christian associations, having been the subject of so much theological dispute, that any appeal to them for analytical purposes in anthropology would at the very least have to specify their meaning rather precisely (see also Scott 2005). But even if one could isolate such meanings in any useful way, it is unclear how they could furnish an analytical vocabulary with which to describe non-Christian practices without Judeo-Christian distortion, or indeed compare them with Christian ones in a noncircular way. Thus, for example, one may query how far Thornton's argument from co-revelations begs its question in just such a way. To the extent that the very notion of revelation is already informed by its theological associations to such phenomena as Christian prophesy, branding West African divination as a form of revelation establishes the analogy with Christianity by descriptive fiat.

In the account of Ifá cosmology that follows, I seek to avoid this sort of circularity in order to expose what is arguably a basic breakdown in the analogy between Ifá and the kinds of Judeo-Christian theological preoccupations mentioned above. I do so by using the key notions of transcendence and immanence, which as we shall see furnish the overall coordinates of Ifá cosmology, in a strictly *heuristic* manner. In particular, I use them to capture the basic idea that the worlds of the gods and of the humans stand at a distance to each other, while yet being able to communicate (if not commune), not least in the ritual of divination, which I shall describe in some detail toward the end of this chapter. What makes orichas so powerful is precisely their ability to traverse the distance from transcendence to immanence so as to inject themselves into the everyday world of humans. Accordingly, the divinatory power of the babalawos resides in their ability to elicit such traversals, particularly by bringing Orula forth to "speak" during the divination. In this sense the contrast between transcendence and immanence captures heuristically the essential cosmological condition with which practitioners of Ifá must reckon—the cosmological "problem" that divination solves for them.

The reason for which it is important to insist on the heuristic character of such a gloss, however, is that this cosmological condition is demonstrably *not* a version of the problem of transcendence so familiar from the history of Christianity. As already noted in relation to Ricoeur's interpretation of Genesis, for example, an abiding concern among Christian theologians and clergy through the ages, as well as the contemporary philosophers and social theorists who have inherited so much of their conceptual vocabulary, has been with the *ontological rupture* that the distinction between transcendence and immanence connotes. From Old Testament depictions of the Creation and Fall, through Christological preoccupations with the nature of the Holy Trinity or the mystery of transubstantiation, to ostensibly secular debates about the relationship between society and the individual, the discontinuity that the distinction between transcendence and immanence sets up has lent the relationship between the two an air of irreducible paradox, mystery, or even miracle. Writing of the central role that such paradoxology played in differentiating Christian dogma and institutions from paganism in late antiquity, the historian Averil Cameron captures the flavor by citing the Christological verse of Gregory the Theologian, archbishop of Constantinople in the late fourth century: "He was human, but God, of the line of David, but the creator of Adam. He was in the flesh, but outside the flesh, born of a mother, but a virgin" (Gregory of Nazianzus, cited in Cameron 1991, 163).

This sort of image of paradox and ontological discontinuity is quite alien to Ifá cosmology. Ifá is premised on a basic *continuity* between the beyond, where divinities ordinarily dwell, and the here and now, in which their influence is effected, not least during the ceremony of divination. So if the transcendence of the divinities in Ifá presents a problem, this ought to be understood as an essentially practical one (a mytho- or indeed cosmo-practical one, to be sure), in contrast to the kinds of ontological conundrums the distinction between transcendence and immanence connotes. It follows that for this distinction to have an analytical, as opposed to merely heuristic, purchase on Ifá it would need thoroughly to be reconceptualized. The (analytical) problem with the "problem of transcendence" in Ifá, if you like, is that it poses no problem, or at least not of the mysterious kind we would ordinarily associate with it. This analytical problem is taken up in the next chapter. As we shall see, recursively reconceptualizing the distinction between transcendence and immanence in the light of their continuous relationship in Ifá cosmology is an important step in the broader task of (recursively) conceptualizing the truths that this relationship, enacted in the ritual divination, engenders. To lay the ground for this analysis, the rest of this chapter is devoted to showing how the contrast between transcendence and immanence plays out cosmologically in Ifá mythology and ritual, including in the ceremony of divination itself.

Myth and Transcendence

Ifá cosmology is presented in the multitude of mythical verses that are associated with each of the 256 divinatory configurations on which the divinatory practice of Ifá is based—the signos, or, as they are called in Lucumí, *oddu.* With the passage of generations, Lucumí language in Cuba became

increasingly ossified into a primarily ritual idiom, with the result that babalawos no longer memorize these mythical accounts as verses (*ese*) in
Yoruba, as their West African counterparts famously do, but rather learn
them as narrative "stories" in Spanish (*historias de Ifá*, or, in Lucumí, *pa-
takí* or *patakín*). However, the role of the oddu as the primary "archive of
knowledge" (Apter 1992, 7) of Ifá cosmology remains. "Everything is in
Ifá" (*todo está en Ifá*), babalawos frequently emphasize, meaning that all
aspects of life are accounted for in one or other of the myths associated
with each of the oddu.

Such accounts take the form of stories that explain what babalawos
refer to as the "birth" of things (*nacimiento*), the idea being that every element of the world refers back to a cosmogonic moment of origin. Matters
as basic as the origin of the world and the species, as specific as the boiling
of water or the color of coconuts, as technical as cures for diseases, as profound as the relationship between life and death, and even as topical as the
invention of the Internet (according to one informant), are all broached in
myths. Crucially, a large proportion of such cosmogonic accounts concern
the "birth" of all sorts of aspects of Ifá worship itself, including specific
elements of its many rituals. All manner of data (e.g., the birth of Orula,
why only men can be babalawos, recipes for magical concoctions, and so
on) are said to be found somewhere in the corpus of Ifá myth. Take, for
example, a myth associated with the oddu Ogunda Meyi with which babalawos explain the relationship between the two principal techniques of
Ifá divination, namely the method involving a divining chain (*ókuele*) and
the more ceremonious form of divination in which palm nuts are used:

> In one of his travels, a babalawo called Popó got sick with open sores, so he
> decided to make a stop near Lake Abaya in Abyssinia. He heard that a Yoruba
> babalawo called Feka lived in a near-by village and was married to a local girl,
> so he went to visit him, hoping for a cure. When they met, Feka recognized the
> sick traveler as being his godfather. Feka succeeded in curing him using his di-
> vining nuts, but he himself fell ill with leprosy in the process. On his deathbed,
> he called his godfather and told him: "I have brought a secret from Egypt so
> that we won't need to fiddle with the nuts all the time. It is a little chain, divided
> in the middle, with four small plates on either side. When I die, go to my grave
> and there you will find the secret of how to make it." The next day Feka died.
> They buried him near the lake, and from his grave grew a tree which bore large
> and oblong fruits. As the fruits fell to the ground, they cracked open saying:
> "ókuele oga oke adafin Feka."

This kind of account, of which there are literally thousands, illustrates two formal themes that speak directly to the role of what we might call "transcendence" in Ifá mythology. First, the ostensibly historical idiom in which the story is told, as an account of events that took place in the distant past in particular African localities, places such myths in a transcendent position with respect to a present state of affairs that they purport to illuminate—in this case, the construction and use of ókuele. Indeed, as the fairytale-like style of the story would indicate, the past of "Africa" in this context can be understood as having existed not only in a quantitative remove in time and space, but also in a qualitative remove: "Africa" in such mythical accounts comes to acquire the luminosity of mythopoeia, taking the role of what Viveiros de Castro has called, with reference to Amerindian myth, the "absolute past" (2007, 157) which "was never present, and therefore never passes" (Viveiros de Castro, pers. com.).

A further and related point regards the role of personification in Ifá mythology. As the story of Popó and his godfather Feka illustrates, the cosmogonic "birth" of things in Ifá is typically associated with particular divine personages whose mythical exploits are depicted in a manner one might call "archetypal," after Mircea Eliade (1991). While this term may have become something of a cliché in discussions of myth, its etymology is entirely apposite to Ifá. On the one hand the Greek "arche," which in pre-Socratic cosmologies has connotations of "beginning," "principle" and "rule" all at once, conveys not only the idea that the divine actions of Ifá myth mark the "birth" of things, but also that such cosmogonic moments have a normative character. So, for example, the story of the birth of the divining chain serves to legitimate its use by babalawos as a proper method of divination, while also providing a justification of its lesser status when compared to the use of divining nuts, from which it is shown to derive in what one might call an abominable fashion, to the extent that the ókuele is bequeathed in a direction that is contrary to the ordinary succession of ritual inheritance—backwards, or upwards, from godson to godfather. On the other hand, mythical narratives of divine action are also "types" inasmuch as their relationship to the daily actions and objects to which they refer is "classificatory" (Bastide 2000, Goldman 2007). If "everything is in Ifá," as babalawos say, that is because in principle each constituent of the world relates to a myth that describes its original birth. Hence mythical archetypes are transcendent inasmuch as they are the original "exemplars" (cf. Needham 1985, Humphrey 1997) to which all worldly elements normatively refer back: godchild to godfather relationships exemplify Feka's relationship to Popó in the story (in view of the inferiority of ókuele, the abominable inversion serves to confirm the normative rule), babalawos' consecration and use of divining chains exemplifies the birth of ókuele and so on.

Indeed, while characters such as Feka and Popó are just two of the myriad mythical personages that appear in the stories of the oddu of Ifá— which include not only named humans but also animals, plants, and other animated natural features or artifacts (such as mountains, rivers, drums, tools)—this principle of classificatory exemplarity is at its clearest when it comes to the mythical depiction of the orichas themselves. The mythical exploits of the orichas, who are by far the most frequent protagonists of Ifá mythology, establish series of classificatory identifications between each of the deities and particular cosmological elements, which are often conceived of in terms of a notion of "ownership." So, for example, Changó is the owner of thunder because Olofin, depicted as the ruler of the orichas, bestowed him this "power" in one of the stories of the oddu Osa Wori. Yemayá owns the sea since, as described in the oddu Iwori Bosa, Olokun ceded his dominion over it and retired to the depths of the ocean which he now owns; and so on for each of the orichas. In this sense the classificatory notion of ownership is the cosmological equivalent of the "anthropological" idea (*sensu* Goldman 2007, 111) that each human being "belongs" to his or her guardian oricha as child does to parent, as seen in the previous chapter.

Since the myths in which the orichas' cosmological associations are established are innumerable, and since their fascination for babalawos (and anthropologists) resides partly in their inordinate level of detail, the nexus of classificatory identifications between orichas and elements of the world is exceedingly complex—an object of lifelong study, as we have seen. Indeed, the irreducible complexity of orichas' classificatory associations is arguably a key aspect of their transcendence as divine exemplars. Possibly even more so than with ancient Greek mythology, the open-ended plethora of mythical narratives associated with each oricha, with potentially endlessly ramifying stories of their divine exploits, effectively lends the orichas an imponderable quality. While the superabundant fund of myth keeps the orichas perpetually beyond mortal grasp, so to speak, it also gives them a biographical "thickness" that makes them literally larger than life: every possible worldly manifestation must, it is assumed, have

118

CHAPTER FOUR

its divine counterpart in the mythical universe of the orichas. Orichas, in this sense, instantiate a standard connotation of "transcendence": there is always more to the world than meets the eye.

Crucial in this respect is the fact that most orichas are conceived as inherently multiple beings (Goldman 2005, 2007). As babalawos and santeros explain, orichas appear in myth in a multiplicity of guises,[2] referred to colloquially as "paths" (*caminos de santo*) or, mainly in the exegetical literature, as "avatars" (*avatares*). To take one of the most vivid examples, Elegguá, the messenger deity charged with taking the offerings of humans to the orichas, appears in Ifá stories in a vast array of forms: while he is most popularly conceived of as a mischievous child, he is just as likely to be described in myth as a fierce warrior, a cantankerous elder, a two-faced trickster, or, in the form of Echú (who is sometimes thought of as a separate deity in his own right), as an antisocial wreaker of havoc (e.g., see Bolívar Aróstegui 1994a, 27–63; Cros Sandoval 2006, 210–22; Brown 2003, 174–75). As an inherent feature of their ontological constitution, these varied and often downright contradictory mythical manifestations only magnify the orichas' transcendent, otherworldly status. Their larger-than-life "thickness" is played out in multiple dimensions—a point that will be taken up in the next chapter.

Ideas about the inherent multiplicity of divine beings are also integral to the process of Ifá divination itself, inasmuch as the oddu configurations on which the system of divination is based are also conceived of as divine beings in their own right, analogous to the orichas. Organized hierarchically (see appendix A), the 256 oddu are grouped in two main categories. First comes the succession of the sixteen *meyi* (Lucumí for "two" of "twin," which refers to their symmetrical configuration as explained below), who are often spoken of as "kings" (*oba*) or "fathers" (*baba*). Then come their 240 "omo" (Lucumí for "child"), which are formed of the binary combinations of the sixteen *meyi* (Héres Hevia 1962, 281–537; cf. McClelland 1966). Each with its own name, the oddu often appear in the stories of Ifá as individual divine beings, each with a personality of its own—albeit one with an, as it were, in-built principle of complexity and self-differentiation due to their paired constitution. While each oddu personage will feature primarily in the narrative "paths" associated with its corresponding divinatory configuration, they may appear also in myths associated with another oddu. For example, in a path of the oddu Oragún (the last in the hierarchy of the sixteen principal oddu), Oragún is described as having invented the use of money after watching one of the other principal oddu,

Obara Meyi, bartering in a market (Holbraad 2005). Given the supreme importance of the oddu in the daily life of worship, babalawos are deeply interested in the nexus of associations between oddu, upon which some of the most esoteric aspects of Ifá ritual rely.

For present purposes, however, we may note that the divine status of the oddu illustrates the character of transcendence in Ifá cosmology in a particularly clear way. Not only are the oddu depicted as having lived and acted in the absolute past of myth, much like the orichas, but accounts of their origin also typically establish close associations between them and the so-called major orichas (*santos mayores*), the most powerful orichas, who were involved in the birth of the universe itself.[3] Such accounts vary, and babalawos themselves are often ambiguous when asked about the mythical genealogy of each oddu. A number of myths, however, depict oddu as either children of Orula or as his "representatives" on earth, charged with bringing order to humanity by the authority of Olofin, the high-god of the sun and ultimate ruler of the affairs of the universe. As one babalawo explained, the oddu can also be considered as guises of Orula himself, analogous to the multiple paths or avatars of an oricha. This, he reasoned, makes sense since the stories that the oddu contain so often are descriptions of Orula's exploits in his many travels as the first babalawo sent to earth by Olofin. Such an interpretation would also accord with practice among Yoruba speakers in Nigeria who, as Bascom reports, refer to the oddu as "roads of Ifa" (Bascom 1991, 40), which concurs with the terminology of "paths" used in Cuba.

Whether one thinks of the oddu as guises of Orula or as his children or representatives, however, the sense of larger-than-life transcendence, which, as we saw in relation to the orichas, is partly a function the inordinate complexity of the mythical accounts associated with each divine personage, is particularly marked in this case. "Ifá does not fit into any one head," babalawos often emphasize (*Ifá no cabe en ninguna cabeza*). What is meant by this is that, since the mythical paths associated with each oddu are of an inordinately large number, even for the most learned babalawos full knowledge of the characteristics of each oddu is in principle impossible to achieve.[4] So while the 256 oddu encompass all that there is in the universe and therefore all there is to know about it, providing a scheme of meticulous classification of the birth of every constituent of the world, that scheme can itself never be fully encompassed by human beings. There is always more to an oddu than any babalawo can know. In this sense the oddu mark a transcendent limit to which babalawos' learning, which as we have seen is the main currency of their ascent in the hierarchy of worship, can only tend.

This principle of transcendence is also enshrined in the heart of Ifá ritual liturgy itself, which will be described in detail later in this chapter. For example, it is with reference to the idea that "Ifá fits in no one head" that babalawos explain why all major Ifá ceremonies require the participation of more than one babalawo—notionally at least four for ceremonious divinations with divining nuts (see below), and at least sixteen for full initiation ceremonies. Since the total fund of knowledge associated with each oddu is in principle unattainable, babalawos are required to multiply their own number in their effort to approximate it by, as it were, putting their heads together.

Indeed, a similar idea is enshrined at the ritual center of the divinatory liturgy of Ifá, in the form of the consecrated divining board upon the surface of which the oddu are marked during divinations, as we shall see below. Circular in shape, the so-called *tablero* (referred to ritually as *atepón*) is deemed by babalawos to be an iconic image of the universe itself (cf. MacGaffey 2000, 18).[5] As if distilling the principle of classificatory exemplarity to its most salient expression, each part of the tablero is meant to correspond to a multiplicity of cosmological elements, forming what in a study of the symbolic topographies of Mongolian scapulomancy has been called a "metonymic field" (Sneath 2009). While such associations are as complex as they are esoteric, their topography takes the form of consecutive divisions of the circular tablero, much as with the circumference of a clock or a compass (Morton-Williams n.d.). Series of cosmological elements (orichas, animals, seasons, times of day and night, cardinal points, parts of the human body and so on) are superimposed on the tablero's four principal parts: the "head" (*lerí opón*), which in Cuba is marked with a cross or sometimes with the figure of Echú, the "foot" (*elese opón*), the "right" side (*otún*), and the "left" side (*osí*). This quadripartite scheme also serves to distribute the 256 oddu, which are localized by means of further subdivisions, starting with Baba Eyiobbe (the first in the hierarchy of *meyi*—see appendix A), whose oddu is marked vertically with two parallel lines drawn from "foot" to "head" at the beginning of all divinations. Thus the cycle of the tablero's circumference can be considered as embodying an inherently elusive limit toward which the exponentially fine-grained classificatory schemes of Ifá (from the four cardinal parts of the tablero to the totality of 256 oddu) can only tend.

One could sum up the character of transcendence that Ifá divinities instantiate by pointing to a fundamental asymmetry in Ifá cosmology. While the divinities, qua archetypes, encompass each of the worldly elements for which they serve as exemplars, they themselves remain constitutionally elusive to human attempts at approximation. What humans can do, however, is to elicit movements in the opposite direction, so to speak, by invoking otherwise transcendent divinities into temporary states of presence or, in that sense, immanence. Indeed, in line with Lévi-Strauss's claim that the role of ritual is to enact continuities where myth posits discontinuities (1981, 625–95; cf. Girard 1976), the aim here is to show that Ifá ritual is fundamentally oriented toward overcoming the forms of transcendence that myth posits, by rendering divinities temporarily present in the world of humans. The manner in which this is achieved in Ifá divination has profound analytical implications for the task of conceptualizing the ontological premises of Ifá cosmology, including, as I have indicated, the relationship between transcendence and immanence itself. We may begin, however, by noting various forms that immanence can take in the ritual contexts of Ifá worship.

Ritual and Immanence

The relationship between myth and ritual in Ifá could be described as one of mutual implication. Myth, as we have seen, justifies ritual, insofar as the "birth" of each ritual procedure is in principle accounted for in the mythical paths of some oddu or other. Conversely, ritual, and particularly divination, serves not only to organize myths, in terms of the scheme of the 256 oddu upon which Ifá divination is based, but also to render them operational in that it makes the telling of myths (and their interpretation) part of the process of divination itself. As we shall see in more detail presently, the oddu, conceived as divine personages, are said literally to "come out" (*salir*) in divination, and it is by virtue of their divine presence during the ceremony that babalawos are able to recount the mythical paths associated with them, and on that basis advise their clients. More than merely a body of abstract knowledge, Ifá mythology is an active force in Ifá worship, constitutive of its mythopractical character.

This mutual embrace of myth and ritual in Ifá divination is related to a broader argument, made by Karin Barber, who, based on her fieldwork in Nigeria, has shown how the orisa, like big-men, are as much dependent on their devotees' ritual attentions as the devotees are dependent on the orishas' divine patronage (Barber 1981). Continuing this line of thinking, one might say that ritual efficacy in Ifá is not just a consequence of the transcendent power of mythical divinities, but also its premise. For while the divinities' power is certainly a function of their transcendent, superhuman quality, that power itself depends on the orichas' ability to make their presence felt in the world of the humans. Since ritual is the chief means by which divine involvement in the world is elicited, ritual may be said to be a necessary condition for the expression of the very idea of mythical transcendence. Indeed, as I want to show, if the power of the orichas resides in their ability to exert influence in the world, then the power of ritual is that of eliciting just such influences. In this sense the power of ritual, and not least divination, is that of rendering otherwise transcendent divinities immanent.

In a comprehensive monograph on oricha cosmology, Mercedes Cros Sandoval discusses one of the most well-known myths about Elegguá, which conveys the role of immanence in worship with the vivid image of a dry coconut with sparkling eyes radiating light:

> Once upon a time, there was an *oba* (king) called Okuboro. Okuboro was married to Echú Añagui. The royal couple had a son called Elegguá. One day, when the prince was a young man, he set forth on a walk with his royal court. Suddenly, he stopped at the crossroads, advanced cautiously a few steps, and stopped again. Three times he took a few steps and abruptly stopped. The courtesans were bewildered. Finally, he made a final stop in front of an object, which was lying on the ground at his feet. The object had two sparkling eyes. To the amazement of his court, the prince picked up a dry coconut from the ground. [The prince] was awed and reverent in the presence of a small dry coconut. Elegguá took the coconut home and told his parents about the vision he had. Nobody believed or paid any attention to his story. Elegguá then cast the coconut behind the front door of the palace, where it remained hidden. One day, a great party was held at the royal house. A light coming from the coconut, which was lying on the ground in the room behind a closed door, bewildered the guests. They were horrified at such an unusual spectacle. Three days later Elegguá died. During his funeral, the coconut shone with such an intense light that everyone feared and respected it. A long time after the death of the prince, the people of the kingdom met with desperate times. The *agua* (elders) gathered together and decided that the ill fortune befalling them was due to the state of abandonment in which they had left the miraculous coconut. They decided to render it homage, but on getting close to it saw that insects had eaten it. They

discussed the poor qualities of the coconut as an object of worship and decided they should worship it but in the form of an *otán*, a stone. From that moment on, they placed an *otán* in a corner of the house, behind a door, as is done nowadays. (Abridged from Cros Sandoval 2006, 215–16)

The otán in question is the consecrated stone that is contained within the figurine of Elegguá, the first major consecrated item neophytes receive in the protracted series of initiatory ceremonies of Santería and Ifá described in the previous chapter. Indeed, as Cros Sandoval also explains, the above myth serves as an account of the birth not only of Elegguá, but also of the practice of using consecrated stones in the worship of the orichas more generally. And it is in the pivotal role of consecration as the sine qua non of all worship that the possibility of the orichas' immanence in the world comes most strongly into play.

As we have seen, at each step on the ladder of initiation neophytes receive particular items that, when properly consecrated, are treated as deities—fed with the blood of sacrificial animals and other offerings, spoken to, and so on. Kept at specific parts of the devotee's home, such items come to form a domestic order of divine presence that reflects the classificatory schemes of orichas articulated in Ifá mythology, as explained in marvelous detail by Brown (2003, 165–286). For example, in line with the origin myth of his consecration, the figurine of Elegguá is typically kept inside a small closet (*canastillero*) behind the front door, protecting the home with the help of the other "warrior" deities, Ogún (patron of iron and warfare), Ochosi (patron of hunting), and Osun (an auxiliary divinity who is said to represent the life of the neophyte), who are also placed in the canastillero. Other orichas, such as Changó, Ochún, Yemayá, Obatalá, or Orula, are placed inside pots (*soperas*) that are decorated with the trademark insignia of the deity and kept on display at a prominent part of the home, in line with their royal pedigree (see Brown 2003 for detail). In this way the home comes to constitute a microcosm of divinities—an intimate arena in which initiates can interact with their orichas on a daily basis, "greeting" them (*saludar al santo*) first thing in the morning, or upon leaving and returning to the home, by sounding bells or other implements that draw their attention, soliciting their help with whatever issues may arise in the ebb and flow of everyday life (e.g., a new job, a hoped-for journey, a love affair, an exam at school) and so on.

Similar forms of intimacy are available to worshipers beyond the home, in the macrocosm of Havana's urban environment, as well as further afield, in the countryside. As we have seen, Ifá mythology posits a complex nexus of identifications between the orichas and particular features of the environment. To borrow the Lévi-Straussian idiom of Marcio Goldman's studies of Brazilian Candomblé, while myth presents such identifications in metaphorical terms, as a matter of classificatory correspondences between worldly elements and their divine owners, in the context of worshipers' ritualized interactions with their natural and social environment these identifications take on a metonymic character (Goldman 2007). In this way, from the point of view of worship, Yemayá inhabits the sea, Ochún inhabits rivers, Elegguá inhabits street corners and marketplaces, Oyá inhabits cemeteries and gusts of wind, and so on.

Signs of the orichas' immanence in the environment are ubiquitous in Havana. Walking on the street, one may see on the ground at a street corner a small package wrapped in brown paper, left there in all likelihood as an offering to Elegguá; a bunch of bananas placed at the foot of a palm tree, maybe with a red ribbon attached, probably placed there by someone as an offering to Changó; on the wall of the Malecón, Havana's seafront promenade, people sit solitarily facing the sea to entreat Yemayá for personal help and protection; or at a riverbank in the outskirts of the city one might see a group of santeros accompanying an *iyawó* (as neophytes undergoing the year-long rite of Santería initiation are called) to perform a ceremony dedicated to Ochún.

Initiation ceremonies themselves provide a further instance of the role of immanence in the ritual life of Ifá. Not only does initiation bestow neophytes with the divine personality of their initiatic signo, which they must express mythopractically as we have seen. It also gives them the right to wear consecrated insignia, such as bracelets (*iddé*) and necklaces (*collares*), which are deemed to contain divine power in their own right. Made with beads of the colors associated with each oricha (green and yellow for Orula, white for Obatalá, red and white for Changó, and so on), these protective items metonymically append orichas onto initiates' bodies. Most important, perhaps, the idea that initiates may embody orichas is starkly expressed in the climactic and most secret ceremony of Santería initiation, the so-called *kariocha*. In this ceremony the tutelary oricha, as "parent" to the neophyte, is "seated" (*asentar*) inside the head of the neophyte. Once the neophyte is fully initiated, this oricha may "mount" (*montar*) his or her "child" during the collective possession ceremonies that santeros call *tambores*, dancing to the rhythms of consecrated drums (*aña*) that are themselves considered as deities.

Such forms of immanence characterize not only the divinatory principle that pervades all aspects of a life of worship, but also the privileged role of divination within it. Babalawos' ability to gauge the circumstances of the orichas' influence in human affairs, as well as to prescribe the means by which to render this influence propitious through offerings (*addimú*), sacrifices (*ebbó*), and other magical remedies, is a function of the immanence of Orula himself, understood as his capacity, as with other orichas, to inhabit the mundane world of humans, allowing them to relate to him directly through divination. Indeed, one might say that, with Orula, macrocosmic and microcosmic orders of immanence coincide. This is because in his case the macrocosmic idiom of "ownership" refers not to some generic natural or social feature to be found in the urban or rural environment at large, but only to the consecrated oracle of Ifá itself, whose paraphernalia are kept within babalawos' homes—that is, within a microcosmic field of divine immanence.

Orula himself inhabits the home in the form of a consecrated stone (otán) which, as with other orichas, is placed inside a luxurious pot, decorated with his trademark colors (green and yellow) and other insignia, which babalawos receive at initiation. Some babalawos explain that the "bunch" (*mano*) of palm nuts (*ikines*, sing. *ikín*) that is also kept inside the pot, and which constitutes the main implement of divination as we shall see, also "is" Orula (see also Bascom 1950; Menéndez Vásquez 1998, 4:131–34). Others claim that the ikines, along with other auxiliary items, including the divining chain that serves as an alternative for more everyday divinations, are only the "voice" through which Orula "speaks." Indeed, some babalawos make a distinction between Orula and Ifá: while Orula "owns" the oracular equipment babalawos use, Ifá is the deity that speaks through this equipment, as a kind of metonymic representative (*sensu* Gell 1998) or personification of Orula.[6] Be that as it may, the tangible presence of Orula that consecration allows is the basic premise of divination, inasmuch as it enables babalawos to communicate directly with him during divinations.

The Cosmological Problem of Divination

In the previous chapter we saw that babalawos lay great store by the superiority of the oracle of Ifá, not least in their long-standing competition with the santeros. As is invariably the case with such matters of legitimation, babalawos justify their claim to divinatory supremacy in explicitly cosmological terms, with reference to the cosmogonic authority of the myths of the divinatory oddu, in which, as we have seen, the birth of all things, including divination itself, is described. Indeed, in terms of the present argument, it is telling that such cosmological accounts of the supremacy of Ifá as a method of divination turn explicitly on a dilemma between transcendence and immanence. In particular, what makes Orula's divinatory authority supreme is the subtle balance that he, more than any other oricha, is deemed to keep between the two poles of absence from the world of the humans and immersion within it.

The origin myth of the oracle of Ifá, presented in the introduction, emphasizes the dangers of Orula's original departure from the world. Overcome with famine and pestilence, as we saw, Orula's children entreat their father to return to earth. Instead, he regales each of them with sixteen palm-nuts, from which point onward "the absence of Ifa from earth no longer mattered, since his children and disciples could communicate with him through [the sixteen palm-nuts] and the other instruments of divination" (Abimbola 1997a, 7). At the other extreme, however, Orula's feted divine impartiality, which according to babalawos sets him apart from the rest of the orichas as final arbiter in divination, is presented as a virtue of his relative *distance* from human affairs. For example, as we saw, babalawos' authority in matters of Santería initiation is justified by the fact that, unlike other orichas, Orula does not himself claim neophytes as his children and is therefore able to distribute humans to their respective guardian orichas disinterestedly. In another such mythical account, Orula's impartiality is explicitly linked to his refusal to participate in full, as it were, immanence in worldly affairs. The myth, which describes the birth of spirit possession, explains why, in contrast to other orichas, Orula does not "mount" human beings (in spirit possession), or, as it is put in the version of the myth that I abbreviate here, why he "does not pass through any head" (this refers to the kariocha ceremony of Santería initiation, in which orichas who do mount devotees are ritually seated inside neophytes' heads, as already discussed):

> After having conceived the earth, and having distributed the *aché* [viz. divine power—see below] to each of the orichas, Olofin (the all-powerful creator deity) gave the orichas the ability to send their form to the earth as an irradiation [*sic*], and to irradiate at the same time through many different people protected by the oricha in question. Each person who received this irradiation stopped being as they were before, and were converted into a being who could say things of

which they themselves were not aware, since they were being possessed by the divinity, mounted by the oricha. When this phenomenon was first introduced things developed normally, but after a while everything began to change. Each person began to think of themselves as superior to the rest, and warfare began, using both weapons and secret knowledge [viz. sorcery]. The warfare began to take its toll on the earth's inhabitants, since each thought of themselves as a god in accordance with the knowledge they had acquired. One day Olofin sent Elegguá to inspect the earth and inform him on how things were. What Elegguá saw made him very angry. He asked one man, "What has caused this war on earth?" to which the man responded, "I am a child of Osain [the fearsome deity of herbs and sorcery], and my father has made me one of his most privileged children, since Osain comes into my head, granting me the knowledge I need, so I am the wisest of all." Elegguá remonstrated with the man about his conceit, telling him that Olofin will not tolerate it and that the wars need to stop. The son of Osain insisted that he was king and that no-one would dethrone him. Annoyed, Elegguá continued his investigation among human beings and, having received similar responses from everyone he spoke to, reported back to Olofin. On hearing this, Olofin decided to send to the earth all of the orichas so that they could ask their respective children to change their behavior. Obatalá went first, but he failed, and after him Olofin sent the rest of the orichas, but each of them failed. Having run out of orichas to send, Olofin remembered Orunmila, and, explaining the gravity of the situation, asked him whether he could bring an end to the war. Orunmila responded, "I promise you that I will fix this war on earth, and fix all the humans, but until I succeed I will not descend [*bajar*] into anyone's head myself." This being the reason for which Orunmila does not pass through any head. (From the oddu Oyekun Di)

Ifá cosmology, then, presents the contrast between what I have been calling transcendence and immanence as a problem of sorts—a twin predicament, if you like. Too much transcendence, imagined as the absolute separation of Orula from the world of humans, spells trouble (famine and pestilence). Too much immanence, depicted as an absolute identification between divinities and humans in the "irradiation" of spirit-possession, can be equally disastrous (warfare and insolence).

For purposes of my overall argument, it is worth noting here the contrast between this cosmological predicament and the kinds of ontological problem with transcendence versus immanence with which we are familiar in the Judeo-Christian intellectual tradition, as discussed earlier. For, in its form, Ifá cosmology presents an *inversion* of Judeo-Christian concerns with ontological rupture. To the extent that such concerns stem from an image of transcendence and immanence as radically, or even absolutely, separate and discrete states, the story Ifá cosmology tells of the dystopian character of "too much" of either of these extremes effectively cancels such an image. Negating the logical limits of absolute transcendence and absolute immanence as cosmological aberrations, Ifá posits the middle ground *between* them as the proper terrain for the interaction of divinities and humans. So, instead of an ontological gap, what we have in Ifá is a cosmological field of relative distances that generate the proper "proportions," to borrow a term from Alberto Corsín Jiménez, of the relationship between divine and mundane orders (Corsín Jiménez 2008; see also Willerslev and Pedersen 2010).

It is within this field of relative distances that the ritual action of divination unfolds. Indeed, the importance of divination as the prime arena in which relationships between humans and orichas are played out is a core message of these foundational negations of the absolute in Ifá mythology. After all, Orula's original departure from the world brought calamity precisely because the well-being of human beings is premised on their ability to enter into relations with Orula, and through him with the other orichas, by means of divination. Moreover, to the extent that divination is the lynchpin of Ifá life, this principle holds more generally for all aspects of worship. Themselves premised upon divination as we saw, rituals of initiation, consecration, sacrifice, magic, and so on all depend on the possibility of establishing direct relationships between humans and divinities (e.g., Orula's speech to the consultant through the oracle, mortals asking the deities for divine favor, feeding them blood, bringing divine power to bear on personal affairs in magic and sorcery). Conversely, the myth about the birth of spirit possession posits Ifá divination as an answer to the perils of too close an identification between humans and divinities. Orula's vow to fix the world by remaining, so to speak, aloof from human beings (refusing to "pass through their heads"), amounts to an affirmation of transcendence as the source of his power. Even the mischievous trickster Elegguá stands aghast at the aberrant image of humans appropriating for themselves the powers of the orichas—possessing, as it were, their possessors.

Admittedly, this contrast between the proportional continuities of Ifá cosmology and the disproportionate ruptures characteristic of transcendence/immanence discourses has far-reaching ramifications, recalling, for example, attempts to paint such a contrast on the larger canvass of the comparative study of world religions in theories of the so-called axial age (e.g., Eisenstadt 1982; see Robbins 2009 for an anthropological commentary). However, since my concern is only with characterizing the cosmological coordinates of Ifá divination, I do not pursue these broader comparative questions here. Rather, I limit myself to a broad ethnographic observation, relating to the aforementioned lack of what we might call mystery (or awe) in babalawos' dealings with the divinities, which may serve to supplement the cosmologically image I have presented.

As noted earlier, one of the symptoms of the ontological ruptures one associates with the transcendence/immanence distinction is the sense of mystery or even miracle associated with its traversal. These quasi-affective correlates of the premise of ontological rupture, so familiar, for example, in the "uncanny" experience of Christian sacraments (Mitchell 1997), are tellingly absent in Ifá. To be sure, divination is a very serious matter indeed for babalawos, and Orula certainly inspires deep respect, as well as fear. But none of this appears to be a matter of awe. Doing fieldwork among diviners in Havana, what is most striking is their matter-of-fact and rather unfussy attitude to their gods. One might even say that babalawos' respect for Orula (as well as for the rest of the orichas) is a function of an essentially "working" relationship with him. In particular, babalawos' capacity to bring Orula forth into immanence during divination conjures no sense of paradox, nor is it the object of wondrous contemplation as, say, the grace of the Eucharist might be (e.g., see Howe 2004). "Coming out" during divination is just what Orula and his oddu do, and babalawos' ability to bring these events about is just a product of the proper exercise of their ritual expertise—a matter of their cosmo-practical skill at managing the relative distances between transcendence and immanence on which the cosmology of Ifá is premised.

The rest of this chapter demonstrates how babalawos negotiate this fine balance between transcendence and immanence, by describing in detail just how Orula's presence is elicited in the liturgy of Ifá divination—the principal ritual solution, as it were, to the cosmo-practical problem of Orula's transcendence. Surprisingly, given the wealth of scholarly attention Ifá has attracted, no sustained account of the whole ceremonial sequence of Ifá divination exists (to my knowledge) in the anthropological literature. In order to complete the ethnographic record, therefore, I have chosen to present a fuller account of the ceremony than is strictly necessary for purposes of the arguments that will be developed in subsequent chapters. Readers who are not interested in the intricacies of the ritual for their own sake can well afford to read the remaining part of the chapter quickly, or even to skip directly to the following chapter, where aspects of the ritual will be discussed more selectively, in order to develop an analysis of its ontological premises, and the particular conceptualization of transcendence and immanence to which they give rise.

The Liturgy of Ifá Divination

Ifá incorporates three related systems of divination that may be distinguished with reference to different technologies employed in each: the *obbi* oracle (in Spanish *los cocos*), using coconut fragments; the ókuele divination, with a divining chain; and the more elaborate method, using divining nuts and a divining tray, which is commonly referred to as the *bajada de Orula* (lit. descent of Orula). The simpler one of the three is the obbi oracle, which involves casting four fragments of a fresh coconut shell. Unlike the other two divinatory methods, the obbi oracle is not exclusive to babalawos since initiates of Santería are also taught how to manipulate and interpret it (Bolívar Aróstegui 1994b, 5–41). As we shall see below, obbi tends to be used by babalawos mainly as part of larger ritual contexts, as a method for making sure that the deities are satisfied with the course of the ritual at each stage. Although ókuele divinations and bajadas de Orula are associated with different types of divinatory ceremony, in structural terms the difference between them is mainly technical. With reference to the myth of the "birth" of ókuele presented above, babalawos often emphasize that the two techniques are variants of a single oracle, and are equally reliable as a way of ascertaining Orula's will. The ókuele, simply easier to use, lends itself more to everyday consultations, while the cumbersome bajadas are reserved for more ceremonious occasions, not least for rituals that involve the major divinations practitioners call itá (see chapter 3), such as initiations, death rites, and so on. Since ókuele divination is regarded, effectively, as an abbreviation of the bajadas, and the intention here is to give as full a picture as possible of the liturgy of Ifá divination, the description will focus on the bajadas.[7]

The Setting and Preparation for the Ritual

Bajadas de Orula are usually held in the house (*ilé*) of a babalawo, most typically that of the consultant's godfather. When, however, the bajada is carried out as part of a larger ritual, such as an initiation ceremony or a funerary rite, a larger house may be rented depending on the number of neophytes, babalawos, and guests participating. Although the whole house may be utilized for the various preparations involved, the ritual itself takes place in a single room (often the living room, unless the house is large enough to accommodate a designated room of worship). Bajadas must involve as a minimum a single consultant (man or woman) and at least four babalawos (but often many more).[8] All costs (including the purchase of sacrificial animals, incidental paraphernalia and herbs, the fees of the babalawos, transportation and rental, snacks for the guests and the babalawos) are paid by the consultant to the godfather, and it is the latter's responsibility to coordinate the necessary purchases and to apportion fees to the rest of the babalawos participating in the ritual according to seniority. The consultant is allowed to bring friends and relatives as she wishes with her into the room where the divination takes place.[9] Babalawos do emphasize, however, that those present should enjoy the full trust of the consultant (they should be "de confianza"), given the delicate nature of the information imparted during the consultation.

Bajadas de Orula (lit. descents of Orula) are so called because, as part of the preparations required for the ceremony, the babalawo in charge of the oracle must literally take the consecrated Orula used for the ceremony (as a rule the deity of the consultant's godfather) down from the shelf where it is usually kept and put it on the floor on top of a divining mat (*estera*). The divining mat is placed on the floor (sometimes with a white sheet spread over it), in a part of the room where there is enough space for the participants in the ceremony to sit comfortably. Personal comfort is considered important in light of the fact that a single ceremony, which may comprise a series of different divinations, may last for a considerable length of time (sometimes, depending on the circumstances, the best part of a day). It is for this reason that the job of manipulating the oracle is usually delegated to the most junior babalawo in the group: sitting on the floor with one's legs wide apart and crouching over a divining tray (placed between the legs) for hours on end is exhausting.

Close to the Orula, the babalawo places the key consecrated items that he will be using during the divination. First comes the divining board, the tablero, which is laid flat on the mat in front of where the babalawo will sit. The tablero, which usually measures 16 inches in diameter by 1–2 inches in depth, is made of hard wood (often mahogany). Its circumference is rimmed so as to keep the all-important divining powder in place on its surface (see below). This circular border is often decorated with repetitive motifs of various kinds, while the four cardinal points are sometimes marked with specific symbols—sun, moon, and so on (Morton-Williams n.d.). Degrees and types of decoration and symbolism vary considerably from tablero to tablero. However, as already mentioned, the "head" (*lerí*) of the tablero is almost always marked with a small cross, so as to allow the circular tray to be oriented in relation to the babalawo, "head" outmost, as well as in relation to the cardinal points (cf. Menéndez Vásquez 1998, 3:235–43, also for diagrams).

Although babalawos rarely make their tableros themselves (they usually buy them from artisans on the market), each babalawo is ritually bound to two tableros, which he receives from his godfather during initiation. As is the case with all ritual objects in Ifá, tableros are consecrated at the time of receipt in a secret ritual which involves washing the object with herbs (*lavar con yerbas*) and "charging" it with potent powders and other magical concoctions (*cargar con acheses*), the preparation of which depends partly on the initiatory signo of the neophyte. The ritual "giving" of the consecrated tableros by the godfather to the neophyte, along with consecrated divining chains as well as the Orula himself, is considered one of the high points of Ifá initiation.

Divining powder (*iyefá*) is then placed on the divining board so as to cover its entire surface. This is considered magically potent in its own right and although it is listed by some babalawos as one of many *acheses* (in this sense, magical powders) that are used in Ifá worship, other babalawos explained to me that its potency is due to the fact that it *contains* a number of other acheses, depending on the initiatory signo of the babalawo using it. Be that as it may, its brownish color is due to the fact that the main ingredient used in the preparation of the powder is dried yam, which is ground and mixed with other substances, including not only acheses but also particular ground herbs as determined by an Osainista (an initiate to the cult of Osain, the deity of herbal remedies and magic). The divining powder is spread on the tray with the help of a small brush (usually an old shaving brush), which may also be "loaded" with acheses.

Once the powder is evenly spread, the babalawo draws two parallel lines from the bottom of the tablero to the top, from *elese opón* (the "feet" of the tablero) to *lerí opón* ("head" of tablero), with the middle and ring finger of his right hand. This represents Baba Eyiobbe, the principal of the 256 oddu of Ifá divination (see appendix A). The bottom-up movement signifies that the consultation is being performed for a living person. In the funerary rites of ituto where a divination is held for the benefit of the deceased, the movement is reversed (top downwards).[10] Then a single horizontal line is drawn from right (*otún*) to left (*osí*), taking care not to cut into the vertical lines of Baba Eyiobbe, thus dividing the surface of the tablero into four quartiles.

After the lines are drawn, Orula is placed at the center of the tablero, on top of the powdered surface. As already mentioned, consecrated Orulas are contained within a clay or, preferably, porcelain pot (*áwere*), which is often decorated with the colors of Orula (green and yellow). Shapes and dimensions vary, though Orula pots rarely exceed 20 inches in diameter (oval or circular) by 15 inches in height. The deity itself resides inside the pot (though some practitioners tend to regard the pot itself as part of the deity), and is usually understood as consisting of the otán, which in this case is a smallish dark river stone, and the divining nuts, referred to as ikines *or adele*. The divining nuts (palm-tree nuts of about an inch long) are divided inside the pot in two "batches" (*manos*) of twenty-one and nineteen nuts respectively.

Having lowered Orula onto the surface of the divining board, the babalawo proceeds to place a number of objects close to it. Upon the right rim of the tray he places a consecrated deer's horn (*irofá*)—though some babalawos commented that what ought to be used is ivory "as they did in Africa." On the left rim he places a cow's tail (*iruke*), once again, a consecrated entity. On either side of the tray are placed two clay bowls (*porrones*) or, more often, güiro-fruit shells (*jícaras*), which are filled with fresh water. Also within reach on the mat the babalawo places his *ibbos*, a collection of small objects the significance of which will be explained presently. Just off the mat are placed two plates, each of which contains four approximately circular pieces of coconut for obbi divination, which must face upwards, with the concave (white) side exposed. A plate with two lit candles is placed alongside the obbi as an offering to Orula.[11] Finally, one of the babalawos prepares four packages, each made with a small rectangular piece of paper (usually brown) containing minuscule amounts of a number of ingredients. The tiny packages are wrapped up tightly and placed on the rim of the tablero.

While these preparations are being made, the atmosphere in the room is generally solemn and the attention of the babalawos in particular is taken up entirely by the serious matter of getting every detail right. While one babalawo attends to the preparation of the tablero, the others are busy preparing other paraphernalia relating to later phases of the ceremony, organizing notes and *libretas* and writing implements, tidying up, and so on. A striking feature on these occasions, difficult to verbalize, is a certain sense of aesthetic pleasure that babalawos seem to draw from their sensory contact with the ritual paraphernalia that they are busy preparing: tiny little bottles filled with potions, butter being scraped with a small knife, delicate sachets of pulverized dried fish carefully emptied into brown paper, extremities of hens being tied up with thread, herbs being smelt and rubbed, the shells of coconuts being broken loudly against the kitchen sink, and so forth. If divination is cosmo-praxis, to enjoy it is to revel in the detail of its technicality.

"Giving Coconut" to Elegguá and Orula: The Obbi Oracle

Once all the ritual implements have been readied a number of preparatory rites are dispensed, before the divination proper can begin. First, one of the babalawos—usually the most junior—"gives coconut" (*da coco*) to Elegguá. As well as messenger (*mensajero*) to the orichas, Elegguá is often hailed as "owner of the paths" (*dueño de los caminos*)—an important idea to which I shall return. In this capacity he is often regarded as a cunning trickster, and santeros who become possessed by him during rituals will typically behave mischievously like children. Nevertheless, one babalawo explained to me, one cannot afford to be deceived by Elegguá's child-like appearance: "really he is a fierce warrior, and anyone who forgets to take him into account must face the consequences."[12] Accordingly, both santeros and babalawos emphasize that all rituals must begin by addressing Elegguá in order to secure his goodwill and protection, and to ensure that he is willing "to open the path" (*abrir el camino*) so that the ritual can proceed without mishaps.

"Giving coconut" is one of a number of ways of achieving this and constitutes an indispensable part of all Ifá rituals. A consecrated Elegguá of one of the babalawos (preferably the one belonging to the owner of the house in which the ceremony is conducted) is placed on the floor close to a wall. With the consultant standing behind him or next to him, the young babalawo bends over the deity and lights a candle for him. Although consultants too are sometimes asked to adulate, it is considered inappropriate to kneel in front of Elegguá. The babalawo then proceeds to chant his moyubba (see chapter 3), invoking orichas and important ritual ancestors, and inviting the consultant to list her dead relatives also (*muertos famili-ares*), while all present respond "ibaé" (translated loosely as "may they rest in peace") in chorus after each name is mentioned. Once the moyubba is completed, the babalawo takes a set of obbi (viz. the four fragments of coconut) and places them on the floor. Dripping fresh water on the floor with his finger "to refresh the path" (*para refrescar el camino*), he ad-dresses Elegguá directly, in Spanish or with further invocations in Lucumí, informing the deity that a bajada is about to commence and asking him for his blessing. The babalawo then proceeds to chant a number of prayers (*rezos*) associated with giving coconut, drawn from the oddu Ochebile, in which the obbi oracle is "born." While doing so, the babalawo uses his thumbnail to pinch off small pieces of the coconut's white flesh, letting them drop on and around the Elegguá.

The focal part of giving coconut consists of the mini divination, carried out with the four fragments. The objective is to ascertain whether Eleg-guá is well disposed toward the ritual that is being carried out. The ba-balawo clasps the four obbi against each other with his hands, close to his waist or crotch.[13] Speaking in the stylized monotone that is typical of such ritual invocations, he asks Elegguá whether he is satisfied (or a question to that effect). He then releases the obbi, letting them drop haphazardly on to the floor. Unlike divination with ikines or the ókuele, the relative location of the coconut fragments is not taken into account, so the four obbi yield only five possible combinations:[14] all four white, that is, with concave part showing (*alafia*); three white and one black, one showing convex part (*otawo*); two white and two black (*eyife*); one white and three black (*okana*); all four black (*oyekun*). While interpretations vary among practitioners, Javier and other babalawos with whom I worked took *alafia* and *eyife* as affirmative responses, *otawo* as inconclusive (making it neces-sary for the babalawo to cast the obbi once again), and *okana* and *oyekun* as negative.[15]

Should Elegguá's reply be negative, the babalawo proceeds to pose questions in order to discover what offering might secure the deity's good-will. Elegguá, like all deities, has particular likes and dislikes when it comes to offerings and sacrifices, and it is up to the babalawos to make ap-propriate suggestions. Questions are followed by obbi casts until an offer is "taken" by means of an affirmative obbi combination (*hasta que lo coja*). Although babalawos typically begin by making modest offers (e.g., fresh water or honey), persistent negative outcomes can create considerable inconvenience, as the babalawo might have to begin to offer more elaborate (and expensive) sacrifices, the ingredients of which may not be readily available. Since the ritual cannot continue until Elegguá is satisfied, it is not uncommon for proceedings to be delayed while the consultant rushes out to find, say, a rooster (or whatever the deity finally accepts).

The next preparatory step before the divination proper begins involves giving coconut to Orula himself. A second mat is placed in front of the Orula being used for the divination, next to the rest of the ritual paraphernalia. The consultant is asked to kneel in front of Orula, accompanied by two babalawos. A third babalawo takes his place behind the divining board, typically sitting directly on the floor, legs wide apart to make space for the board between them, leaning against the wall for comfort. While coconut is being "given" everyone present must also go down on their knees. The two babalawos facing Orula take each a set of obbi prepared earlier from fresh coconut, placing them on the floor. The senior babalawo on the right takes a recipient with water and begins his moyubba. While the dead spirits (*muertos*) are being mentioned, the babalawo on the divining board takes the deer-horn with his right hand and begins rhythmically to tap the floor, next to the divining mat. As with Elegguá, the dead relatives of the consultant also receive a mention. Then, as the babalawo begins to mention the orichas, the babalawo at the divining board switches to tapping the edge of the tablero instead.

Following the moyubba, the senior babalawo begins a procedure known as "praying Obbesá" (*rezar Obbesá*), which involves reciting a number of prayers associated with the oddu of that name. This, it was explained to me, is because in this oddu "the awakening of Orula" is born, in a mythical "path" of Obbesá that explains why Orula chose Obbesá to wake him up in the mornings as a more delicate alternative to Obbeddí, another oddu, who was too abrupt. Prayers of Obbesá are followed by the prayers normally associated with "giving coconut," as described above for Elegguá..

Once this is finished, the two babalawos swap two of their respective four coconut pieces.[16] With the coconut pieces clasped between their hands, they each proceed to touch the consultant's body with them at specific positions, starting from the head and moving down to the feet, and chanting while doing so, in a common ritual procedure known as "touching the parts" (*tocar las partes*).[17] Once this is done, the two babalawos turn toward Orula and cast their respective obbi as with Elegguá. Some babalawos prefer to read the total of eight coconut pieces together (reading them as two "legs" of a single cast, yielding 256 combinations as in ókuele divination). Most, however, treat the two sets of obbi separately, thus effectively carrying out two mini divinations, and twice follow the same sequence as with Elegguá. The procedure ends when Orula is satisfied on both counts.

"Cleaning and Untying Ifá" and "Counting" the Divining Nuts

Now the consultation proper can begin. The young babalawo at the divining board remains seated on the floor, while the rest of the babalawos make themselves comfortable around the area of the divining mat. One of them takes special responsibility for keeping a record of the proceedings in a notebook, making a note of the date, the nature of the ritual being performed, and the results of the consultation. The second mat is removed and a low stool is put in its place for the consultant to sit. Having taken her shoes off, the consultant is invited to put her feet on the edge of the mat. Consultants may not cross their legs, hands, or fingers throughout the consultation, "out of respect for Orula," as babalawos explain. If the consultant is female, a towel or cloth is spread across her knees, also as a mark of respect for the divinity. If a woman is menstruating she may not consult at all.

With everyone settled into their positions, the babalawo at the divining board begins by performing a rite called "cleaning and untying Ifá" (*limpiar y desamarrar Ifá*).[18] He removes the batch of twenty-one divining nuts from Orula's pot and places them in the empty guiro shell (or bowl). Then he takes the nuts in both hands and performs a series of gestures, sometimes chanting softly in Lucumí as he goes along. First he passes the nuts behind his back from right to left. Leaving the nuts in the shell, he performs a series of movements with his hands empty: first he places them on his head, then crosses them over onto opposite shoulders, then onto his legs. He then blows air, raising his hands onto his stomach. Finally he passes his hands through his hair and ends up with the arms extended upward, above his head. Then he takes the nuts once more and presses them against his forehead, chanting "bi ifaru agba untefa" (translated to me as an address to Orula: "he who was born your chief slave walks with you; may you illuminate me").[19] The nuts are finally passed behind the back, this time from left to right.

Next, the young babalawo proceeds to "count" the twenty-one nuts for all to see. He takes five nuts and displays them in the palm of his right hand saying, "Ifá arun oche" (five order Ifá). Then he takes five more in his left hand and shows them, saying, "Ifá ewa orá" (ten anointed[20] give life to Ifá). All ten nuts are placed back in the shell. Then three nuts are shown with the right hand, while the babalawo says, "Ifá eta ogunda" (three paths mark time in Ifá). Two are then shown with the left hand, while he says, "Ifá eyirete" (two figures signal Ifá). Then the babalawo passes one nut in front of his eyes with his right hand and kisses it, saying, "okan chonchon kirufidan kirubeye" (only one delivers the power as a slave on earth). Finally the five remaining nuts are taken in the left hand and shown: "adele marun nincheru Ifá" (five are always guardians of this power). Following each of these stages the other babalawos respond in unison: "otata ikaru ota oyonu" (as these nuts travel they destroy their enemies). Once the counting is finished the rite of "cleaning and untying Ifá" is repeated for a second time.

"Walking the Lands" and the Moyubba

Next the babalawo chants a series of short phrases in a sequence that initiates call "walking the lands" (*caminar las tierras*). Throughout the chanting the babalawo holds the twenty-one nuts in his hands, swaying them on either side of his open legs. The chant is divided into short phrases, each invoking a specific entity in what appears to be an evolutionary order: the sun (identified with Olofin), the creation of the world, intelligence, the sea, earth, plants, animals, humans, the blond man, albinos, the black man, the white man, the "mulato," the *chino* (Asian man), and finally *aché* (translated to me in this context as "the power given to all men by Orula"). The final phrase confirms: "all these are witnesses of Ifá." Once again, "cleaning and untying Ifá" is performed, and the nuts are "counted" once more. The babalawo then places the five remaining nuts on the mat and rubs them first with the back of one hand, then with the other, while the other babalawos sing. Finally he tucks the five nuts underneath the mat. These nuts are deemed to be "witnesses" to the proceedings (*testigos*). The sixteen remaining nuts are placed back in the shell. Then the babalawo removes the pot of Orula from on top of the divining board while chanting further invocations, and takes small amounts of divining powder from the surface of the board and sprinkles it on the floor.

Next the babalawo chants his own moyubba, followed by a long prayer to Orula, soliciting his assistance for the consultation that is about to take place. Once the prayer is complete, the babalawo lifts the guiro shell with the sixteen divining nuts and proceeds to "touch the parts" of the body of the consultant (as described above), who is sitting in front of him. The shell is then handed to the consultant herself, who is invited to "talk to Orula" (*hablar con Orula*) and ask him for benediction. This may be done out loud or whispered close up to the divining nuts. The consultant then returns the shell with the nuts to the babalawo, who raises it above his head while chanting and uses it to indicate the four cardinal points, in the air as well as on the divining board. Meanwhile, all the babalawos sing together. Finally, the babalawo chants in a loud voice: "Ifá lofun ifareo" (Ifá will give an answer). The rest respond: "Addaché!" (translated to me as "another way of saying aché, like a superlative").

Determining the Principal Oddu

The babalawo may now begin the process of "drawing the sign" (*sacar el signo*), that is, casting the divining nuts (a procedure referred to as *atefar*) to determine the oddu (viz. signo) for the divination. Pressing the sixteen nuts together in cupped hands, the babalawo clutches as many as he can with his right hand, lifting them upwards, away from the left hand. Since a single hand can barely hold all sixteen nuts, some tend to remain in the left hand. If one nut remains, the babalawo marks two lines with his middle and ring finger on the powdered surface of the tablero. If two nuts are left, he marks a single line with his middle finger. If either none or more than two are left, the action is considered void.

After making the first of eight marks of the oddu on the tray, the babalawo takes some divining powder from the tray, and, having placed it on the floor, passes his middle finger through it, chanting, "inle alashera otun" (on the ground to the right of me I put the aché). He then touches his tongue with his finger, and draws a line upwards in the middle of his forehead. The other babalawos chant, "niwawaché" (the power has arrived). The babalawo then proceeds to repeat the casting of the nuts consecutively until the seven remaining marks of the signo, referred to formally as *oddu toyale*, are determined.[21] The eight (single or double) marks yielded by this repetitive process are marked on the surface of the tablero in two columns of four (referred to colloquially as *patas*—"legs"), starting from the top right corner and progressing downward to the bottom left.[22] Once the complete oddu is marked on the divining board, the babalawo in charge of keeping record of the proceedings on behalf of the consultant takes a note of it in his note-book. This sign will provide the template of mythical "paths," prohibitions, and admonitions, which the consultant is told about later, during the interpretative phase of the divination, to be discussed in chapters 6 and 7.

The Cacheoro

Once the principal signo of the divination has been marked on the tablero, a brief ceremony referred to as *cacheoro* is conducted. Babalawos I questioned were reluctant to go into much detail, beyond saying that this part of the ceremony is considered a way of honoring Elegguá, and involves erasing the oddu of the divination from the surface of the board in order to "spoil the sign" (*para desbaratar el signo*). The babalawo in charge of the tablero uses the four small packages of brown paper, which up to this point have remained on the rim of the tablero, to gently even out the powdered surface. Once the sign is "spoiled" by erasure in this way, the babalawo divides the board in two by marking a vertical diameter, and then proceeds to mark a series of oddu on either side, including the oddu of the divination, the initiatory signos of the participating babalawos, and a number of other oddu whose presence is deemed necessary for secret reasons. Once all of the required oddu are marked in the powder, the babalawo proceeds to "pray" each of them (*rezar los signos*) by chanting Lucumí verses associated with each, while at the same time rubbing them out with the four packages, using gentle anticlockwise movements. When he reaches the praying of the initiatory oddu of the babalawos present, each rises to "greet" the divining board by prostrating in front of it and kissing its rim.

Once the prayers are over, the babalawo at the tablero unwraps the four brown paper packages, and places them in front of the board so that their contents are exposed. The most junior babalawo then kneels in front of the divining board and drips fresh water into each open package. He rewraps three of the four packages, and, using his right hand, proceeds to touch the head of each babalawo with them, beginning with the babalawo sitting at the divining board. Then the packages are placed next to the warrior deities of the house, after which the young babalawo returns to kneel once again in front of the divining board. The babalawo in charge of the board marks one more oddu on the tablero, and then, with the remaining package, erases it while chanting its "prayers." At this stage the babalawos sing together certain verses associated with the cacheoro ceremony. Once the song is finished, the package is taken out of the house by one of the babalawos and thrown onto the street out of the front door. In the meantime, the babalawo at the divining board sings a song, associated with Elegguá, to "close" (*cerrar*) the ceremony of cacheoro.

Drawing "Witnesses"

Following the cacheoro, two further oddu are drawn with the help of the divining nuts. Considered supplementary to the principal oddu of the divination, these are referred to as "the witnesses" (*los testigos*). Their main role is to allow the babalawo to determine whether the consultant is in a state of what is called *iré* or *osobbo*. From the consultant's point of view, this initial question to Orula is usually the most pressing of all—more so even than determining the principal oddu itself—since it indicates in simple terms whether the consultant's circumstances at the time of the divination are favorable (iré) or not (osobbo). The transient character of either state is indicated by the use of the Castellan verb *estar*, which indicates temporary rather than permanent states of being, when asking whether the consultee "is" iré or osobbo. Lydia Cabrera translates the two terms as "for good path" and "for bad path" respectively (Cabrera 2000, 192). The dynamic sense of a "path" accords with the way both terms are used colloquially: the auspicious state of iré is one that "enters" one's affairs (*entra el iré*), while osobbo is spoken of as a malign influence that hangs "over" the practitioner and ought to be "discarded" (*quitarse el osobbo*). As we shall see when we come to examine the "consultative" part of the divination, which follows the liturgical procedures described here, much of the subsequent course of the consultation depends on the reply the babalawo receives to this crucial question. Thus, the two "witnesses" are normally recorded in the consultant's notebook, usually under the principal oddu, forming a triangle on the page.

The process by which the two "witness" oddu determine whether a consultant is iré or osobbo is an algorithmic operation, the rules of which are secret. In general terms, however, the system works as follows. The 256 oddu form a hierarchy (see appendix A). Within this ranked order, babalawos distinguish two groups: "major" oddu and "minor" oddu. Hence the two witness oddu form four possible combinations of "major" and "minor" (viz. major followed by major, major followed by minor, minor followed by major, and minor followed by minor). Which of these combinations is drawn forms the basis of a procedure called "asking for the hand" (*pedir la mano*). The babalawo gives the consultant two consecrated objects, referred to generically as *ibbo*. For the purposes of determining iré or osobbo, the ibbo used are a walnut-sized river-stone (*otá*), which represents an affirmative answer, and a seashell (*ayé*), representing the negative. (For other types of question, which are posed to Orula after the matter of iré or osobbo has been settled, other ibbo objects may be used.)[23] The consultant hides the ibbo, one in each hand. The babalawo then asks out loud, "is she iré Orula?," and, depending on which of the four major/minor combination of witnesses was drawn, asks the consultant to reveal the contents of either her left of or her right hand. If the stone emerges the consultant is iré; if it is the shell, she is osobbo.

Once iré or osobbo is determined, the procedure of "asking the hand" is repeated for a whole series of further questions to Orula. First the babalawo has to clarify which of a number of types of iré or osobbo "accompanies" the consultee (e.g., in case of iré, good health, financial development, a trip abroad, and so forth, or, in case of osobbo, illness, sudden disaster, gossip, death, or other possible misfortunes). Since the oracle only allows for yes or no answers, this is determined by posing questions separately for each type of iré or osobbo until Orula "takes it" (*hasta que lo coja*), that is, until a positive reply is given. Learning about the dozens types of iré and osobbo that exist, and about the follow-up questions that are appropriate to each, is an important part of the training of babalawos, and experience in such matters counts for a lot. Broadly speaking, however, in cases of osobbo it is necessary first of all to identify the cause of misfortune (e.g., natural cause, hostile sorcery, transgression of a ritual prohibition on the part of the consultant). Next, the babalawo must find out which divine agency is responsible for the consultant's state, that is, for "giving" her the iré or for "defending" her from the osobbo. Questions follow a hierarchical order, from general to particular, first determining whether it is a deity or a dead spirit, and then identifying which particular deity or spirit it is. Orula is then asked what, if anything, the deity or spirit would like to be offered for his or her continuing protection. Deities and spirits have specific preferences when it comes to offerings (*addimú*) and sacrifices (*ebbó*), so the questions are posed accordingly—again, until Orula "takes" a suggestion. Finally, in the case of osobbo, Orula is asked whether the consultant needs to undergo any further remedial actions, such as taking baths or drinking potions prepared with herbs or other potent ingredients, conducting particular types of sacrifice, or, usually in the gravest circumstances, taking specific steps toward initiation.

This sequence of questions, which can often last a considerable length of time, completes the formal part of the liturgy of the ritual. As we shall see in chapter 6 with reference to a detailed example, the end of the formal questioning of Orula typically marks a perceptible change in the atmosphere of the ritual. While "asking the hand," with its repetitive and esoteric formal procedures, is a rather solemn affair that can often feel somewhat monotonous to the consultant and other observers, the mood in the room becomes considerably livelier as the assembled babalawos proceed to engage directly with the consultant and the other participants in the more interactive part of the divination known as "speaking the signo" (*hablar el signo*). As we shall see in later chapters, it is at this stage that the mythical paths of the principal oddu of the divination are recounted and interpreted for the benefit of the consultant. However, in order to prepare for our discussion of this process, and of the character of the truths that are imparted in it, it is necessary first to dwell further into the significance of the liturgy of the ritual and the ontological premises that underlie it. This is the topic of the following chapter.

CHAPTER FIVE

The Ontology of Motion: Power, Powder, and Vertical Transformation

Both transcendence and immanence are relational notions that relate the ground to the grounded beings. If the unconditioned ground is interpreted to be ontologically transcendent to the grounded beings, there arises a task of explicating their relationship that overcomes their *chorismos*. . . . If, on the other hand, the unconditioned ground is interpreted to be ontologically immanent in the grounded beings, their relationship is secured, but the unconditioned status of the ground must be restored. . . . Transcendence and immanence thus defy separation; they exist in tension in any reflective conception of ultimate reality.
— Professor Chin-Tai Kim (1987)

Ontological Non Sequiturs

Chosen more or less arbitrarily from among the countless scholarly treatments of the topic, the above quotation illustrates by way of ethnographic vignette the kinds of knots in which philosophers and theologians typically tie themselves when trying to think through the distinction between transcendence and immanence. Indeed, part of the point of Kim's rather useful article (1987) is to show that the "tension," as he calls it, between the two concepts is an abiding theme in the history of Western philosophy, ranging from philosophical treatments of the sorts of theological concerns I mentioned in the previous chapter through to ostensibly secular metaphysical frameworks of otherwise varied colors. Whether or not such tensions could be resolved conceptually is a philosophical matter that is of no concern to us here. What concerns us is the ethnographic contrast that Ifá presents in this respect, namely the fact that its overall cosmological coordinates, as well as the divinatory practices which they frame, are characteristically free from such conceptual knots. In particular, while the transcendence/immanence pair connotes an ontological rupture, such that passage from one to the other typically acquires an inherently paradoxical or even miraculous character, the relationship between divinities and humans in Ifá cosmology displays a basic continuity, so that the former's traversals into the world of the latter present no conceptual paradox, but rather a mainly practical problem, a challenge that babalawos are able to address by the ritual means of divination.

For present purposes we may express this contrast be means of a distinction between cosmology and ontology (see also Scott 2007, 3–36; Schrempp 1992, 3–16). Cosmology, on this view, refers broadly to the way people imagine the world around them, its various constituents, the relations between them, including people's own position with respect to them, and so on. Ontology, by contrast, refers to the basic principles that can be said to underlie such ways of imagining a world, concerning such analytical abstractions as similarity and difference, continuity and discontinuity, singularity and plurality, and so on. Cosmology, then, pertains to the level of ethnographic description, while ontology pertains to that of anthropological analysis. Or, to put it differently, cosmology constitutes the ethnographic expression of underlying ontological principles that can be extrapolated from it analytically—although one should add, following Michael Scott (2007, 4–5, 18–24), that ontological principles can be extrapolated from other ethnographic fields too (e.g., language, forms of practice, social relationships, or whatever), as we shall see in relation to Ifá divination presently.

The distinction between cosmology and ontology is useful in order to articulate the analytical problem transcendence and immanence in Ifá present. The conceptual pairing of transcendence and immanence, I claim, is premised on an ontology of discontinuity whose cosmological expressions, in Christianity and beyond, include notions of rupture, paradox, mystery, miracle, and so forth. Ifá cosmology, by contrast, is characterized by a relationship of continuity between the realms one would heuristically describe as transcendent and immanent. Ifá cosmology, then, runs counter to the ontology that transcendence and immanence connote. So the question is what ontology can be said to underlie such a cosmology. In particular, is there a way analytically to reconceptualize the ontological premises of the distinction between transcendence and immanence in a way that tallies with the cosmological continuities that are manifest in Ifá?

It will be evident that, in its recursive slant, this way of framing the question runs parallel to the strategy of my overall argument about the concept of truth in Ifá divination. Just as the ethnography of Ifá divination counters assumptions one would ordinarily associate with the notion of truth, and thus requires an analytical redefinition of that concept, so the ethnography of Ifá cosmology (including the cosmological dimensions of divination itself) contradicts standard ontological assumptions about the relationship between transcendence and immanence, and therefore makes it necessary to redefine it. In the final chapter I shall comment further on this parallel and its role in the anthropological stratagems I call recursive. Here, however, we may note that it is just this parallel that makes it so important to attempt to reconceptualize the transcendence/immanence distinction, rather than, say, merely abandoning it, which would surely be another response to its apparent lack of ethnographic "fit" in the context of Ifá. Reconceptualizing the distinction between transcendence and immanence is a necessary step toward reconceptualizing truth itself. And this is because assumptions about the ontological discontinuity marked out by these two concepts—the very assumptions we are here putting up for revision—are integral to the notion of truth that the ethnography of Ifá divination forces us, also, recursively to revise.

This chapter's task, then, is to develop analytically such a conceptualization with reference to the account of the ritual procedure of Ifá divination already presented. In a nutshell, the continuity between the divine and the mundane in Ifá, rendered operational in divination, is the cosmological expression of a basic ontological reversal: rather than thinking of divinities as self-identical entities in a state of ontological rest, Ifá divination and its cosmology require us to think of them as self-differentiating vectors that mark trajectories of ontological motion. Transcendence and immanence, then, are not to be conceived as alternative and mutually distinct "states" that the divinities, as discrete entities, might occupy or travel between. Rather, they should be conceptualized as the relative measures of the transformations that the orichas (including Orula and his oddu) undergo qua vectors of ontological motion. The divinities, in other words, do not travel across ontological distances. They are themselves distances of ontological travel. The basic analytical reversal that this way of thinking of the divinities requires, namely that of giving logical priority to motion over rest, marks out what I shall call the "motile ontology" of divinatory practice in Ifá.

Placing this argument in relation to the broader anthropological literature I have called recursive, it is worth pausing for a moment here to note that its strategy of analytical reversal owes much to a similar reversal

suggested by Marilyn Strathern (see 1988, 1992b). In particular, my attempt to dissolve the age-old theo-ontological problem of transcendence
runs parallel to her influential dissolution of the traditional anthropological problem of social reproduction, which is itself analogous to the problem of transcendence. Ever since Durkheim anthropologists have asked:
How do individuals, conceived as discrete units, come to form enduring
social bonds, conceived as mutual relationships? From the point of view of
Melanesian ethnography,[1] Strathern suggests, the image of units relating
to each other is ill formed in the first place, since in this case persons are
themselves best conceived of *as* relations. In its form, my strategy with
regard to the problem of how beings can move from transcendence to
immanence is identical. From the point of view of Ifá, I say, the problem is
itself ill formed since here divinities just *are* such motions.

Indeed, we may note that the two problems are in a way versions of
each other. The separations between humans and divinities that the idea
of transcendence implies are analogous to separations between discrete
individuals, while the relations between humans and divinities suggested
by the role of immanence in divination are analogous to relations between
people in society. We may also note, of course, that Strathern's Melanesia-
driven "relational" dissolution of the age-old sociological problem does
not get us very far in the case of Ifá (cf. Højer 2004). Simply put, if one
were to say that the problem of transcendence in Ifá is not really a problem because deities and humans mutually constitute each other in the immanent relationships that divination implies, one would be denying the
very condition that leads clients to the diviners in the first place, namely
that the deities *are* transcendent most of the time, so that the diviners'
powers are necessary in order to *elicit* them into immanence. So the motile
ontology I seek to articulate is "post-relational," in a sense proposed by
Morten Pedersen in his own commentary on Strathern's work: it seeks to
extend the Strathernian analytic by *intensifying* its "relational" conceptual
coordinates by asking how relation and, if you like, non-relation (viz. immanence and transcendence) might themselves be related (cf. Pedersen
forthcoming; see also Holbraad and Pedersen 2009, Viveiros de Castro
and Goldman 2008/2009).

The rest of this chapter charts out the ways in which such a motile ontology is fundamental to babalawos' efforts in eliciting divinities into immanence through the ritual of divination. Providing a systematic account
of the oft remarked "dynamism" of Ifá divination,[2] the role of motility in
the liturgy of divination will be examined at three related levels, which

may be labeled respectively as the *practical* level (pertaining to what practitioners of divination do), the *discursive* level (pertaining to what they
say), and the *cosmological* level (pertaining to certain overarching conceptions that inform what they do and say). As we shall see, however, this
three way distinction is one that ultimately undoes itself. While separating
out practical, discursive and cosmological aspects of the ethnography of
divination is a useful heuristic device for the purposes of exposition, once
we get to articulating the principles that underlie all of these aspects, what
we find is an ontology that systematically contravenes the distinctions one
might draw between them. To build such an argument, then, let us begin
by revisiting the liturgy of Ifá divination to explore the constitutive role
motion plays within it.

Motile Practice — A Choreography of Nuts

The liturgical sequence of the ritual of the bajadas examined in the previous chapter can feasibly be described as a kind of choreography. Three
principal classes of *dramatis personae*, so to speak, are brought together
in a space of physical proximity: the consultants, for whom divination
involves a "visit" (*visita*) to the babalawos' consecrated home (*ilé*); the
babalawos, who must be "invited" (*invitar*) to participate in bajadas by
the consultant's godfather; and Orula himself, who must "descend" onto
the divining board in order to "speak" to the assembled participants in the
divination ceremony. Physical proximity, to the point of contact, is emphasized in the ritual repeatedly and in a number of ways. As we saw, the
focal task of "drawing" the signo for the divination is preceded by a number of pronounced ritual actions that emphasize the physical contiguity
of the consultants, the babalawos, and Orula's consecrated paraphernalia:
"greeting" the divining board by prostrating in front of it and kissing its
rim, asking consultants to sit in front of it, placing their feet on the divining
mat throughout the ritual, kissing the divining nuts themselves, "touching"
the consultant's body at specific points with them (*tocar las partes*) and
whispering questions directly to them, manipulating the ibbo figures during the interrogatory phase of the divination, and so on. Indeed, the babalawos and the consultants are all very much aware that in their handling
of the consecrated tools of divination they are literally in the presence of
the deity (witness, for example, the requirement that women should cover
their legs with a cloth during the ceremony "out of respect for Orula"). In

a literal sense, then, divinatory ceremonies can be said to constitute temporary *meetings* of consultants, babalawos, and divinities.

Furthermore, by staying sensitive to the role of motion, one finds that the association between movement and divine potency is pervasive in the liturgy of the bajada. This is particularly clear in observing the way babalawos carry out the various preparatory invocations that come before the casting of the principal oddu. For example, during his moyubba (viz. the long incantation by which the benediction of deities and lineage ancestors is solicited for the ceremony) the babalawo continually taps the divining board with a consecrated deer-horn while mentioning the names of each divine entity, as if to manifest the potency of their divine agency in the consecrated items themselves.[3] The same goes for the ceremony of "walking the lands." Here the divining nuts themselves are used, as the babalawo sways them from one side of his waist to the other while invoking verbally various powerful entities. But perhaps the most striking example is the ceremony of "cleaning and untying Ifá" in which, as we saw, the twenty-one divining nuts are subjected to a series of choreographed sequences of movement, with the babalawo passing them around different parts of his body as he solicits Orula's "illumination." Divine potencies are not merely invoked in the abstract, then, but are rather infused into the mechanics of the divinatory process by means of a variety of simultaneous movements involving the consecrated tools of divination.

These meticulously choreographed connections of movement with divine potency culminate in the process by which the oddu of the divination, along with the two "witnesses," are "drawn" by casting the divining nuts (or casting the divining chain in the case of ókuele divination). Like so many other forms of noninspirational divination, the drawing of oddu in Ifá turns on a key constitutive principle:[4] the oddu as a determinate configuration must emerge out of what could be called a "chaotic event," that is a process that is meant to be kept beyond human control or manipulation. From a technological point of view, this poses the problem of how to infuse "chaos" into the set of 256 discrete possible configurations for which the sixteen divining nuts (or the eight shells of the divining chain) allow. And the solution is found, of course, in motion. The boundaries that render the 256 configurations discrete dissolve indeterminately in a swift continuous motion as the babalawo shifts the nuts from one hand to the other, or, in ókuele, as he lets the chain swing in the air before letting it drop flat on the surface of the divining mat. Orula's ability to "speak" during the ceremony, then, is literally a function of his capacity to move—morphing into different configurations in the hands of the babalawo. Indeed, when it comes to the part of the divination in which the consultant's fortune (iré or osobbo) is determined, the motion of nuts is coupled by that of the ibbo, the consecrated objects that are placed in the hands of the consultant herself, which are "asked for" by the babalawo. In this way, consultants as well as babalawos literally have a hand in the motions by which Orula's pronouncements become determined.

Described in mechanical terms, the outcome of oddu casts represents an equilibrium that results from the interaction of a number of practically imponderable forces, including the power exerted by the babalawo, the weight and friction of the nuts or the chain, gravity, the normal reaction of the surface of the mat on the ground, and so on. Indeed it is worth noting in this connection that if casts seem random, this is because the various vectors of movement that go into determining each outcome are causally independent from each other: were they not, the babalawo could be accused of manipulating the result. Of great importance to babalawos, this principle of propriety is clearly enshrined in the liturgy of the bajada. As we saw, for example, the twenty-one nuts are emphatically "counted" for all to see before the process of casting oddu may begin, and five of them are separated out as "witnesses of Ifá" to ensure the casts are made properly. It is interesting to note, furthermore, that in ritual terms the requirement that these acts go smoothly is underlined by a number of specific strictures relating to possible mishaps that may occur during the casting of the oddu, such as dropping nuts on the floor or getting the divining chain tangled. For example, should the babalawo drop a nut, he must pick it up with his mouth and place it back in its receptacle before he may continue with the proceedings—an action that, as babalawos explain, is also considered a mark of "respect to Orula."

Motile Discourse — Talking of Paths

The second sense in which motion is constitutive of the ceremony of divination is more discursive, and has to do with the multifarious ways in which the notion of "paths" (*camino*, the verb being *caminar*, "to walk") features in the liturgy. We saw, for example, that the invocations performed to prepare for the cast of oddu include the ceremony of "walking the lands," in which the babalawo invokes in a quasi-evolutionary order a whole series of cosmological elements while at the same time shifting all twenty-one divining nuts in a swaying movement with his hands. Babalawos explain that this ceremony recalls Orula's own travels in the different lands in Africa, which are recounted in detail in the mythical stories of the oddu (see Espinosa and Piñero 1997a, 1997b; cf. Frobenius 1913, 248–59; Parrinder 1951, 122; Drewal 1992). (Such myths, of course, are themselves referred to as "paths"—a point that will be taken up in the next chapter, in discussing the role of mythical narrations in the consultative phase of the divination.) Indeed, as we also saw, the oddu themselves can be conceived as "paths" of Orula, much like each of the many guises in which other orichas appear is referred to as a path of the deity. Finally, the term *path* is also used with reference to the consultants, in that their initiatory trajectory, whose course is guided by the oracle of Ifá itself as we saw in chapter 3, is also spoken of in these terms (for example, as when a neophyte is told that his is a "path of Ifá"). Indeed, as Anastasios Panagiotopoulos details in his comprehensive commentary on divinatory imagery in Afro-Cuban religion more broadly, the notion of a path is also used more encompassingly to refer to the total life-course of the consultant, beyond immediate matters of initiation. Noting its affinity to notions of destiny, Panagiotopoulos describes the many images associated with this graphic way of thinking of people's life-trajectories: consultants may be said to "stumble" on their path when they encounter "obstacles," have it "opened," "crossed," or even "broken," experience it as "heavy" or "light," and so on (2011, 37–38, 69, 71–72).

When faced with this kind of terminological confluence one should take care not to overinterpret things. It is certainly tempting to take the multifarious uses of the concept of "paths" as a cue for reading a richly detailed cosmological order on to the divinatory process, and perhaps Ifá worship more generally. In this vein, one would want to ask practitioners for all sorts of clarifications. How do the various senses of "path" relate to one another? What course does each of the paths in question take? What is it that is supposed to travel along them? And so on. In fact, this was my approach during the earlier stages of my fieldwork in Havana. For example, in view of my interest in the role of mythical narration in the divinatory process, I was concerned to find out exactly why the mythical stories associated with each oddu should be thought of as paths. In my mind I developed a number of hypotheses, which I tried out with various informants. Are the myths called paths because they indicate to the consultant what course of action she should take? Or is it because the wisdom imparted in each myth was discovered by Orula on his own travels? Or perhaps each oddu has paths in the same sense as deities have paths, i.e., as distinct guises of a multiplicity? Babalawos generally admitted to having little idea as to whether any of these interpretations was appropriate, and did not seem to attach much importance to my questions (though see Drewal 1992 for extensive commentary on notions of "path" and "travel" in contemporary Yoruba ritual).

Since babalawos generally tend to be very interested indeed in accounting for all manner of detail when it comes to describing the devotional universe of Ifá, one may conclude that the concept of a path does not, in itself, have a particularly "marked" cosmological significance for them—although the data to which it refers (such as myths, deities, initiatory trajectories) certainly do. Its import, I would argue, is more logical: the fact that practitioners find the concept of a path self-evidently appropriate for referring to such diverse data tells us less about *what* they think and more about *how* they think it. Or, to revert to my earlier distinction between cosmology and ontology, it serves as an indication of the ontological parameters that underlie their thinking on these matters. Indeed, from an analytical viewpoint, what makes the concept of paths so intriguing is precisely that, although it lacks much in the nature of explicit content, it has vividly graphic connotations, and particularly the connotation of motion itself. In particular, while specifying relatively little about Orula, the oddu, the myths they contain, or the trajectories of neophytes, the concept of a path associates each of these elements in some sense with the idea of motion.

The fact that both Orula and the oddu should be conceived in such terms is particularly relevant to the question of how best to conceptualize the relationship between transcendence and immanence in divination. Indeed, the notion of paths in this context lends a degree of indigenous support to the suggestion that divinities are to be considered as motions rather than entities—the logical reversal that, as I want to argue, is an analytical corollary of babalawos' ability to elicit these divinities into immanence during divination. For such a suggestion is further supported by the explicit ways in which the notion of paths is emphasized in the ritual of divination. Firstly, as an indispensable requirement in preparation for the divination, the babalawo must perform a libation of fresh water "in order to refresh the paths": "omituto, onatuto . . . ," the babalawo chants as he drips water on to the floor ("fresh water, fresh path . . ."). A second point has to do with the inordinate importance of the messenger-deity Elegguá during divinatory ceremonies (as well as in practically all other Ifá and

Santería rituals). While the close relationship between Orula and Elegguá (or Echú—see chapter 4) has been discussed by a number of scholars, particularly relevant for purposes of my argument here are the ceremonies of "giving coconut" to Elegguá and the *cacheoro*, both of which, as we saw, are prerequisites for a successful bajada.[5] Babalawos invariably give the same explanation for this requirement: "Elegguá opens the paths" (*Elegguá abre los caminos*). When asked to explain this very common statement, practitioners are as vague as they are with regard to the notion of a path itself, though usually they connect Elegguá's "ownership" of the paths, as they call it (*dueño de los caminos*), with his capacity as messenger of the gods (and hence the significance of the four magical offerings that are made to the deity in the cacheoro ceremony). Once again, however, babalawos' vagueness in these matters only serves to underline the apparent self-evidence, for them, of the idea that rendering divinities present and active during divination is a matter of some form of motion. One might even say that the liturgical priority of Elegguá as the "opener" of paths enshrines in ritual terms the logical priority of motion in divination.

Still, it is clearly also the case that such a line of analysis raises more questions than it answers. In what sense exactly are divinities to be thought of as motions? What kind of motion exactly is at issue here? And how is the suggestion that in divination motion might gain logical priority over rest to be understood? To tackle such questions we need to turn our attention to the third, and perhaps deepest, level at which motility features in the liturgy of the bajada, which relates to what practitioners call *aché*. A peculiar concept-*cum*-substance, reminiscent of the Oceanian notion of *mana* that has been the focus of so much debate in anthropology, aché is fundamental to the cosmology of all worship in Ifá. To set the ethnographic parameters of its analysis, we may begin by describing in some detail the multifarious ways in which aché features in the divinatory liturgy in particular.

Motile Cosmology—Aché in Divination

Commenting on Marcel Mauss's famous discussion of mana (2001), Lévi-Strauss argues that the reason why this concept became so interesting to anthropologists was the "the apparently insoluble antinomies" attaching to it, "which struck ethnographers so forcibly, and on which Mauss shed light: force and action; quality and state; substantive, adjective and verb all at once; abstract and concrete; omnipresent and localised" (Lévi-Strauss 1987, 63–64). Seen in such light, aché seems as much of a mana-concept as mana itself. Consider, for example, *El Monte*, the classic monograph on Afro-Cuban religion by Lydia Cabrera (2000). In it, Cabrera mentions aché at eleven separate occasions, and each time characterizes it differently. Sometimes Cabrera writes of aché in the abstract as "grace"[6] (16), "magical power" (99), "all the powers, force, life, the secret of the earth" (103), or "luck" (301). But elsewhere aché appears more concretely as "Orula's grace [kept by the Ifá priest] in his saliva' (106), a "powder that belongs exclusively to a deity" (481), or, yet more specifically, as "*iyefá*, the white powder full of virtues which is spread on to Orula's divining board" (494). Furthermore, aché appears as something with which deities are born (314), or something that may inhere in plants (113), or be invested on objects through consecration rites (103). But rituals themselves may "accumulate" aché through the presence of plenty of initiates (108). Indeed, aché is also the kind of thing that initiates themselves can "have" or "give" (108).

We are faced, then, with a situation similar to the one we confront in relation to the concept of paths: too many analyses and each of them apparently plausible. However, while with paths interpretative possibilities seem superabundant because practitioners' explanations are so sparse, with aché the problem is more that their accounts are so numerous and apparently conflicting—an excess of meaning rather than a lack. Indeed, even if we try to narrow our focus down to the ways in which concepts of aché enter the divinatory process in particular, the problem remains.

Asked how aché relates to divination, babalawos' initial response is most often that aché is the power or capacity (in Spanish usually *poder* or *facultad*) that enables them to divine in the first place: "to divine you must have aché," they say. Conducting the divination, as well as other rituals such as consecration, is also said to "give" the babalawo aché. However, if he uses his office to trick people or do gratuitous evil through sorcery, he may also "lose" it. The importance of aché as an enabling condition or power is enshrined in the liturgy of the divinatory ritual, with babalawos invoking it by name as part of the various incantations that have to be chanted to achieve a successful divination. For example, the long prayers associated with each babalawo's individual moyubba—which, as we saw, are an absolute prerequisite for conducting a divination—are often explained as a way of soliciting the aché of various divine entities, including orichas and ancestral spirits of the lineage. Sometimes this is made explicit by including in the moyubba incantations such as *aché baba, aché bobbo kaleno ocha, aché oluwo, aché ayibbón, aché apetebbí, aché iyalo-cha babalocha, aché bobbo iworo.* While such chants differ from initiate to initiate, this particular sequence was translated to me by one babalawo as an invocation of the "powers" (*poderes*) of Olofin, the orichas, his own godfather, *ayibbón* and *apetebbí* (the closest members of his ritual family), and all other initiates in general. In addition, we also saw that aché is invoked by name at a number of key points of the liturgy of the bajada, including the moment just before the principal oddu is drawn. Culminating his final preparatory moyubba, the babalawo in charge of the divining board calls out loud, "Ifá lofun ifareo!" (translated to me as "Ifá will give an answer!"). At this point the other participating babalawos respond in chorus, "Addaché!," explained to me as superlative evocation of the power of aché.

But while babalawos tend to explain such ritual invocations in rather vague terms—sometimes as appeals for the aché of ritual ancestors, other times as solicitations of the aché of nature, or of the deities, or of Orula— there are also senses in which aché is understood much more precisely, namely as referring specifically to the secret powders that are an indispensable ingredient in just about all Ifá ceremonial, including divination. As we saw, a fundamental principle of all Ifá ceremonial is that, for any given ritual to be effective—for it to work, as it were—the items used must have been properly consecrated. In the case of divination such consecrations crucially involve "charging" or "loading" (*cargar*) each of the paraphernalia—the divining nuts or chain, the tablero, the ibbo objects, and even the shaving-brush that is used to spread divining powder on the tablero—with *acheses.* The Hispanicized plural form of *aché* is appropriate in this context because aché powders are prepared in different ways and according to different recipes, depending on which task is being performed, which magical effect is required, which deity is being consecrated, and so on. Although these matters are strictly secret, it is clear that the sense of "loading" consecrated items with aché is also literal, since token quantities of the powder are in many cases stuffed inside small cavities created for that purpose in the various items that are being consecrated. When I asked what would happen if one were to conduct a divination with "jewish" (*judios*) equipment, as yet-to-be consecrated objects are called, babalawos dismissed the idea.[7] "Orula does not speak with such objects," they said.

As we saw, the aché powder most closely associated with Ifá divination in particular is referred to ritually as *iyefá* or, more colloquially, as *aché de Orula.* Iyefá is used by babalawos in a number of ritual contexts, and is often included as an ingredient for various concoctions involved in magic, sacrifice, and consecration. Significantly, the consecrated pot of Orula that neophytes receive during the mano de Orula ceremony also includes a small envelope containing iyefá. Taken from a stock of iyefá prepared by the neophyte's godfather, this powder is placed inside the pot, alongside the otán-stone and the divining nuts, which together are deemed to "be" Orula, as already explained.

The use of iyefá is at its most visible, however, in the ceremony of divination itself. As we have seen, in bajada ceremonies it is iyefá that is spread on to the divining board, to form the surface upon which the babalawo marks with his fingers the various oddu that emerge during the ceremony—including not only the main oddu of the divination and its two "witnesses," but also the various secret sequences of oddu that are marked on the board as part of the liturgy of the ritual. Here it is worth noting that, in the liturgy of the bajada, iyefá is linked explicitly to the more abstract sense of aché as "power." It should be recalled that, at just about the most focal point of the proceedings, the babalawo, after having drawn the first of the eight marks of the principal oddu on the divining board, places some iyefá on the ground next to the divining board, dips his finger in it and, after tasting it with his tongue, proceeds to mark a line with it on his forehead. As he does so, the rest of the babalawos present exclaim, "Niwawaché!" (the power has arrived!).

This liturgical association of power and powder not only illustrates well the importance of aché in the elicitation of divinities during a divinatory ceremony, but also casts some light on the relationship that is our central concern here, namely between transcendence and immanence in Ifá worship. On the one hand, the divinatory power of the babalawos lies in their ability to render the oddu—whether conceived as divinities in their own right or as paths of Orula himself—immanent during the divination, and thus let Orula "speak." It is just that moment of immanence—when the first mark of the principal oddu emerges or, as babalawos say, "comes out" on the tablero—which is underscored by the exclamation *niwawaché*: the arrival of aché is the emergence of the oddu. On the other hand, that moment is also a direct and very literal function of the use of aché powder. The form that the oddu's appearance takes in the ceremony is that of "marks" (*marcas del oddu*, verb: *marcar el oddu*) in the powdered surface of the divining board. And for those present at the time there is no mistaking the immanent potency of those marks: crouching around the divining board, the babalawos and their consultants are in the presence of a divine being, a symbol that stands for itself if ever there was one (*sensu* Wagner 1986).

The intimate association between the two primary senses of aché in the context of divination—both power and powder, as it were—holds the key for understanding not only the abiding role of motion in Ifá divination, but also its particular character as a basic ontological principle. The role of aché is to provide the conditions for the transformation of divinities as motions from (or better, of) transcendence to immanence and, as such, constitutes a fundamental premise of the motile cosmology of Ifá. In order to show this, however, it is necessary to consider in some detail the analytical problem posed by the two apparently contrasting senses of aché.

An Interlude on the Analysis of Motility—or, the Power of Powder

Much as with mana, as we saw, the meaning that practitioners of Ifá attach to the notion of aché appears excessive. Power and powder, abstract and concrete, concept and thing, it would appear that aché cuts across distinctions that one might otherwise assume are axiomatic, much as Lévi-Strauss remarked of mana. I want to argue, however, that this does not index some kind of antinomy, as Lévi-Strauss would have it. Nor, for that matter, are we faced with an ordinary ambiguity, to be compared, for example, with the English concept of love, which can hardly be said to have a single meaning that incorporates filial and erotic senses. While babalawos certainly distinguish between the different senses in which they use the word *aché*—no one is confused about the difference between power and powder—they also assume (and, if invited, explicitly draw) a clear logical connection between them. On the one hand, to have the power of aché as a diviner one must be properly consecrated as a babalawo and this, most crucially, involves receiving and knowing how to use the consecrated equipment, charged with the powder of aché. No powder no power, so to speak. On the other hand, the secret knowledge required to prepare aché powders and use them for Ifá is possessed only by babalawos—"fathers" of such "secrets," as we have seen. Thus, preparing and using these powders is within the power of babalawos exclusively—so, no power no powder also.

It is worth considering in some detail the logical status of this mutual implication, since it goes to the heart of the apparently anomalous "excess" of aché. To see this, we may imagine two ways of glossing this implication that would make it appear quite unanomalous from a logical point of view, though clearly unusual, or even "irrational," as the old insult has it. The first would be to gloss the implication in causal terms: no powder no power and vice versa, because each is a necessary causal condition for the other. The problem, then, would be simply one of showing why certain people "believe"—to use the hackneyed word—in such seemingly strange causal sequences. We can all understand how, say, gunpowder was a necessary condition for the power of the Conquistadors, and how, conversely, the gunpowder's power was predicated on its Spanish makers' privileged knowledge of how to produce it. Why, then, might Cuban diviners posit this kind of relationship between their power and their powder, given that no causal efficacy seems "actually" to be involved?

The problem with this causal gloss is that it does violence to the ethnography. For on such a causalist account, aché powders and aché power are first posited as discrete elements, conceived as being logically independent from one another, and then related "externally," as philosophers might say, by way of contingent causal relationships. This hardly tallies with what practitioners say. As shown by their reaction to my suggestion that I might start divining with "jewish" equipment, for them the notion of powerless powder, and of powderless power, is not just untenable as a matter of fact, but rather inconceivable as a matter of principle. A babalawo who has not been properly consecrated with aché powder just isn't a babalawo. And powder that has not been prepared properly by a babalawo—father of these secrets—just isn't aché. In other words, the relationship between power and powder is, philosophically speaking, "internal": each is defined in terms of the other (Moore 1922).

So perhaps a better tack might be to gloss the relationship between power and powder as one of mutual implication—a matter, if you like, of logical necessity rather than physical contingency. On this view, the slogan "no powder no power" (and its converse) would be taken as what philosophers call analytic, of the same order as statements such as "the queen is head of state." Just like a queen is no queen unless she is head of state, so a babalawo is not what he is (i.e., does not have the power of aché) unless he has been consecrated with the aché powder (and vice-versa: the aché powder is not what it is unless it has been made by a consecrated babalawo). The question, then, would be what it is about the *meaning* of power and of powder in this context that makes them mutually definable in this way. In other words, why do Cuban diviners consider these two concepts mutually constitutive?

Persuasive though it may seem, however, in that it reflects the internal relationship of power and powder in Ifá, this analysis in terms of logical necessity is just as inadequate to the ethnography as the causal account, though for opposite reasons. The problem here is that by treating the relationship between powder and power as one of logical implication one effectively ignores its irreducibly *practical*, if not causal, character. True, for a babalawo it is enough to contemplate what his power means to know that it required his consecration with aché powder (and vice-versa). But the point is that this logical operation *presupposes* a practical one, since it is only because aché powder is actually efficacious that it can be used to produce babalawos "with aché" (with power). Babalawos only count as such provided they have been consecrated with powder, not because the *meaning* of powder logically implies their power (like the meaning of "queen" implies being head of state), but because the powder itself *gives* them power. (And vice-versa for powder.) In other words, the difference between the relationship of powder and power and that described by an ordinary analytic statement is that while the latter states a conceptual identity, the former implies a real transference, namely, of powder that gives power and of power that makes powder.[8]

So we seem to be confronted with an apparently dismal dilemma: neither causal nor logical glosses seem appropriate to the connections babalawos draw between the two senses of aché. But this only goes to show the Procrustean character of the analytical choices at our disposal. Sure, for as long as one insists on thinking in terms of the choice between causal or conceptual relationships, aché is bound to look like an inherently paradoxical or even antinomous notion (or is it a substance?)—*pace* Lévi-Strauss on mana (and more on this in the next chapter). However, the recursive strategy advanced throughout this book would suggest an alternative conclusion, namely, that what is at fault here is neither aché, nor the bizarrely contradictory "beliefs" babalawos might be said to hold of it, but rather the analytical framework we are bringing to bear upon the matter. If the distinction between causal and conceptual relationships makes aché seem contradictory, then maybe it is that distinction that needs to be questioned. The question, then, would be whether there is an alternative analytical framework that might allow us to conceive of aché in a way that is not contradictory.

Framing the question in this way suggests that making sense of aché is ultimately a matter of analytical footwork rather than ethnographic description. It is precisely because we are landed in contradictions by even our most careful attempts ethnographically to describe, in this case, the connections babalawos draw between aché understood as power and aché understood as powder that the search for a different conceptual framework is forced upon us as an analytical task. The solution to the conundrum aché presents, in other words, is not to be culled from the ethnography itself, but must rather emerge from our own analytical imagination—a point that will be developed in some detail in the concluding chapter of this book. Nevertheless, the ethnography of aché plays a crucial role not only in framing the terms of the analytical problem with which it presents us but also in pointing us in the direction of its analytical solution in rather precise terms. In particular, I suggest, the precise *manner* in which aché transgresses analytical distinctions that may seem axiomatic (such as the distinction between external causal relations and internal conceptual ones) points the way to a corresponding, and correspondingly exact, method for rethinking just those distinctions.

The main clue lies in a basic corollary of the offending distinction, so to speak, between causal and conceptual relations, namely that between concrete objects and abstract concepts. Indeed, consider the implication: If aché seems to defy the distinction between causal and conceptual relations, that is partly because it defies the one between objects and concepts also. If aché powder and aché power were concrete objects, then they could be conceived of as discrete variables, related to each other externally by causal connections. As we have seen, they cannot. If they were concepts, then their connection would be a matter merely of tracing internal (analytic) relationships of logical implication. Again, however, it is not. Indeed, considered in these terms, aché appears to be neither an object nor a concept but rather a bit of both: an indiscrete object and a concept that literally transfers itself, along the lines already discussed. The excess of aché, then, comes down to its transgression of what one might see as the most basic ontological axiom of modernist metaphysics—that most Cartesian of Cartesianisms, so to speak—namely the distinction between ideas and things, concepts and objects.

As well as aligning aché directly with the broader argument about truth in anthropology, which as we saw turns on the analytical implications of precisely these kinds of ontological transgressions (e.g., culture versus nature, representation versus reality), this way of putting the matter suggests an immediate way forward for making sense of the ontological oxymorons with which aché presents us. If aché is to be taken as both what we call a concept and what we call an object, then it follows that the connection between the two sides of its "double aspect," so to speak, is not arbitrary. That is to say, while the ontological status of aché is still obscure due to its apparent excess, we do know one thing: its abstract meaning as "power" is internally related to its concrete nature as powder. It is just such a connection, entailed by babalawos' reversible "no powder no power" formula as we have seen, that renders aché so transgressive. As if by magic, then, the meaning of aché (the concept of power) seems to be literally constituted by the objects to which it would otherwise be assumed simply to "apply" (the powder). Its intension, philosophically speaking, is modified by its extension by what one might call a relation of "hypermetonymy" (imagine a crown that did not just signify royalty, but actually made it—a magical crown, then).

This ethnographically motivated idea that the meaning of a concept might be defined by the concrete characteristic of an object by way of a transgressively internal relation has immediate methodological implications for how our own analysis of aché here can advance. The opportunity for making sense of aché in its very excess is there, in the ethnography of the thing itself: in the aché powder. If babalawos are so clear about the fact that their power to bring divinities into immanence in divination is owed (not quite causally, not quite conceptually, but both) to the powders that are such an active ingredient in their ceremonies, then we may ask: what is it about powder that may give them this power? If aché is both concept and thing, then what, if you like, are the conceptual affordances of its concrete and material characteristics (see also Henare et al. 2007 and Holbraad 2011)? It is in answer to these questions, I suggest, that the most salient contours of the ontological underpinnings of Ifá become apparent.

Motile Ontology—Potential Relations and the Direction of Motion

So what does aché powder *do* in divination? As we saw, spread on the surface of the divining board, powder provides the backdrop upon which the oddu, thought of as divinities, emerge, thus allowing Orula to "speak." Considered prosaically, we may note, powder is able to do this due to its peculiarly *pervious* character, as a collection of unstructured particles—its pure multiplicity, so to speak (cf. Verran 2001, 177–205).[9] In marking the oddu on the board, the babalawo's fingers are able to draw the configuration just to the extent that the "intensive" capacity of powder to be moved (to be displaced like Archimedean bathwater) allows them to do so. The extensive movement of the oddu as it appears on the board, then, presupposes the intensive mobility of powder as the medium upon which it is "registered"—*registro*, in fact, being also one of the words practitioners of Ifá use to refer to the act of divination. Of course, physically speaking, this is always the case—movement presupposes movement. Even if the babalawo marked the oddu with a pencil on a piece of paper, the lead would only leave a mark provided the paper particles reacted accordingly. But the point is that powder renders the motile premise of the oddu's revelation *explicit*, "registered" for all to see by means of a simple figure-ground reversal: oddu figures are revealed *as* a temporary displacement of their ground, the powder.[10]

Now, the first thing to note here is that such a figure-ground reversal offers direct support for the *logical* reversal suggested earlier in relation to the role of movement in the liturgy of bajadas, as well as the notion of paths. If the oddu just *are* the marks they make on aché powder, then the constitution of these divinities as displacements of powder confirms the idea that they are to be thought of not as discrete entities but rather as *motions*. Indeed, this way of thinking of the deities has immediate consequences for the conceptualization of their passage from transcendence to immanence in divination. For even on its own, the idea of deities *as* (rather than in) motion precludes the notion that passing from transcendence to immanence might involve an ontological rupture along the lines discussed earlier. In a logical universe in which motion is primitive, as philosophers might say, what looks like transcendence becomes distance and what looks like relation becomes proximity. Motions through and through, the deities are never divorced from humans, stuck in an ontologically discrete state of transcendence—to say so would be to place limits on the logical priority of motion. But nor does this suggest some form of permanent immanence (if that is where the negation of a transcendent state would leave us—think, perhaps, of Spinoza's immanentism as depicted by Deleuze [1990b]). After all, if deities' immanence in divination turns on their inherently motile character, then such elicitations are never a certain matter. Thus, the cosmo-practical *problem* of divination, discussed earlier, emerges as a question of how properly to harness the motility of the divinities, for there can be no guarantee that their motion will be elicited in the right *direction*, as it were.[11] The relations between divinities and humans that divination is meant to establish, then, are *potential*, and it is only this potential—the potential of directed movement—that aché powder guarantees, as a solution to the genuine problem of the traversals the deities must undergo in order to be rendered present and active in divination.

Nevertheless, while taking us very much in the right direction, so to speak, these considerations do not quite settle the question of how best to conceptualize notions of transcendence and immanence in the motile universe that has emerged from our analysis so far. For while the idea of deities as motions, precipitated by the analysis of aché, may rule out of court the Judeo-Christian worry about ontological rupture that is so alien to Ifá, it is not yet clear how it may capture the more felicitous connotations of the distinction between transcendence and immanence—those that give the distinction its heuristic purchase on Ifá in the first place. As we saw in the previous chapter, the concepts of transcendence and immanence capture abiding ideas in Ifá about qualitatively different manifestations of the divinities—from the larger-than-life majesty of the orichas as depicted in the mythological "beyond" of the absolute past (or the sky), to their matter-of-fact appearance in the here-and-now, through the consecrated enactments of ritual, including, of course, divination. Thinking of the divinities as motions does not in itself do justice to these qualitative differences. On their own, after all, the spatial connotations of motion might suggest that the passage from transcendence to immanence is merely a matter of physical translation, from (or, better, as) somewhere far away, say, to (or as) somewhere near.

To get to the irreducibly qualitative characteristics of the motions in and as which the deities manifest themselves, I suggest, we may dwell further on the idea of potentiality which, as we saw, the notion of motion already entails. In particular, it pays to explore this idea in relation to a series of arguments developed by Eduardo Viveiros de Castro and Marcio Goldman, on the "virtuality" of Amerindian and Afro-Brazilian cosmologies respectively (Viveiros de Castro 1998a, 1998b, 2002, 2005, 2007; Goldman 2005, 2007). As we shall see, drawing on Deleuzian conceptions of "virtuality," "difference," and "becoming" (e.g., Deleuze 1994), Viveiros de Castro and Goldman develop sophisticated analyses of the role of "potential relations" in these cosmological contexts, which serve as comparative references for sharpening our own analysis of motility, and its particular potentials in Ifá.

Viveiros de Castro and Goldman's analyses of these cosmologies turns on a figure-ground reversal that closely parallels the logical reversal powder just performed for us here. Their point (and I paraphrase wildly across texts for the sake of brevity) can be summarized as follows. Anthropologists tend to describe the cosmologies they study as systems of classification. The assumption is that cosmologies are populated by different entities (gods, ancestors, spirits, and so on) that relate to one another in different ways (hierarchically, genealogically, temperamentally, or whatever). Cosmologies can be "charted" by placing these entities in relation to each other in conceptual space—or, indeed, on paper—according to their differences, characterizing their relations in the spaces that are provided—notionally or graphically—between them. Now, try imagining a figure-ground reversal on such a chart, as in an Escher sketch. Cosmological elements now do not feature as self-identical marks relating to each other externally in space (the "scheme," the "paper"), but are rather extended across the spaces that previously divided them. What was assumed to be a scheme of entities now appears as a field of relations, so that the differences that previously distinguished one cosmological element from another extensively now become intensive characteristics of those elements themselves, which are therefore best conceived of as self-differentiating relations. Showing that such a plane of immanence underlies pan-Amerindian notions of myth, spirits, and shamanism, Viveiros de Castro writes:

> [T]he actants of origin myths are defined by their intrinsic capacity to be something else; in this sense, each mythic being differs infinitely from itself, given that it is posited by mythic discourse only to be substituted, that is, transformed. It is this self-difference which defines a "spirit," and which makes all mythic beings into "spirits" too. . . . In sum, myth posits an ontological regime commanded by a fluent intensive difference which incides on each point of a heterogenic continuum, where transformation is anterior to form, relation is superior to terms, and interval is interior to being. (2007, 158)

While Viveiros de Castro does not add the priority of motion over rest to his list, it is clear that such a logical reversal, which I have argued is necessary to make sense of the "intrinsic capacity," in his terms, of Ifá deities to move from transcendence to immanence, is confluent with his argument. Furthermore, the role he has given elsewhere to Amerindian mana-concepts as a premise for what he calls the "transductivity" (161) of spirits and other virtual becomings is largely analogous to the role of aché as a premise for the motility of Ifá "paths" in divination (see Viveiros de Castro 1998a, 79–83, cf. Gray 1996).

A full discussion of these analogies and their possible breakdowns would involve far-reaching comparisons between Amerindian animism and Afro-American polytheism—spirits versus deities, so to speak. Here I shall only use the analogy with Viveiros de Castro's argument on virtuality to make two points—one positive and one negative—that may help to sharpen my own argument on motility. Both points pertain to the question as to how Viveiros de Castro's use of the concept of intensive difference fairs in relation to the problem of deities' transcendence in Ifá, which, as we saw, aché has the power to solve.

First, it will be noted that the point of analogy between the virtual and the motile lies precisely in the idea of potentiality, which is a common corollary of both. As we have seen, if aché forces us to conceive of the oddu of Ifá as motions, it also allows us to think of the oddu as having the potential to take an immanent form in divination, so as to enter into relations with the babalawos that invoke them. In this sense, being motions, oddu are also potential relations, as Viveiros de Castro conceives of them. Analogously, if for Viveiros de Castro spirits are virtual in the sense that they are self-differential, then they too should be construed as potential relations inasmuch as their self-difference just amounts to their inherent potential to "be something other than themselves"—to recall a formulation by Lévy-Bruhl (1926, 76). Indeed, more than just analogous, these two senses of potential relation stand in a relationship of logical implication. For the oddu's potential to enter into relations with humans is *premised* on what Viveiros de Castro calls self-difference. Oddu do not simply travel from the beyond of mythical transcendence to the here of the divining board, for their motion is not one of a self-identical entity. As we have seen, the capacity of oddu to reveal themselves in divination implies a transformation, which resembles the one Viveiros de Castro envisages for Amerindian spirits (although there are contrasts, too, as will be argued presently). Be they conceived as paths of Orula or as deities in their own right, the oddu are posited as characters that live somewhere in the beyond as variable mythical guises, only to be "substituted"—to use Viveiros de Castro's term—during the divinatory ceremony, first as configurations of the palm-nuts and then as marks on the aché powder. In other words, oddu can relate to others, and particularly to human others, just because they can "other" themselves, inasmuch as their motion from transcendence to immanence is premised on their capacity virtually to self-differentiate.

The upshot of this is that the motility of the oddu as they emerge on the divining board should be conceived in a way that merges the spatial connotations of motion with the ontological ones of self-transformation. Aché, then, is the motile space in which ontological transformations happen, and its role on the divining board as a register for the emergence of the oddu through movement is also ontological through and through. In the motile universe of Ifá, the very act of registro on the surface of the divining board, as the babalawo's fingers move through the powder to reveal the oddu, is not an *ex post facto* representation of an already pertaining state of affairs, but rather an act of ontological transformation in its own right, for it is in this act that the oddu "comes out" and is registered as an immanent presence in the divination.

Indeed, such an analysis of aché as both premise and catalyst of transformation can arguably be generalized in Ifá beyond the immediate context of divination. The point can be put with reference to an argument presented by Goldman, regarding what he sees as three distinguishable "logics" or "dimensions" of Candomblé, the Afro-Brazilian cousin of Santería and Ifá.[12] First, Goldman argues, Candomblé involves what he calls a "cosmology," based on a complex system of "metaphoric" classifications.[13] Second, it involves an "anthropology," which places humans amid these classificatory schemes by means of series of ritual substitutions associated with the "metonymic" identifications of sacrifice and possession. And third, it involves a ritualistic logic of "manipulation" (Goldman 2005), in which metaphoric classifications and metonymic identifications are mobilized "pragmatically," as Goldman puts it, at the service of secret magical actions. While Goldman does not provide specific examples from Candomblé, his notion of "ritual manipulations" corresponds directly to what babalawos and santeros in Cuba call *trabajos* (lit. "works"). Witchcrafts in the strict sense of the word, these are covert operations in which varied magical ingredients are mixed and matched according to secret recipes, with a view to bringing about specific desired effects, ranging from the relatively benign (e.g., protection from sorcery, healing of illness) to the more interventionist (love magic, spells against enemies). Elaborating on Roger Bastide's claim that Candomblé practice is characterized by a "will to connect" (Bastide, cited in Goldman 2007, 116–7), Goldman argues that this magical savoir faire displays a logic of what Deleuze called "becoming," in the sense that it involves manipulations that deny "any possible substantial identity" (Goldman 2007, 113).

This logical inversion, which runs parallel to Viveiros de Castro's notion of self-difference, not only contrasts with both the "structural" (viz. metaphoric) logic of Candomblé cosmological classifications and the "serial" (viz. metonymic) logic of Candomblé "anthropology," but also ultimately encompasses both of them. For, as Goldman argues, as soon as one takes into account the focal significance of witchcraft in the practice of Candomblé, one is forced to conclude that the intellectual stipulations of Candomblé cosmology and anthropology are only posited in order to be transformed (to use Viveiros de Castro's language) in the pragmatics of witchcraft, "working as supporting bridges or trampolines for action and creation" (Goldman 2007, 118).

Goldman's thesis about the deterritorialization, as he calls it, of categories in Candomblé witchcraft is fully transposable to the context of Ifá. Indeed, arguably, the implication of Goldman's argument is not so much that the becoming of witchcraft needs to be added as the third and most characteristic dimension of Candomblé logic, alongside the categorial dimensions of "structure" and "series" that it trumps, but rather that the fact that witchcraft *appears* transgressive when placed alongside categorial logic just shows the latter up as an inappropriate analytical frame for understanding Candomblé in the first place (and Ifá by the same token). So the point is not that witchcraft becomings contradict cosmological structures and anthropological series, but rather that the assumption that the latter pair (let alone witchcraft itself) can be understood in terms of structures or series of self-identical categories was wrong from the start. Goldman himself suggests such an interpretation of his argument when he recalls Bastide's observation that Candomblé classifications "are not like our own," inasmuch as they do not operate over entities but rather over "forces and participations" (Bastide, cited in Goldman 2007, 116).

All this would indicate that the idea that in Ifá deities are best understood as motions—denying any possible substantial identity, to use Goldman's expression—can be extended beyond the context of divination as a general ontological premise. For present purposes the most pertinent ethnographic evidence for this has to do with the role of aché, as conceived by practitioners on this broader scale. Goldman touches on the issue at the very outset of his characterization of what he calls "Candomblé ontology":

> [This involves] a kind of monism that postulates the existence of a single *force* [called *ashe*[14]]. Modulations of *ashe* make up everything in existence and capable of existing in the universe according to a process of concretization,

diversification and individualization. Even the *orishas* themselves are no more than a manifestation of a specific modulation of ashe. The multifarious beings and things of the world, stones, plants, animals, human beings . . ., everything "belongs" to the orishas insofar as everything shares this force, simultaneously general and individualized. (Goldman 2007, 110)

Although babalawos in Cuba have not given me such a concerted cosmogony regarding aché, Goldman's synthesis corresponds directly to babalawos' common observation that the orichas and all their worldly manifestations "have aché." Indeed, in line with my earlier argument about aché in divination, we could supplement Goldman's account of aché as a diversified force by positing it also as the premise of diversification itself. Orichas "have aché" precisely to the extent that they are able, qua motions, to "become" the various elements of the world. These elements in turn, "belong" to the orichas just in the sense that they *are them*: they are varied outcomes of the oricha's motile becoming, and hence "have aché" also.

This, arguably, is the significance of the ritual requirement in Ifá (and Santería) that all consecrated items be physically "loaded" with aché powders. This includes not only babalawos' consecrated Orula and the divinatory objects that go with it, as described above, but also all the other deities practitioners receive as consecrated objects at different stages of their initiatory career, as well as the initiates themselves, who are ceremonially "marked" with aché powders at various parts of their body during initiation. Just as the powder babalawos use on their divining boards is powerful as a surface on which Orula's oddu can "come out" in the registro, so consecrated objects and the initiates' marked bodies are powerful ("have aché") as conduits that render the presence of the relevant orichas immanent, particularly as and when this is required in ritual.

Indeed, in the light of our earlier analysis of the role of powder as the pervious ground on which deities manifest literally as immanent figures, it makes sense that powder should also be the active ingredient of consecration. Admittedly, its role as motile ground here is not as graphic. Powder is not itself marked, but rather is either "loaded" in small portions into secret cavities of the consecrated objects associated with the deities, or indeed used to mark the bodies of neophytes. One is tempted to say that the power of these pinches of aché powder is metonymic, provided this is understood as a peculiarly "holographic" instance of metonymy (cf. Wagner 2001). Unlike ordinary metonymy in which a part comes to stand, symbolically, for the whole (e.g., crown for king), the pinches of powder that are used in consecration do not merely stand for the whole from which they are partitioned (which in the case of Ifá consecration is the same iyefá powder that is used, in larger quantities, to cover the divining board). Rather, they literally reconstitute it *as wholes in their own right*—and hence the "holographic" (in the sense of whole-for-whole) character of the metonymic relation. This follows from a second "prosaic" property of powder. As a pure multiplicity of particles, powder is not only pervious, as we saw, but also partible: even pinches of powder constitute wholes, inasmuch as no qualitative difference (other, that is, than quantity) distinguishes them from the wholes from which they were detached (cf. Reed 2007).[15] So, even though in consecration powder does not actually *display* motility as it does in divination, it does retain literally the property (viz. perviousness) that would allow motile deities to be rendered immanent, and thus is powerful in the same sense—albeit, of course, only in principle. Be that as it may, what is clear is that in consecration powder is power in the same sense as it is in divination, namely as a catalyst for the ontological transformation of the orichas, from the transcendence of the "beyond" to immanence in (and as) the consecrated items.

Nevertheless—and moving on to a second point of comparison with Viveiros de Castro's notion of self-difference—it should be noted that the kind of ontological transformation that is at stake in Ifá is in significant ways different from the ones Viveiros de Castro has in mind in the Amerindian context. With reference to Stephen Hugh-Jones's distinction between "horizontal" and "vertical" types of Amazonian shamanism—the former associated, among other features, with hunting, affinity, warfare, reciprocity and anarchic or egalitarian social relations, and the latter with gathering, descent, internal cohesion, heredity and hierarchical social reproduction (1996)—Viveiros de Castro implies that the tendencies of his argument about the virtuality of spirits are "horizontal"(2007, 156). By contrast, Ifá in many ways resembles Hugh-Jones's analysis of vertical shamanism. For example, as we have seen at length, Ifá worship is structured hierarchically, based on the regal prestige of initiation and training in mythical knowledge, with ritual families reproducing themselves along lineage branches, involving principles of ritual kinship, heredity, and so on (cf. Hugh-Jones 1996, 32–47).

Indeed, projected beyond Hugh-Jones's immediate concern with shamanic (or, in our case, divinatory) practice, the contrast between horizontal and vertical cosmological arrangements captures an important difference between Amerindian spirits and Ifá deities. Viveiros de Castro's account of spirits is "horizontal" inasmuch as it is essentially anarchic. Spirits are conceived as endlessly multiplying, like "forests of mirrors," as he writes, and their multiplicity is irreducibly qualitative inasmuch as it implies "modulations of form"–of *ontic* form, we might say, mutating from species to species, from animal to human, minuteness to monstrosity (Viveiros de Castro 2007, 161). Ifá, on the other hand, in accordance with its imperial associations in West Africa, presents the question of deities' potential for transformation in irreducibly vertical or, as practitioners also put it, "hierarchical" terms (e.g., *la jerarquía de los orichas*). What I have in mind here is not primarily the much-debated ranking of deities in the form of a systematic pantheon, whose historical evolution, as David Brown has argued convincingly, is heavily bound up with Christian and other theologizing influences both in Africa and in Cuba (Brown 2003, 114–28; see also Peel 2000).[16] Rather, what makes Ifá vertical is the cosmological premise upon which such rankings are conceived, namely the idea that deities can be characterized by their degree of distance from the human world, which recalls our earlier discussion of transcendence. Brown writes:

[R]ankings along the spirit–matter continuum can be flexible and ambiguous. For example, Echu is, in fact, "everywhere and sees everything": he is a "warrior" of the highly "material" street and forest; he is also right up there as "God's secretary"; at the same time, he is not merely a "mischievous" oricha but is, in one road [viz. "path"], Alosí, the Devil, who manifests himself in this world. . . . Obatalá [sky deity, patron of peace], too, defies ontological confinement. Numerous relatively more "material" and more "spiritual" Obatalás, who are "younger" warrior types or "older" sage types, respectively, populate this continuum. (2003, 127)

So if the orichas are as multiple as Amazonian spirits, each of their paths taking a different ontic form, their multiplicity is nevertheless vertically distributed. They differ from the Amazonian paradigm in that their ontic transformations also imply shifts in what one might call ontological status, since their multiple becomings are inflected hierarchically as a continuum of relatively proximate and relatively distant manifestations. Indeed, the distinction between shifts of ontic form and of ontological status allows us to conceptualize the difference between (horizontal) shamanism and divination, as the respective modes of divine disclosure in Amazonia and in Ifá. The shamanic ability to "call spirits," explains Viveiros de Castro, is a matter of "vision": where nonshamans just see animals in the forest, for example, shamans see spirits (Viveiros de Castro 2007; cf. Pedersen 2007a, 2007b). This makes sense, since the "problem" that spirits present to humans is that there is more to them than meets the nonshamanic eye—qua intensive differences, they are always more than the sum of their ontic snapshot appearances (e.g., the forest animals, which are just a form of their becoming). The problem with the orichas, on the other hand, is not so much that they are invisible but rather that they are not fully "here" in the first place. After all, insofar as the orichas are visible at all, it takes no special powers to see them. The consecrated objects in which they manifest ceremonially, the natural features of which they are patrons, the devotees whose bodies they possess during Santería rituals, as well as the aché powder that Orula marks during divination—all these concretions are there for all to see. The problem is how to elicit the deities' presence in these concrete forms—how to elicit immanence, having posited transcendence. One might say that if the shaman's task is to see what is present, the diviner's is to render present what is already seen.

It follows that while Viveiros de Castro's notion of intensive difference is presupposed by the idea of motility, such a notion is nevertheless insufficient on its own to account for the peculiar verticality of Ifá deities' ontological transformations—Ifá's version of the problem of transcendence. In particular, conceived with reference to the horizontal dimensions of Amerindian shamanism, the distance admitted by this model of virtual becoming is not of a kind that allows us fully to make sense of deities' transcendence in Ifá. A matter of ontic form rather than ontological status, the potentiality of virtual spirits in Amazonia is that of transforming themselves horizontally into what they are not ("becoming-other"), whereas the vertical axis of transcendence to immanence that is so characteristic of Ifá implies transformations that are also constituted as shifts between *orders* of otherness ("becoming-other-kinds-of-other," if you like).

The idea of motility is able analytically to capture these differences between difference. For by distributing virtual becomings across a continuum of *motion*, with its peculiar capacity to self-scale, in terms of the formal relations of distance and proximity (which, as we have seen, the notion of direction implies), we effectively add a second dimension to the concept of becoming itself. Perhaps the clearest way to express this is in terms of the structuralist distinction between syntagmatic and paradigmatic relations (see also Holbraad and Willerslev 2007). Virtual continua relate differences paradigmatically, piling the speciated becomings up as

alternative versions of each other. Motile ones relate them syntagmati-
cally, which is to say that they relate them ordinally, in sequences that
provide them direction in terms of asymmetrical (positional) relations
of before and after. So, no less intensive than their virtual counterparts,
motile differences are nevertheless more complex from a logical point of
view, in that they are able to render two dimensions of difference—paradigmatic form and syntagmatic position—at once. Both dimensions are
needed in order to articulate the problem of transcendence, which, as we
have seen, is so central to Ifá cosmology. Motile deities' transformations
allow them to enter into relations with humans. And the fact that these
transformations scale themselves as changes of ontological status shows
that deity–human relations are not given as cosmological fait accompli
(as virtual relations that are there for those who can see them, as in horizontal shamanism), but rather have to be *accomplished* by transforming
the deities along an intensive, self-differentiating axis that runs from the
relative ontological distance of transcendence to the relative proximity of
immanence. Accomplishing such an ontological transformation of Orula
in particular, in the form of oddu that "come out" on the tablero so that
the babalawo can "speak" them for the beneft of the consultant, is the
ceremonial sine qua non of the process of divinatory consultation. This
process, in which babalawos' trademark claims to truth are brockered, is
the topic of the following two chapters.

Divinatory Metamorphosis: Symbolism, Interpretation, and the Motility of Meaning

Reviewing some of the more influential theoretical perspectives on divination, in chapter 2, I criticized the idea that divinatory truth may be accounted for with reference to the "interpretative openness" that divinatory verdicts sometimes display. When it comes to divination, truth cannot be seen simply as a product of the processes of interpretation that diviners and their clients undergo, since these processes are themselves premised on the idea that their outcomes are true. With a view to advancing my own analysis of babalawos' claim to divinatory truth, I begin this chapter by returning to these ideas to examine a sophisticated version of the argument from interpretative openness, advanced by Dan Sperber. The reason for doing so is partly that Sperber's analysis seems to meet my quick dismissal of cruder appeals to interpretation, though I shall argue that ultimately it does not. More important, however, a critique of Sperber's approach serves as a way of engaging with (rather than just bypassing) the question of interpretation, which is so central to the practice of Ifá. In particular, Sperber's work serves as an entry into a strong anthropological tradition, most prominently developed in his native France, of relating questions of symbolism with formally defined notions about the fluidity of meaning. I am thinking here particularly of Lévi-Strauss's concept of the "floating signifier," which he famously invoked in his commentary on Mauss's discussion of mana.

My return to these classic anthropological debates is motivated by a conundrum that the intimate relationship between interpretation and truth in Ifá divination seems to pose. On the one hand, divinatory truth does indeed emerge out of diviners' copious and skillful efforts at interpretation. The whole success of divination, as babalawos themselves emphasize explicitly, turns on the diviner's ability to interpret the myths of Ifá so as to bring them to bear on the consultant's personal circumstances, and this, as we shall see, can involve a great degree of interpretative laxity on their part, often involving input from the consultant, too. So it would appear that the kind of interpretative openness that Sperber and others emphasize in their analyses does indeed play an important role in babalawos' claims to divinatory truth. On the other hand, however, the role of interpretation in this context is demonstrably *not* the one that arguments from ambiguity such as Sperber's posit. As I shall show with detailed reference to my ethnography of divinatory consultations in Javier's home, babalawos' rhetorical skills are not designed to exploit a putative ambiguity of divinatory pronouncements (the kind of ambiguity, for example, famously ascribed to Pythia's pronouncements at Apollo's oracle at Delphi). Quite the contrary: babalawos' concern is to use the interpretative scope that the divinatory process allows them in order to formulate precise and transparent verdicts that are shown to have direct bearing on their consultants' personal circumstances—verdicts that, as practitioners say, "get to the point." Crucially, the interpretative process by which such verdicts emerge turns not on an inherent ambiguity of the meanings interpreted but rather on their peculiar *fluidity*. To anticipate an expression Javier used when explaining this to me, babalawos' ability to arrive interpretatively at "the truth of things" relies on their skill at "metamorphosing" meanings.

In following chapters I shall connect this ethnographic point to the discussion of the motile ontology of Ifá divination already advanced, in order to show that as an outcome of interpretative metamorphosis divinatory truth itself must be conceptualized in motile terms, as an event. So my critical commentary on the French debate about meaning and its fluidity here is meant, not only to set the terms of my engagement with divinatory interpretation in the latter half of this chapter, but also to prepare the ground for a motile analysis of truth in the chapters that follow. In particular, my aim is to turn the idea of "floating signifiers" on its head for my own purposes. As we shall see, the brunt of Lévi-Strauss's analysis of symbolism—and, after him, Sperber's—is that its mercurial character is due to the fact that symbols, as such, have no meaning and can therefore come to signify anything. By contrast, I want to argue that the data that Lévi-Strauss and Sperber want to call symbolic are characterized by an excess, rather than a lack, of meaning, and thus resist any attempt at symbolic capture. This inherent motility of meaning, as we shall see later, lies at the heart of the processes of interpretation through which babalawos arrive at truth in divination.

The Problem of Symbolism and the Motility of Meaning

In his famous essay on "apparently irrational beliefs" (1985), Sperber advances what he calls a "rationalist" approach to answer the old question as to why people often take the most outlandish data to be true (see also chapter 2). His argument involves two central claims. The first is that strange data (here think of any statement that invites the gloss "symbolic," such as "twins are birds" or divinatory verdicts) are not really as strange as they appear. They are, in fact, just the products of human cognitive mechanisms that allow for learning and creativity, and in particular abilities that involve the human mind's capacity to "store" ideas that are not fully understood (1985, 51). For example, in learning, say, Sperber's theory of symbolism, I may well take it as true that Aborigine clan names (or, indeed, divinatory verdicts) are "symbolic" without being entirely clear as to what the claim amounts to, perhaps because I have not yet fully understood Sperber's definition of symbolism. Similarly, a babalawo's client may be told a more-or-less opaque mythical path of an oddu during a divination and consider it a true account of her own situation without being quite sure how to interpret it. Both cases for Sperber are examples of how people are able to hold representations that have no clear-cut truth-value, since they fall short of having a fully specified meaning. As philosophers might say, such representations do not pick out one and only one proposition.

What is interesting in this claim about the "semi-propositional" character of symbolic representations—this being Sperber's technical term—is that it divests the onus of interpretation from anthropological analysis. To the extent that the meaning of symbolic data such as totemic clan names or divinatory verdicts is opaque by cognitive design, so to speak, anthropologists' attempts at symbolic analysis, that is, attempts to specify one correct meaning over others, are just trips to a never-never land of overinterpretation (Sperber 1975, 48). Interpretation, rather, should be treated as a concern for our informants. Inasmuch as hazy symbolic data are indeed of interest to them, as divinatory verdicts are to diviners and their clients,

they are necessarily subject to interpretation. And such processes of interpretation may well be open-ended, never reaching a definite conclusion,
since the symbolic material to which they are directed may resist being
pinned down propositionally at all. Sperber writes:

> The relativist slogan, the teaching of a Zen master, the philosophy of Kierke-
> gaard, and, generally, poetic texts, [have] content [that] is semi-propositional
> from the start. The speaker's or author's intention is not to convey a specific
> proposition. It is to provide a range of possible interpretations, and to incite
> hearers or readers to search that range for the interpretations most relevant to
> them. The ideas that come as by-products of this search may suffice to make it
> worthwhile, particularly when no final interpretation is ever arrived at. (53)

This certainly captures what goes on in Ifá very well. As we shall see in
detail presently, babalawos themselves are keen to emphasize that a successful divination depends on the diviner's skill in "interpreting" (this is
the word they use—*interpretar*) the paths of oddu given by Orula during
the divination in light of the consultant's circumstances. Moreover, while
babalawos' interpretations are unequivocal in many cases (not least when
it comes to the kinds of regulative matters of initiation, sacrifice, and so on
that were discussed in chapter 3), in others they are understood as being
amenable to continued reinterpretation. Babalawos' taste for "speaking
Ifá"—the quasi-competitive displays of mythical learning in which they
like to engage when they meet—is a prime example. Their ability to re-
fract mundane events through the divinatory mythology of Ifá relies partly
on using their knowledge of relevant divinations as a resource for continual
reinterpretation. Thus, the fugitive babalawo of Javier's godson's story, to
return to the example of "talking Ifá" recounted in chapter 3, was deemed
to be pretending to be dead with reference to the myth about the lion's
funeral that is associated with the man's initiatory signo. Furthermore, as
we shall see, consultants too may reassign meaning to the divinations they
are given by babalawos long after the ritual is done, in light of changing
circumstances that may lend themselves to this kind of hindsight.

Less compelling, however, is Sperber's second move, in which he uses
the notion of semi-propositionality to advance an explanation of symbolic "beliefs." His starting premise is that symbolic data, being semi-
propositional, have no clear-cut truth-value. Since their meaning is hazy
and underspecified in the first place, it is impossible to pin a particular
truth-value on them, true or false. Paradoxically, Sperber suggests, it is just

this ambiguity that allows people to entertain symbolic data as being true. For if symbolic material has no truth-value, then it is a fortiori unfalsifiable. In itself, of course, this is no grounds for supposing that it be taken as true, or "believed," but it does leave the door open, as it were, for the possibility that people might do so. To show how this might work, Sperber makes a distinction between beliefs that are simply represented as facts (e.g., "x is a woman," "roses are red") and beliefs that are represented as commitments to a representation, that is, beliefs about beliefs ("it is true that 'sp,'" where sp stands for a semi-proposition—e.g., "it is true that 'x is a witch,'" "it is true that 'divinatory verdicts are symbolic'"). The former type of belief he calls "factual" and the latter "representational." The point, then, about symbolic data is that they involve representational rather than factual commitment. The analytical advantage gained here is that symbolic data can be entertained as true as long as the representational beliefs within which they are embedded are deemed true, and this latter ascription of truth may have nothing to do with the nature of the embedded belief itself. So, for example, I can reasonably believe that "it is true that 'divinatory verdicts are symbolic'" not on the grounds that I fully understand and assent to the embedded semi proposition ('divinatory verdicts are symbolic') myself, but rather because Sperber and his French ancestors say so, and, since I admire them, I am inclined to trust their anthropological judgment. Similarly for divination:

> What may make it rational to hold a representational belief of semi-propositional content is evidence on its source. Suppose I have plenty of evidence that my parents are truthful, and they tell me that the diviner is truthful but cryptic. Is it not rational, then, for me to believe factually that the diviner speaks the truth, to believe representationally what I understand him to say, and to interpret what he says in accordance with these beliefs? (Sperber 1985, 56)

Now, in chapter 2 we mentioned one criticism of this analysis, due to Boyer, namely that rendering data like divinatory verdicts "rational" cannot in itself be sufficient as a strategy for showing why such data are actually taken as true. Plenty of data that are not, as a matter of fact, taken to be true by anyone—"pigs can fly"—could be shown to be rational on the same grounds (Boyer 1990, 53–54). Furthermore, the appeal to traditional authority (diviners' or others') is transparently subject to an objection from infinite regress. Sure, verdicts may be taken to be true on the grounds that they are divinatory. But why are divinatory verdicts taken to

be true? Because practitioners have it on good authority that they are—
their parents' perhaps. But why do the parents deem them true? Because
of their parents in turn. And so on. Practitioners, on this account, emerge
as either arbitrary or simple.

But there are larger issues at stake in Sperber's analysis. It will be evident from what has been said so far that Sperber's approach to symbolism
is antisemiological, in the sense that for him symbolism "is not a means of
encoding information, but a means of organizing it" (1975, 70). For, as we
saw, on this view the distinguishing mark of a symbol is not in any sense
the peculiarity of its meaning, but precisely the fact that it has no determinate meaning, so that it can be said to function rather like a semantic
variable. Sperber himself indicates, somewhat obliquely, that this position
has its roots in Lévi-Strauss, though, as he emphasizes, Lévi-Strauss was
unable to take matters as far due partly to his insistence on viewing symbolic material on an analogy with language (1985, 84). This point is worth
dwelling upon because, I want to argue, it is by tracing steps from Sperber
back to Lévi-Strauss (from cognitivism to structuralism, so to speak) that
one comes to appreciate the real analytical stakes in the study of symbols
generally, as well as the study of Ifá in particular.

The scope of Sperber's critique is extensive, broaching all areas of inquiry for which Lévi-Strauss is famous (e.g., kinship, "totemism," myth),
areas that cannot be charted here (cf. Sperber 1975, chap. 3; 1985, chap. 3).
But we could make one observation that is, perhaps, in line with Sperber's
thinking. Whether dealing with marriage rules, totemic identifications,
mythical narratives, or what have you, the mark of Lévi-Straussian synthesis turns on the logical priority he gives to systems of relations over dy-
adic correspondences (Lévi-Strauss 1963, 1964, 1966). The maxim is well
known: You look at totemism? Don't expect to get far by wondering what
makes some clan identify with a bear. Look at the systemic relationships
between bears and eagles (and turtles and fishes . . .), and *then* look at the
corresponding relationships between clan A and clan B (and C and D . . .).
However, taken in itself, and notwithstanding Lévi-Strauss's signifier/sig-
nified talk, this conceptual move mediates analysis away from the question
of meaning. According to Sperber, this is because, at the last instance,
questions of meaning (or of "signification") just are questions about correspondences: to ask for the meaning of something is to ask for some other
thing to which it corresponds (an object, a proposition, a word, a sense,
or whatever—cf. Lévi-Strauss 1978, 12). Hence the integrative syntheses
with which structuralist method operates (viz. the compilation and organi-

zation of systems of signifiers) may at most be construed as preliminary to a process of *dis*integration, whereby appropriately positioned members of two or more series are coupled off with each other (signifier to signified). Only at that point would the question of meaning actually be broached. So, insofar as Lévi-Strauss seems to be orientated overwhelmingly toward the first, integrative stage of inquiry, his method seems to be incongruous with his professed goal of interpreting symbolic data. Indeed, as Sperber points out, the symptoms are evident in Lévi-Strauss's analyses:

> Faithful to the terminology of Saussure, [Lévi-Strauss] tends to refer to symbolic phenomena as "signifiers," and one might assume that the investigation is into an underlying code which pairs these signifiers with their "signifieds." Yet, if readers begin looking for the signifieds, they soon realize that the underlying code relates signifiers to other signifiers: there *are* no signifieds. Everything is meaningful, nothing is meant. (1985, 72)

Sperber's solution to the paradox, as we saw, is to do away with the edifice of signification in order to be left with what he takes as Lévi-Strauss's core insight, namely the idea that symbols are best understood in terms of their function (for Sperber a cognitive function) rather than in terms of their meaning (cf. Hénaff 1998, 135–40). I want to take the paradox in a different direction, not least for the simple reason that questions of meaning and interpretation have such pride of place in the practice of Ifá divination, and hence it seems to me that some space must be found for them in analysis, too. It is expedient to sketch out my alternative with reference—or, better, in opposition—to that part of Lévi-Strauss's work that renders the paradox between semiological ends and structuralist means most apparent, namely his discussion of "floating signifiers." Indeed, it is remarkable that in his sustained critiques of structuralism, Sperber omits discussion of the third chapter of *Introduction to the Work of Marcel Mauss*, a *locus classicus* for Lévi-Strauss's thoughts on the meaning of symbols (Lévi-Strauss 1987).

The notion of "floating signifiers" is germane to the question of meaning because it springs from a problematization of the relationship between signifying and signified series.[1] Indeed, I would argue that from the point of view of Lévi-Strauss's theoretical framework, floating signifiers serve to resolve the incongruity between structuralist means and semiological ends. Such a position, however, runs counter to Lévi-Strauss's analysis, since he prefers to project this incongruity as a general problem relating to human evolution (rather than a function of his own theoretical perspective). He puts the problem in terms of a distinction between "symbolism" (which he confusingly interchanges with "language") and "knowledge," in a famous and difficult passage that merits long quotation:

> Whatever may have been the moment and the circumstances of its appearance in the ascent of animal life, language can only have arisen all at once. Things cannot have begun to signify gradually. In the wake of a transformation which is not a subject of study for the social sciences, but for biology and psychology, a shift occurred from a stage when nothing had a meaning to another stage when everything had meaning. Actually, that apparently banal remark is important, because the radical change has no counterpart in the field of knowledge, which develops slowly and progressively. In other words, at the moment when the entire universe all at once became *significant*, it was none the better *known* for being so, even if it is true that the emergence of language must have hastened the rhythm of the development of knowledge. So there is a fundamental opposition, in the history of the human mind, between symbolism, which is characteristically discontinuous, and knowledge, characterised by continuity. . . . It follows that the two categories of the signifier and the signified came to be constituted simultaneously and interdependently, as complementary units; whereas knowledge, that is, the intellectual process which enables us to identify certain aspects of the signifier and certain aspects of the signified, one by reference to the other—we could even say the process which enables us to choose, from the entirety of the signifier and from the entirety of the signified, those parts which present the most satisfying relations of mutual agreement—only got started very slowly. (1987, 59–60; emphases in the original)

The originary/evolutionary dimension may be kept between brackets for present purposes. What is important is Lévi-Strauss's tacit distinction between "having" meaning and "knowing" meaning. All symbols have meaning, he seems to be saying, by virtue of their structural position within a system of (yet more) symbols. In this sense, inasmuch as things like language are systems of symbols, they must come about wholesale, as systems—and hence what Maurice Godelier, in a commentary on Lévi-Strauss, calls the "big bang" theory of meaning (Godelier 1999, 23). However, the meaning of each symbol is not necessarily known. This, it seems, is because the meaning of a symbol is not the type of thing that can be known by gauging relations to other symbols in the system. Rather it is known through a process of comparative coupling: signifier to signified, word to world. And since this process cannot but be piecemeal for "finite" beings, we can speak of a "continuous" accumulation of knowledge.

Thus set up, the problem of meaning presents an intriguing paradox, one that Lévi-Strauss eagerly bites into. Given the intentional character of symbols—their being "about" things—a signifying series (or "system") implies a fortiori a corresponding signified one. This is what I take to be Lévi-Strauss's point when he asserts, in the quote above, that signifier and signified are "constituted simultaneously and interdependently, as complementary units." However, even though the concept of signification implies that this correspondence be constituted "all at once," knowledge, with its laborious bit-for-bit coordinations, lags behind ineluctably at actually *establishing* that correspondence. So there is a circle to be squared here. How can knowledge both presuppose and produce correspondence? How, indeed, can two series (signifier and signified) be both isomorphic and asymptotic?

Lévi-Strauss's solution comes in two moves. First, he divests himself of responsibility by casting the problem in terms of the "human condition," as I already pointed out:

> [A] fundamental situation perseveres which arises out of the human condition: namely, that man has from the start had at his disposition a signifier-totality which he is at a loss to know how to allocate to a signified, given as such, but no less unknown for being given. There is always a non-equivalence or "inadequation" between the two, a non-fit and overspill which divine understanding alone can soak up; this generates a signifier-surfeit relative to the signifieds to which it can be fitted. (1987, 62)

Lévi-Strauss's second move is acrobatic and can be explained as follows. If the signifier series is characterized by an excess of meaning relative to the corresponding signifieds, and if the correspondence must nevertheless be maintained, then, from a formal point of view, an open option is to add a second dimension to the one-dimensional series of signifiers, so as to accommodate the overflow of meaning. And, given that for Lévi-Strauss this overflow is determined temporally, as a time-hiatus folding instantaneous signification over a piecemeal accumulation of "knowledge," it makes sense to posit that extra dimension as a temporal one. Thus, the expansion of the signifier series across time allows for *change* in the semantic content of signifiers, that is, a serial (viz. temporal) revaluation of signifiers at different times. In this sense signifiers are seen as having the capacity to "float" relative to corresponding signifieds, without being anchored to any one of them permanently. We arrive, then, at a position that is remarkably close to Sperber's, whereby a class of "signifiers" (or "representations") is given the peculiar characteristic of being able to mean various different things at different times because inherently they mean nothing in particular. Moreover, Lévi-Strauss and Sperber agree that the kinds of data anthropologists usually call symbolic, and in particular data related to magic, myth, mystical knowledge and so on, belong to that class.

There are many difficulties with this view (for a wide-ranging critique see Godelier 1999, 23–29). Staying at Lévi-Strauss's abstract level of exposition, however, the central problem is this. Say we accept the conceptual tools that Lévi-Strauss brings to his argument (such as signification, systemic matrices, and knowledge by semantic correspondence), but strive to stay neutral as to what theoretical agenda these concepts should be mobilized for. From such a standpoint, Lévi-Strauss's choice to bridge the gap between having meaning (signifying series) and knowing meaning (signifier-signified correspondence) by floating the *signifiers* appears arbitrary at least. A converse solution seems just as effective. For one may well follow Lévi-Strauss in saying that signifying and signified series are interdependent from the start (due to the intentional structure of signification, as we saw), and then proceed to locate the swelling of meaning at the level of the signified rather than that of the signifier. On this view, change and instability (the "float") would not be a function of relations of signification, but would become rather a property of the signified, the *floated signified*, as Gilles Deleuze puts it (1990a, 49). Or, to express the point in terms of the signifying series also, the possibility of change would not be appended as a byproduct of a "symbolic function," but rather instated as a part of symbolic meaning itself: change would not be *of* the meaning, it would *be* the meaning. Consequently, the paradoxical time-lag between signification and knowledge that lies at the heart of Lévi-Strauss's analysis would be rendered in terms of the difficulty of designating inherently *fluid signifieds* by means of *stable signifiers*. Indeed, insofar as "knowledge" is understood, with Lévi-Strauss, as the piecemeal identification of stable signifier-signified correspondences, then it would entail a cumulative *loss* of meaning since such correspondences would be established at the expense of the fluidity of the signified. To "know" symbolic data, then, would be necessarily to misrecognize them as being in a state of rest— knowledge by arrest, if you like.

The main advantage of this alternative analysis of symbolism is that it

sticks rather closer to the way symbols are understood by those who entertain them. Consider the main object of Lévi-Strauss's discussion, namely
the Oceanic concept of mana, which we have already encountered in the
discussion of aché (mana's West African and Afro-American cousin) in
the previous chapter. Drawing on Mauss's discussion, as we saw, Lévi-
Strauss is impressed by polysemy—"the apparently insoluble antinomies
attaching to the notion of mana" (Lévi-Strauss 1987, 64). For him, this
extreme malleability of mana-concepts makes them prime examples of
floating signifiers:

> Force and action; quality and state; substantive, adjective and verb all at once;
> abstract and concrete; omnipresent and localized. . . . Indeed *mana* is all those
> things together; but is that not precisely because it is none of those things, but a
> simple form, or to be more accurate, a symbol in its pure state, therefore liable
> to take on any symbolic content whatever? (1987, 64)

Well, not necessarily. Mauss's seminal phenomenology of mana need not
be inverted in such a way—or not, at least, without a structuralist axe
to grind (cf. Mauss 2001, 133–49). Why not take mana-concepts at face
value by interpreting their polysemy as a function of the fluidity of mana
itself? If, in speaking to ethnographers or to each other, Austronesians
were prepared to mention/attribute/perceive (words fail!) mana in a variety of contexts, then it is fair to assume that for them mana just was the
type of thing/quality/relation that can be relevant in all these different
contexts—relevant, moreover, in similar or different ways in each case.
This does not make mana-talk less meaningful, but more so.[2]

   Such a suggestion would also accord with the conclusions we reached
in the previous chapter with respect to aché. As we saw, the manifest polysemy of aché—both power and powder—is a function not of a lack of
meaning but of an excess of it. What makes aché so powerful is precisely
the fact that it transgresses distinctions one might otherwise take to be
axiomatic, including the very dualities that underlie Lévi-Strauss's attempt
to analyze mana-terms, such as signifier versus signified, language versus
world, concept versus object, and so on. As people in Oceania might put
it, mana-terms are "too hot to handle" (Mauss 2001; cf. Sahlins 1985,
18–19). And as we also saw, the transgressive character of these terms
forces upon us the analytical shift toward the idea of motility. Thought of
as self-differentiating motions rather than self-identical entities, notions
such as aché or mana can be deemed to be *both* force and action, quality

and state, concept and object, with no logical contradiction. Indeed, to
the extent that the structuralist distinction between signifier and signified
can be added to the list of binaries that the motile self-differentiations of
mana transgress, we may note that ultimately the choice between floating
signifiers and floated signifieds, which I have used to gain a critical vantage
on Lévi-Strauss's analysis, is itself also false. By virtue of its meaning *as*
float, mana floats "excessively" also across any divide between itself and
its putative signifiers: again, it is neither signifier nor signified because, qua
motile, it is both.

Taking, like Sperber, a cue from Lévi-Strauss's suggestion that mana-
terms demonstrate in extreme form the characteristics of all of the data
anthropologists have called symbolic, I now want to show that this kind of
motility is at the heart of the process by which babalawos are able to arrive
at truth during divination. As babalawos themselves emphasize, processes
of interpretation, which anthropologists would see as symbolic operations
par excellence, are at the heart of diviners' ability to arrive at true verdicts.
In the next chapter I shall argue that such an analysis of divinatory interpretation in Ifá demonstrates that the motility of these operations constitutes the major premise for an analysis of divinatory truth. As a function
of interpretation, divinatory truth itself has to be understood in motile
terms. In order to build toward this analysis, the rest of the present chapter
is devoted to exploring the role of interpretation in divinatory consultations, showing how the motility of meaning is so central to it. We may
begin by picking up the description of the divinatory ritual from where we
left off in chapter 4.

Interrogating Orula

Once the formal liturgy by which babalawos invoke Orula and his oddu
into presence is complete, and the principal oddu for the divination has
been "drawn" along with its two "witnesses," the babalawos proceed to
pose a series of specific questions to Orula. This is a part of the consultation that is referred to as "asking the hand," and involves the consultant
hiding selected objects (the so-called ibbo) in each of her hands. This process of interrogation may be illustrated by an extract from one of the many
consultations I witnessed in Javier's home. It was an ordinary consultation
conducted with the ókuele (the divining chain) for one of Javier's god-
daughters, a good friend of Javielito's and mine. She was a woman in her

thirties who had received kofá from the old man some months earlier, and was now saving up for her initiation into Santería as a daughter of Ochún, the sensual oricha of love and rivers. While Javier and Yolanda, as I shall call her, sat at the table, Javielito and I sat on Javier's bed, watching the proceedings. The consultation lasted almost an hour, which is not unusual for such proceedings. Here I present some extracts.[3] The principal oddu drawn for the consultation was Obbeyono:

JAVIER: [In a chanting, high pitched voice] Is she iré Orula? [casting the ókuele]. No. He says you are osobbo.

YOLANDA: Ai! I knew it already! [turning to Javielito and me].

JAVIER: Let's see what is happening to you. [chanting] *Ófo* (loss) Orula? [casts ókuele] No. [silence]

JAVIER: *Árun* (illness) Orula? [casts again] Yes. [turning to Javielito with concern]. He says yes . . . [turning to consultant] Orula says that your osobbo is of illness. [silence]

JAVIER: *Árun otonowa* (illness "from the sky," explained to me by Javielito as a "normal" form of illness) Orula? [casts] No.

JAVIER: *Kafetí lerí* (illness due to her own head) Orula? [casts] No.

JAVIER: *Ikan burukú otá* (sorcery) Orula? [casts] Yes! [to the consultant] He says sorcery. [silence]

JAVIER: Let's see who is going to protect her. *Ocha oniré* (is it one of "minor" deities who will bring her iré) Orula? [casts] No. [a number of questions follow asking individually for other divinities: Orula himself, Olokun (deity of deep waters), Eggun (spirits of dead), Oddua (creator god). All receive negative replies].

JAVIER: San Lázaro *oniré* Orúla? [casts] Yes.

YOLANDA: Is it San Lázaro[4] godfather?

JAVIER: He says yes.

YOLANDA: You know, they told me! The other day I was sitting by the sea at the Malecón [the seaside boulevard in Havana] and this woman came up to me [a stranger[5]] and told me that she could see an osobbo on top of me, but that I shouldn't worry thanks to San Lázaro. [To me:] Remember I told you?! How was it she said to me? I should go to cleanse myself (*hacer limpieza*) at the foot of San Lázaro or something like that, I didn't take much note.

JAVIER: Let's see if it is that. Is that what San Lázaro wants Orula? [casts] He says no. Let's see . . . Is there something that he wants Orula? [casts] Yes.

A total of six questions are asked trying to identify an acceptable offering (flowers, prayers, alcohol, tobacco, a larger sacrifice, coconut milk). This provokes some discussion between Javier and his son, as they both rake their brains to remember San Lázaro's likes and dislikes. Finally Javier hits upon it: the deity wishes the consultant to procure a consecrated necklace of San Lázaro (one made of maroon beads—his designated color, though there was some disagreement between the two men over this), and wear it for her protection from sorcery and illness.

JAVIER: [looking for his cigarettes] Well, now let's speak . . .

As Javier's line of questioning illustrates, babalawos are allowed some scope for maneuver during the interrogative stage of consultation. Within overall liturgical constraints on the form of the questioning (viz. starting with iré/osobbo, then determining the particular type of fortune involved, and so on), babalawos are free to make decisions of their own regarding both the order and content of the questions they ask of Orula. Babalawos themselves emphasize two considerations. First, questions should be posed in the light of the principal signo of the divination. For example, when it comes to identifying the deity responsible for the consultant's good or bad fortune, it makes sense to begin by asking about deities who are known to be closely connected to the oddu drawn. Such connections are made in the light of the content of the myths associated with the oddu in question, in which particular divinities may feature prominently. Second, the wider circumstances of the consultant may also be taken into consideration. Thus, if the consultant is known to practice Spiritism, the babalawo may begin by looking for her divine protection among spirits of the dead (*muertos*) rather than among the orichas. Or, to take a different example, should the babalawo be aware that the consultant has recently come into some money, he may well begin by asking Orula whether the consultant's iré or osobbo is related to financial matters. The input of such circumstantial considerations becomes all the more important when the diviner and his client know each other well, be it simply through previous interaction, perhaps in divinatory consultations, or often through stronger ritual bonds to do with initiation.

While, as babalawos openly acknowledge, such sources of information can be of great aid to specifying interpretatively the significance of any given divination, there is a further way in which circumstantial considerations come into play during consultations—one which babalawos tend to be less keen to discuss. As noted in chapter 3, even ordinary consultations have what I called a "regulative" aspect, in that the verdicts of the oracle may channel the consultant through to further rituals, including costly initiation ceremonies. Specific verdicts to this effect are understood as binding, and consultants ignore them at their peril. Inevitably, babalawos have an interest in persuading clients to undergo such rituals, both because of the large quantities of money involved and because of the prestige of acquiring godchildren in large numbers. Thus, it is not uncommon for babalawos to solicit divinatory verdicts prescribing further rituals by posing appropriate questions to the oracle, for example, early in the proceedings of the divination inquiring about possible initiatory steps (see Holbraad 2005). Javier's relatively modest proposals of offerings to San Lázaro in the above example, then, are not necessarily typical of babalawos' practices in general.

Be that as it may, the scope for babalawos' interpretative judgment becomes even wider in the next phase of the divinatory proceedings. Here babalawos begin to "speak the signo" (*hablar el signo*) of the divination, first recounting some of its mythical "paths" to the client, and then interpreting the significance of each for her or him. At this stage one might note an inverse correlation between liturgical structure and interpretative scope in the ritual as a whole. Although the consultant is expected to sit respectfully on her chair throughout the consultation, the babalawo for his part, by the time he comes to speak the signo, tends to adopt a more relaxed demeanor, perhaps getting up, pouring himself coffee or lighting a cigarette. In general, while earlier stages of the proceedings are kept deliberately formal, by the time the signo's paths begin to be recounted and interpreted, babalawos and their clients tend to interact more informally. Indeed, the consultation often lapses into ordinary conversation as, together, diviner and consultant work on interpreting the significance of the divination—a process in which *babalawos'* interpretative skills really come into their own.

"Speaking the Signo," "Interpreting the Paths"

"Ifá is interpretation, we always say that," Manolo, one of Javier's most successful godchildren, once told me. "In order to speak the signo it is not enough just to know the stories. You also have to know how to explain them, to make the point clear to people [the consultants]." A second extract of Yolanda's consultation with Javier may give an idea of the kind of activity to which Manolo was referring. It is taken from the later, more relaxed part of the proceedings, when her divinatory signo for the consultation was "spoken." Over a period of about twenty minutes, Javier covered a good deal of ground, recounting four different stories—all paths of the oddu (viz. signo) cast, Obbeyono. His discussion of the second of the paths went as follows:

JAVIER: Let me tell you, never mind your osobbo—San Lázaro will take care of that as long as you thank him. People like it when this signo comes up, and it has been coming up a lot in these times. It speaks of a trip.

YOLANDA: [Laughter] That's what everyone wants!

JAVIER: [Drawing on his cigarette] Ifá says that in Lucumí land, in Africa, there was a territory that was owned by Ogún [the fearsome "warrior" deity of iron], and with his machete he'd cut down the people when they tried to enter. It so happened once that he felt someone was penetrating the border, so he took his machete and went to meet the intruder. But when he arrived he saw San Lázaro struggling with his crutches and took pity, so instead of attacking he got to work opening the cripple's path across the land with his machete. It is from that time on that San Lázaro has always been thankful to Ogún. When people get this signo in their itá [the long divination conducted for neophytes as part of their initiation], we usually say that they are travelers. But in this case, Orula is just telling you of the possibility of a trip.

YOLANDA: If only... But every time that things look up, something comes along and spoils my luck (mi suerte).

JAVIER: Let's see if Ogún wants something to open your path. [casts ókuele]. No. He says he doesn't want anything. In any case, when you go home you should attend to your Ogún, give him rum to drink, but not too much in case he gets drunk and then he can't help you [laughter—note that the consultant has received a consecrated Ogún as part of "receiving the warriors" years earlier]. Everyone wants to travel, no?

With reference to this example, it is important to preempt hasty conclusions as to the importance of intersubjective negotiations of meaning in divinatory interpretation, that is, the kind of arguments from interpretative openness with which I began the discussion of this chapter. In this connection, we may note first of all that, although Yolanda's dialogical interjections in the above snippet are hardly unusual, such an active input on the part of consultants is by no means a prerequisite for a successful divination. I have witnessed consultations in which the client stayed almost completely silent throughout. And although babalawos do generally admit that they prefer it when their clients affirm, negate, or comment upon their interpretations, it was never suggested to me that this is necessary for "speaking the signo." When asked, babalawos merely concede that such interventions may sometimes allow them to deliver Orula's diagnoses more accurately. When I probed Yolanda herself on this matter, when later debriefing her on her consultation with Javier, she explained that her intention had been to help the babalawo "get to the point" (ir al grano), thus allowing him to pursue lines of interpretation that illuminated her circumstances more directly.

This point is borne out by babalawos' tendency to focus on the more elementary features of the myths when they construct interpretations. Contrary to the claim that Pythian ambiguity is central to babalawos' mode of interpretation (e.g., Matibag 1997), the above example illustrates a concern for transparency and simplicity which in my experience is entirely characteristic. From the story of San Lázaro's travels, Javier concludes, in a matter-of-fact style, that the consultant should be mindful of the possibility of a journey (which, as everyone knows in Cuba today, might lead to emigration). Interpretation sticks to basics, so to speak, the object of the exercise being not so much to expand creatively on "the ambiguities between the lines," as Matibag puts it, but rather to *extract* from them a clear message: a moral, a diagnosis, an admonition, a prohibition (Matibag 1997, 151–52; see also Parkin 1991, 183, and particularly Graw 2009). As far as babalawos are concerned, the yardstick of a good "orator of Ifá" (*orador de Ifá*), as they sometimes say, is above all his skill at bringing the myths to bear on their clients' personal circumstances with some precision. Javier illustrated this to me with a vivid account that merits full quotation:

[To consult] you need to know how to speak, to be an orator of Ifá, to manage the *metamorphosis*, as we call it. . . . You might come to me and from one story I can tell you three things. But you go to someone else and they might tell you ten, knowing how to get the most out of the oddu (*sacarle provecho*). Here in Cuba we've had great orators. There was one guy . . . who was famous when I was young. Once I was in an itá [initiatory consultation] with him; he was arrogant but with good reason since he knew more than anyone else, plus his signo [his initiatory oddu] was Obbeché, which means "parrot," so he had the gift of speaking Ifá just by his signo. The other babalawos were speaking the signo [viz.

of the consultation]—I did too—but at some point he just stood up and said: "Now listen to me!" and turning to the neophyte [curtly], "The fridge in your house is broken!" [The neophyte], bewildered, goes, "Yes, it is." The babalawo turns to the rest: "Did you hear that?"—that was his way of teaching. We wondered how Ifá can speak of the guy's fridge. So he explained himself—I think the oddu was Obara Meyi: "Ifá says that there was an island where fishermen lived, but all their fish kept rotting. Close by there was another island which always had snow, so the fishermen brought snow from there to put their fish in." And so with metamorphosis he says that in the house there must be a fridge, and since the neophyte had turned out osobbo, that it must be broken. Do you see how it works?

In light of Javier's illustration, one might say that babalawos' interpretative skill in divination turns on two related elements, namely the scope of the data that they can draw upon interpretatively and their ability to "make the most" of it, as Javier put it, so as to extract a verdict such as "your fridge is broken"—a verdict the relevance and precision of which is such that even fellow babalawos are impressed. In terms of scope, the primary condition for a babalawo's ability at speaking the signo is his intimate knowledge of the mythical paths associated with it. As discussed in chapter 3, the prime index of a babalawo's divinatory ability is his "learning" (*conocimiento*), which consists partly in memorizing as large a number of myths as possible, in order to be able to draw upon them in divination—a chief field of competition between babalawos, as Javier's comments about the old master's extravagance also convey. Moreover, we see here also an illustration of how babalawos are free to go beyond the myths themselves, to draw on whatever other information they deem relevant to the consultation, both within the confines of the consultation and further afield. For example, Javier's account illustrates how Orula's answers during the earlier "interrogative" stage of the consultation are also taken into consideration when speaking the signo. While it was with reference to the myth about the fish and the snow that the babalawo of Javier's story discerned that Orula was speaking about the consultant's refrigerator, the myth is further interpreted in light of the condition of osobbo identified previously so as to offer a more specific interpretation: the fridge is broken. In this way, all manner of data obtained during the interrogation of Orula may be weaved into babalawos' subsequent interpretations.

Indeed, babalawos' scope for interpretation is further widened by the notion, often repeated by babalawos, that "Ifá speaks past, present, and future" (*Ifá habla pasado, presente, y futuro*). As babalawos explain, the paths of myth do not specify times, so their potential field of reference is, so to speak, untensed: narrowing down whether a verdict relates to something that happened, is happening, or will happen is a matter of interpretative insight. Recalling the earlier extract from Javier's consultation, the consultant's defeatism with regard to her "luck" at travel (expressed with implicit reference to past frustrations) was in no way taken to invalidate Javier's suggestion. Rather, it projected travel as a possibility of which to be aware in the future. Should the consultant have been more immediately involved in travel plans at the time, Javier might well have delved further into the story of San Lázaro and Ogún in order to arrive at an interpretation that would have been more directly relevant to her circumstances (see also Abbink 1993).

A consequence of this element of openness is that interpretation often continues beyond the ritual confines of the consultation. Consultants in particular, concerned as they are with the specifics of the matters at hand, tend to leave divinatory sessions with food for thought. Thus it is not at all rare for consultants to reinterpret verdicts for themselves, in light of changes in their own circumstances well after their consultation. For example, a mother of two once confided in me her agitation when it dawned on her that problems that one of her sons had recently been having with the police had been mentioned by a babalawo months in advance, though she was not able to recognize the significance of the verdict at the time: "Orula had spoken of problems with the law (*la justicia*) in the family, but I didn't take notice. Now look what happened!"

Conversely, such iterative interpretations also help to accommodate or take the sting out of skepticism with regard to the truth of babalawos' pronouncements. As will be discussed further presently, clients who visit babalawos with a half-hearted or even critical view regarding the efficacy of the oracle are not unusual. Some may have doubts about diviners in general, while others may be unsure of the abilities or the credentials of a particular babalawo. One often finds in such cases that clients may leave a consultation with their doubts intact, but nevertheless remember the verdicts on a "who knows" basis. If at some later stage something that appears relevant does occur, they may recall the diviner's original pronouncements approvingly.

Motile Meanings in Divination

At this point it may appear rather as if the scope-enhancing character of divinatory interpretation is ultimately just a way of maximizing the possibility of babalawos hitting upon a verdict that their clients can accept as true—a suggestion that would essentially be a variant of the familiar arguments from ambiguity already discussed. Indeed, I have to admit that during my research I found somewhat frustrating the frequency with which babalawos would appeal to such dicta as "Ifá speaks past, present and future" when particular suggestions made in a divination failed to hit the mark with clients. Every time babalawos got something wrong, it seemed, they had a get-out clause. Could their claims to truth really be so transparently disingenuous? And could their clients really be so naive?

It will be noted that such suspicions are based on intuitions that also informed Evans-Pritchard's argument on "secondary elaborations of belief," discussed in chapter 2. The supposed get-out clause of "Ifá speaks past, present and future," for example, does look very much like the sort of secondary elaboration that allows babalawos to excuse their failings in a circular manner (Diviner: "Orula speaks of travel"—Client: "No chance!"—Diviner: "Well, sometime in the future then . . ."). In chapter 2, however, I argued that, even on its own terms, such an account fails to explain why people believe what diviners tell them. If, as Evans-Pritchard demonstrated *contra* Lévy-Bruhl's notion of "primitive mentalities," practitioners of divination are able to think in as commonsense a manner as the rest of us, there is no reason in principle to assume that they could not break Evans-Pritchard's putative circle of mutually supporting mystical beliefs. Such an assumption amounts to charging the Azande (and by the same token the practitioners of Ifá in Cuba) with a form of dogmatism—one that remains unexplained by Evans-Pritchard's argument from circularity.

More to the point, however, I would suggest that such an imputation would be based on a misunderstanding of the relationship between interpretation and truth in babalawos' rhetorical practice. To see this is so, we may note that the idea of the interpretative freedoms enjoyed by babalawos providing "get-out clauses," "secondary elaborations" and the like, takes for granted familiar ways of thinking about truth—the ones I have glossed as representationist. According to such views, the success of a babalawo's verdict in divination would depend on whether or not it represented the world as it actually is, that is, on whether it stated a fact. Interpretation, then, would turn on babalawos' scope for maximizing the domain of facts that might satisfy their putative verdicts. To use the example, when Yolanda rebuffed the oracle's suggestion that travel was in the cards for her, Javier was able to preserve the putative truth of the verdict by projecting it as a representation of future and as-yet-unforeseen events. If this is what he was doing, it would indeed be a disingenuous move on his part, and Yolanda would be naive to go along with it. While, on this analysis, Javier's claim to truth should reside in his ability as a diviner to arrive at verdicts that represent facts, what he would effectively be doing is making sure that what counts as a fact in the first place is wide enough to corroborate his verdict—indeed any verdict. The Pythian trick, as it were.

Quite apart from being somewhat contemptuous of Javier and Yolanda, such an analysis misconstrues the relationship between truth and interpretation in Ifá. In particular, what the examples of babalawos "speaking the signo" show is that in divination the representationist assumption that truth has logical priority over interpretation is systematically *inverted*. According to the representationist image, we may note, the job of babalawos is imagined as that of deciphering a truth-claim that is already given by the oracle in the form of a myth, interpreting its meaning for the consultant in order to show in what sense it might be true or, in other words, to specify what putative fact it expresses. Hence, for example, the myth of San Lázaro's passage through the land of Ogún would itself be understood as a divinatory truth-claim, given in the cryptic form of a mythical narrative, and Javier's subsequent suggestion that Yolanda would be traveling in the future would be understood as an interpretation of the myth's content for the benefit of the consultant. Truth comes first, followed by interpretation.

By contrast, our analysis of the manner in which divinatory verdicts are derived from the process of consultation shows that when babalawos insist that "Ifá is interpretation," they mean what they say. What we see in the examples of "speaking the signo" is not an interpretation of a prior truth given in the form of a myth. After all, the myths in themselves do not claim to represent anything about the consultant—if they are "about" anything they are about San Lázaro, Ogún, rotting fish, snow, and so on. Rather, we see myths serving as templates for a series of interpretative procedures by which divinatory truth-claims are *arrived at*. As Javier so vividly illustrated with his story of metamorphosis, the objective of these procedures is not to decipher a myth, but rather to *relate* it with as much precision as possible to the personal circumstances of the consultant—what Graw calls the "consultational quality" of the oracle (2009). Guided by the myth about the fishermen, as well as the prior diagnosis of osobbo and whatever other circumstances he might deem relevant, the babalawo's objective is to arrive at a verdict that is of immediate personal relevance to the consultant.

According to this image, then, diviners' verdicts emerge at the moment at which a myth is successfully related to the consultant's circumstances—or, to use the language of Ifá, at the moment these otherwise independent "paths" are made to meet. Crucially, seen in the light of Javier's emphasis on the role of "metamorphosis" as the key to babalawos' interpretative acumen, the language of "paths" here speaks directly to the inherently *motile* character of meaning in this context, in the sense I outlined earlier in my critique of Sperber and Lévi-Strauss's discussions of symbolism. Babalawos' expertise in relating the mythical paths of divinatory signos to the personal circumstances of consultants—their life-paths—through interpretative metamorphosis does not turn on a capacity of such meaningful data to represent elements of the world. Rather than appealing to ineluctably abstract and potentially immutable qualities of meaningful data (viewed as "semi-propositions," "floating signifiers," or indeed "secondary elaborations"), babalawos' interpretative transformations deploy meanings concretely, as things of the world that move and interact with each other in "metamorphosis" (see also Henare et al. 2007; Holbraad and Pedersen 2009). Just as Orula himself may "meet" the consultant owing to his concrete movement as a collection of consecrated objects, so his "words," expressed as myths, intersect with the path of the consultant in the act of "speaking the signo," in which babalawos perceive their own interpretative forte. Conversely, the consultant's path intersects the narrative of the myth insofar as his or her personal concerns orient the questions (explicit or implicit) that Orula's mythical utterances are meant to answer. The points at which these two moving orders of meaning meet correspond to the verdicts of divination.

So, the marvel of Javier's story of metamorphosis—indeed the very point of emphasizing the word—is not that a myth about fishermen could, *per impossible*, represent facts about the state of repair of a consultant's fridge.[6] It is rather that, on Orula's divinatory authority, two otherwise independent (and in that sense mutually irrelevant) trajectories of meaning are mutually transformed, by way of the babalawo's interpretative skill as an orator of Ifá, to produce a verdict that is of immediate relevance to the consultant. In the light of the consultant's circumstances (he has a fridge, he is osobbo), a narrative about fishermen, their rotting fish, and the snow they collect from an island, becomes a message about his broken fridge. Similarly, in Yolanda's case, Orula's story about San Lázaro and Ogún in Africa becomes a message about her travel prospects with San Lázaro's aid and protection. Far from reflecting upon the world to capture its facts by way of representational "arrest," meaning here partakes in the fluidity of the world in its own right. The significance of such an understanding of meaning becomes fully apparent, as we shall see, when it comes to conceptualizing the truth-claims that emerge out of the process of divinatory consultation. This is the task of the next chapter.

CHAPTER SEVEN

The Event of Truth: Coincidence, Revelation, Bewilderment

In the previous chapter I explained that babalawos conceive of their ability to pronounce truth as an effect of their elaborate interpretative efforts, and showed how such acts of interpretation work in practice during divinatory consultations. Emerging out of the process of interpretation, divinatory truth turns on babalawos' skill in "metamorphosing" their mythical knowledge, making the myths speak to the circumstances of their clients. But if divinatory truth is an outcome of babalawos' management of mythical and other meanings during the divination, then how is truth itself to be conceptualized in the context?

This question recalls the critical discussion of the anthropological debate about symbolism and its relationship to truth already discussed. Sperber's account of how people are able to "represent" symbolic data (including divinations) as true is premised on the idea that such data lack a clear-cut meaning—a notion that goes back to Lévi-Strauss's concept of "floating signifiers" able to take on shifting meanings because of their inherent vacuity. Building on my earlier discussion of aché as a Maussian mana-concept, I suggested that the characteristic fluidity of symbols might be better conceived as an effect of the inherently self-transformational, or excessive, character of meaning. The process of divinatory interpretation in Ifá may be seen as supporting such a view insofar as babalawos' interpretative efforts are directed not at deciphering an unclear meaning, but rather at transforming it—"metamorphosing" it—so as to channel its inherent motility in a particular direction, making its path meet that of the consultant. One may ask, then, where this motile image of interpretation leaves the question of truth—the question that motivated Sperber's analysis. In particular, if Sperber, following Lévi-Strauss, conceives of the truth of symbolic data as a function of their properties as representations (viz. their inherent ambiguity as "semi-representations" or "floating signifiers"), then how might truth be conceived as a function of the motility of meaning? If truth in divination is the product of the transformational motion of meaning, after all, then it too must be conceived in motile terms.

In order to develop such a motile analysis of truth in contrast to ordinary assumptions about its representational character, we may begin by returning to the distinction between questions of "why" and of "how." As we saw in chapter 2, this was the distinction by which Evans-Pritchard sought to theorize the difference between the "magical reasoning" of divination and the "common sense" of his readers. As I propose to show, that distinction provides a good starting point for articulating the deep logical divergence between representational truth-claims, which correspond to the question of how, and motile ones, which correspond to that of why. Indeed, as an attempt to articulate the logic of divinatory truth in contrast to that of representation, one might say that this return to Evans-Pritchard rehabilitates the Lévy-Bruhlian agenda that motivated his argument. If Lévy-Bruhl's core intuition about the alternative logical premises of magical thought survives in Evans-Pritchard's argument about why questions, my task here is to build on the latter's insights in order to take Lévy-Bruhl's line of thinking further than the idea of "participation"—an idea that in itself is probably not discriminating enough to furnish the logical coordinates of divinatory practice (see also Holbraad 2007, 200; cf. Goldman 1994).

Coincidence, Paths, and the Event of Truth (or Bewilderment)

Admittedly, much of the substance of Evans-Pritchard's distinction between how- and why-questions is not particularly relevant to our purposes, not least because Ifá oracles are in fact called upon to answer all sorts of questions that have little to do with the kinds of instances of misfortune Evans-Pritchard was addressing. In what sense, for instance, should questions regarding the advisability or timing of an initiation ceremony be thought of as "why" rather than "how"-questions? Certainly, if, as James

Laidlaw has suggested (Laidlaw 2010), Evans-Pritchard's argument centers primarily on the Azande's concern with allocating moral responsibility and blame, it is hard to see its relevance to the more prosaic and regulative uses of Ifá divination. More significant, to my mind, are two key insights that underlie Evans-Pritchard's distinction, both of which pertain to the formal properties of why-questions rather than their content or subject matter.

First, there is mileage to be had out of Evans-Pritchard's suggestion that the role of divinatory truth-claims is to *relate* things—according to him, events to personal histories. In the light of the motile analysis of interpretation offered in the previous chapter, the suggestion is immediately attractive. Babalawos themselves, we saw, make clear that bringing things into relation (in this case making the "paths" of myths meet those of individual consultants) is their major skill in consultations. What I want to show, then, is that Evans-Pritchard's distinction between why- and how-questions most basically turns on a difference between two orders of relation, and this difference has consequences for the way we may think about the character of paths in Ifá and how they meet to enunciate truth in divination (and how they may fail to do so, too).

Consider Evans-Pritchard's characterization of the distinction. How-questions are cast in causal terms, by linking events linearly in logical sequences, consequent to antecedent: "this happened because that happened . . . ," and so on. Such links we may call relations of *conjunction*. Why-questions, on the other hand, seem to pertain to something like a hidden dimension, squeezed laterally *in between* linear conjunctions: when all causal chains are said and done, as tightly as can be, there is still space enough to ask "why" as an extra question ("Why *me*? Why *now*?" asked the Zande brewer). This "extra" quality is just the product of the logical shift involved in relating causal chains to data that lie outside of them—outside by definition, since positing further causal links would keep analysis at the level of the how.

But what kind of relation could that be? The clue lies in Evans-Pritchard's second key insight, namely that common sense (viz. the how-logic of causation) tends to brush off diviners' and clients' why-questions as matters of coincidence. Notwithstanding its normative vacuity, the concept is graphically dynamic: we call coincidences those events that constitute a singular outcome of two or more *unrelated* causal series. (I walk into a bar and find you there "by coincidence," if the events that brought me there were causally independent of the events that brought you.) This may

A. *Conjunction*   B. *Coincidence*

(causal links)   (non-causal interactions)

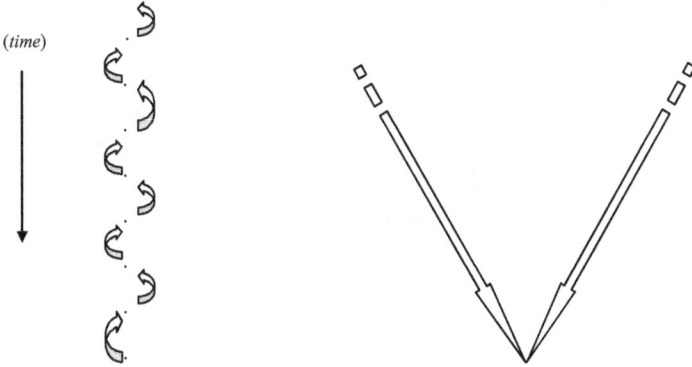

(*time*)

· : *event,* ⋐ : *causal link* (consequent to antecedent), ⬛⟹ : *trajectory of motion*

FIGURE 7.1. Conjuction ("how") as causation and coincidence ("why") as non-causal motility.

seem like a negative way of characterizing why-relations, since the obvious distinguishing mark of coincidence (as opposed to conjunction) is that it is *non*-causal. However, a more formal analysis reveals the positive, dynamic facets of Evans-Pritchard's insight.

A key point to note, somewhat abstractly for now, is that coincidences involve interaction. Coincidental relations do not pan out as ordered series like causal ones do, but are rather constituted at the *intersections* of causal series, as illustrated in figure 7.1. From this it follows that the points of intersection that constitute coincidental relations correspond to events, since they represent meeting-points of series that are in motion. Since causal chains themselves comprise events—that is, alterations over time –, their meetings properly constitute temporary collisions of trajectories. One may say, then, that coincidences are best glossed oxymoronically as non-causal interactions, or, more poetically, as *pure effects*.

These initial abstract considerations allow for an analysis that goes beyond the distinction between how- and why-questions. On this view, the difference between conjunction and coincidence is not one of the meaning or content of different categories of questions, but rather a purely formal antithesis. If an Evans-Pritchardian "common sense" works on identifying the conjunctions that link events to their causes, divination works laterally at establishing collision-points between causally independent trajectories of events. It follows, therefore, that the distinction can also be put in terms of an opposition between rest and motion. As we have defined it, the difference between causal conjunctions and non-causal interactions comes down to the difference between giving logical priority to series of isolated—or at least distinct, and in that sense stable and discrete—events, and starting with continuous trajectories of motion. So from this point of view common sense and divination are diametrically opposed: while the former is given events as determinable points and then must work at linking these points in an implicitly temporal order to form chains of them (thinking causally, from consequent to antecedent), the latter is given motion as the raw material, so that its job becomes one of *arriving at* events, which in this case are constituted as temporary definitions at the vertices of motion.

All this would probably sound like logical overdrive—an excessively precious distillation of Evans-Pritchard's comments—were it not for the fact that it accords so well with the analysis of divinatory ontology advanced in earlier chapters. In fact, the reversal of giving logical priority to motion over rest that underlies Evans-Pritchard's distinction is the same as the one that was formulated to account for babalawos' capacity to elicit Orula into presence during the ritual of divination. Moreover, in line with my earlier analysis of the motility of meaning in divinatory interpretation, just as one has to think of the divinities as self-differentiating motions in order to make sense of their ontological transformations from relative transcendence to relative immanence, so one has to think of the paths that diviners make collide in their consultations as self-differentiating trajectories of meaning in order to make sense of the manner in which these coincidental collisions enunciate truth. Note the formal similarity in either case. The problem of the ritual invocation of Orula that precedes the consultation is to elicit the presence of an otherwise transcendent oricha, and the solution is to channel, by ritual means, his self-transformational trajectory in the direction of immanence. Similarly, the problem of the consultation itself is to generate collisions of otherwise unrelated (and in that sense mutually transcendent) paths, and the solution is to channel, by means of the oratory of interpretation, their motile courses so at to make them meet. The "achievement" of truth, then, is formally similar to the invocation of Orula in the ritual: a matter of generating proximity in the face of distance. Indeed, as versions of each other, the two concerns are also interconnected sequentially: first, Orula has to be made present in order to "speak" in the form of an oddu, and then the mythical paths associated with the oddu have themselves to be "spoken" by the babalawo so as to generate, through interpretative metamorphosis, a verdict for the consultant.

Such a motile analysis of the whole sequence is motivated directly by the pervasive role of motility in the liturgy of Ifá divination, discussed in the previous chapters. The prominence of motion at so many levels of divinatory liturgy, practitioners' multifarious references to paths, as well as their richly fluid conception of aché and the deployment of the powders associated with it, are all constitutive elements of this motile ontology. Indeed, in light of the formal definition of coincidence that we have culled from Evans-Pritchard, the explicit formality of the concept of paths is particularly enticing here, in that it allows us to outline in relatively precise terms the role of coincidental relations in Ifá divination.

A first point relates to what I previously called the chaotic character of diviners' casts. As we saw, casts (whether with nuts or with the divining chain) constitute a temporary equilibrium of a number of imponderable forces. Babalawos are expected to keep the various trajectories of motion that produce each cast (the movement of the chain and of their hand, the friction of the nuts, and so on) in causal isolation from each other — they are supposed to refrain from weighting the action, as it were. The casts, then, are a perfect example of coincidence in every sense of the word. Nonetheless, an important analytical difference is involved. In terms of the commonsense non-causal notion of coincidence, oracular casts can be seen as nothing but random events. Our formal definition, on the other hand, enables us to fill this logical-*cum*-normative void: here casts can be understood with reference to the dynamic (motile) premises of the coincidental relations that they involve.

This distinction between two senses of coincidence (negative-causal versus positive-motile) has a purchase on practitioners' own views on the efficacy of their oracles. Practitioners, as we saw, are adamant that oracles only work provided that the babalawo and his ritual paraphernalia are all properly consecrated. Uninitiated charlatans who just procure unconsecrated ("jewish") equipment can only pretend to divine, they say, since "Orula is not even there," as one babalawo remarked. So, in the hands of impostors, divinatory casts are fake in that they constitute nothing more than random events — coincidences in the "common" sense. What makes genuine casts different is that in them Orula is indeed "there" and able to "speak," delivering verdicts through the divining nuts (or chain), in the form of determinate oddu configurations.

What is crucial here is that Orula's immanent presence in the ceremony is stipulated in motile terms. Orula is there and able to speak in the form of oddu, insofar as his path, manifested as a tangible collection of ritual paraphernalia, *meets* with the path of the babalawo (and also, at certain key moments, with that of the consultant). This liturgical choreography of motion, as we saw, culminates in the event of the oddu cast—the expression of Orula's presence and his ability immanently to "speak." Given that such a conceptualization is motile through and through, as was shown in relation to the significance of aché in this process, we may conclude that from the practitioners' viewpoint oddu casts constitute coincidences understood as noncausal interactions—meetings—of trajectories of movement.

Sequentially, such a motile logic underlies also the process of interpretation that follows the casting of the oddu, through which Orula's verdicts get determined interpretatively for the benefit of the consultant. We may recall that practitioners' path-talk refers not only to the consecrated paraphernalia of Orula himself, but also to what he "says" during the divination. So just as the corporeal actions that divination involves (the casting of the oddu, as well as the series of ritualized acts that precede it) can be conceptualized as a coincidental interaction of trajectories, so can the interpretative interrogation of Orula upon which the latter parts of the consultation turn. In particular, drawing on the analysis of the previous chapter, the process of interpretation can be conceived as an interaction between, on the one hand, the paths of iré/osobbo (plus their subsequent ramifications in further questioning) and, following the interrogatory part of the ceremony, the mythical paths that are then narrated when the oddu is "spoken," and, on the other hand, the personal life-trajectory of the consultant—her or his "path of life" (*camino de vida*), including her or his path within the ritual life of the religion, in terms of initiation and so on.

Such an analysis has immediate implications for the conceptualization also of *truth* in this context. In particular, viewing divinatory truth-claims as singular events that emanate from temporary collisions of otherwise independent paths of meaning implies a wholesale departure from representationist accounts of divinatory truth familiar from the literature. For if, as we saw in the previous chapter, the motile character of divinatory meanings colliding with each other in the motions of interpretative metamorphosis is nonrepresentational, then the same must go for the truth-events to which these collisions give rise. Truth, in this very concrete sense, is the outcome not of representation but of transformation. So, here is my suggestion. If divinatory verdicts emerge where the trajectories of paths meet, then why not use these collisions of meaning to define divinatory truth itself? On this view, divinatory interpretation delivers truth strictly in the sense that it *brings together* initially separate strands of meaning (paths) in such a way that both of them get transformed temporarily so as to constitute a divinatory verdict. Thus truth itself would be seen as a direct function of proximal motion—the capacity that motile meanings have to interact with one another at moments of motile coincidence.

The implications of this view will be fleshed out in more detail in due course. As an immediate advantage, however, we may note that it sticks to the letter of what practitioners say on the topic. Recall, for example, Javier's illustration of divinatory interpretation with the story of the arrogant babalawo's mastery of "metamorphosis." According to Javier, the babalawo was able to arrive at the most bizarrely mundane truth-claim (that the consultant's fridge is broken) precisely by establishing meeting points between the myth of the fishermen and the personal circumstances of the consultant, thus transforming both of them gradually ("metamorphosing" them) so as to produce a verdict. As a story about the wonders of the metamorphoses of divinatory oratory, this was also a story about the proper emergence of divinatory truth.

Just as significantly, however, a motile analysis of truth is also borne out by cases in which divination is judged to have failed. Certainly, Javier's story about the broken fridge is impressive—after all, he told it to illustrate how divination "works." And as we saw also in chapter 3 in relation to babalawos' mythopractical interpretations of all manner of mundane events, this kind of exaltation of the marvels of Ifá's capacity to illuminate people's lives is a favorite pastime, not least among the initiates themselves. Nevertheless, as Evans-Pritchard showed for the Azande (1976, 154–63), in Ifá dissatisfaction with divinations is far from uncommon. Horror stories abound among practitioners probably as much as felicitous tales about the supreme credibility of Orula's oracle, with people frequently lamenting how far divinations they were given diverged from how things turned out to be. Indeed, as Kristina Wirtz has shown in detail, complaints and mutual accusations regarding each other's failures are also a mainstay among the diviners themselves, as they tussle competitively for prominence within and between ritual lineages, as well as against santeros and other outsider competitors (2007, 186–94). Considering babalawos' adamant claims about the powers of Orula, it may not be surprising that divinations that are deemed as failures provoke reactions ranging from confusion to indignation, and can sometimes cause considerable distress to the consultants involved. To take one of the many examples I encountered, this is what a young woman told me after a long and particularly detailed itá divination she received as part of her mano de Orula (kofá) ceremony:

> It was terrible. [The babalawos] told me that I'm a daughter of Ochún, but that's obvious.[1] But after that they said many things that have nothing to do with me. . . . That I will never prosper until I kneel at my mother's feet and ask for her forgiveness. What is that? I've spent the past hour talking and crying with my mum, trying to work out what I've done to her. I asked her for her forgiveness but she didn't give it because I haven't done anything! We've always been so close, and none of this is going to change that.

Traditionally, anthropologists keen to make sense of native belief systems, so called, have felt that such stories pose a problem. Indeed, if one assumes that the diviners' statement is best construed as a representation of the woman's relationship to her mother, then her vehement denials are certainly problematic: the woman appears not to believe in the divination, so, inasmuch as divination is construed as part of a local system of "belief," such a case requires explanation. Ingenious analytical footwork such as Evans-Pritchard's "secondary elaborations" are then produced, as we have seen.

However, I would argue that if anything is false here, that is the anthropological worry that such analyses are designed to assuage. Distressing as they may be, divinatory fiascos such as this do not pose the kind of crisis-of-representation problem that lurks behind anthropologists' analytical worry that divination might be shown up as a sham to the people who would otherwise believe in it. Consider the way in which the young woman expresses her distress at what the babalawos told her. Nothing in what she says suggests that what is at issue for her is a question of belief. For a start, the very intensity of her distress, tinged with indignation rather than doubt, suggests that at issue for her is not a disbelief in what the priests told her, but rather a sense of sheer bewilderment that the truth of what she was told is not apparent to her. Her hour-long agony in trying to "work out" what she must have done to her mother to account for the divinatory admonition suggests that, far from doubting the oracle, the woman is convinced that its pronouncements *must* be true—her bewildered question being, how so. This would bear out the crucial point about the inherent indubitability of divination, conveyed in chapter 2 by my imaginary dialogue between the Zande practitioner and his doubting friend—a point to which I shall return at length in the next chapter.

Here, however, we may note the telling way in which the woman describes her sense of bewilderment. What was so disconcerting about the babalawos' pronouncement was not that is was false, but rather that she was unable to discern its relevance to her. "What is that?" she says. Effectively, what the babalawos failed to do on this occasion is what the babalawo of Javier's fridge story was supposed to have done so well, namely to deliver a verdict that *connected* with the woman's personal circumstances. So, the effect of their forceful delivery (which displayed none of the interpretative equivocations about, say, future possibilities that, as we have seen, are possible on such occasions) is to put the woman on a spin, searching herself for ways to make the diviners' verdict have a purchase on her own life. In begging for her mother's forgiveness even without a notion as to why she might be required to do so, she is not only displaying her assumption that what the diviners said must be true, but also provoking her mother to come up with something on which to latch the divination. Rather than a matter of the world giving the lie to the divination, the divinatory fiasco is experienced as a failure of the two to connect—to "meet." So the woman is left, effectively, trying in vain to complete herself the interpretative process by which such a truth-event could come to pass.

Motile Truth, Representation, and Their Mutual Eclipse

The motile characterization of truth that I have offered may have an air of vacuous mysticism about it. Such an impression, however, is arguably owed to the fact that thinking of truth in this way brings to light those aspects of truth-ascription that notions based on representation take for granted (this goes to vacuity) and thus obscure (and this to mysticism). Consider the representationist account of truth for a moment. Truth, we tend to think, is an attribute of representations that reflect facts. It involves, we may therefore assume, a comparison between representations and facts in order to ascertain a match of some sort. This notion, however, is hardly unproblematic. Much epistemology, for example, is concerned with articulating exactly how such matches might be conceived (e.g., philosophers talk about "correspondence" and "coherence" as two alternative ways of thinking about this question). Indeed, without going into the question in much depth, it is easy to see the problem. Think, for example, of the notion of comparison here. Presumably, if ascribing truth to a given proposition involves comparing it to a fact, then one would need to have also a criterion for deciding which fact is the relevant one. But it does not take much to realize that, whatever it might look like, such a criterion would itself involve the very same process of truth-ascription it would purport to facilitate. To select one fact over another as the most relevant for deciding on the truth of a representation is itself a way of making a prior truth-claim about the facts in question. Deciding on how to match a representation to a fact, then, already presupposes a somehow more "initial" process of matching, which in turn would presuppose another even more initial one, and so on. So we seem to be landed in an infinite regress of ever more initial truth-matches.

Reminiscent of so much philosophical debate, this kind of logical problem is arguably a symptom of a deeper and more abiding conceptual conflict involved in representationist intuitions about truth. On the one hand the representationist account posits truth as a relational property, by attributing it onto representations that stand at a certain relation to facts (a matching-relation). On the other hand, the things that are supposed to be related in this way are taken as belonging to distinct ontological camps: representations *versus* facts. The difficulty that arises, then, is one that is said to be typical of dualist ontological schemes in general, namely the so-called problem of interaction: how can tokens of distinct ontological types be brought into relation with one another, as, for example, truth-matches would require? It is in the light of this problem that the representationist account both takes for granted and obscures the "initial" truth-matches that we have been pointing to. Initial liaisons between representations and facts need to be assumed in order to render the matching-relations of truth-ascription possible. But they need to stay untheorized since their ontological anomaly as half representation and half fact is logically scandalous (cf. Latour 1999, 2010).

These kinds of logical problems often have solutions, of course, and my argument regarding divinatory truth is not meant to have a bearing on the philosophical question as to whether or not the representationist quandary is soluble. I only claim that Ifá divination turns on an alternative account of truth, and that this alternative can be defined conceptually in terms of its freedom from that particular quandary. This is because what

THE EVENT OF TRUTH

fails to register in the representationist account—the *initial position* of truth—is now foregrounded as the basis for the very different conceptualization of truth that we have been exploring. If truth turns on temporary collisions or meetings between moving trajectories of meaning, there is no ontological anomaly to contend with, and hence no circularity either: unlike "matches," the meetings in question are constituted as relations between tokens of the same ontological type.

It should be emphasized that the foregoing is not meant to add to, and much less improve on, the representationist account. Rather, it constitutes a departure from it, for the notion of truth that it articulates is not the one we are used to worrying about, whether intuitively or philosophically. I venture to call the truth in question "revelatory" (though on the caveat that the word be purged of its Judeo-Christian connotations of mystery or miracle, discussed in previous chapters). For at issue here is not the veracity of the way things are thought about or represented, but rather the capability that things—moving, motile things—have to reveal themselves in particular ways, when they come into relation with each other: the affect of proximal motion. Indeed, this should not be read merely as a metaphor, since "things" in this context does not refer (only) to objects or entities, but more broadly to all meaningful data that, as such, register, and can interact, in motion and as motion (see also Manning 2009). So what I have in mind in talking of revelation here is far from mysterious. Consider conversation: your ideas reveal themselves to me as they collide with, and thus transform, my own "in exchange," just like my analysis of Ifá divination reveals itself to you when you "put your mind to it." Taking the mystery out of it, one may cast the truth-claims of divination as being revelatory in terms of the modification that results when two initially independent strands of meaning are brought together.

At this point it may also be objected that such an analogy between divination and ordinary conversation is more worrying than it is reassuring. After all, what the analogy seems to suggest is that *all* meaningful data must a fortiori be construed as giving rise to "truth" whenever they are brought into relation with one another, and such a consequence should surely render the very notion of truth vacuous. Indeed, note that this difficulty is a symmetrical inversion of the problem of interaction that we encountered in our commentary on the representationist account. If there the problem was that the ontological divide between representations and facts meant that tokens of each could not consistently be brought in truth-relations to one another, the problem here seems to be that the ontological continuity of meaning-trajectories makes it necessary that every time any particular pair of trajectories of meaning relate they should do so to produce truth. So one may fairly wonder whether the conceptual machinery of motion overdetermines the argument. If all transformations of meaning can be considered as revelations of truth, as has been suggested, after all, then in what does the diviner's special claim to truth consist?

But on this one can bite the bullet. One can well admit that *as long as they are viewed on a motile premise* all collisions of meaning-trajectories are ipso facto true in the motile sense we have been developing. One would have to add, however, that the reason why truth-claims are not in general posited automatically as true in this way is that only very few of them carry their motile credentials, as it were, on the sleeve, as they do so concertedly in Ifá divination. Let me explain.

Assume that it is right to suggest that the representationist account presupposes the motile one because it takes for granted initial truth-matches, that is, matches that from a motile viewpoint register as coincidental intersections of meaningful trajectories. Even so, the fact is that once these meetings are granted, the conditions for the machinery of representation are in place. No matter how they came about, the meetings in question can now be isolated as discrete data and treated on the familiar representational mold. So, to take the earlier example, in full conversation your ideas may reveal themselves as they collide with my own (they may constitute truth-events on the motile account). But this does not stop me from abstracting away from the trajectories that lead up to these transformative collisions of meaning, and representing your ideas as statements of distinct propositions about things. Indeed, it is probably fair to say that these kinds of representational judgments dominate my thinking during conversation, and that motile considerations remain dormant as a background condition. This is arguably because the representational mold dominates thinking generally, and there are good reasons why this should be so, including even good evolutionary reasons, if one is inclined to think in these terms.[2] Certainly Cubans do this all the time like the rest of us, and so did the Azande, recalling Evans-Pritchard's point about the ubiquity of commonsense thinking in their everyday lives.

However, our analysis suggests that this kind of truth reckoning is not only different from the motile one, but also logically incompatible with it. As we saw, the motile truths-events that are defined at the intersections of meaning-trajectories are suppressed in the representationist account as ontological anomalies. Conversely, the propositional truths that fall under the remit of representation are willy-nilly blotted out of the universe of motion that divinatory revelations presuppose, as we saw, for example, in the case of the young woman's experience of divinatory fiasco. From this incompatibility follows an either/or clause, whereby representational truth-ascription unavoidably eclipses colliding trajectories and vice versa—a form of "obviation" that closely parallels Wagner's analysis of the "dialogical" character of the relationship between convention and invention, discussed in chapter 1. It further follows that the dominion of representational thinking lodges itself *at the expense* of motile truth-events, by obviating them as hidden premises. Hence the motile account of truth is rendered non-vacuous not because its general applicability is dented as such, but because it is habitually obscured.

These considerations allow us to clinch the argument on divination. What distinguishes the interpretative procedures of Ifá from ordinary conversations is just the fact that divinatory proceedings meticulously and deliberately *maximize* the scope for treating verdicts as motile truth-events.[3] We already have seen the various discursive and liturgical constituents of this logic—the purposeful and cosmologically marked emphasis on motion in the divinatory ritual, the conceptualization of paths at so many different levels, the multiple consecratory uses of aché, and so on. But, again, arguably the most focal element—the one that makes most visible the motile character of oracular truth-claims—is the act of casting the palm nuts (or the chain), by which the divinatory configurations are said to "come out." As we saw, coincidence is pivotal to this process, and both yes/no and mythical verdicts turn on this, as prescribed by the divinatory liturgy and its technologies of motion. Casts, then, are truth-events par excellence since they just *are* temporary equilibriums that emerge from non-causal interactions between salient movements: Orula's (his consecrated paraphernalia), the babalawo's (his hands), and the consultant's (hands and other parts of her body).

Again, note, a possible objection suggests itself. Even if we accept that the motile model of truth might be tenable in some circumstances, surely merely physical events like casts of divining chains cannot fit the bill. For, unlike the processes of interpretation that follow them, casts do not bring together trajectories that are meaningful as such: what *meaning* could there be in a mere hand movement or a chain-swing? Furthermore, on this view the fact that practitioners are prepared to attach such significance to

"merely" coincidental outcomes (by virtue of the elaborately meaningful paths of each oddu) is taken just as an indication of the dogmatic and
arbitrary character of divinatory belief.

In light of our previous argument, however, it may be clear that this
kind of straight-minded objection amounts merely to a flat refusal to take
the motile premise of Ifá seriously. Oddu meanings appear as arbitrary
semiotic appendages on "mere" physical movements only if one takes for
granted that meaning is separable from its material manifestations. Such
an assumption, however, just iterates the representationist ontology by in-
sisting that meaning can be thought of only as an abstraction.[4] Our motile
analysis denies this. Since on a motile premise we can accept that meanings just are parts of the world, we can also accept that parts of the world
(like moving hands and divining chains) can *be* meanings—not as signs
that "have" meaning, but as instantiations of meaning pure and simple, as
was argued earlier, specifically with reference to aché and its role in eliciting the oddu into presence. The problem then becomes one of *revealing*
what meanings the given movements instantiate, and this is a matter of
bringing relevant meaning-trajectories together by coincidence, to give a
truth-event. Divinatory casts, then, set the conditions for just such a process, by bringing a meaningful oddu into immanence in the divinatory fray.
And the subsequent transformation of the oddu's paths in the rhetoric of
interpretation brings the process into fruition for the consultant's benefit,
delivering the verdict.

Skepticism and Misunderstanding

To conclude this chapter, I want to suggest that an advantage of this analysis is that it also puts the commonsense (skeptical) view of divination into
perspective. Although, as I have sought to show, the role of coincidence
in divination allows for verdicts to be understood on a motile premise, in
no way does it *force* such a view. As any skeptic can attest (and plenty of
anthropologists have done so, as we have seen), divinatory verdicts can
perfectly well be severed logically from the trajectories of motion out of
which they emerge, and treated as ordinary representational truth-claims,
as we also saw in the example of ordinary conversation. Thus viewed, verdicts are just straightforward statements of fact. They differ from more
mundane statements only in being entirely unsubstantiated (they are, after all, arrived at quite "randomly") and, sometimes, in describing facts

that seem bizarre, regarding exotic things like sorcery, iré and osobbo, the influence of divinities, and so on.

The point, however, is that such appeals to representational reason in no way contradict the motility of truth as it is construed in divinatory practice. They simply talk past it. One's feelings about the truth or falsehood of divinatory verdicts seen as representations have no bearing on those verdicts' claim to the motile truth we have been articulating in relation to the ethnography here, since the very concepts of truth that are at issue in each case are different. In the next chapter I elaborate on this ontological difference (ontological since it pertains to two alternative conceptions of what truth *is*) by picking up my suggestion in chapter 2 that representational concepts of truth are unable to capture the definitive feature of divination, namely that its claim is to indubitable truths. As we shall see, the motile conception that we have been advancing here is at the heart of this notion of indubitability. So, again, the skeptic who doubts diviners' claims to truth and the practitioner who assumes that they are true by definition are not disagreeing about the nature of divinatory truth. Rather, they are talking about different kinds of truth altogether, only one of which is divinatory. At issue is not a disagreement at all, but rather a misunderstanding.

To prepare for this argument, we may note that the point about misunderstanding projects rather revealingly on the ethnographic ground. The perspectives that I have been designating as skeptical and divinatory for the sake of the present argument do not correspond tidily to particular groups or individuals in Cuba—or anywhere else probably. This is hardly surprising, given that while the two perspectives eclipse one another (in the sense that they are not held concurrently with respect to the same conceptualization of truth), each of them makes sense in its own terms, so that it is perfectly possible for people to oscillate between them with no contradiction or, as it is said, cognitive dissonance. We noted, for example, that in Cuba one frequently meets people who admit to visiting babalawos or other diviners occasionally, without taking very seriously or "paying much attention" to what they say (this particular expression, *sin hacerles caso*, in Spanish also has connotations of disbelief). Often, people who participate in the world of Ifá and other popular forms of divination in this half-hearted way explain their visits to diviners as mainly a matter of taste. "I am not really a believer in these things you study," a good friend of mine in Havana once told me, "but I like to go sometimes just to listen to what they [the diviners] say." A sense of intrigue, as well as the sheer beauty of a well-performed divination, is no doubt part of the

attraction. Equally, however, such attitudes bear out the notion that interest in contemplating the revelatory truths that oracles provide is in no way
incompatible with the fact that oracular truth-claims are nevertheless not
worth "believing" in the representational sense, that is, that they are not
to be taken as sources of accurate "information." In the next chapter we
shall see that babalawos express this clearly themselves, not least in order
to fend off unscrupulous fellow initiates who may try to dupe clients into
thinking that information, in this sense, is what they offer.

Here, a coda to my earlier story of the young woman who was offended
by a babalawo's divinatory admonition that she owed her mother an
apology may serve to illustrate the point. Some weeks after that harrow-
ing experience, I met with the woman again and asked for her thoughts
on what had happened in the ceremony. "That guy was just shameless" (*el
tipo fue un descarado*), she said dismissively:

> Didn't you see how disrespectfully he was talking to me? . . . That's not how
> babalawos should behave. [These guys] charged all that money [for the kofá
> ceremony] and in the itá they were speaking from the books [referring to
> inexperienced babalawos' practice of consulting with the aid of published com-
> pendia of oddu and their myths] and saying all sorts of things that had nothing
> to do with anything. I'll never have anything to do with them again. I know it's
> not padrino's fault, he thought they were good [referring to the fact that the
> neophyte's godfather is charged with inviting appropriate babalawos to par-
> ticipate in the ceremony]. He'll know best, but for me those gentlemen weren't
> *babalawos*. (*El sabrá mejor, pero pa' mi aquellos señores no eran babalawos.*)

The point of the tirade is hardly to dispute the official initiatory credentials
of the "shameless" priest—as an uninitiated female, the woman has no
authority to do so (hence the respectful deference to her padrino—"he'll
know best"). Nevertheless, the logic is clear. The babalawos' failure to deliver truth in the consultation is taken as grounds to doubt, not the integrity of the process of divination, but rather that of the men who conducted
it. If they failed to deliver truth, that is because they were incompetent,
and to that extent they just were not being proper babalawos. In this way,
the logic of what a genuine, and ipso facto successful, divination would
involve remains immune to criticism. By implying that the purportedly
divinatory verdicts were, in retrospect, hardly divinatory at all, the woman
effectively upholds the integrity of genuine babalawos and, by implication at least, the notion of truth on which it rests. To interpret her criti-

cism as a breach with the logic of divination as such would be equivalent to doubting whether, say, "love thy neighbor" is an inherent principle of Christian practice on the grounds that many Christians (including priests) are less than loving to their neighbors, or whether respect for the law is a fundamental premise of liberal democracies because their citizens (including parliamentarians) sometimes act unlawfully. Indeed, the fact that the woman continued to visit her godfather and other diviners in the months that followed her bad experience at the itá illustrates this characteristically. When I last saw her, she told me enthusiastically that she was now saving up for her own initiation into Santería as a daughter of Ochún.

CHAPTER EIGHT

Definition and Obligation: The Truth of the Oracles

The motile analysis of Ifá divination advanced in the previous chapter has taken us a long way away from the notion that diviners' claim to truth is representational. In this chapter I bring the analysis of Ifá divination to a close by addressing the question that originally motivated it, namely the question of indubitability. As was suggested in chapter 2 with reference to the existing anthropological literature on divination, the alterity of divinatory truth resides not in the fact that practitioners' belief in it appears irrational, but rather in the fact that practitioners treat it as somehow lying beyond the very opposition between belief and doubt. What makes divinatory truth-claims so special for them is that they are inherently indubitable. This, I suggested, presents a formidable analytical challenge. Given that the verdicts diviners offer appear to be no different from ordinary truth-claims, and therefore hardly seem to be immune to doubt, how might one account analytically for the notion that they are indubitable, without making practitioners of divination seem merely dogmatic in stipulating that they are? Since representations are inherently open to doubt, I concluded that a requirement for such an analysis would be to posit divinatory truth-claims as something other than representations.

In the previous chapter we saw that a motile analysis of Ifá divination fulfills this requirement amply. While representational takes on truth presuppose that meaning can be conceived in a state of rest, forming propositions that can be compared to states of affairs in the world (i.e., the fact-giving match), our motile analysis is premised on the idea that meanings are in a state of flux, transforming each other as and when they collide. The question that arises, then, is whether a nonrepresentational analysis of this kind can account for the notion that divinatory truths are indubitable. In what follows I show that it can, by exploring the logical implications of thinking of truth as a transformation of meaning. If diviners are in the business of transforming meanings, I argue, what they are effectively doing is enunciating novel *definitions*. And if divinatory verdicts are to be thought of as a species of definition, it follows that, notwithstanding their surface similarity to fact-giving (or at least fact-claiming) representations, they are much closer to statements whose truth is "analytic" (i.e., statements such as "all bachelors are unmarried men," which are true, precisely, "by definition") and are therefore indubitable. The difference is that while ordinary analytic truths offer definitions of things (concepts, objects, properties, etc.) that already exist, divinatory verdicts invent definitions for *new* things.[1] As we shall see, the ontological effects of such inventive definitions have important consequences for the way we conceive of the normative power of divination—its ability to compel action on the part of the consultants—discussed in chapter 3. In order to set this argument on its tracks, however, we may begin by demonstrating its major ethnographic premise, namely that practitioners of Ifá assume that the truths of divination are inherently indubitable.

No Lies, No Mistakes

In the previous chapter we saw in some detail that, even when despondent about divinations they deem to have failed, practitioners of Ifá assume that, as such, genuine divinatory verdicts are not open to the kind of doubt one might express about everyday statements of fact. Here I focus on what babalawos themselves say on the matter. Indeed, if one might say that consultants' stances, such as that of the woman of the previous chapter, turn on a more-or-less implicit assumption that divinations do not offer the kind of truth that is open to doubt, babalawos are entirely explicit on this point. Recall, for example, the conversation that took place in Javier's home when his godchild Rogelio, himself a babalawo, came to discuss rumors that one of his own godchildren had gone into hiding, letting it be known that he was dead. Taking the man's underhanded behavior merely as confirmation of the treacherous characteristics of Obbesá, his signo of initiation, Rogelio punctuated his analysis with a phrase that babalawos often use to emphasize the power of their art: "Orula makes no mistakes" (*Orula no se equivoca*). Another assertion one hears often in such contexts, as well as during consultations by way of emphasizing to consultants the weight of Orula's divinatory pronouncements, is that "in Ifá there are no lies" (*en Ifá no hay mentiras*).

It is important to note that babalawos' frequent repetition of such phrases is not intended as some kind of wide-eyed advertisement of the wonders of divination, but rather as a matter-of-fact statement of its basic premise—analogous, perhaps, to a soccer fan saying that football "is a game of two halves" or a cook saying "it is all in the ingredients." For example, when Rogelio uses the idea that Ifá makes no mistakes to underline that his miscreant godchild had what was coming to him because of his signo of initiation, Javier's assent is formulaic: "It's true that Orula makes no mistakes. We are the mistaken ones. If it isn't today it will be tomorrow." The two men are exchanging statements of the obvious. On this basis we may conclude that the "obvious premise" of divination is its infallibility. To say that Orula's verdicts can be neither mistaken nor deceitful is effectively to bar the possibility that they might be false. So if verdicts cannot be false, to doubt them is what philosophers call a category mistake: to doubt a divinatory verdict is to treat it as if it were not a verdict. For babalawos the very notion of an oracular error is an oxymoron.

Notably, as indicated by Javier's further adage, "we are the mistaken ones," this is perfectly compatible with the oracle's verdicts being subjected to equivocations of various types, since practitioners make a clear distinction between Orula's immunity from criticism and the babalawos' own shortcomings as human operators of the oracles. Indeed, the charges of incompetence or dishonesty that were discussed in the previous chapter are commonplace both among babalawos, insofar as competition for prestige and clientele involves discrediting colleagues, and among those clients who are dissatisfied with a babalawo's services for one reason or another (cf. Bascom 1941; Horton 1964; Turner 1975, 217; Mendonsa 1976, 191–92; Fortes 1987, 11). "The *babalawo* is a human being, and that means he's imperfect," I was told by one practitioner.

The most telling conversation I had during fieldwork on this matter was with Javier's son Javielito about "exploitative" babalawos, as he called them (cf. Holbraad 2004a). One of his main complaints against such babalawos, he said, was with the way they seek to impress their clients by attaching Orula's verdicts to specific dates or people's names (e.g., "your daughter will fall ill next Tuesday," or "the witch is your neighbor, Maria"):

I don't give people dates: Ifá speaks past, present, and future, and gives advice, but [consultants] should know for themselves their own situation and act on it as they see fit. . . . Some [babalawos] do give them, but that's just showing off, and clients complain when things don't turn out that way. How can they [the babalawos] know these things? Ifá doesn't work like that.

How are we to understand the claim that "Ifá doesn't work like that"? Why can Ifá give "advice" but not dates and names? When I asked Javielito to elaborate, he reverted to a point we have already discussed, and which babalawos tend to repeat like a mantra in such conversations, namely that "Ifá is interpretation," implying that interpretation of itself could not yield specific names and dates. Admittedly, the implication is moot since, as we saw, in fact Ifá *is* used to give unambiguous "yes" or "no" answers to specific questions posed to it by the diviner during the interrogatory part of the ceremony in which the ibbo objects are used in "asking the hand." Arguably, however, the import of babalawos' normative insistence on such terms as "advice" (*consejo*) and "interpretation" (*interpretación*) has more to do with the question of infallibility than with ambiguity. By adding dates and names, allegedly exploitative babalawos present Orula's verdicts as statements of fact that may be verified or falsified according to how things actually turn out. "Advice," by contrast, may be interpreted, or even acted upon, but not doubted in the sense statements of fact can.

Similarly, as we saw in the previous chapter with reference to Javier's consultant's travel prospects, the idea that "Ifá speaks past, present and future" also serves as a normative mitigation of fallibility. My experience during the itá divination that was carried out as part of my own mano de Orula initiation ceremony was to me rather poignant in this respect. When I queried—in falsifying mood!—the oracle's contention that I am prone to impotence, one of the babalawos reminded me with macho gusto that I have no children after all. "And don't forget,' he added with emphasis, "Ifá speaks past, present, *and future*."

The normative rhetoric is important here. For Javielito's dispute with babalawos who give names and dates could be cast precisely as a dispute over whether or not oracular pronouncements ought to be taken as fal-sifiable truth-claims. As we have seen, those who practice divination are no more barred from taking oracular verdicts as statements of fact than anthropologists, and this may be readily exploited by babalawos who wish to "show off"—presenting divination as a miraculous ability to guess the future. No wonder, then, that babalawos should find it necessary to stress normatively that the oracles' pronouncements are not affirmations that might, least of all in principle, be falsified by facts.

Divination and Definition

So with Ifá we are landed in the analytical *impasse* that was explained in chapter 2. How to make sense of the idea that Orula's verdicts are, as such, indubitable, given that they look so much like ordinary (inherently doubtful) statements of fact, and so unlike the kinds of truths that one would recognize as indubitable? In line with the overall approach to alterity taken throughout this book, I argue that this predicament indicates that we have reached the limits of our ways of thinking about indubitability and the assumptions about truth that underlie them. What is needed, in other words, is a way of conceptualizing truth that removes the semblance of absurdity from the claim that statements such as "you are bewitched," "your fridge is broken," or "you are prone to impotence" are inherently beyond doubt.

In the analysis of motility in the previous chapter, the verdicts of Ifá were shown to consist in transformations of meaning. Now, this idea, of new meanings being brought about through the collisions that oracles engender, immediately suggests the notion of *definition* as a possible conceptual gloss for the truth-claims oracles produce. Certainly, thought of as an event, or even an *act*, the concept of definition would capture rather well the idea of a meaning being brought about—as, for example, when a mathematician defines a variable by providing it with a value (let x equal such-and-such) or an anthropologist defines a new piece of jargon. And what would make this line of inquiry particularly promising for our purposes is the fact that, as we have seen in relation to the philosophical idea of analyticity, the concept of definition brings us in the vicinity, at least, of the indubitable—what is true "by definition," as we saw, is true beyond doubt. So the question would be: how might a divinatory verdict such as "you are bewitched," which so looks like an ordinary statement of fact, be conceived as a form of definition? And what implications would this have for the conceptualization of truth itself in this context?

The first thing to note in this connection is that much of the philosophical literature on concepts of definition is of little help here. For while a survey of these discussions is beyond the scope of the present argument

(though see Robinson 1950), it may be fair to say that, at least within analytical philosophy of language, debates about definitions focus overwhelmingly on the question of "adequacy," and this is a notion that seems to rule
out of court any interest in how definitions might bring *new* meanings
about. Rather, questions of adequacy appear mainly to be concerned with
how meanings that already exist as a stock may or may not relate to each
other. So here is a horse, to take one of the standard examples favored by
analytical philosophers, and the problem is to decide whether and how
a sentence like "quadruped with a flowing mane and tail" may serve to
define it. Importantly, appeals to truth-conditions are prominent in these
discussions. Since we *have* a sense of what a horse is, defining it must be
a matter of getting this sense right, using terms that hold true of horses,
such as "quadruped." On this conservative view, then, definition must at
the very minimum be a species of truth-claim, understood in the ordinary
sense: a predicative assertion of important—or maybe "essential"—facts
about the *definiendum*.[2] And hence our analytical disappointment: on this
species of definition we are back with representations and the doubts to
which they inherently give rise.

But what of *inventive* definitions? It is remarkable that philosophers,
who do nothing if not muster powers of clear thinking and creativity in
order to *change* what and how we think, should presume a stock of meanings that is given. Maybe defining a horse is just a matter of articulating
truly a sense one already has. But who could even begin to have a sense
of a Platonic form, a monad, or sense data before philosophers ventured
to define them? Indeed, those philosophers who have followed Nietzsche
in thinking of philosophy as an "untimely" enterprise, have sought reflec-
tively—inventively—to theorize invention (e.g., Heidegger 1968; Deleuze
1994; cf. Nietzsche 1997). And so have those anthropologists who see the
creation of new meanings not just as a philosophical prerogative, but as an
irreducible aspect of social living, as discussed in chapter 1 in relation to
the work of Roy Wagner and others (see also Ardener 1989).

So let us distinguish between inventive definitions and the ones with
which analytical philosophy is mainly concerned—call them "conventional," following Wagner's terminology. I want to argue that, when cast
in relation to questions of definition, and notwithstanding Wagner's own
apparent unease with the topic, the distinction between invention and
convention pertains directly to the question of truth. Conventional definitions, we saw, are a species of representational truth-claims. As an example of what I take to be an inventive definition, consider a definition of

the notion of "inventive definition" itself—as pudding to my proof. Let us define inventive definition as a speech-act that inaugurates a new meaning by combining two or more previously unrelated meanings. I did it just now: taking the meanings "speech-act," "inauguration," "novelty," and "meaning," I combined them to inaugurate a new meaning—new relative to the conventions of conventional definition—that may be called "inventive definition." In fact, in order to underline the novelty of the definition in this context, I shall adopt the neologism "infinition," which was suggested to me by Viveiros de Castro (pers. comm; see also Holbraad 2008). The term is apposite partly because, as a verbal noun, it highlights the active and transformative character of these kinds of definition, and partly because the etymological association with the grammatical class of the "infinitive" connotes that what is at issue in such acts of definition is the creation of *concepts* –"to run," "to think," "to define," indeed, "to infine" are infinitives insofar as they express the conceptual correlate, as it were, of the actions they designate. (As we shall see presently, the term's connotation of infinity is also relevant.)

Now consider whether this kind of definition is a species of ordinary truth-claim. If it were, "speech-act," "inauguration," "novelty," and "meaning" would all have to be construed as properties that predicate "infinition," like "quadruped" and "flowing mane" predicate "horse." Our definition of "infinition" would be deemed adequate insofar as it picked out properties that hold true of such definitions (viz. that they are speech-acts, they inaugurate, and so on). But this would be contradictory. The notion that *definiens* must pick out properties of their definiendum implies that the definiendum is not new: it must already be there to be picked at, as it were, acting as a reference by which its definition may be checked for truth.[3] Posited as a condition for its own definition, the definiendum takes logical precedence over its definiens, and hence the latter cannot be said to inaugurate it. So, since infinitions are defined inventively as inaugurations—*as inventions of (new) meanings*—it follows that, unlike conventional definitions, inventive definitions are not predicative truth-claims.

Let us then spell out the implications of treating divinatory pronouncements as infinitions. We have seen that, in "speaking the signo" during the divinatory consultation, diviners interpretatively transform the myths of the oddu cast so as to arrive at a verdict that speaks directly to the personal circumstances of the consultant. Hence, the diviner's job is to establish specific relations between the consultant and the meanings that he is able interpretatively to extract from the oddu—recalling Javier's notion that skillful babalawos "get the most out of the oddu." So, to take my own example, the verdict "you are prone to impotence" established a relation between me and impotence. Treating this as an act of infinition implies that "impotence" here is not to be understood as a predicate that might "hold true" of me. Rather, it is a meaning that during divination is related to me so as to *redefine me*. By telling me that I am prone to impotence the oracle renders a specific relationship to impotence part of my definition as a person. Or, put in philosophical terminology, the oracle renders my relationship to impotence "internal": much like a bachelor is defined by being unmarried, so I am defined by being prone to impotence (though on balance I'd rather my fridge were broken . . .).

In sum, rather than ascribing to the consultant a set of properties that may be falsified in light of experience, divination *defines the consultant as a new kind of person*. From being a person who stands in no particular relation to impotence, the oracle transforms me into a person who is prone to it. Similarly, as trivial as it may seem (and triviality is arguably part of the reason why the pronouncement seemed at once bemusing and impressive according to Javier's account), the verdict "your fridge is broken" renders having a broken fridge part of the definition of the consultant as a person. To ask whether such a shift is "true" or "false"— to "doubt" it—is to misunderstand the strictly tautological character of such assertions. Divinatory verdicts are true by definition, and therefore beyond doubt, just because they *are* definitions. The fact that practitioners of Ifá might be as liable as anthropological analysts to fall into the trap of treating them as doubtful statements of fact explains why babalawos put such normative emphasis on the requirement that the oracles' pronouncements be understood as infallible (viz. no lies, no mistakes).

Now, this way of thinking of divination may seem awkward or over the top. Maybe a concept can be defined afresh, but can the notion of invention really be stretched to include people as well? For, more than just meanings (e.g., infinitions), consultants are flesh-and-blood persons, and it is unclear how as such they can be "brought together" with meanings such as "impotence" or "broken fridge." In fact, is this talk of oracles' ability to transform people not metaphysically suspicious? For it would seem that what is being propounded here is a particularly extreme version of social constructivism (magical or oracular constructivism if you will), based on the extravagantly idealist notion that entities of the world can be brought in and out of existence by mere human fancy—divinatory or otherwise.

Such appeals to common sense, however, are all too easy in their professed transparency. Instead of reducing to the absurd our claim that oracular verdicts have ontological effects, appeals to common sense just alert us to the fact that the sense of divination, with its seemingly bizarre entailment that assertions may be indubitable at the level of logical principle, is quite uncommon—uncanny even, given the "magical" connotations (cf. Bracken 2007). Let me go over the ground to clarify this.

What differentiates predicative (conventional) from nonpredicative (inventive) definition, and what makes the latter rather than the former appropriate to the analysis of divination, is that predication presupposes the "common" distinction between word and world, while invention does not. As we saw, the truth-functional character of conventional definitions is premised on the logical priority of their definienda. And although this logical priority does not imply that the definienda in question exist (defining unicorns as "horses with horns" does not mean that they exist), it does imply the existence of a domain of entities—the "world"—from which conventional definitions may draw their truth-values. By contrast, inventive definitions do not presuppose the existence of a world of entities: such a world is their conventionalized outcome. When the oracle of Ifá defines me as a person who is prone to impotence, it is not speaking of an entity existing out there in the world, of whom certain properties may be said to hold. Such a construal would imply that the definition in question is conventional and open to doubt—precisely that which babalawos are so keen to deny. But neither does the inevitable consequence—namely, that in defining me the oracle is *bringing me about as a new person*—imply the idealist notion that the world's constituents exist insofar as people (such as diviners or anthropological analysts) think or speak of them. For, just like the notion of conventional definition, idealism is premised on a logical distinction between word and world, concept and thing—in other words, precisely that distinction which the motile logic of invention obliterates (see also Latour 1999, 2010).

Recalling our central point about the inherently "excessive" character of the motile ontology of Ifá—excessive in that it transgresses even the arch-Cartesian binary of concepts versus things—we may say that the notion of infinition implies a logical universe of trajectile elements the very constitution of which involves traversals of just such distinctions. Motile equivalents to Latour's "hybrids" (1993) or "factishes" (2010)—indeed, vectors whose hybridity unfolds in ontological motion—infinitions admit only of paradoxical glosses when expressed in terms of what Latour calls "modernist" ontology: concepts-*cum*-things, one has to say, although one would prefer to render the ontological hyphens as *vectors* to mark the analytical departure (not least from Latour himself) that our motile analytic seeks to establish. Infinitions, then, as "concepts↔(*cum*)↔things."

Indeed, this essentially negative defense against the charge of an idealist oracular constructivism can be complemented by a positive one. Why claim that infinitions must ipso facto have ontological effects, bringing forth the objects they define as existing entities? Well, consider the alternatives. One would be to claim that when I, for example, define infinitions as inventions of new concepts I am merely giving a name to a phenomenon that already exists—indeed, how else could I appeal, for example, to Plato and his forms as a convincing precedent of what I have in mind? But this is contradictory. If infinitions already exist then they do not exist as *new* concepts, which is what they are defined as. Infinitions may be logically quirky, but not as quirky as having the capacity to preexist themselves!

The alternative would be to claim that the concepts that infinitions inaugurate are just that: *mere* concepts. This treats inventive definitions on a par with "unicorn," "the golden mountain," or "the current king of France" and other such butts of analytical philosophers' jokes as, at most, senses with no reference, in philosophical parlance. This renders their purported ontological effects, quite literally, fanciful. Such a move, however, is just a throwback to the commonsense frame, which insists on treating concepts as representations (here read "sense") to be contrasted to the world (here read "reference"). The problem is not only that this begs the question; it is also that to treat infinitions as representations implicitly pastes over their putative novelty. The assumption that the ontological effects of infinitions must be measured against the world of "evidence" that gives them their epistemic purchase precludes novelty on two counts. For one thing, the world to which inventive definitions might refer is presumed to be already given (as an evidential benchmark, so to speak), so any question of their ontological effects *upon* such a world is already foreclosed. Second, and more to the point, such epistemic litmus tests ("does the new concept refer to an existing entity or not?") implicitly deny the novelty of the concepts they purport to measure against the world. The suggestion that an infinition might turn out not to have a referent gives logical priority to the putatively new concept (read "representation") over the world to which it may or may not refer. Thus for the question of an infinitions' reference even to be raised the supposedly novel concept must be taken as already given; its novelty, *qua* infinition, must be effaced.

Provided this reductio of the alternatives is fair and the alternatives are exhaustive,[4] it follows that by accepting the notion that definitions can be invented we willy-nilly accept that such inventions must have ontological effects—they must bring forth, into existence, the entities they define. As we shall see in the conclusion, the notion that infinitions have an onto-logical purchase, literally bringing the entities they define into existence, has far-reaching implications, not least for the practice of anthropological analysis itself. Before turning to these broader concerns, however, I want to show that the analytical perspective offered by the notion of infinition allows us also to make sense of what I have called the "regulative" role of divination in Ifá—its role in organizing the internal affairs of worship by imposing obligations on consultants.

Divination and Obligation

The remit of the oracle of Ifá extends well beyond its consultative uses. More than just providing clients with true verdicts relating to their per-sonal circumstances, divination also effectively regulates key aspects of worship, issuing edicts as well as verdicts. In chapter 3 we saw the ways in which the regulative force of the oracle operates in two related fields. First, divination lies at the heart of the structural arrangements of wor-ship insofar as it determines neophytes' initiatory course from one stage of consecration to the next, particularly by means of the ceremonious itá divinations conducted as part of initiations. Second, the signo that babala-wos are given at the itá of their own initiation serves as a life-long template for their comportment in life—the "mythopractical" injunction of what they call "living the signo."

Notably, however, it is not possible to draw a sharp distinction between consultative and regulatory aspects of divination. On the one hand, itá div-inations, in which the regulative role of the oracle becomes most apparent, also serve as ordinary consultations. Both the examples I have been using in this chapter (viz. the broken fridge and impotence) are drawn from itá divinations, and these pronouncements do not differ in any substantial way from the kinds of verdicts babalawos might give a client in an ev-eryday ókuele consultation, such as Javier's pronouncement on Yolanda's travel prospects. Conversely, ordinary consultations invariably involve a normative dimension, insofar as they serve not only to gauge the personal circumstances of the consultant, but also to enunciate the means by which to influence their course. Diagnosis and remedy are enshrined alongside each other in the liturgical order of divinatory consultations, particularly when Orula is questioned about the consultant's state of fortune by means of "asking the hand" with the ibbo. For example, in the extract from Yolanda's consultation we saw that, having determined that she is in a state of osobbo due to sorcery, Javier subsequently finds out from Orula that San Lázaro would protect the consultant from sorcery and disease provided she procured one of his consecrated necklaces. Once an action of this sort is prescribed by Orula, the consultant is obliged to carry out the remedy lest she offend the orichas involved and/or Orula himself. So the dire consequences of acts of "disobedience" in matters of initiation are just as much invoked in the context of ordinary consultation.

The pervasive normative dimension of divinatory verdicts is arguably a direct corollary of the motile logic on which they are premised. To be sure, this could be grasped intuitively. If divinatory verdicts act to redefine consultants as new people, then it seems to stand to reason that these new people should act in accordance with the ontological constitution that the oracle makes for them. For example, if by "marking a path of Ifá" for Javier in the itá of his mano de Orula ceremony, Orula redefined Javier as the kind of person that should be a babalawo, then Javier's subsequent initiation would be just a way of acting out his (newly defined) nature. However, while this way of thinking of the matter is basically right, it is also rather too quick. In particular, it makes short shrift of the notion of obligation in this context. If acting in accordance with oracular edicts is merely a matter of following one's ontological constitution, then in what sense are the edicts normative at all? Furthermore, how are we, along these lines, to make sense of the very notion of "disobedience" and of the fact that consultants often take a long time to fulfill the oracle's original edict? Recall, for instance, that both Javier and Javielito became babalawos several years after their respective itá had "called" them to initiation.

More than by a simple intuitive link-up, I suggest, the motile logic of divinatory verdicts and their normative force are connected by necessity: the infinitions that divination effects, in other words, *logically entail* the actions that they appear normatively to prescribe. The challenge, then, is to show how a verdict such as "Orula says you have a path of Ifá" could entail that the neophyte in question actually undergoes the initiation. And note that this would be a marked departure of the old Humean axiom of "no is implies an ought," which arguably underwrites the notion of obligation as it is ordinarily understood. Hence by demonstrating that in divinatory truth *ought* is the logical corollary of *is* one also formulates a motile alternative to our commonsense notion of obligation, thereby extending the sense of the alterity of divinatory truth. In order to unfold this argument we may start with the commonsense notion.

Imagine you tell your child (god forbid) "you are made to be an anthropologist." Just like Orula's call to Ifá, this is a truth-claim about a person that has implications for the future. As it stands, however, such a statement entails no actual influence over the child's future—other than parental desire, perhaps, its description of what the child is "made to be" holds no sway over what the child will actually become. In order to yield such an influence, what you would need to do is replace what looks like a descriptive statement (viz. you "are" made to be an anthropologist) with a normative one (must needs, you *ought* to become an anthropologist). Thus, in ordinary ways of thinking about normativity the notion of obligation is conceived as an extra ingredient of sorts—one that comes in to compensate for the fact that "merely" descriptive truth-claims about the future do not, as such, imply that what they claim must actually come to pass. Hence, on this view, divinatory verdicts would be deemed obligatory just to *compensate for the absence* of any ineluctable logical link between what one is told to do (divination) and what one actually does (initiation, offerings, living the signo, and so on). Divination does not imply action, it would seem, so it may as well compel it.

Now, before formulating the motile alternative, we may pause here to make explicit some of the premises that underlie this commonsense view of obligation. For a start, note that obligation on this ordinary understanding is taken as a means of regulating *choice*: it only makes sense to oblige someone to act in a certain way (e.g., to get initiated) if he may have acted otherwise. Thus obligation is posited against the background of a set of distinct possible courses of action, including the prescribed course and its assumed alternatives. In the case of divinatory "calling" the alternative that seems to motivate obligation in the first place is a state of *in*action, namely the fact that potential neophytes have *not yet* been initiated, and this state of affairs may be taken as logically distinct from the prescribed action, that is, initiation itself. So the commonsense take on divinatory obligation also implies a particular view of temporal distribution according to which actions and/or inactions succeed each other as logically discrete phases, conceived as units (cf. Strathern 2004; Holbraad and Pedersen 2009).

What unifies these logical snapshots is that they are ascribed to a single "agent." So if obligation presupposes a series of discrete actions distributed over time, it also presupposes a single perduring subject who either performs them or fails to do so at different times. In other words, the commonsense notion of obligation is premised on a straightforward Aristotelian analysis of change, whereby a single "subject" perdures through an alteration of its "predicates" at different times. Applied to initiation, this would be spelled out as follows:

Before the oracle's call the person (subject) does not have a
path of Ifá (predicate)
After the oracle's call the person (subject) has a path of Ifá (predicate)

Straightforward as it is, talk of perduring subjects and altering predicates here should alert us to the possibility that this view of obligation may be quite inappropriate for analyzing the normative force peculiar to divinatory verdicts, since Ifá, as we have seen, turns on a logic that precludes subject/predicate distinctions. In fact, by inaugurating *new meanings*, divinatory pronouncements may be said to turn the Aristotelian analysis of change inside out or, better, back to front. Rather than imagining that definition must start with a subject (definiendum) upon which predicates (definiens) may be applied, the infinitions that oracles effect take the definiens as raw material out of which a definiendum may be crafted afresh by a process of synthetic combination, as per our motile analysis of divinatory truth.

It follows that understanding the nature of the obligations the oracles impose requires a wholesale departure from subject-predicate assumptions. So we may ask: With what logical image are we left if we discard such assumptions? What would obligation look like if it were not parsed as a digital alteration of a subject's predicates? To answer these questions it pays to drill a little further into the subject-predicate analyses to which they are counterposed.

As we saw, such standard analyses of obligation imply a specific image of change itself. Most important, for my argument, this image presents change as an essentially *derivative* phenomenon: changes are broken down in terms of a temporal succession of putatively more basic logical units, which, crucially, are not in themselves subject to change. On the one hand, the substrate that guarantees the unity of the phenomenon of change (viz. the subject) is posited as a perduring and self-identical entity. On the other, the predicates that hold of it at different times do not in themselves change either: they succeed each other as discrete self-identical states that, with respect to themselves, remain static—change, after all, occurs only in their relations to the subjects they predicate at different times.

So, in line with the abiding logical reversal on which our motile analysis has been based (viz. movement before rest), one may wonder whether the Aristotelian model could be denied so as to render change *non*-derivative. What if one took the basic logical unit for the analysis of change to be *changes themselves*? This would effectively invert the analytical task: the problem would not be how to account for the fact that things change, but rather to show how changes can become stabilized as "things." Indeed, this is a problem we have already begun to solve in our analysis of infinition. As we saw, for this inverse idea of changes yielding things to make sense one has to deny the (otherwise) axiomatic distinction between a subject and its predicates (e.g., a man and whether he has a "path of Ifá") in favor of a logical universe of concepts↔(*cum*)↔things that in divination combine with each other to define new concepts↔(*cum*)↔things (e.g., the man with a path of Ifá). So we already have an account of how these elements come about, and this begs our present question nicely: is this account compatible with the analytical reversal that divinatory obligation seems to force upon us, namely that the basic units that make up infinitions (the person, the notion of an initiatory path, and so on) are changes rather than stable entities?

The contrast between nonpredicative (viz. motile) and predicative images of change, cast in terms of the logic of divinatory transformation, is depicted in figure 8.1. Three features should be emphasized. First, the symmetry along the lateral axis of 8.1a indicates that this logical universe presents the consultant and the notion of an initiatory "path" as elements of the same formal order (if not the same ontological *kind*), namely as the trajectories of change I have branded also as concepts↔(*cum*)↔things. And note that the same goes for the altered trajectory that results from their collision, that is, the infinition of the consultant as a man who has a "path" of Ifá (his invention as a person that has to become a babalawo)—this too is a trajectory of ontological change, modified by the collision of trajectories that produced (viz. infined) it. A second point follows, namely that according to this view change occurs continuously: Instead of a "digital" disjunction of a property and its negation before and after the change

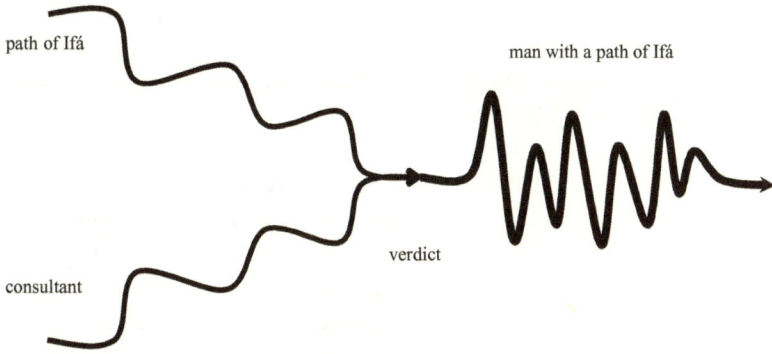

a. Motile transformation

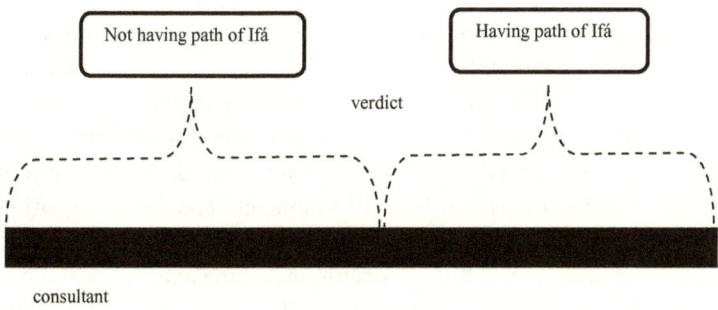

b. Aristotelian predicative change

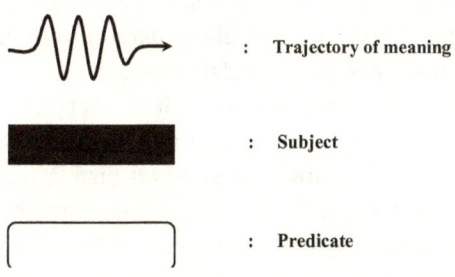

: **Trajectory of meaning**

: **Subject**

: **Predicate**

FIGURE 8.1. Parsing divinatory obligation: motile transformation versus predicative change.

as in 8.1b, what we have here is an "analogue" collision of trajectories of meaning that produces more of the same, that is, a further trajectory (cf. Bateson 2002, 103). So the novelty that the change produces should here be thought of as the kind of novelty *transformations* bring about, the creation that ensues when things differentiate themselves by combining with others (cf. Viveiros de Castro 1998a, 15–17). After change, it is changes all the way down—to recast a familiar anthropological saying (Geertz 1973a, 28–29). Indeed, this is a further sense in which the neologism of "infinition" is apposite. If the constituents that make for the transformations that an infinition involves are themselves further transformations, then one can say that, by their nature, infinitions are implicated in series of modulations of meaning that extend into infinity (see also Holbraad 2008). Indeed, insofar as any particular infinition is *defined* in terms of the modulations that, as it were transitively, lead up to it, one may say that infinity is constitutively contained within it (cf. Riles 1998).

From this idea of continuous transformation follows the third and, to our purposes, most significant point, which has to do with choice. As explained earlier, the idea of choice turns on subject-predicate logic, since choices are premised on logical distinctions between possible courses of action that can be distributed discretely over time.[5] So choice is incongruent with our motile image. Indeed, to imagine change as a continuous modulation of further changes is to imagine a world that is "determinist" to the point of asphyxia. If the trajectories that make up a transformation are *seamlessly* connected, and no data other than trajectories influence their course (changes all the way down), their courses could *not but* be as they are. For to imagine an alternative course (as one must if one is properly to speak of choosing) is conceptually to *interrupt* a change in order to intercalate its putative alternative. And this would be to render the change discrete—effectively, to "conventionalize" it as a subject (see above). In other words, each trajectory of meaning is as it is because the trajectories that it combines are as they are because of yet further trajectories, and, since this regress is infinite, each trajectory *cannot but* be as it is.

Such an image of pure actuality, as we may call it, allows us to formulate a motile account of obligation. True, this image leaves no space for a concept of obligation that is bound up with the option of choice. But this is its virtue for our purposes (see also Holbraad 2010b). For the notion, for example, that having a "path of Ifá" marked by the oracle implies that the potential neophyte *has to* undergo the initiation can be rendered in purely motile terms. On such an analysis the divinatory verdict that says "you have a path of Ifá" does not *pre*scribe a course of action in the face of possible alternatives, but rather *de*scribes (or pre*dicts*) a course that cannot but be as it is, since it is trajectile in the way I have just explained. On the oracle's say-so, becoming a babalawo is something one "has to" do in the sense of having the ceremony ahead of one, as a necessary constitutive element of who one is (rather than in the ordinary normative sense, where "have to" is synonym to "ought to"). Were the term not too loaded, we would say that on a motile view what seems like obligation is constituted as *destiny* in the strict sense: what one "has to" do is one's destination, a destination that is given by the trajectories of meaning that oracles bring together so as to redefine the people who consult them.[6]

Initiation as Ontological Transformation

At this point it is worth pausing to consider the implications of this analysis of the normative force of divination for the notion of initiation itself. In particular, I would suggest that such an analysis speaks directly to a rather intuitive notion one often meets in anthropological discussions of initiation rites, namely that the point of such ceremonies is to transform neophytes ontologically—to make them different kinds of people: from boys to men, laymen to diviners, and so on (e.g., Van Gennep 1960; Turner 1969; Bloch 1992). Now, the idea of transformation is hardly alien to what babalawos have to say about the importance of initiation. As we saw in chapter 3, babalawos describe initiation as the "birth of a king," and elaborate in a number of ways on the effects of such a birth (initiation gives you aché, health, a longer life). Furthermore, such notions of transformation also have structural implications, effecting a gradual accumulation of relationships, both with deities (including with one's own signo of initiation, which has to be "lived") and with ritual kin in the context of the lineage and the family.

In an important sense, these relational transformations (viz. human-oricha, human-human, and signo-human) make initiation analogous to divination, to the extent that the latter also turns on babalawos' ability interpretatively to establish relationships between consultants and the mythical features of the oddu. Moreover, the notion that such interpretative relationships in divination serve to redefine the consultant, transforming his or her ontological constitution, implies that they are to be understood, philosophically speaking, as internal. One is therefore led to consider whether the analogy of initiation with divination holds in this respect as well. Since it is divination that precipitates initiation, can one say that the internal relationships that characterize the former are *carried over* to the latter—are they, from the point of view of their motile logic, *transitive*?

Again, to see that they are, consider the opposite case, namely the suggestion that the relations that initiation brings about are logically "external." On such a view, a neophyte's relationship to the divinities that he "receives" in initiation (as well as the rest of the relationships this entails, with kin and signo alike) would have to be conceived in predicative terms. The neophyte comes to "have" the deities (the godfather, the signo) like a subject "has" predicates (or "properties"). However, while such a position seems perfectly tenable in itself, it is inconsistent with the idea that the initiation ceremony, through which the neophyte comes to acquire all these new relationships, was obligated by the oracle's call in the motile sense. Treating these relationships in predicative terms amounts to treating the neophyte as a logical subject, "conventionalizing" him as a discrete entity. This would *sever* the motile trajectory of obligation at its most crucial point, namely the point at which the ceremony prescribed by Orula is actually carried out—the point of the oracular edict's "consummation," if you will. Thus, treating initiatory relationships as external would be to introduce a logical break between divination and initiation (viz. continuous trajectory versus discrete subject), whereas the whole point of a motile analysis of obligation is to dissolve such a separation. In a motile analysis, as we have seen, obligation is a function of the motility of the action of divination itself: the modulation of transformations that the oracle effects is one of *directing* the neophyte toward his initiation, by redefining him as someone who "has to" do it.

In effect, on this motile image, the temporal lag from divinatory "call" to ceremony is rendered a *logical feature* of initiatory transformation: time unites divination and initiation as seamlessly connected moments on a trajectory of motile modulation, rather than separating them as discrete actions. So when practitioners speak of the initiatory course of Ifá as a "path" they are being more telling than metaphorical: practitioners move from one ceremony to the next as paths whose course is set by divinatory stricture (see also Panagiotopoulos 2011). Defined by the oracles, each practitioner's path (or better, each practitioner-as-path) unfolds in the course of initiation, as a unique, continuous and therefore "purely actual" transformation. Mixing a metaphor, we may say that oracles regulate ini-

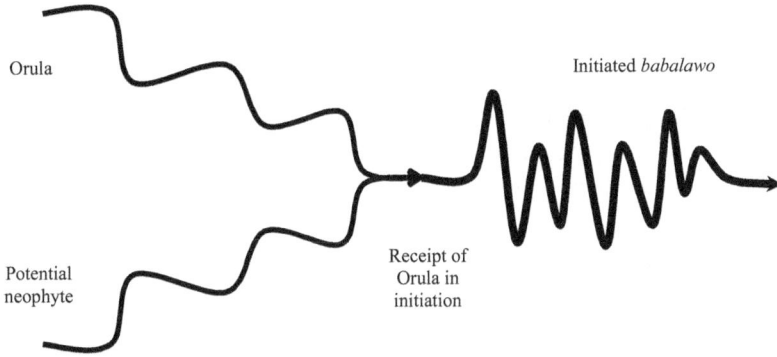

FIGURE 8.2. Initiatory transformation in Ifá.

tiation by channeling neophytes' paths like dams that harness a river. And the paths are as they are "obligatorily" in the (uncommon) sense of having their course marked by oracles that preclude the possibility of choice itself—precluding, if you like, the possibility of possibility.

So, by virtue of its own motility, the model of oracular obligation presented in figure 8.1a duplicates itself in the initiation ceremony that it precipitates, as seen in figure 8.2. It should be clear that the relations involved here, between deities and humans (or, in full Ifá initiation, also between the initiatory signo and the neophyte babalawo), are indeed internal. By being received, the deities *transform* the neophyte into someone who "has" them. This logical analysis casts in rigorous terms ethnographic hints at ontological transformation, such as the idea that initiation is a regal "birth" that gives aché. Inasmuch as these characteristics are gained by virtue of receiving the deities, they can only be thought of as characteristics that *define* the neophyte, and definition is the hallmark of internal relation.

Equivocations

To conclude this analysis of initiation, I want to defend it from a strong objection, namely that it exoticizes the actual experience of initiation as it pans out in Ifá practitioners' lives. A case can certainly be made for this complaint. As set out, the whole argument about the ontological transformations that divination and initiation effect has taken the form of a detailed elucidation of the motile logic of divinatory infinitions. Insofar as initiation ceremonies are indeed precipitated by the oracles and the motile obligations they induce, this may make sense. But is this not an altogether idealized image of what actually goes on when a practitioner decides to undergo initiation? "Decision" is used advisedly here because from the practitioner's perspective—as opposed to that of the oracle, on which the analysis has focused—that seems to be exactly what initiation involves. Indeed, this is how both Javier and his son put the matter. Both allowed a number of years to pass before they acted on Orula's initial call to Ifá. Javier admitted to being quite happy to enjoy his life as an Abakuá in Matanzas, while Javielito said quite openly that for many years following his "call" to Ifá (which came when he was still a child) his attitude was one of "disinterest." So while the oracle may present initiation as the inevitable outcome of Orula's call, the actual people involved do not seem to see their progression from the "call" to its consummation as ineluctable. Indeed, if practitioners had no choice in the matter, as I seem to have suggested, why would babalawos raise the specter of the orichas' divine wrath as a sanction against "falling into disobedience"? Fear and anxiety appear to be methods for *keeping* potential neophytes on the straight and narrow ("path"), and this indicates that, contrary to my analysis, things *could* have taken a different course.

What is more, they often do. Notwithstanding the obligations divinatory "calls" impose, there are plenty of men in Havana who at one time or other were told by diviners that they have a path of Ifá and nevertheless remain uninitiated, often because they cannot afford to pay for the ceremony, or even because they ignored the oracle's prescription, as Javielito admitted doing for several years. Just as telling is the converse case, namely babalawos whose initiation seems to have been owed more to personal choice than to divinatory obligation. For example, in the late 1990s, when Ifá was enjoying its first period of effervescence in the wake of years of suppression by the state authorities, some men treated Ifá initiation as a lifestyle choice—an element of their "street cred," along with owning a motorbike or designer clothes (Holbraad 2004a). These new initiates were rarely inclined to invest much time in learning how to practice as babalawos, so that for many of them initiation hardly marked a transformation at all—let alone an ontological one.

Notably, however, such initiates did tend to admit that they would rather keep their lapses to themselves in the presence of more senior babalawos, who would be sure to criticize them for their "lack of respect"—*falta de respeto*. Indeed, if we may call them that, those "lifestyle babalawos" I spoke to were rarely at ease with their stance. Knowing that their "disobediences" and "disrespects" were subject to criticism, and expecting them to attract divine sanctions, they were themselves typically embarrassed and apprehensive about their behavior. So, the fact that these behaviors form an important part of the picture of Ifá practice in Havana does not warrant the conclusion that the motile logic of Ifá as I have outlined it exoticizes what actually goes on when a practitioner decides to undergo initiation. On the contrary, inasmuch as acts that are not in line with oracular obligations are perceived as deviant not only by orthodox babalawos but also by those who commit them, the ethnography confirms the import of the logic of Ifá for practitioners.

But there is also a principled reason for resisting the charge that a motile analysis relies on an overly exotic account of initiation. For the contrast between the logic of divinatory obligation and people's capacity to contradict it on which the charge is based is strictly analogous to a contrast examined earlier in relation to the oracles' claim to truth. As we saw in the previous chapter, the fact that diviners' truth-claims are stipulated as indubitable does not mean that they are never actually doubted. Like anthropologists who write on divination, practitioners too may wonder whether what oracles say is "really true." As we saw, however, for babalawos who take such pains normatively to emphasize that the oracle is infallible this is just a misunderstanding: to doubt whether an oracular pronouncement is true is to doubt whether it is an oracular pronouncement.

The same holds for the obligations that the motile logic of the oracles induces. It *is* perfectly possible to view initiation as a matter of choice—a discrete possibility of action to be weighed against alternatives, or even just ignored. However, such reversals of the priority of obligation over choice in Ifá amount to a form of logical *denial*, in the psychological sense of the word. To weigh what one "has" to do against possible alternatives is to deny the special sense in which one has to do it (as one's motile destiny), conventionalizing obligation as a predicative "ought." Or, putting it in the earlier formula, to treat initiation as a matter of choice is to treat it as if it were not, properly speaking, an initiation at all. Again, the only way to bar this logical avenue is normative: enter notions of disobedience, disrespect, and the fear of Orula's wrath. In view of how serious the matter of initiation is to the life of the cult, it is hardly surprising that the normative stakes, and the emotive responses they induce for practitioners, should rise in such a fashion.

More generally, one could say that the analytical strategy that has led us to develop the present argument about the analytics of motility, infinitions, and ontological transformation is one that, in a sense, *obeys Orula*. Rather than setting up the alterity of Ifá worship as a series of ethnographic "phenomena" that require anthropological "explanation" (Why should practitioners of Ifá think that their rituals are able to elicit transcendent deities into immanence? Why should they think that the truths these deities give them in divination are beyond doubt? Why should they think that initiation turns them into different kinds of persons?), we have instead obeyed the logic of the ethnography by taking its peculiar character for granted. Given that practitioners of Ifá think and act in ways that do indeed appear quite peculiar—in fact, as has been shown, they appear absurd—from the point of view of commonsense assumptions that inform the anthropologist's own thoughts and actions, how far do we need to depart from these assumptions in order to make sense of Ifá, removing its semblance of absurdity? And what new assumptions must take their place? As a conclusion, the next chapter is devoted to exploring the implications of this strategic shift for the practice of anthropology itself. In particular, its aim is to explore what I shall call the "metarecursive" potential of such a strategy. If, as we have seen, the dividend of our analysis of Ifá has been a new way of conceptualizing the notion of truth, then to what extent can such a notion elucidate the very process by which it was arrived at? What, in other words, is *anthropology*'s peculiar claim to truth, and how does it relate to the analytics that our study of Ifá divination has precipitated?

Anthropological Truth

In the introduction I explained that a key motivation for this book's argument would be to take seriously the analogy between babalawos and intellectuals, which so often surfaces in the literature on Ifá. I suggested that doing so serves a recursive agenda on two levels. The first one, which pertains to the relationship between ethnographic materials and analytical concepts, opens the way for the second, further recursive step, which pertains to the relationship between analytical concepts and the procedures through which they are derived. Throughout the book, I have so far concentrated on the first task, by proposing a recursive analysis of the concept of truth with reference to the alterity of Ifá divination in Cuba—truth being the common-yet-different concern of diviners and intellectuals that gave rise to the analogy between babalawos and intellectuals in the first place. The outcome of this process has been to develop a suitably "altered" concept of truth, branded with the neologism "infinition" to underline the alteration.

To move on from there to meta-anthropological questions about the recursive relationship between anthropological analysis and ethnography constitutes, so to speak, a metarecursive step: what difference does reinventing the concept of truth in the light of Ifá make to the way one thinks about truth in anthropology? For the very idea that the study of Ifá might require the analyst to replace one notion of truth with another is itself a claim about the kind of truth that anthropological analysis may yield. Indeed, it is with this metarecursive step that the fecundity of the analogy between diviners and intellectuals really comes into its own. In the argument of the preceding chapters, the recursive revision of truth that is occasioned by the ethnography of Ifá has been directed specifically at the representationist assumptions that have informed the scholarly literature on divination:

CONCLUSION

How does one need to revise one's assumptions about what counts as truth in order to avoid the habitual conclusion that divination comprises merely a set of absurd "beliefs"? Metarecursive questions, on the other hand, turn the light on recursive analysis as such, by asking how the altered concept of truth that this recursive process engenders (viz. truth as infinition) relates to the kind of claim to truth that recursive analysis itself might make. This pertains to a broader concern with the character of truth in anthropological reasoning: How might the revised concept of truth that the analysis of Ifá has yielded shed light on the forms of reasoning that such an analysis involves? How, in other words, might a concept of truth derived recursively from the work of Cuban diviners modify the way we think of our work as intellectuals in anthropology?

This concluding chapter takes up these metarecursive questions. By this stage their answer may seem predictable, or even banal. For it takes little to notice that there is a direct correspondence between the outcome of the preceding chapters' recursive argument, namely the conceptualization of truth as an event of conceptual invention, and the process by which it was derived. It may appear, even, as if the metarecursive argument can be derived directly from this relationship: the argument has exemplified itself, one might want to say, by reproducing its content (truth as infinition) in its form (again, truth as infinition). And yes: in a broad and basic way, this would sum up the conclusion this final chapter seeks to establish, namely that, like divination, recursive anthropology is indeed in the business of infinition.

Nevertheless, it would be an error to suppose that such a conclusion follows logically from the recursive argument about the conceptualization of truth in divination.[1] The correspondence between the content of that argument (divination as infinition) and its form (anthropology as, in some sense, also infinition) is as deceptive as it is revealing, arguably hiding much that is different in the character and role of infinition in the two cases. The problem is formally identical to one I identified in chapter 1 when commenting on Wagner's argument on invention. In that context I argued that the coincidence of the content of Daribi ethnography (culture as invention) and the form of its analysis (anthropology as invention) was a matter of strategy rather than logical necessity. So, to set on its tracks the argument on infinition in anthropological thinking, we may begin by dwelling a little on its strategy.

The parallel with Wagner's argument on invention is close. Indeed, the distinction between recursive arguments from ethnography and their metarecursive dividends can be mapped onto it directly. Wagner's recursive argument proceeds in three steps. First, Wagner establishes that anthropologists assume conventionally that cultural differences are to be understood as differences in conventions. Second, he shows that this assumption can be contradicted ethnographically, since what makes the Daribi (and other non-Westerners) different is the fact that the things that anthropologists would recognize as their "culture" are in fact the opposite of convention, since they are oriented toward subverting conventions (taken as "innate") so as to generate (artificially) inventions. Third, Wagner goes on to revise the concept of culture in the light of this ethnographic difference (this being the recursive move), so as to generate a novel analytical standpoint from which "culture" incorporates invention as a process of differentiation from convention. As I pointed out, this recursive argument then acts as a resource for a further and logically separate move on Wagner's part, namely that of characterizing that argument itself as an example of anthropological invention. The reason why this metarecursive move is strategic (rather than a necessary logical consequence) is that it could have been occasioned by a different body of ethnography altogether—one that might not focus on cultural processes of invention at all: *any* contradiction between initial assumptions and ethnographic description (i.e., any case of alterity, as I shall be defining it more formally in what follows) could do. While Wagner is not explicit about this himself, I suggested, the strategic advantage of the analogy between content and form in his argument is that it facilitates an anthropological comparison: the ethnographic inventions he describes and the analytical inventions he performs in doing so are placed alongside each other, in comparative relief—the apogee, arguably, of a metarecursive tack.

   In parallel to this strategy point for point, the argument on anthropological truth I now want to advance is also meant to supplement it. This is partly for the reasons explained in the introduction, namely that Wagner's recursive analytic, as well as those of Strathern, Latour, Viveiros de Castro, and others, places the notion of truth at an unwarranted distance. But it is also because getting a handle on the role of truth in recursive anthropological arguments allows us to add something to the Wagnerian idea that such arguments are examples of "invention." Indeed, in the light of the analysis of divinatory truth in the last chapter, it will be clear that the notion of infinition is itself a transformation of Wagner's idea of invention—its modulation in the key of truth. So, to mix the metaphors further, my attempt to fill a gap in the recursive literature involves deepening it a little first.

In what follows, the argument on infinition in divination is treated as a resource for articulating by comparison the notion of truth on which such recursive arguments rely, and the kinds of reasoning to which it gives rise. Just as Wagner's meta-anthropological argument puts Daribi inventions and their anthropological analysis side by side, as versions of each other, so I want to put babalawos' infinitions on a level with my own. Indeed, if this leveling effect relies partly on treating the ethnography of divination as an analytical resource (its recursive transformation, performed piecemeal in the preceding chapters), it also involves treating that analysis as an ethnographic one. So I begin by treating the argument of the previous chapters in just this way (as an ethnographic example of recursive analysis at work), with a view to making explicit the character of its claims to truth. Metarecursively, I shall be drawing on the content of this argument in order to articulate its form, and, in doing so, compare the two. Of key concern here will be the contrasts, as well as the continuities, between the roles of infinition in the two cases. Crucially, this will involve comparing the respective stances toward alterity in either case, since, as I have noted in relation to Wagner, it is the problem of ethnographic alterity that raises the requirement of analytical invention on the part of the anthropologist. To the extent that questions of ontological alterity are also at the heart of Ifá divination, as we have seen in earlier chapters, the question of alterity has a direct purchase on the contrast between the two activities.

Divination and Anthropology

At the outset in this book, I made clear that the analogy between divination and anthropology (or intellectual work more generally) is due to the fact that both activities are centrally and explicitly concerned with truth. Much of the main body of the book has been devoted to corroborating and clarifying this claim with regard to divination, using the majesty of Ifá as the case in point. In devoting so much ethnographic energy to just one side of the analogy, however, I have taken the other for granted as a matter of course. It is only because one assumes that anthropology is eminently concerned with truth that comparing it along those lines with divination is interesting or revealing. Even my relatively brief discussion of the trajectory of truth in anthropology—from evolutionism to constructionism and so on—gained its place in chapter 1 as an account of *how* truth has been a concern for anthropologists. *That* it has been so was taken as obvious.

Why this ethnographic self-assurance? Would a proper analogy not require a more symmetrical approach, not just in the epistemological sense made famous by Latour (1993), but also for the sheer balance of ethnographic detail? Certainly, as Latour and others have demonstrated with their own ethnographies of academic practice—including studies of documents not unlike the pages if this book (Riles 2006)—revealing ethnographically the properties of academic research takes as much work as doing it. Yet there is one sense in which the ethnographic asymmetry of my account may be justified. For one of the differences between diviners' and intellectuals' concern for truth lies precisely in its degree of transparency.

Divination and anthropology are indeed about truth in equal measure (though it remains to be seen in what sense this may be so). But one way in which anthropology, like other intellectual work, is different from divination is that it is also concerned with making this concern explicit—it is, as it were, constitutively concerned with its concern for truth. This, I take it, is what we have in mind when we say that intellectual work of this kind takes the form of "argument"—the *logos* in "anthropology" enshrines this. The notion of argument is no doubt complex, embedded in "knowledge practices" (*sensu* Strathern 2005) whose elucidation would take me into matters of formal logic as well as more public-spirited debates in science and technology studies, which is further than I can go here. I merely wish to highlight that rendering a concern with truth obvious is constitutive to what we mean by "argument." Making an argument, we take it, involves bringing to the surface of a text the procedures by which its truth is established, rendering transparent—even "sign-posting," as it is said—features relating to logic, validity, scope, consistency, evidence, coherence, and so forth. One might even want to say that the peculiar modus operandi of arguments rely on the idea that an argument's claim to truth consists in the manner in which it is shown: a "strong" argument is one that shows, or "performs," its strength in this sense—rather like Greek men, famously for Michael Herzfeld (1988), are only proper men by virtue of showing that they are.

To see the contrast with divination, consider the sting in characterizing the style of a piece of intellectual work as "oracular," as self-consciously Anglo-Saxon intellectuals often do for the writings of "Continentals." In effect "oracular" points to an absence of argument in the text: it presumes truth, failing to *display* a sufficient concern with it; in other words, it states truth rather than establishing it. Seen in this light, anthropologists' traditional worry about the epistemic credentials of divination amount to a worry about why people might "believe" in diviners, given their characteristic lack of *argument*—actual and, more disconcertingly, possible. And my critical move against this literature has turned on this idea as well. I argued that rather than take the failure of divinatory truth to comply with standards of intellectual argumentation as a sign of its epistemic deficiency, we should take it as a clue to its basic alterity. If diviners do not argue for their truth-claims in the way we do, say, when we talk about them, that is because their truth-claims are of a sort that requires no argument.

So a basic ethnographic difference between the concern for truth in divination and in anthropology lies in its ethnographic tractability. While in divination one has to "find" the concern with truth, in anthropology it is given at the surface—its "obviousness" is one of its ethnographic characteristics. Hence the asymmetry: if the overall task of the preceding chapters has been to find the concern for truth in divination, revealing the peculiar characteristics that make it so different from our own concerns in doing so, the task of this final chapter is rather to "read off" the kinds of truth-claims that this analysis has made from the arguments that have made them explicit. In retracing these traces of (and as) argument, my concern is to see how the contrast between representational and infinitive truth that they articulate plays itself out in that very articulation. In particular, I want to show that the character of infinition in this mode of anthropological reasoning, comparable but different to its character in divination, is owed to the peculiar nature of the analytical challenge that ethnographic alterity presents. It is the difference between the ways in which alterity enters into divination and into recursive anthropological analysis that accounts for the different character and role of truth as infinition in the two cases.

To see this we may return to the beginning. I started chapter 2 by explaining that its task would be to create the "elbow space" for a new way of looking at divinatory truth. This conjures the image of a kind of analytical competition—perhaps of a race to anthropological success, or even of a commercial enterprise of sorts, in which competing accounts of divination struggle to establish their own niche in a crowded market of approaches; here are the alternative products for making sense of divination, and here's mine, and here's why it is better. Given the intellectual character of the exercise, one may assume that criteria of truth would be at the heart of this kind of pitch. Loosely and intuitively, one may expect that arguing for a new approach to divination would involve showing that existing ones are in one way or another wrong, and then raising the prospect of a better one, where what makes for a "better" approach is understood, in some sense, as its superior claim to truth. It may well be that this intuition goes back to one's caricatured memory of school, with its right and wrong answers to questions on the blackboard. Still, it seems to capture something basic about the arguments developed in chapter 2. One after the other, competing approaches to divination are shown to be deficient, and then the "desiderata" for a better approach are proposed.

So we may ask: on what notion of truth does this tack of argument rely? The answer is not straightforward since the argument unfolds as a complex sequence of claims to truth and judgments upon them. The first point to note, however, is that a large part of this sequence of reasoning relies on a straightforwardly representationist notion of truth. Key to this is the question that both motivates and directs the sifting of competing accounts of divination, namely how far each of them is able to reflect divinatory phenomena as they are—a clear-cut question about the relationship between representations and facts. The question surfaces in the argument in a number of ways, which are strung together sequentially.

Initially, it motivates an ethnographic premise, namely that, for its practitioners, what makes divination important is that it delivers truth. As a putatively "empirical" claim, this was established already in the introduction by drawing on the historical and ethnographic literature on Ifá in West Africa and Cuba, and then reiterated in chapter 2 with reference also to scholarship on other forms of divination. This statement of ethnographic "fact" then serves as the basic criterion that guides the review of existing analytical approaches to divination. It does so in two distinguishable ways.

First, it serves as a criterion of relevance. Reviewing the literature, I identify broadly three "competitor" approaches (viz. functionalism, symbolism, and speech-act theory) and show how each fails to engage with the question of truth head on. Note that this is not an argument about the truth or falsehood of these approaches, since their claims to truth may be credible in their own terms (e.g., it may be true that certain forms of divination promote social order). The critical point is only that the facts they purport to identify in divination are not the ones that mark out the empirical remit of my own argument—simply, they are not "about" the aspects of divinatory phenomena which my argument seeks to address, namely practitioners' concern for truth.[2]

Second, the argument turns to approaches that engage directly with the question of truth. In doing so it raises the representational truth-stakes. My dispute with Evans-Pritchard and Boyer, put forward as a way of diagnosing a basic divergence of approach to just this question, is comfortably cast as a truth-functional disagreement over the representation of divinatory phenomena. What is most basically "wrong" with their analyses, I suggested, is that, in seeking to account for why people might "believe" that divination delivers truth, they effectively assume that divinatory claims to truth must be of a kind that is inherently open to doubt. This contradicts what arguably makes diviners' verdicts so special for the practitioners themselves, namely that their verdicts are understood as such to be beyond doubt. So what we seem to have here is a straightforward dispute about the representation of the facts of divination: Evans-Pritchard and Boyer represent divinatory truth to be one way; I demonstrate that in fact it is another; hence I pronounce their account of divination to be "false."

So far so good, one might say. If what is wrong with existing accounts of divination is that they misrepresent its claim to truth, presumably the solution is simple: replace them with an account that represents it correctly—in particular, one that represents it as inherently indubitable. Notably, on such a view Evans-Pritchard's and Boyer's broader anthropological question regarding practitioners' "belief" in divination would be basically right. Its only fault would be that it was formulated somewhat inaccurately. In view of my empirically minded correction, rather than asking why practitioners believe that oracles give them the truth, they should be asking why they might believe that the truth the oracles purport to give them is indubitable—the only difference between the "apparent irrationality" in the two cases being that the latter is more extreme.

Yet this is not how the argument of chapter 2 proceeds. Instead of seeking to remedy the faults of earlier representations of divination by recommending a better one, and then adjusting the analytical questions that ride on it accordingly, the tack of the argument is to intensify the perception of the faults to such a degree as to show them up as insoluble, and thus to undermine the analytical edifice that is built upon them. To this end, the argument takes a modal turn, to demonstrate that accounts such as those of Evans-Pritchard and Boyer misrepresent divinatory truth, not by way of mere empirical inaccuracy, but rather by logical necessity.

This involves showing two things. First, that the *only possible* way to represent divinatory truth-claims is as purported representations of facts. As I showed, while a number of ways of thinking about indubitable truths are available, none of them can be applied to divinatory verdicts. Such verdicts, in other words, do not meet criteria of indubitability as we know them. Whatever way you look at them, they look like ordinary statements of fact. Second, however, if this is so, we are stuck with doubt as an inherent property of the verdicts. This is because statements of fact have the possibility of doubt built into them, as a corollary of the very notion of representation. Representations are inherently doubtful since the ontological "gap" between them and the world they purport to reflect leaves the possibility of error open as a matter of logical principle.

Taken together, these two arguments reduce to the absurd the idea that divinatory verdicts are indubitably true. If our *best shot* at describing verdicts as true is to describe them as representations, then the putatively empirical claim that they are understood as indubitable by practitioners themselves is logically incoherent. To say "divinatory verdicts are indubitably true representations" is to state a logical oxymoron. So if that is the best way we can find to describe the ethnography of divination, we are effectively imputing to our informants not an apparently irrational belief but a form of absurdity: if we know what truth means at all in this context, we know that it cannot count as indubitable.

It is with this move from belief to absurdity that the argument of chapter 2 takes its recursive turn. On the back of my discussion of the recursive strategies of Wagner, Viveiros de Castro, and others in chapter 1, I suggested that reducing our description of divinatory truth to the absurd effectively lifts the burden of the "problem" of divination from the shoulders of our informants and shifts it onto our own, as analysts. True, one could conceivably stick with charging the absurd idea of indubitable representations on the tab of our informants. But note the crucial difference. A "belief" that, say, oracles give truth may indeed appear irrational (e.g., why should a random event like the tossing of coconut shells be deemed a source of truth?), but one can at least *conceive* of it as being true. Its apparent irrationality comes down to a form of disagreement: one side believes that oracles give truth while the other does not. The two positions turn on the same concept of truth (namely truth as representation) and the disagreement is about how best to apply it (about whether one can ascribe truth to oracles or not). Not so for the charge of absurdity. Here the problem is that, as far as the putative belief can be formulated at all, it is

properly speaking altogether *inconceivable*. To ascribe to those who practice divination the belief that oracles give representations that are immune
to doubt is to ascribe to them a nonsense of the order of "bachelors are
married" or "2 + 2 = 3." The problem, then, ceases to be one of a putative
disagreement and becomes one of sheer and necessary incomprehension.
Precisely because we *know*, as a matter now of logical principle, that representational truths are inherently doubtful, we *cannot know*, even with
the best description we can muster, *what* the other side is supposed to be
holding. We have nothing to say, then, about what practitioners of divination believe, save one thing: If our best representation of their belief is
that divination gives truth, then the concept of truth that is stake for them
must be different to the one we have had to take for granted when describing it. To paraphrase Sperber against himself, there are no native "semi-
propositions" to be found: just our own non-propositions about them.

So the real effect and significance of the reductio of our best accounts
of divination is to reduce to the absurd the very project of anthropological representation. And hence the recursivity: a logical repatriation
of the problem of alterity. The problem lies not with what "they" might
think (*sensu* Bloch 1998), and neither, therefore, with how we might best
represent it—describe it empirically, explain it positively, interpret it relatively, appreciate it respectfully, and so on. Rather the problem lies with
us: whatever it may be that they say or do, let alone think or believe, we
are not equipped to represent it. To use a mentalist metaphor, alterity is
exposed as a projection of our own thoughts onto the inside of our forehead—or, to switch to a more classical image, a shadow play that figures
on the walls of our cave. Indeed, the effect of alterity thus construed is
similar to the one Socrates was supposed to have induced in his interlocutors in dialogues such as the *Republic*, with his relentless questioning
of the assumptions that lay behind what they thought they already knew,
namely *aporia*. The dual connotation of the Greek word captures well the
predicament of alterity: not only a feeling of puzzlement, but also a sense
that it is borne of one's lack of resources[3]—the poverty of thought that in
English too we call "being at a loss."

Before going on to examine the particular demands that this way of
construing the problem of alterity places on anthropological analysis—
its particular consequences for the way we think about anthropological
truth—we may consider its immediate dividends with respect to the recursively minded literature reviewed in the introduction. The turn that

my argument from absurdity forces is basically consonant with the message of this literature, namely that ethnographic alterity is a function of our own conceptual inadequacy. However, I would suggest that arriving at this conclusion by way of the kind of reductio argument we have just reviewed helps to further specify this thought. Recursive analyses tend to be presented as if they were somehow irrelevant to anthropologists' traditional concern with the truth of their representations of the people they study. Viveiros de Castro, as we saw, puts it explicitly: "the concept of objective truth (along with those of representation and nature) is part of the rules of *that* game [viz. anthropological representation], not the one being proposed here" (2002, 116, original emphasis). In an important sense, of course, this is true. The whole point of the kind of reductio I have performed is to show that alterity is indeed that which cannot be represented.

However, the point is also that, if this is what alterity is, then the way to find it is by *showing* how attempts to represent it fail. As we have seen in our review of the strategy of the argument of chapter 2, while the outcome of the reductio of indubitable representations is the aporia of nonrepresentation, the means for reaching it are thoroughly representational. Like negative theology, we reach that which cannot be represented by showing how all attempts to represent it fail. Albeit through its failure, then, representational truth acts as the necessary diagnostic of alterity: without it the recursive turn remains logically unmotivated.

This first sense in which truth (in this case representational truth) is relevant to recursive analysis has far-reaching implications, both strategically (to show why recursivity is anthropologically advisable and defend it from its critics) and substantially (to pinpoint its particular character and scope more precisely). On the matter of strategy, the idea that the failures of representation force recursivity upon us by logical necessity provides a significant supplement to the recursively minded arguments that were explored in the chapter 1. With reference to the work of Wagner, Strathern, and Viveiros de Castro, I showed that their suggestion that ethnographic alterity precipitates the need recursively to rethink our own means for conceptualizing it was motivated as a matter of what might be described as analytical felicity. Wagner, for example, posed the problem of treating Daribi culture in terms of conventions as a matter of ethnographic distortion, which fails, as he puts it in *Habu*, "to make . . . provision for creativity within the culture it purports to represent" (Wagner 1972, 3). Strathern, similarly, talks about the need to "displace our metaphors" as a matter of achieving the goal of "adequate description" (1988, 12). Most explicitly, Viveiros de Castro emphasizes the moral and political implications of failing to do so—a failure to recognize our constitutive misunderstandings of others' meanings turns their "culture" into an "epistemic teratology [of] error, illusion, madness [and] ideology" (2002, 130). By contrast, the argument from absurdity presented here shows that, more than a matter of analytical felicity, recursive attention to our own misunderstandings is a matter of logical necessity.

This adds an effective weapon for defending the recursive approach from the habitual quips of error, illusion, and madness that are made against *it*. As we saw, critics who find the recursive insistence on conceptual alterity tiresome are fond of making arguments from preposterousness in classical empiricist style: "surely the Melanesians/Amerindians/etc. don't think that . . . ," they say, holding up their hands in triumph to show that they exist.[4] The force of such criticisms turns on an Ockham's razor sort of a choice: between the options of (e.g.) supposing that Amazonians might really define peccaries as humans, and assuming that they must know that the two are different, such critics prefer to credit the Amazonians with a modicum of "common sense." Arguments from what I have called analytical felicity can only counter this choice on grounds of its lack of imagination, as a matter, ultimately, of moral preference: you may wish to credit people with common sense, would go the reply, but I would rather credit what they actually say (e.g., in a given situation, that peccaries are human). By contrast, the strategy pursued in chapter 2 bars commonsense chauvinism by reducing *it* to the absurd. If your very best shot at even describing divinatory truth lands you in a contradiction—the nonsense of saying that divinatory verdicts are both representations and inherently beyond doubt—then it is you who needs to think again.

Most revealing, however, is how the argument from absurdity meets the charge that often rides on such hardnosed appeals to common sense, namely that of "exoticism." Like relativists, goes the complaint, those who present the challenge of anthropological analysis as a matter of conceptual alterity are committed to exaggerating differences at the expense of palpable similarities. Even if we accept that in certain circumstances people might really think that peccaries are human (or that divinations are indubitable), it is an outrageous exaggeration to base one's whole account of them on such data, since we all know from experience that even the most remote and exotic-looking peoples go about their lives most of the time much as we do—Evans-Pritchard established this contra Lévy-Bruhl's philosophical exoticism of different "mentalities," as we saw, many years ago.

In chapter 1 I noted the basic misapprehension involved in this line of complaint, namely the assumption that recursive analyses are even in the business of providing accurate representations of the people studied. One might also note the prejudicial premise of holism that such criticisms presuppose—as if all analytical proposals by anthropologists had to draw their strength from the completeness of their scope (see also Holbraad 2009, 2010a). Again, however, I would suggest that defining the problem of alterity as a failure of representation helps to sharpen the response. As we have seen, this approach depends on displaying alterity by copiously going through all the ways in which it could (though ultimately cannot) be represented. Far from being assumed or exaggerated, difference is "proved" by taking the assumption of *similarity* to its limit—taking the representations that we would assume have a purchase on our ethnography as seriously as they can be taken, in order to show in precise terms where, how and why they nevertheless lead us into absurd positions. To put it by analogy to Karl Popper's famous argument on the value of falsifying scientific propositions, recursive analysis proceeds, not by seeking to verify some first principle of alterity, but rather by submitting the prior supposition of similarity to systematic testing so as to determine the exact degree to which it may or may not be carried.

This also shows why recursive analysis is in no way incompatible with the obvious observation that alterity is hardly an all-encompassing predicament, and that the people we study are in all sorts of ways eminently comprehensible to us. For there is no reason to suppose that, in sifting through our ethnographic representations so as to expose their possible limitations, we might not find many ways in which they *do not* lead to us to the absurdities of contradiction. The balance between successful and unsuccessful representations, in this sense, is a contingent matter, to do with the character of the ethnography in each case, as well as of the repertoires of analytical concepts we bring to it. One can certainly conceive of a situation where the "fit" between analytical assumptions and ethnography was perfect, just as one can imagine a situation in which it was entirely absent. Still, it is demonstrable that well-nigh all ethnography lies somewhere in between these poles of radical commensurability and incommensurability (cf. Povinelli 2001). Notwithstanding critics' accusations to the contrary, recursive analyses are sensitive to this complexity, since they stand or fall by the precision with which they are able to chart it.

This observation provides a useful handle onto the main body of my ethnographic account of Ifá divination in Cuba. In chapters 3–8 I substantiated ethnographically the notion that divination issues in indubitable truths, a claim that in chapter 2 was put forward only in a putative way, for purely critical purposes, as an empirical hypothesis. And true, in initiating this ethnographic journey in chapter 3, I made explicit my intention of bringing the alterity of divinatory truth to the surface of my account, prefacing it with the story of my first encounter with Javier and the puzzling effects it had on me. However, in line with the comments already made, my attempt to diagnose the alterity of divination is not made at the expense of similarity, but rather in terms of it. So, for example, the account in chapter 3 of the pervasive role of truth in the life of Ifá, as well as the development of these themes in the chapters that follow it, is cast in terms of a series of ethnographic claims the truth of which can be ascertained in a straightforwardly representational sense. Most obviously, these include such "raw data" as dates, events, indigenous terms, accounts of rituals and myths and so on, all of which can be judged for accuracy with reference to facts as they are in Cuba. These data, moreover, also carry a series of further claims that are pitched at a higher level of abstraction, including generalizations about the structure of cult organization, estimations of how "typical" or "representative" particular actions or forms of behavior might be, and so on. These too are presented as claims whose value can be judged by representationist criteria of truth.

Far from being suppressed, these descriptive representations furnish the ethnographic starting-point for my attempt to pinpoint the senses in which babalawos' concern for truth diverges from our attempts to represent it. The analytical procedure is the same as the one rehearsed in a hypothetical and programmatic manner in chapter 2 with reference to the putative observation that divinatory truth is indubitable. Only now the analysis is blown up to proper ethnographic scale, to include (as far as possible) the whole terrain of data that comprise babalawos' concern for truth and the pivotal role that divination, as a source of truth, plays in their life. Much of the data turns out to be transparent indeed. For example, there seems to be no issue with claiming that Javier was initiated in 1967 with Mejias as godfather—although, even in this simple statement of fact, what exactly "godfather" might mean would raise further questions.

Other data may be treated as transparent and unproblematic for the purposes of the argument, although one might suspect that, had the argument been directed elsewhere, they may have presented problems of their own (e.g., the observation that Ifá lineages are exclusive to men will appear less straightforward when set alongside babalawos' common suggestion that they have no need of women in their lineages because they "give birth" to each other themselves—how far can one's initial assumptions about what counts as a man incorporate this notion without contradiction?). And then there are data that are deliberately shown not to be transparent at all, by following the reductio procedure of chapter 2.

This procedure is evident in the text at different scales, both within and across the ethnographically led analyses of chapters 3–8. In particular, the overall arc of the argument about indubitability unfolds piecemeal from chapter to chapter, with the ritual, cosmological, and ontological dimensions of divination explored in detail before reaching the crux of the argument in chapter 8, where the key claims that Ifá "tells no lies" and "makes no mistakes," and all that rides on them, are addressed. Each step in filling out this ethnographic picture, however, involves its own struggles with alterity. Hence, chapters 4 and 5 are about exploring the contradictions implied in viewing divination in terms of the distinction between transcendence and immanence. Similarly, chapters 6 and 7 begin to dismantle the idea that divinatory truth can be viewed as a property of representations with reference to the inherent "motility" of interpretation and truth in the process of divinatory consultation. Pivotal to each of these arguments is the effect of aporia, which in each case is brought to the surface deliberately by showing how our descriptions of the "phenomena" involved are incoherent unto themselves.

One could summarize the overall outcome of the ethnographic engagements of these chapters by contrasting it to what is perhaps the default image of the role of ethnography in anthropological analysis. Notwithstanding recent critical assessments (e.g., Chua, High, and Lau 2008; Engelke 2009), a prevalent image of the role that ethnographic description plays in anthropological argument recapitulates a dispotif that is pervasive when it comes to thinking about "science" more generally, namely that of empirical evidence supporting theoretical propositions. Ethnography, on this view, is imagined as an act of charting out a "field" of data with descriptive precision, in order then to "build" theory upon them. The image presented by our recursive analysis is perhaps closer to that conjured by notions of "deconstruction"—which, in Jacques Derrida's formulations, laid store by the theoretical fecundity of aporia much as we have here (e.g., Derrida 1992). But rather than merely reversing the image of analysis founded—"constructed"—on the surface of descriptive data, the recursive image summons a different topology altogether. Here the field of data can be imagined as a curved surface whose intensive torsions measure degrees of relative representational transparency and opacity. More like black holes than Latourian black boxes, these suctions of sense register in our ethnographic descriptions as failures of representation: not a lack of correspondence with the facts, but an inability even to express them without contradiction.

Yet, in line with Derrida, I now want to argue that these contradictions are indeed fecund: they furnish the elements with which analysis turns its own aporias into something productive. What I have in mind is, of course, a version of the notion of truth as infinition, although, as we shall see, the analogy with divinatory operations inflects it somewhat differently. In order to see how infinitions work in this context, the key point to note at the outset is that the absurdities that motivate them, nonsensical though they may be, are not devoid of content. To take our central example, saying that divinatory truth is indubitable may be a contradiction insofar as we are bound to the assumption of truth as representation. Nevertheless, the terms in which the contradiction is set up—our best shot at ethnographic description—have an immediate and specific *heuristic* purchase, and this in three ways. First, while expressing a misunderstanding, they also specify the concepts that generate it. It is the concept of representational truth that renders indubitability inconceivable. Second, this suggests a way out of the *impasse*. If the concept of truth as representation is the fly in the ointment here, then *that* is the concept that requires our analytical attention. Third, the terms of contradiction also provide a criterion for analytical success. Whatever the analytical attention that yields it might be, its result will be happy if what it generates is a way of thinking about truth that allows us to represent the truth of divination as indubitable. A successful analysis, then, would be one that removes the contradictions that our initial descriptions of the ethnography involve, so as to generate representations that are transparent. What we have here, in other words, is a representational litmus test: if we can arrive at a position of being able to say "divinatory truth is indubitable" without contradiction, we know we are there.

Our ethnographic misunderstandings, then, provide both the tools and the compass for recursive analysis, framing its beginning and its end alike in terms of representational criteria of truth (failure and success respectively). But what comes in between? The answer to this question has already been given in chapter 8, where the recursive analysis of divinatory truth is concluded. There, the contradictions to which the problem of indubitability gives rise were resolved by redefining the concept of truth in such a way as to remove them. The passage from absurdity to transparency, then, took the form of a revision of concepts. What must truth *be* for us to be able to state without contradiction that divinations are beyond doubt? Answering this question, as we saw, involves replacing the contradictory notion of representation with a new one, namely that which I branded as infinition.

It is at this point that the metarecursive comparison between divination and anthropology comes fully into its own: as an act of reconceptualization, the process which led our analysis to the concept of infinition parallels the very process this concept helps to articulate, namely babalawos' own acts of reconceptualization. This metarecursive analogy was noted in chapter 8: to show how thinking of divinatory verdicts as inventions of new meanings (infinitions) might make sense, I explained how such a thought exemplifies itself in the act. Our effort to conceive of truth in a way that does not mire us in the contradictions of representationism relies on the possibility of inventing a new concept by relating previously unrelated ones "internally," bringing them into relationships that mutually modify the meanings of the concepts involved. Hence the parallel: Where the diviner is able to transform his clients by altering the meaning of their personal circumstances in the light of the mythical paths of the oddu, the anthropologist transforms his own concepts by altering them in the light of the exigencies of ethnographic description.

In a moment, by way of closing, I shall address important contrasts between these two procedures. First, however, we may note that the parallel between them allows us to further characterize the process by which the recursive movement from aporia to clarity unfolds in anthropological analysis. As was noted in the analysis of divinatory truth-claims in chapters 7 and 8, conceptualizing truth as infinition involves criteria of truth that are different from those of representation. What makes a verdict true is not its (inherently doubtful) "match" with the facts, but rather its success in redefining them in a way that is recognized as relevant and revealing by the consultant. At issue is the cogency of redefinition as opposed to the accuracy of representation. This is also how infinitions differ from representations in anthropological analysis. Taking as raw material the concepts in which our heuristic (contradictory) descriptions of the ethnography are cast, we use them to generate new meanings that are conceptually coherent, that is, free of internal contradiction. So, as in divinatory infinition, truth in our analytical infinitions becomes a matter of internal cogency rather than external match. Only here the cogency is judged in terms not of its relevance to the experiential narrative of a consultant's path of life but rather of its relevance to the analytical trajectory developed by the anthropologist. To show that thinking of diviners' verdicts as infinitions makes sense, I had to demonstrate how such a notion is coherent with the other arguments developed in the course of my analysis (the motile logic of divinatory interpretation, the deities' constitution as vectors of ontological transformation, and so on). Crucially, this involved exploring the logical assumptions and consequences of these arguments, to show how they are modified by the proposed infinition (if notions of truth as representation presuppose an ontological distinction between word and world, then where does the notion of infinition leave this distinction? How does this relate to the argument on the motility of meaning? And so on).

So, what takes place between the representationally defined start and end points of recursive analysis are procedures whose truth is anything but representational. Again, the parallel with divination bears out this point, suggesting that the stakes in this form of anthropological reasoning are distinctively *ontological* (see also Viveiros de Castro 1998b, 2010; Henare et al. 2007; cf. Evens 2008). Just like the diviner's myth-based verdicts amount to an interference with the ontological constitution of the consultant, so the infinitions that the alterity of ethnography precipitates shift the ontological coordinates of the concepts that we use in our analyses. What emerges out of this analytical procedure, in other words, are answers to ontological questions: What counts as truth? What counts as meaning? What relationship between word and world do they imply? What counts as obligation in this context?

Hence the notion of alterity as misunderstanding rather than disagreement, explained earlier, can be parsed as a properly ontological divergence. Where representationist accounts of anthropological truth present "cultural difference" as a disagreement over how to apply a given concept to the world (an epistemic question, to do with what philosophers call the "extension" of a concept),[5] the infinitive account proposed here posits alterity as a divergence between alternative ways of conceptualizing things (an ontological question, to do with the "intension" of concepts). Let me underline here that such a take on alterity has no mentalist, culturalist, or other "territorial" implications: the ontological multiplicity that it posits (different concepts of x, rather than different applications of the concept of x) is in no way to be distributed across different people's heads, cultures, habituses, or what have you. That is the territorialized imaginary of belief and representation (Whose belief? Whose representation? Where? When?). At issue only are the conceptual divergences that we need to posit (that is, infine) in our analyses in order to make sense of the (otherwise) territorialized data that interest us. Ontologies, then, are not phenomena out there to be found. They are the analytical artifices through which such searches proceed (see also Venkatesan et al. 2010).

Ontography as Antidivination

I have proposed the term *ontography* to describe this form of anthropological analysis, in order to indicate its investment in charting out alterity in terms of ontological difference (Holbraad 2003, 2009). In the light of our discussion, we may lay out its manner of proceeding as series of methodological instructions—the terms of engagement with alterity, so to speak. Lest this checklist for anthropological truth appear too bold, let alone formulaic, I would invoke the analogy with divination to suggest that this is, effectively, the anthropological equivalent of a divinatory ritual—and ritual in Ifá is nothing if not bold and formulaic (compare with the account of the liturgy of divinatory ceremonies provided in chapter 4):

Step 1: Describe your ethnography as well as you can, using all the concepts at your disposal in order to represent it as accurately as possible. Use ordinary representational criteria of truth to judge the accuracy of your descriptions: match them with the facts as you found them in the field.

Step 2: Scan your descriptions for logical contradictions. Occasions in which your descriptions tempt you to say that your informants are being "irrational" are good candidates for logical scrutiny. When you can show the contradictions involved, you have identified "alterity."

Step 3: Specify the conceptual conflicts that generate the contradictions. Which concepts are involved? What are the associated assumptions, corollaries, concomitants, consequences, and so on? How do they relate to the more transparent and logically unproblematic parts of your ethnographic description? Answering these questions provides you with the heuristic tools you will need for step 4.

Step 4: Experiment with redefining in different ways the concepts that generate contradictions. Ask questions of the form "What if x were thought of as . . . ?" "What does y need to be in order that. . .?" Modify the meanings of your concepts by bringing them into different relationships with each other. Your criterion of truth is the logical cogency of your infinitions. This involves two minimum requirements: (a) that your infinitions remove the contradictions that motivate them; and (b) that they do not generate new ones in relation either to each other or to other parts of your ethnographic descriptions. Your aim is to straighten out the logical torsions of your ethnographic account, not merely to displace them.

NB (*remember!*): While the concepts you are infining in these ways are derived from your (variously un/successful) descriptions of the ethnography, responsibility for your acts of reconceptualization is your own. Your ethnography won't give you the answers, only the terms with which to generate them. Feel free to draw on fellow anthropologists, philosophers and other thinkers for inspiration and comparison but again, remember the following:

Step 5: The litmus test for gauging the success of your recursive, motile, infinitive, and ontographic analytical experiment is its transparency with respect to *your ethnography*. This means that, while your infinitions' claim to truth resides in their logical cogency, the final test they have to pass is representational: If and only if your infinitions allow you to articulate true representations of the phenomena whose description initially mired you in contradiction, your work is done.

Show your thinking.

The analogy between these methodological instructions and the ceremonial order of a divination is offered only half tongue-in-cheek. Indeed, much of its metarecursive value lies in its facetiousness. For putting things in this way also serves to convey a point that is as important as it is obvious: anthropology and divination are not the same activity. I do not propose to go into all the ways, in turns blatant and revealing, in which this is the case. I leave it to the reader to imagine the wealth of suggestive analogies and contrasts a *tout court* comparison would bring to light—deities as concepts, consecration as argument, divinatory casts as ethnographic happenstances, and more. To close, I focus only on a chief breakdown in the analogy, which speaks most directly to the abiding concern of this book with the role and character of truth in divination and in anthropology.

Consider the axis of the comparison, namely the analytical substitution of infinitive for representational truth that we have proposed in both cases. For divination, where a standard analysis would present babalawos as using their mythical learning to derive accurate representations (diagnoses, predictions, and so on) of their clients' personal circumstances, we have proposed instead that they use it as a resource for changing (viz. infining) their clients themselves, transforming their meaning as persons. For anthropology, we have substituted the standard idea that anthropologists use their analytical concepts and procedures in order to represent (describe, explain, interpret) the people they study ethnographically with the suggestion that, provoked by their inability to describe it without conceptual confusions (viz. the problem of alterity), they use their ethnography as a resource for transforming (viz. infining) recursively their analytical concepts and procedures. Putting it in this way, however, makes it clear that the role or, better, the *direction* of infinition in each case is different. In a nutshell: while diviners use myths to transform the world (recursive) anthropologists use the world to transform their analytical concepts; while the babalawo learns the myths to change life, the anthropologist learns his ethnography (life too, in a sense) to change his conceptual repertoire (myths, too, in a sense).

So, notwithstanding the parallel of infinition, divination and anthropology are in a sense each other's opposites. One could go so far as to call recursive anthropology a form of anti-divination, or perhaps "reverse divination" (cf. Kirsch 2006). For imagine what divination would look like on a straight analogy with recursive analysis: a form of reverse ontogeny, so to speak, in which babalawos would use their knowledge of the lives of their clients to transform the orichas and their mythical paths, changing the "births" of things and Orula's mythical testimony to the origins of their creation in the light of the world they are supposed to have brought forth. Notwithstanding Barber's point that, in practice, devotees' actions can have an effect on the makeup of their cosmologies (Barber 1981), from the point of view of the logic of Ifá divination, such an image is, if not an abomination, then at least a cosmological non sequitur. While I have never put the scenario to babalawos (in fact, I am not sure how I would have even expressed it had I tried to do so), our account of the power divination has for them suggests a plausible response: Ifá is so powerful, babalawos say, because "everything is in it"—everything we see (and all that we do not see) in this world is "born" in one or other of Orula's oddu. Indeed, in a strict sense, the power that the oddu give them, as mortal babalawos, it precisely that of iterating the cosmogony of Ifá through further acts of, if you like, *ontogony*: the infinitions they perform in divination effect ontological transformations, making new people, by *re*creating the world in and through the images of its originary creations (a major cosmic responsibility, to be sure).

Thus construed, however, the breakdown of the analogy with anthropology cuts both ways. If anthropology is an anti-divination, then is divination not also an anti-anthropology? At least, I would suggest, divination presents a direct reversal of the recursive agenda that has been elaborated throughout this book. For what the notion that "everything is in Ifá" effectively denies is the problem of alterity that precipitates such an agenda. Alterity, as we saw in chapter 4, is indeed a constitutive feature of Ifá cosmology, inasmuch as the cosmological coordinates within which divination operates posit an ontological separation between the world of myth "beyond" and the world of mortals "here and now." As argued at length in chapter 5, however, the whole point of divination is that this alterity presents no logical "problem," as it does, for example, in Christian theology. Deities (including the oddu and their mythical paths) are so powerful precisely because they are defined as the kinds of beings that can *traverse* ontological distance—indeed, I argued, they *are* trajectories of ontological traversal. Alterity, in this sense, is internal and constitutive to them.

Not so for recursive anthropology. For here the analytical force of infinition is provoked for precisely the opposite reason: it is the anthropologist's *inability* to traverse the ontological distance between his analytical concepts and the ethnography they purport to articulate that motivates the recursive exercise of conceptual invention. Alterity is indeed a "problem" in this case, insofar as it is posited as an external predicament that conditions the project of anthropological analysis—a wall of absurdity that our attempts to make sense of ethnography (sometimes) hit against.[6] Again, the image that a straight analogy with divination would yield is indicative of the difference: rather than the kind of ontography we have been setting forth, an anthropology that would treat alterity on the mold of divination would have also to be conceived as a project of "ontogony." Proceeding from the premise that "everything is in anthropology," it would draw on its repertoire of analytical concepts (conceived here as complete and all-embracing, like the oddu) in order to recreate ethnography in its image. This, indeed, would be just an extreme—because ontologically inflected and empowered—version of what representationist anthropology has always been doing. Precisely the predicament that this book has sought recursively to avoid, only worse. It would be a kind of radical conceptual colonialism (*sensu* Viveiros de Castro 2011) in which anthropology assumed not that people the world over can be represented in our own terms but rather that they can be ontologically transformed by them.

Ultimately, then, the difference between anthropology and divination can be described also as a difference of temperament or attitude. In chapter 1 I contrasted babalawos' supreme confidence in their own ability to pronounce truth with anthropologists' deflated sense of angst on this score in recent, post-crisis-of-representation years. This book has been about articulating an anthropology free of this angst, bringing babalawos' orientation toward truth to bear recursively upon our analytical procedures, to generate a suitably revamped understanding of truth that can be placed at their center. I hope that some of the babalawos' confidence in this respect rubs off on anthropology in the process. Still, something of the old angst remains, only now in the guise of a certain humility—one that I think has always been at the core of anthropologists' worries about representation, only robbed of much of its creative potential. Unlike babalawos, whose myths allow them constitutively to have an answer for everything, the form of anthropological truth that I have sought to articulate is one that proceeds from the premise that we do not know everything. It is this humble realization in the face of others' lives—in the face of our ethnography—that precipitates our creativity. Our capacity for truth, then, is a function of this kind of concerted humility.

On Humility

In his peer-review of the manuscript of the preceding chapters, Eduardo Viveiros de Castro noted somewhat playfully that he found amusing the "strong Kantian accent" of many of my reasonings.[1] "Sometimes," he continued,

> I was led to imagine [the manuscript] as a kind of latter day *Critique of Anthropological Reason.* [Chapter 2], for instance, reads as a version of the "antinomies of reason"; and the job done in [the conclusion] looks amazingly like a "transcendental deduction" sort of argument. The whole project of the author, as a matter of fact, made me think of a Kantian-like effort to establish the conditions of possibility of all anthropological knowledge.

While I am no expert on Kant, I think I recognize the analogy—one that would be preposterously flattering to me, where it not so clearly targeted at the style rather than the substance of my anthropological "reasonings." At any rate, the nub of Viveiros's comment lies not so much in the analogy itself as in the irony that it implies. After all, as he notes, what is amusing about my "Kantian accent" is that it should be used to articulate what is, as he puts it, a "keenly post-critical" argument. Indeed: if a Kantian turn of thinking connotes expectations of transcendental necessity, settling upon the "conditions of possibility of all knowledge" and so on, the substance of my argument seems to cut in the opposite direction, toward ethnographic contingency and the unsettlingly recursive effects that it may have on an anthropological thinking always on the move. So how, we may ask with Viveiros, do these seemingly contradictory impulses—critical form, as it would seem, versus post-critical content—tally with each other?

The query is a pointed one. For it speaks directly to the claim with which I ended my meta-anthropological argument on truth in the conclusion, regarding the stance of humility which, as I suggested, captures what is most deeply at stake in the recursive motion of anthropological thinking. Indeed, Viveiros's congenial amusement with the form of my argument could be expressed also as a reservation over just this claim. Just how humble exactly, one may ask, is the idea that conclusions about the nature of anthropological reasoning as such, including the claim about its constitutive humility itself, can be drawn recursively from the ethnographic contingencies of Cuban divination? Again: the putative humility of allowing ethnographic contingency to *transform* anthropological assumptions seems to grate against the—after all—rather grandiose idea that such a process of transformation might issue in a meta-anthropological argument about the conditions of possibility of anthropological reasoning in general.

By way of epilogue, I want briefly to show why I think there is no contradiction here. In particular, I shall make three points that, taken together, show that a concern with conditions of possibility is indeed integral to the kind of recursive anthropology I have sought to articulate, but *no more* integral than the idea that such a concern could *not* aspire to set the conditions of possibility of "all possible" anthropological knowledge. The humility of recursive anthropology, then, is a humility also about the claims of recursive anthropology, including the recursive claim about humility itself. I take the three points in turn, with reference to Viveiros's tease on my Kantianism.

1. *Post-Kantianism*. The analogy between Kantian critique and recursive anthropology as I have articulated it can be expressed in terms of Kant's famous metaphor of the Copernican Revolution. Broadly put, Kantian critique is "Copernican" in the sense that it sources the conditions of possibility of knowledge, not in the object of knowledge, but rather in the subject. Thus, the experience of the world is taken as given (fixed relatively, in that sense, like a Copernican sun), and the problem becomes one of deducing the categories of thought that are necessary for its understanding. Now, already in this minimal sense, we may note, the motion that this kind of "revolution" implies is indeed recursive. Rather than taking categories of thought and using them to say things about the world, Kantian critique takes the experience of the world and uses it to say things about our categories of thought—a quintessentially recursive move. Indeed, replace

"world" with "other," "experience of the world" with "ethnography," and "categories of thought" with "analytical concepts," and the above account of Kantian critique becomes a fair description of recursive anthropology.

And hence the Kantian accent. For while the motion of thought marked by my recursive argument may not be transcendental, it is certainly deductive, in first deriving the underlying assumptions upon which ethnographic (mis)descriptions rest, as well as critical in then showing up the logical problems, if not the antinomies, that may render those assumptions inappropriate. Without putting too fine a point on it, one might say that the kind of recursive argument I have sought to articulate depends on exposing ethnographic materials to the same kind (if not order) of logical analysis as Kantian critique applies to the experience of the world in general. In fact, one might even say that anthropological recursivity is in an important respect *post*-Kantian, recalling Pedersen's usage of "post" talk (see chapter 5), inasmuch as it involves also an *intensification* of Kantian-style critique. The monumentality of Kant's endeavor, after all, is owing to his Newtonian conviction that the source of critique could only be one, namely the sensible world as subject to the apperceptions of a transcendental Ego. The impulse of recursive anthropology is post-Kantian, then, in that it effectively *multiplies* the sources of critique by a factor, as it were, of ethnographic alterity. *Any* ethnographically described world, on this post-critical image, can provide a basis for the kind of recursive analytic Kant reserved for Newton's.

2. *Non-Kantianism.* It is, of course, just this passage from Newtonian universality to ethnographically driven alterity that also makes the project of recursive anthropology profoundly *non*-Kantian. For the principal effect of multiplying the sources of critique in this way is precisely to *break down* Kant-style monuments to reason—the critique of Critique, if you like. The Kantian aspiration to determine the conditions of possibility of *all* knowledge turns on the idea that such conditions can be extrapolated from the experience of a uniform world governed by universal laws, as in the Newtonian image. So, the necessity, metaphysically speaking, of transcendental categories of understanding is corollary to the singular reality of the world whose apprehension they condition. By contrast, as we have seen throughout this book, recursive anthropology draws its strength and creativity from the contingencies of ethnographic alterity. And since the manifestations of alterity are as multiple, in principle, as the ethnographic record is vast, it follows that the analytical concepts that are derived re-

cursively from them are contingent upon the ethnographic specificities of each case, *and necessarily so.*

We may note here that the humbling, non-Kantian effect that such a constitutive commitment to ethnographic contingency involves could fruitfully be compared to Durkheim's famous attempt to relativize Kant's categories by rendering them as empirically variable social facts. Certainly, the move from transcendental necessity toward empirical contingency in the two cases seems parallel. The difference, however, lies in the manner in which contingency is articulated in either case. For Durkheim, the contingency of social categories is itself an empirical matter. As products of collective representation, categories may vary from one society to another, so the analyst's job is to describe these social facts in all their variety. By contrast, as we have seen, the recursive turn in anthropology is motivated by the fact that just this kind of variability may well *resist* description—the problem of alterity. At issue, in other words, are not the categories of those we purport to describe, but rather our own when our attempts to do so fail.

We have, then, a recipe for a form of contingency considerably more radical than Durkheim's. Rather than containing it at the level of ethnographic description, the recursive move allows the contingency of ethnographic alterity to transmute itself to the level of analysis. So if Durkheim follows Kant in englobing contingency in an a priori framework of analytical forms (society for transcendental ego, collective for subject, social fact for category of understanding, and so on), recursive anthropology departs from both of them in rendering all analytical forms contingent upon the vagaries of ethnographically driven aporia. Indeed, it is by virtue of just such a non-Kantianism that recursive anthropological arguments can, depending on the ethnographic circumstances, engender explicitly *anti-*Kantian (anti-Newtonian, anti-Durkheimian, or anti–anything else) conceptualizations. So, to the extent that ethnographic alterity may contradict just the kinds of assumptions Kant or Durkheim might take for granted, it has the power recursively to show *them* up as contingent and present them with alternatives. While I have not sought to target it directly at Kant or Durkheim, my Ifá-driven argument against representationism and for the motility of truth could furnish an example.

3. *Post-recursivity, non-recursivity, or even anti-recursivity.* This, then, is also why such a recursive argument could hardly pretend to set the conditions of possibility for all knowledge, anthropological or otherwise.

Wedding its *faux*-Kantian aspiration to rigor to the ethnographic contingencies that precipitate it, the recursive move is just that: a move—as contingent, time-bound, and subjunctive as any. So, for example, my own derivation of the motile logic of infinition is contingent on the particular challenges of alterity presented by the ethnography of Ifá divination. To the extent that different ethnographic materials (e.g., another form divination, or a non-divinatory practice otherwise oriented toward truth) would present different forms of alterity, one can expect the recursive analytical effects derived from them to be different. In fact we saw instances of just this kind of difference, noting in chapter 5, for example, the transformations that Melanesian- or Amerindian-derived conceptualizations must undergo when transposed onto the ethnographic contingencies of Ifá cosmology and ritual. For these were hardly criticisms, say, of Strathern and Viveiros respectively, as "authors" of the conceptualizations in question. If such recursive conceptualizations are wedded to the ethnographic contingencies that precipitate them, then transposing them to different ethnographic settings must also precipitate a *further* reconceptualization. Comparison, as it were, as transformation (see also Holbraad and Willerslev 2007; Holbraad and Pedersen 2010).

And the same, finally, goes for the metarecursive argument about anthropological recursivity itself, elaborated in the conclusion. Now, as I made clear, the force of that argument does not derive directly from the contingency of Ifá divination. Rather it derives from the contingency of the analytical choices and strategies that contingency precipitated— hence its "meta"-recursive status, based also, as we saw, on a meta-ethnographic description of the argument elaborated throughout this book. Still, contingency remains the motor, albeit at the second order. For Ifá divination (or for that matter any other first-order ethnography) might well have been shown to present different analytical challenges from the ones I have identified and sought to deal with—a different form of alterity, perhaps, or another kind of problem altogether, as yet unspecified, or even none at all. In such a case, up for grabs both ethnographically and meta-ethnographically, my metarecursive argument about anthropological recursivity would itself invite further transformation. Where such a post-recursive prospect might lead is a question that must remain open—constitutively so (though possibly only for now). Certainly, from the contingently recursive standpoint at which my argument temporarily rests, perching on a branch like Lévi-Strauss's famous Sioux bird from

Totemism,[2] a future non- or even anti-recursive turn cannot be excluded, just as they cannot yet, in their constitutive ethnographic contingency, be conceived. What we have, in effect, is a machine for thinking in perpetual motion—an excessive motion, ever capable of setting the conditions of possibility for its own undoing. Or not, as the case may be.

Appendix A

The Naming and Ranking of
Divinatory Configurations

The 256 configurations upon which Ifá divination is based are as fundamental to the oracle of Ifá as star signs are to astrology. Although the divinatory techniques are designed to ensure that each oddu is equally likely to occur on any given occasion (on a probability of 1/256), the oddu are not as evenly weighted in the minds of practitioners. Babalawos distinguish between sixteen "principal" oddu and 240 derivative configurations. What distinguishes the principal oddu from the rest is that they are configured symmetrically on the vertical axis, that is, they have identical "legs." The four binary variables of each leg give sixteen possible configurations, each of which has its own name. Accordingly, the principal oddu bear the names of their distinctive leg configuration, followed by the word *meyi*, which is Lucumí for "two" or "twin" (Bascom 1991, 42). For example, the configuration II I I II (reading from top to bottom) is called Iwori. Hence the repetition of this figure in both legs corresponds to the principal oddu Iwori Meyi. The names of the remaining 240 oddu are similarly composite, since in principle they are derived by combining the names of their two legs, reading from right to left. So, for example, the oddu "Osá Trupo" is made up of Osá (II I I I) in the right leg, and Otrupon (II II I II) in the left leg. In practice, however, a large proportion of the oddu are referred to by surrogate names, usually substituting one or both of the legs' names with another word associated with the corresponding principal oddu. Some babalawos dismiss this as force of habit, while others explain that pro-

TABLE A.1 **Names and ranks of the oddu of Ifá divination as used in Cuba.**

I I I I *Eyiobbe* (1)	I I II II *Iroso* (5)	I I I II *Oggunda* (9)	II I I I *Otura* (13)
II II II II *Oyiekún* (2)	II II I I *Ojwani* (6)	II I I I *Osá* (10)	I I II I *Irete* (14)
II I I II *Owori* (3)	I II II II *Obara* (7)	II I II II *Iká* (11)	I II I II *Oché* (15)
I II II I *Oddí* (4)	II II II I *Okana* (8)	II II I II *Otrupo* (12)	II I II I *Ofún* (16)

nouncing the full name of certain "strong" oddu (*signos fuertes*) can be dangerous (see also Maupoil 1943, 411–12).

The distinction between principal and derivative oddu is conceived of in hierarchical terms. The sixteen principal oddu are often referred to as "kings" (*oba*) or "fathers" (*baba*), and are thought of as superior to the rest, which are sometimes referred to as their "children" (*omo oddu* or *omoluo* or *hijos*). But hierarchical distinctions are made also within each category: the sixteen principal oddu are ranked one by one as listed above, and their "children" can be ranked accordingly, by matching the principal rankings algorithmically (see McClelland 1966 for a detailed discussion of ranking among the Yoruba, and Héres Hevia 1962, 281–537 for Cuba).

As is evident from the list, ranking follows a logical pattern, as oddu are organized in pairs of "mirror" configurations (I I I I → II II II II; II I I II → I II II I; etc.). Indeed, in conversation babalawos can get quite excited about these patterns and seem to derive satisfaction from exploring the relationships between configurations, using technical terms to describe mirror images, inversions, and the like (e.g., *abbure, contrabbure*).[1] Referring to these formal relationships, one babalawo marveled at the fact that ultimately "[one] can derive the rest of the *letras* from any single one." (*Letras*, meaning literally "letter," is a term also used to refer to the oddu, particularly among babalawos in technical contexts.)

Although the formal elegance of the system is certainly appreciated for what it is, the significance of the relationships between oddu (hierarchical or otherwise) is also substantialized in mythical terms. Indeed, the language of personification used to describe these relationships (such as kings, fathers, children) is quite literal, since each oddu corresponds to—or "is," in babalawos' more ambiguous parlance—a divine being. The individual oddu feature in a plethora of Ifá myths, much like the deities of the pantheon. While an analysis of these myths would be impossible here, it is worth noting two distinct ways in which babalawos refer to the oddu when exploring the mythical relationships between them. On the one hand, any given oddu (conceived of as a mythical character) may appear in a "path" of another oddu, in one of many mythical accounts formally associated with it. Particularly important in this context is the fact that oddu are said to be "born" (*nacen*) in other oddu. In principle, then, the formal derivations that are said to connect the 256 oddu to each other can be complemented by tracing quasi-formal genealogical relations between them.[2]

On the other hand, the relationships between oddu are also the explicit subject matter of myths. Countless mythical paths describe the exploits of each individual oddu in the sacred cities of Africa and beyond, wherein they appear as kings, warriors, diviners, as guises of the orichas, including Orula himself, or as deities in their own right. A number of these stories concern a whole repertoire of relationships between oddu, as well as between oddu and orichas (kinship, friendship, enmity, envy, alliance). A prime example of this is the story of how, despite being the youngest of the sixteen oddu kings (the 16 principal oddu), Baba Eyiobbe was placed at the top of the hierarchy of oddu by Olofin. The story appears as one of the paths of the oddu Eyiobbe itself:

> Olofin [the highest ranking divinity, patron of the sun] in this path was blind and had the habit of meeting up with the meyi [the 16 principal oddu]. Oragún [surrogate name for Ofún, the last of the meyi] customarily sat on Olofin's side. One day Olofin announced to the meyi that he would decree what rank each should have. On the chosen day Eyiobbe sat himself next to Olofin since Oragún was always arriving late. Olofin's idea was to give the first rank to Oragún, sat as he

was always close by him. But, being blind, he just turned to his side and ended up giving the first rank to Eyiobbe. Then he carried on giving the ranks around the table successively to the rest of the *meyi*. When Oragún arrived the ranks had already been given and only the last one, where there was illness, death, and other calamities, was left for him.

Appendix B

"Papers of Ifá": An Example

"Papers of Ifá" (see chapter 2) do not always include the same kind of information. As a general rule, however, one may distinguish four kinds of data that may feature on them. Following the name and visual representation of the relevant oddu, there may appear:

1. A prayer (*rezo*) associated with the oddu in question, which invariable appears in Lucumí and is memorized as such by the babalawo. These days initiates are rarely able to translate the prayer word for word, and are often unable to specify its precise meaning.

2. One or more proverbs (*refránes*), written either in Spanish or in Lucumí, which often summarize or present the moral of the myth that follows, as, for example, the proverb "money is cursed" corresponds to the path of the oddu Oragún concerning the origin of money mentioned in chapter 4.

3. One or more myths, that is, paths of the oddu. These appear in Spanish, though they are often littered with key terms in Lucumí, which tend to add to their esoteric feel for practitioners (as well as anthropologists). Myths vary in length from a few lines to one or more pages (the paper shown in figure B.1 lists three relatively short myths). Longer myths may include detailed descriptions of ritual acts "born" in the oddu, including recipes for magical concoctions of various kinds, songs to be sung during the performance of the ritual (*suyeres*), related ritual prohibitions, and other such data. Relevant details sometimes appear as "notes" (*notas*) at the end of the mythical narrative.

4. A recipe for an offering (*addimú*) or, most typically, a sacrifice (*ebbó*) associated with the oddu. These usually appear as lists of ingredients, using Lucumí terminology (note the mixture of Spanish and Lucumí terms in the example of figure B.1).

```
        I I
        0 0    Otunché
        I I
        0 I
```

① Tres hermanos fueron al cielo a vera Olofin y este les dio aché de plumas y las trajeron sujetas en las manos y los tres perdieron las plumas y entonces fueron al cielo para lamentarse de la perdida y Olofin les dijo: Ya la gracia está concedida.

② Ebbo
Un gallo, 1 machete, vaina de flamboyan, eku, eya, epo, $6·30.

Patakin
Este era un cazador que fue donde esta el rey dentro del monte a cazar y el rey le preguntó que hacia dentro de sus montes y él le dijo que iba a buscar comida, entonces el rey le dio dos vainas y le dijo: Cuando llegues a tu casa siembralas y tendras que comer pero no le comuniques tus secretos a nadie y fue para su casa y lo hizo, entonces tuvo de todo. Lo llamó el rey y le dijo que sabia que tenia un secreto que era mas rico que todo el mundo, le dijo que si lo decia al rey entonces él seria mas rico que este, se lo arranco y fue al monte otra vez y le preguntó que hacia en sus montes otra vez, este le dijo que se habia acabado porque lo habia vendido y se arranco la cabeza.

③
Un hombre pobre tenia una mujer y ocho hijos pero un dia la mujer le parió otro y da la casualidad que ese mismo dia parió la mujer del rey pero murió y entonces el rey dictó un bando para que la mujer que hubiera parido ese dia se presentara en palacio y a ella la llevaron ante el rey el cual le ofreció riquezas contal de que le ayudara su hijo recien nacido el esposo fue a casa de Orunmila el cual le dijo que tenia que bañar a su mujer antes que otro lo hiciera, pero el no lo hizo así mientras tanto el rey le preparo un baño y mando al marido que la bañara pero como era un baño de echiceria la mujer se quedó con el rey.

nota.
Aqui la mujer le ruega la cabeza al marido, ese dia la mujer no hace nada, tiene que visitar el santisimo. Esta persona nadie la considera siempre tiene un problema que lo agobia, siempre tiene algo pendiente. El awó de este Ifá está autorizado a rogarle la cabeza a la señora.

FIGURE B.1. A sample "paper of Ifá."

Notes

Preface

1. The influence on my thinking of Latour, Strathern, Viveiros de Castro, and Wagner has been the most abiding during the writing of this book. Having only belatedly discovered the work of Evens, who has been advancing confluent arguments for decades (e.g., 1983, 2008), I realize that a more prominent engagement with his writings would have served to sharpen my argument further.

Introduction

1. For a similar line of ethnographic argument regarding the notion of knowledge, see Crook 2007.

2. In the case of the Azande that he famously describes, from the lowly rubbing-board to the prestigious benge poison oracle (Evans-Pritchard 1976, 120).

3. Throughout this book tonal accents are omitted from the spelling of Yoruba terms for the sake of simplicity, following the conventions of the Cuba-centric scholarly literature. Also note that I follow the convention of spelling the Yoruba term for deity as *orisa* and the Cuban term as *oricha*.

4. William Bascom, for example, reports that during his field research in twentieth-century Nigeria Ifá diviners cited "a myth according to which the method [of merindinlogun] is based on what the River Goddess Osun learned about divination while she was living with Ifá" (1991, 11)

5. When referring to Yoruba diviners I use the term *babalawo* for both singular and plural instances. In reference to initiates in Cuba I follow the indigenous practice of Hispanicizing the plural as *babalawos*.

6. With close ties to the dynasty of Ife kings (the *Ooni*, who traced direct ancestry to Oduduwa), the central shrine of Ifá was located at Ife and was run by a hierarchy of babalawo led by the *Araba*, the ritual head of the cult (Bascom 1991,

93–94). While the relationship between the principal shrine at Ife and the Ifá cults of other polities was not structured formally, and this may well have allowed the cult to spread more freely with the characteristically peripatetic movement of babalawo from one area to another (Peel 1990, 343–44), the cult of Ife maintained its preeminent position both ritually and, by extension, politically. As Horton has argued, the cult of the Ooni's diviners at Ife was not only more elaborate than its equivalents in other towns, but was also most likely associated with guild-like groupings of babalawo that included representatives from other polities (Horton 1979, 123). Furthermore, a period of apprenticeship at Ife was considered an important marker of prestige for babalawos operating elsewhere, and not least for those aspiring to act as royal counsels in their home polities. So since, as Horton argues, "all major political problems in individual states were referred, at some stage or other, to the local Ifá diviners . . ., allegiance to and influence from Ife must always have been at least a potential factor in the political verdicts of these local operatives" (124).

7. The term is said to derive from *Yaraba*, the Hausa ethnonym for the population of Oyo (Matory 1999, 82). As Matory shows, the idea of "the Yoruba," uniting Ife, Oyo, Egba, Ilesa, Nago and other groups under a single ethnic identity, was actively forged by a Creole cultural elite that emerged in and around Lagos toward the end of the nineteenth century. Comprising freed slaves and other returnees from Brazil, Cuba, and elsewhere (often via Sierra Leone) who took up prominent positions in British-run parts of the West African coast primarily as administrators or independent traders, this literate elite included a number of prestigious and well-traveled babalawo. While some of these returnees converted to Christianity, Ifá was enshrined at the pinnacle of what was called "Yoruba traditional religion" in the ethnological literature produced through the interaction of a self-consciously Yoruba intelligentsia with European administrators and scholars from the late nineteenth century onwards.

8. For recent overviews and discussions on the trajectory of the literature on Afro-American culture and religion see Yelvington 2001 and Palmié 2007.

9. For a vivid illustration of this point, see Barry Hallen's account of the difficulties he encountered when he tried to explain his search for African philosophy to a group of Yoruba herbalists who became his main informants (Hallen 2000, 5–7).

Chapter One

1. Bloch treats social constructivism as a variant of diffusionism (2005, 7), which in a sense, as we shall see, it is. From the point of view of their respective stance to truth, however, the two need to be distinguished for reasons that will be explained.

2. Proponents of the so-called psychic unity of mankind thesis, such as Edward Burnett Tylor, would add that all humans had this capacity in equal measure, although this was a matter of debate (Tylor 1920).

3. This tendency was perhaps strongest in America, where, with the foundational influence of Franz Boas, the nascent subfield of "cultural anthropology" was rooted partly in the Teutonic humanism of the *geisteswissenschaften* and the broader Herderian critique of the Enlightenment from which it stemmed. But Europeans too, drawing particularly from Durkheim a strong Rousseauian line on the distinctive characteristics of the "social," were sensitive to basic breakdowns in the analogy between anthropological modes of inquiry and natural scientific ones.

4. The latter suggestion had been tabled controversially much earlier in the twentieth century by the French philosopher and ethnologist Lucien Lévy-Bruhl, and had been elaborated further by the British social anthropologist E. E. Evans-Pritchard, as we shall see in the next chapter.

5. As Steven Sangren (2007) has pointed out, the shame of not having gotten around to conducting such a study has so far been deemed lesser than the embarrassment doing so would no doubt cause.

6. I borrow the term "representationism" from Richard Rorty (1991), though its currency is in any case wide.

7. See, for example, Hutchins 1995 and Pedersen 2007a for critical review.

8. For example, the positivist outlook of Durkheimian sociology did not stop Marcel Mauss from using Maori prestations as a vantage point from which to criticize modern markets any more than the relativist premise of Boasian culturalism dictated to Margaret Mead that she should use her fieldwork among adolescent girls in Samoa to show up the peculiarities of American parenting (Mauss 1990; Mead 1961).

9. It is worth noting that the sense in which culture is an invention for Wagner is in a way directly opposite to the sense in which it can be, famously, for Hobsbawm and Ranger, when they write of "invented traditions" (1983). Hobsbawm and Ranger's core observation is that practices that may seem "traditional" typically turn out to be recent inventions that act to legitimate present practices by establishing a sense of continuity with an often fictitious past. In terms of Wagner's argument, the claim amounts to the idea that conventions typically purport to be older than they actually are. What is being invented for Hobsbawm and Ranger are not inventions in Wagner's sense, but rather new and suitably old-looking conventions. While the "invented traditions" argument is highly persuasive in its own terms (though see also Sahlins 1999), therefore, it should in no way be confused with Wagner's, which is that the very assumption that people are bound always to control the vagaries of history by appeal to the stability of convention (putative or otherwise) may in some cases have more to do with the analyst's needs than with those of the people he studies.

10. Wagner's technical term for these creative acts of transgression is "obviation" and, following *The Invention of Culture*, he devoted his *Lethal Speech* (1978) to developing this concept with reference to Daribi mythology. As Wagner remarks

(1981, xvi), taken together, *Habu, The Invention of Culture*, and *Lethal Speech* form a trilogy that presents a sustained treatment of the "dialectic" of convention and invention.

11. It is for this reason that calling Wagner a genius, be it true or not (and more on truth later), is at least more interesting than calling Mozart one. While even the latter claim must involve a kernel of expressive invention (it is not, after all, a *mere* tautology), it is clear that more than two centuries of citing Mozart as an archetype of genius have made the claim itself something of a cliché, which is to say, not much more than a statement of already established convention. Calling Wagner a genius, by contrast, is "controversial" (and hence interesting) to the extent that it raises novel possibilities for what being a genius might involve, as well as putting Wagner himself in a new light.

12. The term *recursivity* has wide and varying applications in mathematics, linguistics, computer programming, and elsewhere. As Helen Verran (2001, 89–91) points out, it became widely used as a metaphor in popular culture as well as social theoretical discourse in the 1980s (e.g., Strathern drew her usage from Nancy Munn [1986, 156–57]). In general terms, *recursivity* is defined as a property of definitions, proofs, or algorithms that contain forms of self-reference (an online computer hackers' dictionary illustrates this with a joke: when you search for "recursion" the first hit you get reads "see recursion"). My usage here inflects this idea: I use the term to refer to operations whose formal properties are modified by the contents on which they operate. For example, imagine an algorithm whose sequence of instructions changes in light of each result it produces; or, to recall Wagner on invention, a concept that changes every time it is used to express something. Such a usage, drawing on Strathern to say something slightly different, also exemplifies itself.

13. It is worth noting that Viveiros de Castro's recursive publication strategy, so to speak, of drawing metatheoretical implications from previous ethnographic work is analogous to Wagner's move from the ethnography of *Habu* to the "epistemology" of *The Invention of Culture*. In fact, exemplarily recursive in its agenda, Viveiros de Castro's earlier body of work advances an argument that also runs parallel to Wagner's. The particular character of human-animal relationships in Amazonian animism, branded synthetically as "perspectivist" (see also Stolze Lima 1999) precipitates an analytical realignment of the distinction between culture and nature, whereby the concept of culture (rather than nature) becomes the site of universal similarity, and that of nature (rather than culture) becomes the site of relative difference. This "multi-naturalism," as Viveiros de Castro calls it (1998a, 1998b), recalls Wagner's suggestion that, for Melanesians and other non-Westerners, culture is what is "innate," while nature is "artificial." "The relative native," then, can be read as an attempt to draw out further the recursive implications of such conceptual realignments for the practice of anthropology: What does an anthro-

pology that adopts the "multi-naturalist" premise of Amerindian cosmology look like? For the author's own commentary on Wagner, as well as Strathern, see Viveiros de Castro 2009.

14. The article is published in Portuguese with the title "O nativo relative." The passages presented here were translated in draft by me and kindly revised and refined by the author.

Chapter Two

1. For a detailed review of the recent literature on divination in Africa in particular, see Devisch in press. For a selection of studies broaching such issues from an interdisciplinary perspective see Curry 2010.

2. Detienne attributes the expression to Andrew Lang (see Detienne 1981, 28), though in anthropology its most notorious use is Dan Sperber's (1985).

3. Robin Horton elaborated influentially the Popperian distinction between "closed" and "open" systems of thought in order to make a stark opposition between "African traditional thought" and "Western science" (Horton 1967). To this extent, my criticisms of Evans-Pritchard may also apply to Horton.

4. It may be objected that the relevant statement here—that is, the statement that is stipulated as indubitable—is not "you are bewitched" but rather "the oracle having said so, you are bewitched," and that by placing the claim of bewitchment within the logical scope of a genuine divination in this way the statement does indeed become analytic. However, it does not. To see this, consider the statement spelled out in full: (1) oracular statements are true; (2) the statement "you are bewitched" is oracular; therefore, (3) it true that you are bewitched. *Ex hypothesi* (1) is analytically true. But (2) is not—as we saw in our imaginary Zande dialogue, whether any given statement is genuinely oracular is a matter of fact that is always open to doubt. So (3) is not analytically true either since it is premised on a factual claim, namely (2). The problem, in other words, is that the analyticity of the idea that oracular statements are true does not rub off to any particular statement, since whether any such statement is indeed oracular seems always and in principle to be open to doubt.

5. The term *representation* is used here as a generic and philosophically loose category, to include indiscriminately statements, utterances, propositions, sentences, and so on. There are two reasons for doing this. The first is in order to bypass the technical debate among philosophers as to which of the aforementioned candidates should properly be thought of as bearers of truth and falsity (e.g., see Soames 1999, 13–19). Second, the term is fashionable in anthropology and allows one to connect with current debates within the discipline, as already demonstrated in the previous chapter.

6. This logical predicament of representation premises the broader ontotheological condition Paul Ricoeur famously called the "hermeneutics of suspicion" (1970, 32–35). For more on this see chapter 4.

Chapter Three

1. "Washing" a deity constitutes a cheap alternative to full initiation to Santería, and has become relatively common among younger generations of babalawos.

2. In ascending hierarchical order, the full list of ceremonies includes: (1) receipt of "mano de Orula" ("bunch of Orula"), whereby the consecrated pot of Orula, the patron god of divination, is "given" to the neophyte, though in incomplete form since the "bunch" of twenty palm nuts that is given at this stage is deemed not to be enough to divine with—twenty-one nuts comprise the complete set; (2) initiation to Santería, which is considered a prerequisite for Ifá initiation, even though the ceremony is performed by santeros, so that the neophyte is effectively included in an alternative cult structure before "entering Ifá"; (3) full Ifá initiation, when the neophyte becomes a babalawo by receiving the Orula in complete form and can henceforth act as diviner; (4) receipt of *guanaddo* (or *cuchillo*—the "knife"), which entitles babalawos to perform sacrifices of four legged animals; (5) certain subsequent ceremonies that bestow specific "powers" on the initiate, such as the receipt of Olofin, the all-powerful patron of the sun. For a discussion of the historical evolution of this ceremonial sequence in Cuba see Brown 2003.

3. The death rites of ituto and *honras*, when the oracle is consulted in order to ensure the future well-being of the deceased babalawo, may be considered a category in themselves. The "warriors" include Elegguá (messenger god and "owner of the paths"), Ogún (patron of smithery and war), and Ochosi (god of hunting), who are given together with Osun, considered a symbol of the neophyte's personal well-being.

Chapter Four

1. Such questions are staple not only to the ever growing anthropological literature on Christian conversion in colonial and postcolonial contexts, but also, for example, to the longstanding historical corpus on the origins of Christianity in the midst of Judaic and pagan religious practices in late antiquity (e.g., Brown 1981; Bynum 1995).

2. There are some exceptions to this general observation, notably the case of Oyá, the goddess of winds and cemeteries, who is closely associated with the personification of death, *ikú*, and is an emphatically singular being.

3. Some babalawos reserve the term *oricha* only for these "major" creator deities (particularly Olofin—sometimes identified with Olodumare—Oddúa, Orula, Obatalá, and Osain), distinguishing them from the rest of the divinities (Elegguá, Ochosi, Ogún, Changó, Ochún, Yemayá, Oyá, and so on) to whom they refer as *ocha*.

4. Babalawos sometimes set the figure of 101 as the notional limit of the amount of paths each oddu may have, although one babalawo explained to me that since hardly anyone gets to learn so many ($101 \times 256 = 25,856!$), it may well be that different oddu may have fewer or more than that. Indeed, the habitual expectation is that a babalawo should know at least sixteen paths for each oddu ($16 \times 256 = 4096$). In practice, however, babalawos' knowledge of paths is distributed unequally, so that any individual babalawo may often know more than sixteen stories for some oddu (particularly Baba Eyiobbe and the other meyi, as well his own initiatory signo), while falling well short of the quota for others. Interestingly (given that one would expect the frequency of each oddu to be random), some babalawos explained to me their relatively scant knowledge of paths for certain oddu by saying that they rarely occur during divination (*hay oddu que salen poco*).

5. Based on West African materials, Robert Pelton claims the role of the divining board in Ifá is "iconographic," as an "an icon of man's place in the cosmos" (1980, 149, and 148–56 *passim* on Ifá iconography). Similar points are made in Frobenius 1913, 248–59, 282–87; Maupoil 1943, 184–94; and Bascom 1991, 33–34, for West Africa; and Héres Hevia 1962, 308–54; Argüelles Mederos and Hodge Limonta 1991, 90–91; and Menéndez Vásquez 1998, 3:235–67, for Cuba.

6. A young initiate who takes an interest in contemporary Yoruba practices in Nigeria, explained that, "properly speaking," the deity who is most closely associated with the oracle is Agboniregún, while Ifá is best understood as an impersonal force that guides diviners during ceremonies. However, older practitioners with whom I spoke were more inclined to treat Agboniregún as "a title," or praise-name, of Orula (see also Bascom 1991, 108; on Yoruba praise names in Nigeria see Barber 1991).

7. My description draws on personal observation of approximately thirty-five divinations (including ókuele as well as bajadas), as well as information obtained from "papers of Ifá" (see chapter 3) entrusted to me by babalawos. Given the secret character of much of the content of these documents, and in accordance with my informants' express wishes, I omit details of the chants of the prayers (*rezos*, *suyeres*, and other ritual knowledge—see also Appendix B), the ingredients of magical recipes, and the mechanism through which oddu configurations are used to determine answers to particular questions during the consultation. My informants are satisfied with this arrangement since only with such esoteric knowledge included could my description serve as a guide to practice in the hands of a noniniti-ate (*aleyo*). Thus, what follows is essentially a detailed description of those aspects

of a divinatory ceremony that any noninitiate (client or observer) is able to see just by going to consult a babalawo.

8. On some informants' account, the minimum number is three.

9. I use "she" throughout in order to avoid the unwieldy use of "she or he," and in view of the fact that, while consultants can be of either gender, the larger proportion is female (see chapter 3).

10. Indeed, in the case of ituto ceremonies, the tablero is omitted and the oddu are marked on ash which is placed directly on the ground.

11. Generally, to all saints one lights two candles apart from the guerreros and el muerto (dead spirits) who take one.

12. Natalia Bolívar refers to a path of the oddu Okana in which "Olofin [tells Elegguá]: 'You being the smallest of all and my messenger, shall be the grandest on the Earth and in the Sky, and it will be impossible to do anything without counting on you' " (Bolívar Aróstegui 1994a, 27, my translation).

13. On the connection between divination and genitals and fecundity see Guanche 1983, 366.

14. Bolívar describes an alternative mode of interpretation, called *apere-tí*, which takes the relative position of the obbi into account (Bolívar Aróstegui 1994b, 16–41). Babalawos assured me that this is not used in Ifá, and I have never witnessed it myself.

15. For example, Bolívar Aróstegui 1994b, 12–15, and Guanche 1983, 389–90, provide diverging accounts of obbi interpretation, and practices I witnessed among different babalawos and santeros during fieldwork were not always consistent.

16. I was unable to ascertain the reason for this.

17. This act is common in a variety of ritual contexts in Ifá, whether it be carried out with coconut or other ritual items. Babalawos are particularly meticulous at this performance when it comes to sacrifices, whereby the sacrificial animal itself is used to "touch" the client's "parts." The order followed usually is forehead, neck, front and back part of shoulders, hipbones, outside and inside of hands, knees, and, finally, the feet (see also Bascom 1991, 60–68; Cabrera 1994; de Souza Hernández 1998).

18. One babalawo explained to me the significance of this rite with reference to an Ifá myth, though I have not been able to corroborate this account. Apparently there was once a babalawo who was brought up by Olokun, the ferocious deity of deep waters. Olokun was adamant that his protégé should never learn how to practice Ifá. Changó, the virile god of thunder, arrived one day and, seeing the difficulties that the local villagers were facing, decided to teach the babalawo how to divine in order to be able to help his neighbors. Changó said, "You have been bound up by Olokun and to unbind yourself you have to do this," and showed the babalawo how to pass the divining nuts behind his back.

19. My translations of Lucumí ritual speech are based on Spanish translations that babalawos gave me, as well as those contained in "papers of Ifá" that I was shown.

20. This may well be a reference to the practice of rubbing the nuts in palm oil (*manteca de corojo*), which is deemed part of the regular care that initiates owe their Orula. In the case of Orula such maintenance work should be undertaken on Sunday mornings.

21. Ókuele divination is simpler in that, instead of drawing out the process of determining each of the eight parts of the oddu sequentially, it allows babalawos to cast oddu in one fell swoop. The chain, which is 30–50 cm long, has eight oblong fragments of coconut shell (roughly 1–4 cm long) attached to it. The diviner holds the chain from the middle, so that the chain's two "legs," each with four shells, hang on either side of his fingers. Allowing the chain to swing freely in the air, he lets it drop onto a flat surface (usually a straw mat). Each shell has a front (its concave, lighter side) and a back (the convex, darker side), so that the outcome of each cast is "read" as a determinate configuration of the front or back of the eight shells (*boca arriba/abajo*).

22. The opposite direction is followed if the divination is conducted for the benefit of a dead spirit—for example, in the funerary rites of ituto.

23. It is said that a babalawo should have sixteen different ibbo corresponding to various types of questions. However most babalawos tend to work with four or five, including a small bone from a goat's hoof (one previously sacrificed to Elegguá), and a head of a hen previously sacrificed to Orula.

Chapter Five

1. Though her dissolution of the problem of social reproduction is driven specifically by the recursive potential of Melanesian ethnography (e.g., ceremonial exchange, kinship practices, initiation ceremonies), Strathern's reinvention of Euro-American distinctions between society and individual builds on earlier critiques advanced in relation to of South Asian materials (particularly Dumont 1970 and Marriott 1979).

2. See Díaz Fabelo 1960, 29–30; Idowu 1962, 5–6; Pelton 1980, 127–63; Argüelles Mederos and Hodge Limonta 1991, 89–91; Menéndez Vásquez 1995, 41–42.

3. In the case of ordinary consultations, the babalawo moves the divining chain itself up and down, in a dangling movement over the divining mat.

4. For an application of the distinction between regulative and constitutive rules to Zande oracles, see Ahern 1982; cf. Humphrey and Laidlaw 1994, 117–21.

5. For discussions on the close relationship between Orula and Elegguá see Frobenius 1913, 229–32; Idowu 1962, 80–85; Pelton 1980, 133–63; Bascom 1991, 103–7; Barnet 1995, 45–49; Staewen 1996, 4; Cabrera 2000, 76–88.

6. Translations from the Spanish text are mine.

7. Consecration is often referred to as a 'baptism' (*bautizo*) with obvious Christian connotations.

8. Hubert and Mauss express exactly this point when they write that the idea of mana "not only transforms magical judgements into analytical judgements but converts them from a priori to *a posteriori* arguments, since the idea dominates and conditions all experience" (Mauss 2001, 156). Saul Kripke put the possibility of a posteriori analyticity on the philosophers' table almost a century later, though not much to our use here since mana-terms such as aché are anything but "rigid designators"—as the terms of a posteriori analytic truths, for him, must be (e.g., "water is H_2O"; 1980, 48–49, and see chapter 2 above for more on Kripke).

9. In her detailed study of Yoruba concepts of number and quantity, Helen Verran suggests that Yoruba do not designate quantities by aggregating discrete entities, but rather view quantity as one of the "modalities" through which any particular object may be characterized as an object in the first place. Quantity, according to this view, is not a more abstract designation of the object quantified, but rather one of the attributes that give the object its concrete mode of existence as what Verran calls a "sortal particular." Such a view accords with my analysis of aché powder here, since it would imply that multiplicity is at the core of the very definition of powder as a "sortal," rather than an accidental attribute that can be abstracted from it. However, I do not wish to put too fine a point on this, since Verran's study concerns notions of quantification that can be read off Yoruba language and found among children and adults in contemporary Nigeria, whereas my analysis concerns the particular associations that aché has in the practice of divination as I witnessed it in Cuba.

10. I have made a parallel argument regarding the role of money in Ifá cosmology (Holbraad 2005).

11. For an illuminating account of the logical implications of the notion of direction, framed in terms of the philosophy of evolution, see Ingold 1986, 12–13.

12. While Goldman notes that his informants as a rule emphasize the Bantu origins of their Candomblé practices (pers. com.), the cosmological commonalities of Candomblé with the (putatively) Yoruba-based practice of Ifá in Cuba are widely accepted and well documented (e.g., see Brown 2003, 115; cf. Palmié 2002, 159–62).

13. Translations from the original Portuguese are my own.

14. Ashe is how *aché* is spelt in the literature on Brazilian Candomblé. *Oricha* is spelt *orisha* (see below).

15. While displaying holographic properties as I have indicated, such an absence of "structure" also distinguishes my notion of "partibility" from Melanesianists' use of the mathematical concept of "fractality" (cf. Wagner 1991; Gell 1998, 137–40; Strathern 2004). A fractal object is one that reproduces structural features at different scales. The "partibility" of powder, however, comes down to the fact that it reproduces an *absence* of structure at *whatever* scale gradation.

16. Brown points out that the "hierarchical protocols" that practitioners associate with the orichas "can shift, depending upon socioritual context" (2003, 128). He

explains: "Formally, the ranking oricha elder, Obatalá, is the 'highest,' and Ochún is the 'smallest' or most junior. Yet, these relationships are fluid, since alternate *patakín* (legends) relativize and turn upside down, at least momentarily, any given hierarchy. In one important story, little Ochún, manifesting as the unprepossessing buzzard, saves the world from a scourge when all others have failed, demonstrating that 'a junior can be . . . the elder among elders' " (Brown 2003, 128, citing Ecún 1986, 141). Clearly this is not to argue that Ifá cosmology is less vertical, in Hugh-Jones's terms, than practitioners represent it, but rather to show that its vertical coordinates are not fixed.

Chapter Six

1. I borrow the term *series* from Gilles Deleuze's inspiring exposition of Lévi-Strauss's argument in the "Eighth Series of Structure" of *The Logic of Sense* (Deleuze 1990a, 48–51).

2. If one may hazard a guess without further discussion, it seems reasonable to think that the move to "floating signifiers" is only motivated by a perspective that posits the apogee of meaning, roughly speaking, as a state of perfect and permanent correspondence of signifier to signified. Whether such fits are possible at all, and whether—as Lévi-Strauss claims (1987, 61)—it is the job of science to deliver them, are open questions (although see Latour 1987 for a classic ethnographic refutation of such a view).

3. The extracts are reconstructed from detailed notes taken during and just after the consultation. Relevant explanations are provided in square brackets and translations from ritual Lucumí are included, where necessary, in parentheses. Words spoken in Spanish are translated directly into English.

4. San Lázaro de las Muletas (Saint Lazarus of the Cruches, identified with Babalú Ayé in Lucumí) is considered a highly potent "major" deity, patron of the sick and needy, and is depicted as a cripple himself. The annual pilgrimage to the Catholic sanctuary of Saint Lazarus at Rincón, an old leprosy clinic south of Havana, is one the most attended religious ceremonies in Cuba (Sierra Torres 1995; Zamora 2000).

5. This is a common phenomenon in Havana. It is not at all unusual for people at various stages of their "development" (*desarroyo*) as Spiritist mediums to practice their seership on strangers that they meet on the street (Espirito Santo 2009).

6. Consider the implications for myths in particular. Recalling Lévi-Strauss's analysis, in his "late" period of the *Mythologiques*, of myth as an inherently self-transformational register of signification (e.g. 1981), a motile view of mythical "paths" in Ifá does suggest a marked departure from certain familiar anthropological models, which tend to depict myths as metanarratives of sorts, the job of which may be to explain things (as Frazer and Tylor had claimed; cf. Cohen 1969,

338–39), to reinforce the solidarity of social groups (Durkheim 1995), to prescribe a blueprint for stable social organization (Malinowski 1948), to soak up the "threat of history" by referring reality back to an archetypal order (Eliade 1991), or to do so by imaginatively obviating the contradictions that render society unstable (Lévi-Strauss 1977, part 3; Bloch 1992, 99–105). In particular, the emphasis that divinatory interpretation places on the telling of myths as a temporal activity is incongruous with the premise of approaches such these, namely that myths are most fruitfully viewed as representations that are limited to reflecting upon reality (in whatever way) rather than partaking of it. From the viewpoint of divinatory interpretation myths are no more abstract or representational than, say, the data that make up practitioners' life-paths. For example, in the extract from Yolanda's consultation above, the path of Obbeyono that tells the story of San Lázaro's meeting with Ogún need not be construed as fundamentally different to, say, the consultant's personal frustrations in her attempts to travel. Both data refer to events or states of affairs that are meaningful, and both can be thought about or narrated at particular times and places (see also Basso 1996).

Chapter Seven

1. This refers to the crucial question posed in itá divinations of the kofá (mano de Orula) ceremony, as to which of the santos is the neophyte's "guardian angel," as discussed in chapter 3. It is not unusual for neophytes to expect the answer they receive, since a guardian angel's influence is often deemed to be clear in the neophyte's personality.

2. It is argued, for example, that the ability to align our thoughts with our environment (i.e., to judge representations for truth) is an indispensable condition for acting effectively, and ultimately for what evolutionary theorists call "surviving" (Sperber 1996, 98–11 and *passim*; Rappaport 1999, 406–437).

3. I would not want to suggest that motile notions of truth are always obscured in ordinary conversation or other nondivinatory contexts. Psychoanalytic consultation might provide a counterexample, though I shall not argue the case here. On the connection between psychoanalysis and divination (or phenomena related to it) see Jung 1989; Fortes 1981; Turner 1967; Humphrey 1976; and, most recently, Devisch forthcoming).

4. Note that the alleged ontological distinction here is slightly different from the one we encountered in our discussion of divinatory interpretation. If there representationism amounted to assuming an ontological gap between representations and the world (i.e., as an issue regarding the metaphysics of semantics), here the distinction is drawn between representations and the worldly vehicles through which they get expressed (at the semiotic level: signified versus signifier). However, since a motile analysis denies a shared premise of these variants of representation-

ism, namely that meanings are irreducibly abstract, it is reasonable to expect that it should serve as a tenable alternative to semiotic representationism also. On such a view, oddu are not arbitrary signifiers of abstract (signified) meanings, and nor therefore does the system of 256 oddu constitute a semiotic code. Rather, the relationship between the material manifestation of oddu during the divination and its meaning (as expressed in mythical paths and so on) can be thought of as analogous to the relationship between a person and his personality: there is no arbitrariness because the oddu just *is* its meaning, for those who are acquainted with it (the babalawos who "study"). This is borne out by the fact that each oddu is properly considered a deity in its own right, as well as practitioners' complex accounts of the genealogical underpinnings of the relationships between the various oddu (see appendix A). So, inasmuch as oddu in Cuba are commonly referred to as "signs of Ifá" (signos), then these signs, quite literally for practitioners, *speak for themselves*—again, recalling Wagner (1986).

Chapter Eight

1. For a confluent argument about the role of novelty in Mongolian divination see Swancutt 2006.

2. I adopt the standard distinction in the philosophical literature between *definiendum* and *definiens* (e.g., Robinson 1950). The former is the object of definition, while the latter is its means.

3. The notion of "being there" merely conveys the idea of logical priority in order to distinguish conventional from inventive definitions. No *immediate* ontological consequences are at stake, so at least the better-known conundrums within analytical philosophy regarding the possibility of making truth-claims about nonexistent entities are bypassed. To take the most influential example, perhaps, consider Russell's *Theory of Descriptions* (Russell 1905). Russell held that it is possible to make truth-claims about nonexistent entities (e.g., unicorns) without fear of contradiction, because, contrary to grammatical appearances, such truth-claims do not *refer* to the entities they denote. For example, the claim "unicorns are horses with horns" does not refer to unicorns, and hence does not depend on their actually existing for it to have meaning. For the claim can be restated by replacing the apparent reference to unicorns with a description of a variable: "anything that is a unicorn is a horse with a horn," thus predicating unicorns without committing to their existence.

Nevertheless, even restated as descriptions, conventional definitions retain their predicative character. The difference is merely that on Russell's ingenious theory the subject of predication is a variable rather than an entity or class of entities (putative or actual). So the distinction between a subject and its predicates remains, and so does the logical priority of the former over the latter. Indeed, this logical priority does have ontological consequences, though they are weaker than the ones Russell—and, after him, most notably Quine (1953)—sought to avoid. For the view that *definienda* are variables rather than entities is itself premised on a distinction between entities and their predicates, since the very notion of a variable implies a domain of entities from which the variable may draw its values. Indeed, for Russell such a distinction between a "world" of entities, on the one hand, and the statements that can be made about it on the other (which would include definitions) ought to be the starting point for straight-thinking philosophers, and indeed is part of what *motivates* the theory of descriptions. As he wrote, "[l]ogic must no more admit a unicorn than zoology can; for logic is concerned with the *real world* just as truly as zoology, though with its more abstract and general features" (Russell 1996: 209, my emphasis).

4. It will be clear that this argument is closely related to "ontological arguments" in theology. Since such arguments are notoriously difficult to pin down I offer my own somewhat tentatively. As Bertrand Russell put it, "it is easier to feel convinced that [ontological arguments] must be fallacious than it is to find out precisely where the fallacy lies" (1946, 609).

5. For a classic argument on the analogy between temporality and modality (i.e., between different times and different possible worlds) see Lewis 1986, 202–4 and *passim*.

6. In contrast to well discussed cases in West African ethnography, notions of "destiny" or "fate" did not show up as a salient part of cosmology or practice in my research on Cuban Ifá (though see Panagiotopoulos 2011 for ways in which they do). Not only are references to such ideas largely absent in babalawos' discourse, but also in Cuba adoration of *orí* (the head), which the Yoruba consider the locus of individual destiny, is not prevalent (Bascom 1991, 71–74; Lawal 1985). As the Cuban babalawo Fran Obbeché told me, Yoruba practitioners visiting Cuba in recent years have found this absence perplexing. Nevertheless, to the extent that the analytical metaphor of "destiny" sheds light on the practice of Ifá divination in Cuba, it may also be relevant in thinking of the ways in which indigenous notions of destiny have been conceptualized in the West African literature. A particular problem there has been how to tally the eschatological connotations of European words like "destiny" or "fate"—not least the idea that they are "inexorable" or "foreordained" (Herskovits, cited in Fortes 1981, 22)—with the widely reported use of divination as a means not only to gauge it, but also to modify it by means of the sacrifices and other offerings that diviners are able to prescribe for the benefit of clients (e.g., for the case of Yoruba Ifá see Bascom 1991, 60–62, 113–19). It may be noted that on a motile analysis the paradox disappears. On such a view one's destiny is indeed preordained, in the sense that one's future trajectory is already contained, as it were, in one's past since that too is trajectile. But this motile version of determinism hardly precludes the "freedom" to influence the future by divination and sacrifice, precisely because motile divinatory predictions, including the

prescriptions of sacrifice, are *constitutive* of one's destiny. Destiny, in other words, is the outcome rather than the condition of divination.

Conclusion

1. I have suggested just such a syllogism in earlier publications (e.g., Holbraad 2008). Here I wish to correct the error.

2. Having said this, there is also a rider on this claim, namely that the facts about divination in which I am interested are inherently more significant than the facts illuminated by these approaches, and this because truth is the overriding concern for practitioners of divination—another empirical claim on my part.

3. I thank Paraskeyi Nastou for making this point.

4. A philosophical conversation stopper famously proposed by G.E. Moore in defense of common sense (Moore 1939).

5. The extension of an expression is its reference. Intension is harder to define, but for present purposes it can be understood as a description of sufficient and/or necessary criteria for determining the extension of a given expression (see Chalmers 2002). So, for example, if I ask you what a peccary is and you point one out to me ("there's one!"), you are giving me the meaning of "peccary" in terms of its extension. But if you explain to me that a peccary is a pig-like animal that lives in South America, you will be giving me the intension of the term. Loosely, we may say that a term's extension depends on empirical considerations, while its intension depends on conceptual ones.

6. It may be observed that this lends a peculiarly Judeo-Christian hue to the recursive challenge in anthropology: as I suggested in chapters 4 and 5, the problem of the radical ontological alterity of a (divine) Other, often expressed as a mysterious "gap" between trasncendence and immanence, is characteristic of this particular theological tradition. This may be another facet of the "Christianity of anthropology," to recall Cannell's phrase (2006).

Epilogue

1. Quotations are taken directly from Viveiros de Castro's reviewer's report to the editorial board of the University of Chicago Press. I am hugely grateful to him for allowing me to cite this document, using it as a foil, as he might say, for these retrospective reflections on the argument developed in the previous chapters.

2. "Everything as it moves, now and then, here and there, makes stops. The bird as it flies stops in one place to make its nest, and in another to rest in its flight" (Lévi-Strauss 1964, 98).

Appendix A

1. Note that the term *abbure* is normally used as kinship term to refer to ritual sibling relationships within religious families (see chapter 3). However, when used to talk about the oddu, babalawos are equivocal as to whether the term should be understood as an indication of the siblingship of the oddu in question. Generally, genealogical relations between oddu are understood to feature more in the contents of the myths themselves, rather than as series of formal relations between configurations of signos.

2. Note here that neither the formal derivations based on comparing the oddu as configurations, nor the quasi-formal connections derived from genealogical sequences need be cyclical. Just as each oddu is related formally to more than one other oddu (its inversion, its mirror image, and so on), so each oddu may be associated with a number of myths describing the birth of other oddu. Thus both systems of relations are "open" in form.

Works Cited

Abbink, Jon. 1993. "Reading the Entrails: Analysis of an African Divination Discourse." *Man* (N.S.) 28 (4): 705–26.

Abimbola, Wande. 1965. "The Place of Ifa in Yoruba Traditional Religion." *African Notes* 2 (2): 3–4.

———. 1973. "The Literature of the Ifa Cult." In *Sources of Yoruba History*, ed. Saburi O. Biobaku, 41–62. Oxford: Clarendon Press.

———. 1997a. *Ifa: An Exposition of Ifa Literary Corpus.* New York: Athelia Henrietta Press.

———. 1997b. *Ifa Will Mend Our Broken World: Thoughts on Yoruba Religion and Culture in Africa and the Diaspora.* Roxbury: Aim Books.

———. 2000. "Continuity and Change in the Verbal, Artistic, Ritualistic, and Performance Traditions of Ifa Divination." In *Insight and Artistry in African Divination*, ed. John Pemberton III, 175–81. Washington, DC: Smithsonian Institution Press.

Ahern, Emily M. 1982. "Rules in Oracles and Games." *Man* (N.S.) 17 (2): 302–12.

Akinnaso, F. Niyi. 1992. "Schooling, Language, and Knowledge in Literate and Non-literate Societies." *Comparative Studies in Society and History* 34 (1): 68–109.

Andreu Alonso, Guillermo. 1995. *Los Araras en Cuba: Florentina, la Princesa dahomeyana.* La Habana: Editorial de Ciencias Sociales.

Appiah, Kwame A. 1992. *In My Father's House: Africa in the Philosophy of Culture.* Oxford: Oxford University Press.

Apter, Andrew. 1987. "The Historiography of Yoruba Myth and Ritual." *History in Africa* 14:1–25.

———. 1991. "The Embodiment of Paradox: Yoruba Kingship and Female Power." *Cultural Anthropology* 6 (2): 212–29.

———. 1992. *Black Critics and Kings: The Hermeneutics of Power in Yoruba Society.* Chicago: University of Chicago Press.

————. 1995. "Notes on Orisha Cults in the Ekiti Yoruba Highlands: a Tribute to Pierre Verger." *Cahiers d'Études Africaines* 35 (138/139): 369–401.

Ardener, Edwin. 1989. *The Voice of Prophecy and Other Essays.* Edited by Malcolm Chapman. Oxford: Basil Blackwell.

Argüelles Mederos, Anibal, and Ileana Hodge Limonta. 1991. *Los llamados cultos sincréticos y el espiritismo.* La Habana: Editorial Academia.

Argyriadis, Kali. 2005. "El desarrollo del turismo religioso en la Habana y la acusación del mercantilismo." *Desacatos* 18:29–52.

Argyriadis, Kali, Renée de la Torre, Cristina Gutiérrez Zúniga, and Alejandra Aguilar Ros, eds. 2008. *Raíces en movimiento: prácticas religiosas tradicionales en contextos translocales.* Guadalajara: El Colegio de Jalisco /CEMCA/ IRD/ CIESAS/ ITESO.

Argyrou, Vassos. 2002. *Anthropology and the Will to Meaning: A Postcolonial Critique.* London: Pluto Press.

Asad, Talal. 1993. *Genealogies of Religion: Discipline and Reasons of Power in Christianity and Islam.* Baltimore: Johns Hopkins University Press.

Austin, John L. 1962. *How to Do Things with Words.* Edited by James O. Urmson. Oxford: Clarendon Press.

Awolalu, Omosade J. 1979. *Yoruba Beliefs and Sacrificial Rites.* Longman: London.

Ayorinde, Christine. 2004. *Afro-Cuban Religiosity, Revolution, and National Identity.* Gainesville: University Press of Florida.

Barber, Karin. 1981. "How Man Makes God in West Africa: Yoruba Attitudes Towards the 'orisa.'" *Africa: Journal of the International African Institute* 51 (3): 724–45.

————. 1991. *I Could Speak Until Tomorrow: Oríkì, Women and the Past in a Yorùbá Town.* Edinburgh: Edinburgh University Press.

Barnes, Sandra T. and Paula Girshick Ben-Amos. 1997. "Ogun, the Empire Builder." In *Africa's Ogun*, 2nd expanded ed., ed. Sandra T. Barnes, 39–64. Bloomington: Indiana University Press.

Barnet, Miguel. 1995. *Cultos afrocubanos.* La Habana: Ediciones Unión.

Bascom, William R. 1941. "The Sanctions of Ifa Divination." *Man* IXXI (1/2): 43–53.

————. 1950. "The Focus of Cuban Santeria." *Southwestern Journal of Anthropology* 6 (1): 64–68.

————. 1980. *Sixteen Cowries: Yoruba Divination from Africa to the New World.* Bloomington and Indianapolis: Indiana University Press.

————. 1991. *Ifa Divination: Communication Between Gods and Men in West Africa.* Bloomington: Indiana University Press.

Basso, Keith H. 1996. *Wisdom Sits in Places: Landscape and Language Among the Western Apache.* Albuquerque: University of New Mexico Press.

Basso Ortíz, Alessandra. 2005. *Los Gangá en Cuba.* La Habana: Fundación Fernando Ortíz.

Bastide, Roger. 2000. *Le Candomblé da Bahia (Rite Nagô)*. Paris: Plon.

Bateson, Gregory. 2002. *Mind and Nature: A Necessary Unity*. Cresskill, NJ: Hampton Press.

Benedict, Ruth. 1934. *Patterns of Culture*. New York: Houghton Mifflin.

Bloch, Maurice. 1974. "Symbols, Song, Dance and Features of Articulation: Is Religion an Extreme Form of Traditional Authority?" *Archives Europeenes de Sociologie* 15:55–81.

———. 1992. *From Prey into Hunter*. Cambridge: Cambridge University Press.

———. 1998. *How We Think They Think: Anthropological Approaches to Cognition, Memory and Literacy*. Boulder, CO: Westview Press.

———. 2005. "Where Did Anthropology Go? Or the Need for 'Human Nature.'" In his *Essays on Cultural Transmission*, 1–20. Oxford: Berg.

Boas, Franz. 1940. *Race, Language, and Culture*. New York: Macmillan.

Bohannan, Paul. 1975. "Tiv Divination." In *Studies in Social Anthropology: Essays in Memory of E. E. Evans-Pritchard by His Former Oxford Colleagues*, ed. John Beattie and Godfrey Lienhardt, 149–66. Oxford: Clarendon Press.

Bolívar Aróstegui, Natalia. 1994a. *Los orishas en Cuba*. La Habana: PM Ediciones.

———. 1994b. *Opolopo owó: los sistemas adivinatorios de la Regla de Ocha*. La Habana: Editorial de Ciencias Sociales.

Boyer, Pascal. 1990. *Tradition as Truth and Communication*. Cambridge: Cambridge University Press.

———. 1994. *The Naturalness of Religious Ideas*. Berkeley: University of California Press.

———. 2000. "Functional Origins of Religious Concepts." *Journal of the Royal Anthropological Institute* (N.S.) 6 (2): 195–214.

Bracken, Christopher. 2007. *Magical Criticism: The Recourse of Savage Philosophy*. Chicago: University of Chicago Press.

Brandon, George. 1993. *Santería from Africa to the New World: The Dead Sell Memories*. Bloomington: Indiana University Press.

Brenner, Louis. 2000. "Muslim Divination and the History of Religion of Sub-Saharan Africa." In *Insight and Artistry in African Divination*, ed. John Pemberton III, 45–59. Washington, DC: Smithsonian Institution Press.

Brown, David H. 2003. *Santería Enthroned: Art, Ritual, and Innovation in an Afro-Cuban Religion*. Chicago: University of Chicago Press.

Brown, Peter. 1981. *The Cult of the Saints: Its Rise and Function in Latin Christianity*. Chicago: University of Chicago Press.

Bruun Jensen, Casper and Kjetle Rödje, eds. 2009. *Deleuzian Intersections: Science, Technology, Anthropology*. New York: Berghahn.

Bynum, Caroline Walker. 1995. *The Resurrection of the Body in Western Christianity, 200–1336*. New York: Columbia University Press.

Cabrera, Lydia. 1994. *La medicina popular de Cuba: medicos de antaño, curanderos, santeros y paleros de hogaño*. Miami: Colección del Chicherekú en el Exilio.

————. 2000. *El monte*. Miami: Ediciones Universal.

Cameron, Averil. 1991. *Christianity and the Rhetoric of Empire: The Development of Christian Rhetoric.* Berkeley: University of California Press.

Cannell, Fenella. 2006. "Introduction: The Anthropology of Christianity." In *The Anthropology of Christianity*, ed. Cannell, 1–50. Durham, NC: Duke University Press.

Capone, Stefania. 1999. "Les dieux sur le Net: l'essor des religions d'origine africaine aux Etats-Unis." *L'homme* 151:47–74.

Carrier, James G. ed. 1992. *History and Tradition in Melanesian Anthropology.* Berkeley: University of California Press.

Chalmers, David J. 2002. "On Sense and Intension." In *Philosophical Perspectives 16: Language and Mind*, ed. James Tomberlin, 135–82. Oxford: Blackwell.

Chua, Liana, Casey High, and Timm Lau, eds. 2008. *How Do We Know? Evidence, Ethnography, and the Making of Anthropological Knowledge.* Newcastle-upon-Tyne: Cambridge Scholars Publishing.

Cicero, Marcus Tullius, 1997. Nature of the Gods *and* On Divination. Translated by C. D. Yonge. Essex: Prometheus Books Publishers.

Cohen, Percy S. 1969. "Theories of Myth." *Man* (N.S.) 4 (3): 337–53.

Cohen, Peter F. 2002. "Orisha Journeys: The Role of Travel in the Birth of Yorùbá-Atlantic Religions." *Archives de Sciences Sociales des Religions* 117 (January–March): 17–36.

Corsín Jiménez, Alberto, 2008. "Well-Being in Anthropological Balance: Remarks on Proportionality as Political Imagination." In *Culture and Well-Being: Anthropological Approaches to Freedom and Political Ethics*, ed. Alberto Corsín Jiménez, 180–200. Ann Arbor: Pluto Press.

Corsín Jiménez, Alberto and Rane Willerslev. 2007. "'An Anthropological Concept of the Concept': Reversibility among the Siberian Yukaghirs." *Journal of the Royal Anthropological Institute* (N.S.) 13 (3): 527–44.

Crook, Tony. 2007. *Anthropological Knowledge, Secrecy, and Bolivip, Papua New Guinea: Exchanging Skin.* Oxford: Oxford University Press.

Cros Sandoval, Mercedes. 2006. *Worldviews, the Orichas, and Santería: Africa to Cuba and Beyond.* Gainesville: University Press of Florida.

Curry, Patrick, ed. 2010. *Divination: Perspectives for a New Millennium.* Farnham: Ashgate.

D'Andrade, Roy G. 1995. "Moral Models in Anthropology." *Current Anthropology* 36 (3): 399–408.

de Boeck, Filip, and René Devisch. 1994. "Ndembu, Luunda and Yaka Divination Compared: from Representation and Social Engineering to Embodiment and Worldmaking." *Journal of Religion in Africa* 24 (2): 98–128.

Deleuze, Gilles. 1990a. *The Logic of Sense.* Translated by Mark Lester. London: Athlone Press.

———. 1990b. *Expressionism in Philosophy: Spinoza*. Translated by Martin Joughin. New York: Zone Books.

———. 1994. *Difference and Repetition*. Translated by Paul Patton. London: Athlone Press.

Deleuze, Gilles, and Felix Guattari. 1996. *What Is Philosophy?* New York: Columbia University Press.

Derrida, Jacques. 1992. "Force of Law." In *Deconstruction and the Possibility of Justice*, trans. Mary Quaintance, ed. Drucilla Cornell, Michael Rosenfeld, and David Gray Carlson, 3–67. New York: Routledge.

de Souza Hernández, Adrián. 1998. *El sacrificio en el culto de los orichas: ebbó, animales, materiales y plantas*. La Habana: Ediciones Ifatumó.

Detienne, Marcel. 1981. *L'invention de la mythologie*. Paris: Gallimard.

———. 1996. *The Masters of Truth in Archaic Greece*. Translated by Jeffrey Lloyd. London: Zone Books.

Devisch, René. 1985. "Perspectives on Divination in Contemporary Sub-Saharan Africa." In *Theoretical Explorations in African Religions*, ed. Wim van Binsbergen and Matthew Schoffeleers, 50–83. London: Routledge.

———. 1991. "Mediumistic Divination among the Northern Yaka of Zaire: Etiology and Ways of Knowing." In *African Divination Systems*, ed. Phillip Peek, 112–32. Bloomington: Indiana University Press.

———. In press. "Recent Approaches to Divination in Africa: The Bodiliness of Acute Discernment." In *The Wiley-Blackwell Companion to African Religions*, ed. Elias Bongmba. Oxford: Blackwell.

———. Forthcoming. "Of Divinatory *Connaissance* among the Yaka of Congo." In *Reality Reviewed: Dynamics of African Divination*, ed. Wouter van Beek and Philip Peek. Leiden: Brill.

Dianteill, Erwan. 2000. *Des dieux et des signes: Initiation, écriture et divination dans les religions afro-cubaines*. Paris: Editions de l'EHESS.

———. 2002. "Deterritorialization and Reterritorialization of the Orisha Religion in Africa and the New World (Nigeria, Cuba and the United States)." *International Journal of Urban and Regional Research* 26 (1): 121–37.

Díaz Fabelo, Teodoro. 1960. *Olorun*. La Habana: Ediciones del Departamento de Folklór del Teatro Nacional de Cuba.

Douglas, Mary, ed. 1970. *Witchcraft Confessions and Accusations*. London: Tavistock.

Drewal, Margaret Thompson. 1992. *Yoruba Ritual: Performers, Play, Agency*. Bloomington: Indiana University Press.

Dumont, Louis. 1970. *Homo Hierarchicus: The Caste System and its Implications*. London: Weidenfeld and Nicolson.

Durkheim, Emile. 1995. *The Elementary Forms of Religious Life* (1912). Translated by Karen E. Fields. New York: Free Press.

Ecún, Obá (Cecilio Pérez). 1986. *Itá: mitología de la religión "Yoruba."* Gráficas. Maravillas.

Eisenstadt, Shmuel N. 1982. "The Axial Age: The Emergence of Transcendental Visions and the Rise of the Clerics." *Archives Europeennes de Sociologie* 23 (2): 294–314.

Eliade, Mircea. 1991. *The Myth of Eternal Return, or, Cosmos and History* (1954). Translated by Willard R. Trask. London: Arkana.

Engelke, Matthew. 2007. *A Problem of Presence: Beyond Scripture in an African Church.* Berkeley: University of California Press.

———. 2009. *The Objects of Evidence: Anthropological Approaches to the Production of Knowledge.* Oxford: Wiley-VCH.

Espinosa, Félix, and Amadeo Piñero. 1997a. *Ifá y la creación.* La Habana: Ediciones Cubanas.

———. 1997b. *La leyenda de Orula.* La Habana: Ediciones Cubanas.

Espirito Santo, Diana. 2009. "Developing the Dead: The Nature of Knowledge, Mediumship and Self in Cuban Espiritismo." PhD thesis, University of London.

———. 2010. "Spiritist Boundary-Work and the Morality of Materiality in Afro-Cuban Religion." *Journal of Material Culture* 15 (1): 64–82.

Evans-Pritchard, E. E. 1976. *Witchcraft, Oracles, and Magic Among the Azande.* Abridged from 1937 ed. by Eva Gillies. Oxford: Clarendon Press.

Evens, Terrence M. S. 1983. "Mind, Logic, and the Efficacy of the Nuer Incest Prohibition." *Man* (N.S.) 18 (1): 111–33.

———. 2008. *Anthropology and Ethics: Nondualism and the Conduct of Sacrifice.* Oxford: Berghahn Books.

Favret-Saada, Jeanne. 1980. *Deadly Words: Witchcraft in the Bocage.* Cambridge: Cambridge University Press.

Ferme, Mariane C. 2001. *The Underneath of Things: Violence, History and the Everyday in Sierra Leone.* Berkeley: University of California Press.

Fernández Robaina, Tomás. 1990. *El negro en Cuba, 1902–1958.* La Habana: Editorial de Ciencias Sociales.

Feyerabend, Paul K. 1975. *Against Method: Outline of an Anarchistic Theory of Knowledge.* London: New Left Books.

Fortes, Meyer. 1981. *Oedipus and Job in West African Religion* (1959). New York: Octagon Books.

———. 1987. "Divination: Religious Premises and Logical Techniques." In *Religion, Morality and the Person: Essays on Talensi Religion*, ed. Jack Goody, 1–21. Cambridge: Cambridge University Press.

Fortes, Meyer, and Germaine Dieterlen, eds. 1965. *African Systems of Thought.* Oxford: Oxford University Press.

Frazer, James. 1911. *The Golden Bough: A Study in Magic and Religion*, pt. 1, vol. 1, *The Magic Art and the Evolution of Kings.* London: Macmillan.

Freeman, Derek. 1983. *Margaret Mead and Samoa: the Making and Unmaking of an Anthropological Myth.* Cambridge: Harvard University Press.

Frobenius, Leo. 1913. *The Voice of Africa*, vol. 1. London: Hutchinson.

Garfinkel, Harold. 1967. *Studies in Ethnomethodology.* Englewood Cliffs, NJ: Prentice-Hall.

Geertz, Clifford. 1973a. *The Interpretation of Cultures.* New York: Basic Books.

———. 1973b. "Thick Description." In his *The Interpretation of Cultures.* New York: Basic Books.

———. 1998. *Art and Agency: An Anthropological Theory.* Oxford: Clarendon Press.

Gellner, Ernest. 1985. *Relativism and the Social Sciences.* Cambridge: Cambridge University Press.

Gilroy, Paul. 1993. *The Black Atlantic: Modernity and Double Consciousness.* Cambridge: Harvard University Press.

Girard, René. 1976. "Differentiation and Undifferentiation in Lévi-Strauss and Current Critical Theory." *Contemporary Literature* 17 (3): 404–29.

Goldman, Márcio. 1994. *Razão e diferença: afectividade, racionalidade e relativismo no . pensamento de Lévy-Bruhl.* Rio de Janeiro: Editora UFRJ.

———. 2005. "Formas do saber e modos do ser: Observações sobre multiplicidade e ontologia no Candomblé." *Religião and Sociedade* 25 (2): 102–20.

———. 2007. "How to Learn in an Afro-Brazilian Spirit Possession Religion: Ontology and Multiplicity in Candomblé." In *Learning Religion: Anthropological Approaches*, ed. David Berliner and Ramon Sarró, 103–20. New York: Berghahn Books.

Godelier, Maurice. 1999. *The Enigma of the Gift.* Translated by Nora Scott. Cambridge: Polity Press.

Graw, Knut. 2009. "Beyond Expertise: Reflections on Specialist Agency and the Autonomy of the Divinatory Ritual Process." *Africa: Journal of the International Africa Institute* 79 (1): 92–109.

Gray, Andrew. 1996. *The Arakmbut of Amazonian Peru. I: Mythology, Spirituality, and History.* Oxford: Berghahn.

Guanche, Jesús. 1983. *Procesos etnoculturales de Cuba.* La Habana: Editorial Letras Cubanas.

Hagedorn, Katherine J. 2001. *Divine Utterances: The Performance of Afro-Cuban Santeria.* Washington, DC: Smithsonian Institution Press.

Hallen, Barry. 2000. *The Good, the Bad, and the Beautiful: Discourse about Values in Yoruba Culture.* Bloomington: Indiana University Press.

Hallen, Barry, and J. Olubi Sodipo. 1997. *Knowledge, Belief, and Witchcraft: Analytic Experiments in African Philosophy.* Stanford, CA: Stanford University Press.

Hallpike, Christopher R. 1979. *The Foundations of Primitive Thought.* Oxford: Clarendon Press.

Haraway, Donna. 2007. *When Species Meet.* Minneapolis: University of Minnesota Press.

Hart, Keith, 2001. "Cultural Critique in Anthropology." In *International Ency-clopedia of the Social and Behavioral Sciences*, ed. Neil J Smelser and Paul B. Baltes, 5:3037-41. New York: Elsevier.

Hearn, Adrian H. 2008. *Cuba: Religion, Social Capital and Development.* Durham, NC: Duke University Press.

Heidegger, Martin. 1968. *What Is Called Thinking?* Translated by J. Glenn Gray. New York: Harper and Row.

Hénaff, Marcel. 1998. *Claude Lévi-Strauss and the Making of Structural Anthropol-ogy.* Translated by Mary Baker. Minneapolis: University of Minnesota Press.

Henare, Amiria, Martin Holbraad, and Sari Wastell, eds. 2007. *Thinking Through Things: Theorising Artefacts Ethnographically.* London: Routledge.

Heres Hevia, Manuel. 1962. *Libro blanco para la Orden Caballeros de la Luz.* La Habana.

Herrnstein Smith, Barbara. 2005. *Scandalous Knowledge: Science, Truth and the Human.* Edinburgh: Edinburgh University Press.

Herskovits, Melville J. 1958. *The Myth of the Negro Past.* Boston: Beacon Press.

Herzfeld, Michael. 1988. *The Poetics of Manhood: Contest and Identity in a Cretan Mountain Village.* Princeton NJ: Princeton University Press.

Hobsbawm, Eric J., and Terence O. Ranger, eds. 1983. *The Invention of Tradition.* Cambridge: Cambridge University Press.

Holbraad, Martin. 2003. "Estimando a necessidade: os oráculos de ifá e a verdade em Havana." *Mana* 9 (2): 39–77.

———. 2004a. "Religious 'Speculation': The Rise of Ifá Cults and Consumption in Post-Soviet Havana." *Journal of Latin American Studies* 36 (4): 1–21.

———. 2004b. "Response to Bruno Latour's 'Thou Shall Not Freeze-Frame.'" Avail-able online: http://nansi.abaetenet.net/abaetextos/response-to-bruno-latours-thou-shall-not-freeze-frame-martin-holbraad.

———. 2005. "Expending Multiplicity: Money in Cuban Ifá Cults." *Journal of the Royal Anthropological Institute* 11 (2): 231–54.

———. 2007. "The Power of Powder: Multiplicity and Motion in the Divinatory Cosmology of Cuban Ifá (or *Mana*, Again)." In *Thinking Through Things: The-orising Artefacts Ethnographically*, ed. Amiria Henare, Martin Holbraad, and Sari Wastell, 189–225. London: Routledge.

———. 2008. "Definitive Evidence, from Cuban Gods." *Journal of the Royal Anthropological . Institute* (Special Issue *Objects of Evidence*, ed. Matthew En-gelke, S93–S109.

———. 2009. "Ontology, Ethnography, Archaeology: An Afterword on the Ontog-raphy of Things." *Cambridge Archaeological Journal* 19 (3): 431–41.

———. 2010a. "The Whole Beyond Holism: Gambling, Divination and Ethnogra-phy in Cuba." In *Experiments in Holism: Theory and Practice in Contemporary Anthropology*, ed. Ton Otto and Nils Bubandt, 67–85. Oxford: Blackwell.

———. 2010b. "Of Ises and Oughts: An Endnote on Divinatory Obligation." In *Divination:. Perspectives for a New Millennium*, ed. Patrick Curry, 265–74. Farnham: Ashgate.

———. 2011. "Can the Thing Speak?" *OAP Press, Working Paper Series #7.* Available online: http://openanthcoop.net/press/http://openanthcoop.net/press/wp-content/uploads/2011/01/Holbraad-Can-the-Thing-Speak2.pdf.

Holbraad, Martin, and Morten A. Pedersen. 2009. "Planet M: The Intense Abstraction of Marilyn Strathern." *Anthropological Theory* 9 (4): 371–94.

Holbraad, Martin, and Rane Willerslev. 2007. "Transcendental Perspectivism: Anonymous Viewpoints from Inner Asia." *Inner Asia* 9 (2): 329–45.

Hollis, Martin, and Steven Lukes. 1982. *Rationality and Relativism.* Oxford: Basil Blackwell.

Horton, Robin. 1964. "Kalabari Diviners and Oracles." *ODU* 1 (1): 3–16.

———. 1967. "African Traditional Thought and Western Science." *Africa* 37 (1–2): 50–71, 155–87.

———. 1971. "African Conversion." *Africa* 41:85–109.

———. 1979. "Ancient Ife: A Reassessment." *Journal of the Historical Society of Nigeria* 9 (4): 69–150.

Horton, Robin, and Ruth Finnegan, eds. 1973. *Modes of Thought: Essays on Thinking in Western and Non-Western Societies.* London: Faber and Faber.

Hountondji, Paulin J. 1983. *African Philosophy: Myth and Reality.* Translated by Henri Evans and Jonathan Rée. Bloomington: Indiana University Press.

Howe, Leo. 2004. "Late Medieval Christianity, Balinese Hinduism, and the Doctrinal Mode of Religiosity." In *Ritual and Memory: Toward a Comparative Anthropology of Religion*, ed. Harvey Whitehouse and James Laidlaw, 135–54. Walnut Creek, CA: Altamira Press.

Hugh-Jones, Stephen. 1996. "Shamans, Prophets, Priests and Pastors." In *Shamanism, History, and the State*, ed. Nicholas Thomas and Caroline Humphrey, 32–75. Ann Arbor: University of Michigan Press.

Hume, David. 2000. *A Treatise of Human Nature.* Edited by David F. and Mary Norton. Oxford: Oxford University Press.

Humphrey, Caroline. 1976. "Omens and Their Explanation among the Buriat." *Archives Européenes de Sociologie* 17:21–38.

———. 1997. "Exemplars and Rules: Aspects of the Discourse of Moralities in Mongolia." In *The Ethnography of Moralities*, ed. Signe Howell, 25–47. London: Routledge.

Humphrey, Caroline, and James Laidlaw. 1994. *The Archetypal Actions of Ritual.* Oxford: Clarendon Press.

Hutchins, Edwin. 1980. *Culture and Inference: A Trobriand Case Study.* Cambridge: Harvard University Press.

———. 1995. *Cognition in the Wild.* Cambridge, MA: MIT Press.

Højer, Lars. 2004. "The Anti-Social Contract: Enmity and Suspicion in Northern Mongolia." *Cambridge Anthropology* 24:41–63.

Idowu, Bolaji E. 1962. *Olodumare: God in Yoruba Belief*. London: Longmans.

Ingold, Tim. 1986. *Evolution and Social Life*. Cambridge: Cambridge University Press.

Jackson, Michael D. 1978. "An Approach to Kurango Divination." *Human Relations* 31 (2): 117–38.

———. 1989. *Paths Towards a Clearing: Radical Empiricism and Ethnographic Inquiry*. Bloomington: Indiana University Press.

Johnson, Samuel. 1921. *The History of the Yorubas*. London: George Routledge and Sons.

Jules-Rosette, Bennetta. 1978. "The Veil of Objectivity: Prophesy, Divination, and Social Inquiry." *American Anthropologist* 80 (3): 549–70.

Jung, Carl G. 1989. Foreword to *The I Ching or Book of Changes* (1951). London: Arkana.

Karp, Ivan, and D. A. Masolo, eds. 2000. *African Philosophy as Cultural Inquiry*. Bloomington: Indiana University Press.

Keane, Webb. 2007. *Christian Moderns: Freedom and Fetish in the Mission Encounter*. Berkeley: University of California Press.

Kelly, José A. 2011. *State Health Care and Yanomami Transformations: A Symmetrical Ethnography*. Tucson: University of Arizona Press.

Kirsch, Stewart. 2006. *Reverse Anthropology: Indigenous Analysis of Social and Environmental Relations in New Guinea*. Stanford, CA: Stanford University Press.

Kripke, Saul. 1980. *Naming and Necessity*. Oxford: Blackwell.

Kroeber, Alfred L. 1952. *The Nature of Culture*. Chicago: University of Chicago Press.

Kuhn, Thomas S. 1962. *The Structure of Scientific Revolutions*. Chicago: University of Chicago Press.

Kuper, Adam. 2000. *Culture: The Anthropologists' Account*. Cambridge: Harvard University Press.

Lachatañere, Romulo. 1961. "Las creencias religiosas de los afrocubanos y la falsa aplicación del término brujería." *Actas del Folklore* 1 (5): 11–15.

Laidlaw, James. 2010. "Agency and Responsibility: Perhaps You Can Have Too Much of a Good Thing." In *Ordinary Ethics: Anthropology, Language and Action*, ed. Michael Lambek, 143–64. New York: Fordham University Press.

Latour, Bruno. 1987. *Science in Action: How to Follow Scientists and Engineers through Society*.Cambridge Mass.: Harvard University Press.

———. 1993. *We Have Never Been Modern*. Translated by Catherine Porter. London: Prentice-Hall.

———. 1999. *Pandora's Hope: Essays on the Reality of Science Studies*. Cambridge: Harvard University Press.

―――. 2004. "Why Has Critique Run Out of Steam? From Matters of Fact to Matters of Concern." *Critical Inquiry* 30 (2): 225–48.

―――. 2005. "'Thou Shall Not Freeze-Frame,' or, How Not to Understand the Science and Religion Debate." In *Science, Religion, and the Human Experience*, ed. James D. Proctor, 27–48. Oxford: Oxford University Press.

―――. 2010. "On the Cult of the Factish Gods." In his *On the Modern Cult of the Factish Gods*, trans. Catherine Porter and Heather MacLean, 1–66. Durham, NC: Duke University Press.

Law, R.C.C. 1973. "Traditional History." In *Sources of Yoruba History*, ed. Saburi O. Biobaku, 25–40. Oxford: Clarendon Press.

Lawal, Babatunde. 1985. "Orí: The Significance of the Head in Yoruba Sculpture." *Journal of Anthropological Research* 41:91–103.

Leach, James. 2003. *Creative Land: Place and Procreation on the Rai Coast of Papua New Guinea*. New York: Berghahn Books.

Lévi-Strauss, Claude. 1963. *Structural Anthropology*. Vol. 1. Translated by Claire Jacobson and Brooke Grundfest Schoepf. London: Allen Lane the Penguin Press.

―――. 1964. *Totemism*. Translated by Rodney Needham. London: Merlin Press.

―――. 1966. *The Savage Mind*. Oxford: Oxford University Press.

―――. 1977. *Structural Anthropology*. Vol. 2. Translated by Monique Leyton. Middlesex: Penguin Books.

―――. 1978. *Myth and Meaning*. London: Routledge and Kegan Paul.

―――. 1981. *The Naked Man*, vol. 4 of *Mythologiques*. Translated by John and Doreen Weightman. Chicago: University of Chicago Press.

―――. 1987. *Introduction to the Work of Marcel Mauss*. Translated by Felicity Baker. London: Routledge and Kegan Paul.

Lévy-Bruhl, Lucien. 1926. *How Natives Think*. Translated by Lilian A. Clare. London: . George Allen and Unwin.

Lewis, David. 1986. *On the Plurality of Worlds*. Oxford: Basil Blackwell.

Lukes, Steven, 2000. "Different Cultures, Different Rationalities?" *History of the Human Sciences* 13 (1): 3–18.

MacGaffey, Wyatt. 2000. "The Cultural Tradition of the African Forests." In *Insight and Artistry in African Divination*, ed. John Pemberton III, 13–24. Washington, DC: Smithsonian Institution Press.

Mahmood, Saba. 2004. *Politics of Piety: The Islamic Revival and the Feminist Subject*. Princeton, NJ: Princeton University Press.

Malinowski, Bronislaw C. 1926. "Anthropology." *Encyclopedia Britannica*, 13th ed., 131–40.

―――. 1948. "Myth in Primitive Society." In his *Magic, Science, and Religion and Other Essays*. Boston: Beacon Press.

Mamet, David. 1997. *True and False: Heresy and Common Sense for the Actor*. New York: Pantheon Books.

Marcus, George E., and Michael M. J. Fischer. 1986. *Anthropology as Cultural Critique: An Experimental Moment in the Human Sciences.* Chicago: University of Chicago Press.

Marriott, McKim. 1979. "Hindu Transactions: Diversity without Dualism." In *Transaction and Meaning: Directions in the Anthropology of Human Issues*, ed. Bruce Kapferer, 109–42. Philadelphia: Institute for the Study of Human Issues.

Masolo, D. A. 1994. *African Philosophy in Search of Identity.* Bloomington: Indiana University Press.

Mason, Michael A. 2002. *Living Santería: Rituals and Experiences in an Afro-Cuban Religion.* Washington, DC: Smithsonian Institution Press.

Matibag, Eugenio. 1997. "Ifá and Interpretation: An Afro-Caribbean Literary Practice." In *Sacred Possessions: Vodou, Santería, Obeah, and the Caribbean*, ed. Margarite Fernández Olmos and Lizabeth Paravisisni-Gebert, 151–70. New Brunswick, NJ: Rutgers University Press.

Matory, J. Lorand. 1999. "The English Professors of Brazil: On the Diasporic Roots of the Yoruba Nation." *Comparative Studies in Society and History* 41 (1): 72–103.

———. 2001. "El nuevo imperio yoruba: textos, migración y el auge trasatlántico de la nación lucumí." In *Culturas encontradas: Cuba y los Estados Unidos*, ed. Rafael Hernández and John H. Coatsworth, 167–88. La Habana and Cambridge, MA: CIDCC Juan Marinello and CELDR Universidad de Harvard.

———. 2005. *Sex and the Empire That Is No More: Gender and the Politics of Metaphor in Oyo Yoruba Religion.* New York: Berghahn Books.

Maupoil, Bernard. 1943. *La geomancie à l'ancienne côte des esclaves.* Paris: Université de Paris.

Mauss, Marcel. 1990. *The Gift: Forms and Functions of Exchange in Archaic Societies.* Translated by W. D. Halls. London: Routledge.

———. 2001. *A General Theory of Magic.* Translated by Robert Brain. 1972 ed. by Hubert and Mauss. London: Routledge Classics.

Mbembe, Achille. 2001. *On the Postcolony.* Berkeley: University of California Press.

McClelland, Elizabeth M. 1966. "The Significance of Number in the Odu of Ifa." *Africa* 36:421–31.

Mead, Margaret. 1961. *Coming of Age in Samoa* (1928). New York: Morrow Quill Paperbacks.

Mendonsa, Eugene L. 1976. "Characteristics of Sisala Diviners." In *The Realm of the Extra-Human: Agents and Audiences*, ed. Agehananda Bharati, 179–95. The Hague: Mouton.

———. 1982. *The Politics of Divination: A Processual View of Reactions to Illness and Deviance Among the Sisala of Northern Ghana.* Berkeley: University of California Press.

Menéndez Vásquez, Lázara. 1995. "Un cake para Obatalá?!" *Temas* 4:38–51.

———. 1998. *Estudios afro-cubanos*. Vols. 1–4. La Habana: Editorial Félix Varela.

Miller, Ivor L. 2009. *Voice of the Leopard: African Secret Societies and Cuba*. Jackson: University Press of Mississippi.

Mitchell, J. Clyde. 1956. *The Yao Village*. Manchester: Manchester University Press.

Mitchell, Jon P. 1997. "A Moment with Christ: The Importance of Feelings in the Analysis of Belief." *Journal of the Royal Anthropological Institute* (N.S.) 3 (1): 79–94.

Montejo, Esteban. 1968. *The Autobiography of a Runaway Slave*. Edited by Miguel Barnet. New York: Pantheon.

Moore, George Edward. 1922. "External and Internal Relations." In his *Philosophical Studies*. New York: Harcourt, Brace.

———. 1939. "Proof of an External World." In his *Philosophical Papers*, 127–50. London: Allen and Unwin.

Moore, Henrietta. 2005. "The Truths of Anthropology." *Cambridge Anthropology* 25 (1): 52–58.

Moore, Omar K. 1957. "Divination—A New Perspective." *American Anthropologist* 59:69–74.

Morris, Brian. 1997. "In Defense of Realism and Truth: Critical Reflections on the Anthropological Followers of Heidegger." *Critique of Anthropology* 17 (3): 313–40.

Morton-Williams, Peter. 1964. "An Outline of the Cosmology and Cult Organization of Oyo Yoruba." *Africa* 34 (3): 243–61.

———. 1966. "Two Studies of Ifa Divination: Introduction to the Mode of Divination." *Africa* 36 (4): 406–8.

———. n.d. "The Ifa Divination Board: What Do Diviners Say?" Unpublished manuscript.

Mudimbe, Valentin Y. 1988. *The Invention of Africa: Gnosis, Philosophy, and the Order of Knowledge*. Bloomington: Indiana University Press.

Munn, Nancy D. 1986. *The Fame of Gawa: A Symbolic Study of Value Transformation in a Massim Society*. Cambridge: Cambridge University Press.

Myhre, Knut C. 2006a. "Divination and Experience: Explorations of a Chagga Epistemology." *Journal of the Royal Anthropological Institute* (N.S.) 12 (2): 313–30.

———. 2006b. "The Truth of Anthropology: Epistemology, Meaning, and Residual Positivism." *Anthropology Today* 22 (6): 16–19.

Needham, Rodney. 1972. *Belief, Language and Experience*. Chicago: University of Chicago Press.

———. 1985. *Exemplars*. Berkeley: University of California Press.

Nicolau Parés, Luis, and Roger Sansi, eds. 2011. *Sorcery in the Black Atlantic*. Chicago: University of Chicago Press.

Nietzsche, Friedrich. 1997. *Untimely Meditations*. Edited by Daniel Breazeale, translated by R. J. Hollingdale. Cambridge: Cambridge University Press.

Obeyesekere, Gananath. 1992. *The Apotheosis of Captain Cook: European Mythmaking in the Pacific*. Princeton, NJ: Princeton University Press.

Ochoa, Todd R. 2010. *Society of the Dead: Quita Manaquita and Palo Praise in Cuba*. Berkeley: University of California Press.

Ortíz, Fernando. 1906. *Los negros brujos*. Madrid: Editorial América.

———. 1921. "Los cabildos afrocubanos." *Revista Bimestre Cubana* 26:5–39.

Palmié, Stephan. 1995. "Against Syncretism: 'Africanizing' and 'Cubanizing' Discourses in North American *òrìsà* Worship." In *Counterworks: Managing the Diversity of Knowledge*, ed. Richard Fardon, 73–104. London: Routledge.

———. 2002. *Wizards and Scientists: Explorations in Afro-Cuban Modernity and Tradition*. Durham, NC: Duke University Press.

———. 2007. "Is There a Model in the Muddle? 'Creolization' in African American History and Anthropology." In *Creolization and Diaspora: Historical, Ethnographic, and Theoretical Perspectives, ed.* Charles Stewart, 178–200. Walnut Creek, CA: Left Coast Press.

Panagiotopoulos, Anastassis. 2011. *The Island of Crossed Destinies: Human and Other-than-Human Perspectives in Afro-Cuban Divination*. PhD dissertation, University of Edinburgh.

Park, George K. 1963. "Divination and Its Social Contexts." *Journal of the Royal Anthropological Institute* 93 (2): 195–209.

Parkin, David, 1991. "Simultaneity and Sequencing in the Oracular Speech of Kenyan Diviners." In *African Divination Systems: Ways of Knowing*, ed. Philip Peek, 173–90. Bloomington: Indiana University Press.

Parrinder, Geoffrey. 1951. *West African Psychology: A Comparative Study of Psychological and Religious Thought*. London: Lutterworth Press.

———. 1970. *West African Religion*, New York: Barnes and Noble.

Pedersen, Morten A. 2007a. "Talismans of Thought: Shamanist Ontologies and Extended Cognition in Northern Mongolia." In *Thinking Through Things: Theorising Artefacts Ethnographically*, ed. Amiria Henare, Martin Holbraad and Sari Wastell, 141–67. London: Routledge.

———. 2007b. "Multiplicity without Myth: Theorizing Darhad Perspectivism." *Inner Asia* 9 (2): 311–28.

———. Forthcoming. "The Task of Anthropology Is to Invent Relations. For the Motion." *Critique of Anthropology*.

Peek, Philip, ed. 1991. *African Divination Systems: Ways of Knowing*. Bloomington: Indiana University Press.

Peel, John D. Y. 1984. "Making History: The Past in the Ijesha Present." *Man* (N.S.) 19:111–32.

———. 1990. "The Pastor and the 'Babalawo': The Interaction of Religions in Nineteenth-Century Yorubaland." *Africa: Journal of the International African Institute* 60 (3): 338–69.

———. 2000. *Religious Encounter and the Making of the Yoruba.* Bloomington: Indiana University Press.

Pelton, Robert D. 1980. *The Trickster in West Africa: A Study of Mythic Irony and Sacred Delight.* Berkeley: California University Press.

Pina-Cabral, João de. 2009. "The All-Or-Nothing Syndrome and the Human Condition." *Social Analysis* 53 (2): 163–76.

Plantinga, Alvin. 1964. "Necessary Being." In *Faith and Philosophy: Philosophical Studies in Religion and Ethics*, ed. Plantinga, 97–110. Grand Rapids, MI: William B. Eerdmans.

Povinelli, Elizabeth A. 2001. "Radical Worlds: The Anthropology of Incommensurability and Inconceivability." *Annual Review of Anthropology* 30:319–34.

Quine, Willard Van Orman. 1953. "On What There Is." In his *From a Logical Point of View*, 1–19. New York: Harper and Row.

Rappaport, Roy A. 1979. "The Obvious Aspects of Ritual." In his *Ecology, Meaning, and Religion*, 173–222. Richmond, CA: North Atlantic Books.

———. 1999. *Ritual and Religion in the Making of Humanity.* Cambridge: Cambridge University Press.

Reed, Adam. 2007. "'Smuk Is King': The Action of Cigarettes in a Papua New Guinea Prison." In *Thinking Through Things: Theorising Artefacts Ethnographically*, ed. Amiria Henare, Martin Holbraad and Sari Wastell, 32–46. London: Routledge.

Ricoeur, Paul. 1970. *Freud and Philosophy: An Essay on Interpretation.* Translated by Denis Savage. New Haven, CT: Yale University Press.

———. 1998. "Thinking Creation." In *Thinking Biblically: Exegetical and Hermeneutical Studies* by André LaCocque and Paul Ricoeur. Translated by David Pellauer. Chicago: University of Chicago Press.

Riles, Annelise. 1998. "Infinity Within the Brackets." *American Ethnologist* 25 (3): 378–98.

———, ed. 2006. *Documents: Artefacts of Modern Knowledge.* Ann Arbor: University of Michigan Press.

Robbins, Joel. 2009. "Is the *Trans-* in *Transnational* the *Trans-* in *Transcendent*? On Alterity and the Sacred in the Age of Globalization." In *Transnational Transcendence: Essays on Religion and Globalization*, ed. Thomas J. Csordas, 55–72. Berkeley: University of California Press.

Robinson, Richard. 1950. *Definition.* Oxford: Clarendon Press.

Rodrigues, Raymundo Nina. 1988. *Os africanos no Brasil* (1905). 7th ed. Brasília: Editora da Universidade de Brasília.

Rorty, Richard. 1979. *Philosophy and the Mirror of Nature.* Princeton, NJ: Princeton University Press.

———. 1991. "Introduction: Antirepresentationalism, Ethnocentrism, and Liberalism." In his *Objectivity, Relativism, and Truth*, vol. 1 of *Philosophical Papers*, 1–20. Cambridge: Cambridge University Press.

Rosaldo, Renato. 1989. *Culture and Truth: The Remaking of Social Analysis*. Boston: Beacon Press.

Routon, Kenneth. 2008. "Conjuring the Past: Slavery and the Historical Imagination in Cuba." *American Ethnologist* 35 (4): 632–49.

Russell, Bertrand. 1905. "On Denoting." *Mind* 14:479–93.

———. 1946. *History of Western Philosophy*. London: Allen and Unwin.

———. 1996. "Descriptions." Extract from his *Introduction to Mathematical Philosophy* (1919) in *The Philosophy of Language*, 3rd ed., ed. A. P. Martinich, 208–314. New York: Oxford University Press.

Sahlins, Marshall. 1985. *Islands of History*. Chicago: University of Chicago Press.

———. 1995. *How "Natives" Think, about Captain Cook for Example*. Chicago: University of Chicago Press.

———. 1996. "The Sadness of Sweetness: The Native Anthropology of Western Cosmology." *Current Anthropology* 37:395–528.

———. 1999. "Two or Three Things That I Know about Culture." *Journal of the Royal Anthropological Institute* (N.S.) 5 (3): 399–421.

Sangren, Steven P. 2007. "Anthropology of Anthropology? Further Reflections on Reflexivity." *Anthropology Today* 23 (4): 13–16.

Schneider, David M. 1968. *American Kinship: A Cultural Account*. Chicago: University of Chicago Press.

———. 1984. *A Critique of the Study of Kinship*. Ann Arbor: University of Michigan Press.

———. 1995. *Schneider on Schneider: The Conversion of the Jews and Other Anthropological Stories*. Edited by Richard Handler. Durham, NC: Duke University Press.

Schrempp, Gregory. 1992. *Magical Arrows: The Maori, Greeks, and the Folklore of the Universe*. Madison: University of Wisconsin Press.

Scott, Michael W. 2005. "'I Was Like Abraham:' Notes on the Anthropology of Christianity from the Solomon Islands." *Ethnos* 70 (1): 101–25.

———. 2007. *The Severed Snake: Matrilineages, Making Place, and a Melanesian Christianity in Southeast Solomon Islands*. Durham, NC: Carolina Academic Press.

Searle, John R. 1969. *Speech-Acts: An Essay in the Philosophy of Language*. Cambridge: Cambridge University Press.

Shaw, Rosalind. 1985. "Gender and the Structuring of Reality in Temne Divination." *Africa* 55:286–303.

———. 1991. "Splitting Truth from Darkness: Epistemological Aspects of Temne Divination." In *African Divination Systems: Ways of Knowing*, ed. Philip M. Peek, 137–52. Bloomington: Indiana University Press.

Sierra Torres, Guillermo. 1995. "La fiesta de San Lázaro: variaciones, adaptación y popularidad." *Caribbean Studies* 28 (2): 404–13.

Silva, Sónia. 2011. *Along an African Border: Angolan Refugees and Their Divination Baskets*. Philadelphia: University of Pennsylvania Press.

Sneath, David. 2009. "Reading the Signs by Lenin's Light: Development, Divination and Metonymic Fields in Mongolia." *Ethnos* 74 (1): 72–90.

Soames, Scott. 1999. *Understanding Truth*. New York: Oxford University Press.

Southwold, Martin. 1979. "Religious Belief." *Man* (N.S.) 14:628–44.

Sperber, Dan. 1975. *Rethinking Symbolism*. Cambridge: Cambridge University Press.

———. 1985. *On Anthropological Knowledge*. Cambridge: Cambridge University Press.

———. 1996. *Explaining Culture: A Naturalistic Approach*. Oxford: Blackwell Publishers.

Spiro, Melford E. 1987. *Culture and Human Nature*. Edited by Benjamin Kilborne and L. L. Langness. Chicago: University of Chicago Press.

Staewen, Christoph. 1996. *Ifa: African Gods Speak*. Hamburg: Lit Verlag.

Steiner, Franz B. 1954. "Chagga Truth: A Note on Gutmann's Account of the Chagga Concept of Truth." *Africa* 24:364–69.

Stengers, Isabelle. 2000. *The Invention of Modern Science*. Translated by Daniel W. Smity. Minneapolis: University of Minnesota Press.

Stolze Lima, Tânia. 1999. "The Two and its Multiple: Reflections on Perspectivism in a Tupi Cosmology." *Ethnos* 61(4): 107–131.

Strathern, Marilyn. 1980. "No Nature, No Culture: The Hagen Case." In *Nature, Culture and Gender*, ed. Carol MacCormack and Marilyn Strathern, 174–222. Cambridge: Cambridge University Press.

———. 1988. *The Gender of the Gift: Problems with Women and Problems with Society in Melanesia.* Berkeley: University of California Press.

———. 1990. "Artefacts of History: Events and the Interpretation of Images." In *Culture and History in the Pacific*, ed. Jukka Siikala, 25–44. Helsinki: Finnish Anthropological Society.

———. 1992a. *After Nature: English Kinship in the Twentieth Century*. Cambridge: Cambridge University Press.

———. 1992b. "Parts and Wholes: Refiguring Relationships in a Post-Plural Society." In *Conceptualizing Society*, ed. Adam Kuper, 75–104. London: Routledge.

———. 2004. *Partial Connections*. Updated ed. Walnut Creek, CA: Altamira Press.

———. 2005. *Kinship, Law and the Unexpected: Relatives are Always a Surprise*. Cambridge: Cambridge University Press.

Stroeken, Koen. 2008. "Believed Belief: Science/Religion versus Sukuma Magic." *Social Analysis* 52 (1): 144–65.

———. 2010. *Moral Power: The Magic of Witchcraft*. New York: Berghahn Books.

Swancutt, Katherine. 2006. "Representational vs. Conjectural Divination: Innovating out of Nothing in Mongolia." *Journal of the Royal Anthropological Institute* 12 (2): 331–53.

Tambiah, Stanley J. 1985. *Culture, Thought and Social Action*. Cambridge: Harvard University Press.

———. 1990. *Magic, Science, Religion, and the Scope of Rationality*. Cambridge: Cambridge University Press.

Thompson, Robert Farris. 1983. *Flash of the Spirit: African and Afro-American Art and Philosophy*. New York: Random House.

Thornton, John. 1992. *Africa and Africans in the Making of the Atlantic World, 1400–1680*. Cambridge: Cambridge University Press.

Trouillot, Michel-Rolph. 2002. "Alter-Native Modernities: Caribbean Lessons for the Savage Slot." In *Critically Modern: Alternatives, Alterities, Anthropologies*, ed. Bruce Knauft, 220–40. Bloomington: Indiana University Press.

Turner, Victor. 1967. *The Forest of Symbols*. Ithaca, NY: Cornell University Press.

———. 1969. *The Ritual Process*. London: Routledge, Kegan and Paul.

———. 1975. *Revelation and Divination in Ndembu Ritual*. Ithaca: Cornell University Press.

Tylor, Edward B. 1920. *Primitive Culture* (1871). New York: G. P. Putnam's Sons.

Van Gennep, Arnold. 1960. *The Rites of Passage*. Translated by Monica B. Vizedom and Gabrielle L. Caffe. London: Routledge and Kegan Paul.

Venkatesan, Soumhya, Michael Carrithers, Karen Sykes, Matei Candea, and Martin Holbraad. 2010. "Ontology Is Just Another Word for Culture: Motion Tabled at the 2008 Meeting of the Group for Debates in Anthropological Theory." *Critique of Anthropology* 30:152–200.

Vernant, Jean-Pierre, ed. 1974. *Divination et Rationalité*. Paris: Seuil.

Verran, Helen. 2001. *Science and an African Logic*. Chicago: University of Chicago Press.

Viveiros de Castro, Eduardo. 1992. *From the Enemy's Point of View: Humanity and Divinity in an Amazonian Society*. Chicago: University of Chicago Press.

———. 1998a. "Cosmological Perspectivism in Amazonia and Elsewhere." Four lectures delivered at the Department of Social Anthropology, University of Cambridge, February 17–March 10.

———. 1998b. "Cosmological Deixis and Amerindian Perspectivism." *Journal of the Royal Anthropological Institute* (N.S.) 4 (3): 469–88.

———. 2002. "O nativo relativo." *Mana* 8 (1): 113–48.

———. 2003. *And*. Manchester: Manchester Papers in Social Anthropology.

———. 2005. "The Gift and the Given: Three Nano-Essays on Kinship and Magic." In *Genealogy Beyond Kinship: Sequence, Transmission, and Essence in Eth-*

nography and Social Theory, ed. Sandra Bamford and James Leach, 237–68. Oxford: Berghahn Books.

———. 2007. "The Crystal Forest: Notes on the Ontology of Amazonian Spirits." *Inner Asia* 9 (2): 153–72.

———. 2009. "Intensive Filiation and Demonic Alliance." In *Deleuzian Intersections: Science, Technology, Anthropology*, ed. Casper Bruun Jensen and Kjetle Rödje, 219–55. New York: Berghahn.

———. 2010. *Metafísicas caníbales: líneas de antropología postestructural*. Translated from the original French by Stella Mastrangelo. Buenos Aires: Katz Editores.

———. 2011. "Zeno and the Art of Anthropology: Of Lies, Beliefs, Paradoxes and Other Truths." Translated by Antonia Walford. *Common Knowledge* 17 (1): 128–45.

Viveiros de Castro and Márcio Goldman. 2008/2009. "Slow Motions: Comments on a Few Texts by Marilyn Strathern." Translated by Ashley Lebner. *Cambridge Anthropology* 28 (3): 23–42.

Wagner, Roy, 1972. *Habu: The Innovation of Meaning in Daribi Religion*. Chicago: University of Chicago Press.

———. 1978. *Lethal Speech: Daribi Myth as Symbolic Obviation*. Ithaca, NY: Cornell University Press.

———. 1981. *The Invention of Culture*. Revised and expanded ed. Chicago: University of Chicago Press.

———. 1984. "Ritual as Communication: Order, Meaning, and Secrecy in Melanesian Initiation Rites." *Annual Review of Anthropology* 13:143–55.

———. 1986. *Symbols That Stand for Themselves*. Chicago: University of Chicago Press.

———. 1987. "Figure-Ground Reversal Among the Barok." In *Assemblage of Spirits: Idea and Image in New Zealand*, ed. Louise Lincoln, 56–63. New York: George Braziller.

———. 1991. "The Fractal Person." In *Big Men and Great Men: Personifications of Power in Melanesia*, ed. Maurice Godelier and Marilyn Strathern, 159–74. Cambridge: Cambridge University Press.

———. 2001. *An Anthropology of the Subject: Holographic Worldview in New Guinea and Its Meaning and Significance for the World of Anthropology*. Berkeley: University of California Press.

Werbner, Richard P. 1973. "The Superabundance of Understanding: Kalanga Rhetoric and Domestic Divination." *American Anthropologist* 75:1416–40.

———. 1989. "Tswapong Wisdom Divination: Making the Hidden Seen." In his *Ritual Passage, Sacred Journey: The Process and Organization of Religious Movement*, 19–60. Washington, DC: Smithsonian Institution Press.

West, Harry G. 2007. *Ethnographic Sorcery*. Chicago: University of Chicago Press.

308   WORKS CITED

Whyte, Susan R. 1997. *Questioning Misfortune: The Pragmatics of Uncertainty in Eastern Uganda.* Cambridge: Cambridge University Press.
Wikan, Unni. 1990. *Managing Turbulent Hearts: A Balinese Formula for Living.* Chicago: University of Chicago Press.
Willerslev, Rane, and Morten A. Pedersen. 2010. "Proportional Holism: Joking the Cosmos into Shape in North Asia." In *Experiments in Holism: Theory and Practice in Contemporary Anthropology*, ed. Ton Otto and Nils Bubandt, 262–78. Oxford: Blackwell.
Willet, Frank. 1967. *Ife in the History of West African Sculpture.* London: Thames and Hudson.
Wilson, Bryan R., ed. 1974. *Rationality.* Oxford: Basil Blackwell.
Wilson, Richard A. 2004. "The Trouble with Truth: Anthropology's Epistemological Hypochondria." *Anthropology Today* 20 (5): 14–17.
Winch, Peter. 1967. *The Idea of Social Science and its Relation to Philosophy.* London: Routledge and Keegan Paul.
Winkelman, Michael, and Philip M. Peek, eds. 2004. *Divination and Healing: Potent Vision.* Tucson: University of Arizona Press.
Wirtz, Kristina. 2007. *Ritual, Discourse, and Community in Cuban Santería: Speaking a Sacred World.* Gainesville: University Press of Florida.
Wood, Micahel. 2005. *The Road to Delphi: The Life and Afterlife of Oracles.* London: Pimlico.
Yelvington, Kevin A. 2001. "The Anthropology of Afro-Latin America and the Caribbean: Diasporic Dimensions." *Annual Review of Anthropology* 30:227–60.
Zamora, Laciel. 2000. *El culto de San Lázaro en Cuba.* La Habana: Colección La Fuente Viva.
Zeitlyn, David. 1990. "Prof. Garfinkel Visits the Soothsayers: Ethnomethodology and Mambila Divination." *Man* (N.S.) 25: 654–66.
———. 1995. "Divination as Dialogue: Negotiation of Meaning with Random Responses." In *Social Intelligence and Interaction: Expressions and Implications of the Social Bias in Human Intelligence*, ed. Esther N. Goody, 189–205. Cambridge: Cambridge University Press.
Zempleni, Andras. 1995. "How to Say Things with Assertive Acts? About Some Pragmatic Properties of Senoufo Divination." In *Beyond Textuality: Asceticism and Violence in Anthropological Interpretation*, ed. Gilles Bibeau and Ellen E. Corin, 233–48. Berlin: Mouton de Gruyter.

Index

factishes, 48–49, 222

facts, 21, 36–37, 40, 72, 210, 217–18, 221, 253, 277n4; and definitions, 219; ethnographic, 243–44, 250, 252, 255, 277n4, 287n2; and representations, 21, 73–74, 177, 193–95, 205–7, 214, 215, 243, 245, 252; social, 263. *See also* relations

falsehood. *See* truth

familia de Ifá (family of Ifá), 93, 97, 98, 231

Febles, Miguel (Odí Ka), 105–6, 107, 108

figure/ground reversal, 44, 162, 164

floating signifier, 173–74, 179, 182–84, 194, 196–97, 283n2

form and content, xviii, 6–7, 21, 42, 46, 79, 198, 238–40, 252, 260

fractality, 282n15

Fran (Obbeché), 100, 286n6

Frazer, James, 55

functionalism, 26, 56

fundaments. *See* Ifá

Geertz, Clifford, 84

gender: in Santería, 82. *See also* Ifá

Genesis, 112–13

Godelier, Maurice, 180, 182

god-parenthood, 80, 93–98; hierarchy in, 13, 93. See also *ahijado*; kinship; lineages; *madrina*; *padrino*

Goldman, Marcio, 117, 124, 163, 166–68, 282n12

Graw, Knut, 193–94

Greek men, 241

Gregory of Nazianzus, 114

guanaddo. *See* Ifá initiation

guerreros (warrior deities), 87, 90, 91, 98, 123, 188, 278n3, 280n11

habu, 39–40, 42, 44, 47

hacerse Ifá. *See* Ifá initiation

Hallen, Barry, 274n9

Hart, Keith, 35

Havana, 75, 79, 80, 83, 88, 101, 107, 123–24, 127, 151, 185, 234, 235

heavens (*orun*), 4, 6

Herskovits, Melville, 11

Herzfeld, Michael, 241

heuristic usage, 113–14, 145, 148, 163, 252–55

hierarchy: in *cabildos*, 13; initiatory, 90–98; of questions to Orula, 142; in vertical

shamanism, 169–70. See also *babalawos*; god-parenthood; *oddu*; *orichas*

Hobsbawm, Eric, and Terence Ranger, 275n9

holography, 168–69, 282n15

homosexuality, 82. *See also* Ifá

honras. See Ifá

Horton, Robin, 4, 274n6, 277n3

how-questions. *See* why-questions and how-questions

Hugh-Jones, Stephen, 169, 283n16

Hume, David, 66, 225

humility, xxiii, 259, 260–65

Humphrey, Caroline, 116–17

hybrids, 49, 222

ibbo, 133, 142, 148, 150, 155, 184, 217, 225, 281n23

iddé (consecrated bracelets), 124

idealism, 221–23

Ifá: alterity of, 236, 237; birthday of (*cumpleaños de*), 82; consecrated items in, 82, 93, 97, 123, 125, 133, 141–42, 148–50, 155, 168; cosmology, xxii, 4, 8, 79, 108, 109–30, 144–48, 153–57, 163–65, 172; ceremonies (*plantes*), 80, 96, 101, 102; in Cuba, xx, xxi, 55, 79, 88–89, 95, 99, 114–15, 119, 189, 211, 234–35, 278n2; ethnography of, 54, 55, 73; "everything is in," 8, 115, 257; fundaments (*fundamentos*) of, 82; funerary rites (*ituto, honras*), 82, 92, 103, 130, 131, 133, 278n3, 280n10, 281n22; gender and sexuality in, 85, 93, 96, 115, 137, 148, 212, 280n9, 280n13; historiography of, 8; *iporiawó* (Ifá illumination) in, 106; lies and deception in, 77–78; and money, 75–76, 83–84, 88–89, 93, 94, 101–2, 03, 107, 118–19, 187, 212, 282n10; names of, 100; "old style" (*al antiguo*), 76, 84; and politics, 4–5, 6, 98–99, 170, 274n6; sacrifice (*ebbó*) and offerings (*addimú*) in, 83, 88, 97, 106, 118, 123, 124, 128, 142, 156, 185–86, 270, 280n17, 281n23, 286n6; and Santería, 12, 85; secrets in, 77–78, 93, 105, 106–8; "talk" (*hablar Ifá*), 76, 83, 102–4; in West Africa, xx, 3–11, 79, 98, 115, 119, 170, 273n4, 279n6, 286n6. See also *babalawos*; *ese Ifá*; *familia de Ifá* (family of Ifá); hierarchy; knowledge; *oddu*; Orula

www.ingramcontent.com/pod-product-compliance
Lightning Source LLC
Chambersburg PA
CBHW022136020426
42334CB00015B/912